Libraries and Information

This book should be returned by the last date stamped above.
You may renew the loan personally, by post or telephone for a
further period if the book is not required by another reader.

www.wakefield.gov.uk

wakefieldcouncil
working for you

7 0 0 0 0 0 0 0 3 4 2 7 7 1

SUNDIAL
IN THE SHADE

SUNDIAL
IN THE SHADE

THE STORY OF BARRY RICHARDS:
THE GENIUS LOST TO TEST CRICKET

ANDREW MURTAGH

To Lin Murtagh, my wife.

Without whom I would probably not be here today.

First published by Pitch Publishing, 2015

Pitch Publishing
A2 Yeoman Gate
Yeoman Way
Durrington
BN13 3QZ
www.pitchpublishing.co.uk

A CIP catalogue record is available for this book
from the British Library.

ISBN 978 178531-010-2

Typesetting and origination by Pitch Publishing

Printed in Great Britain

Contents

'Hide not your talent. They for use
were made.

What's a sundial in the shade?'

Benjamin Franklin

Foreword
by Tim Rice

SOUTH Africa's Barry Richards is simply one of the greatest batsmen cricket has ever seen, whose talents have at times been bracketed with those of Sir Donald Bradman, Sachin Tendulkar and his namesake Vivian. The comparison would have been made more often but for the well-known tragedy of his career: it coincided almost exactly with his country's period of isolation from the cricket world, 1970-1991, as a result of apartheid. This meant that he only played four Test Matches, all against Australia, all of which were won by South Africa, and his contribution of 508 runs at an average of over 72 was a major factor in this triumph. After that magnificent success, the door slammed shut on South Africa's international cricket and by the time it was prised open again, Barry had retired. He played first-class cricket until 1983, notably for Hampshire and South Australia, and nearly every time he went to the wicket, his admirers could not but wonder what might have been.

I have had the honour of knowing Barry as a friend for many years and have even played in a couple of extremely minor club matches which he graced with his presence. He was long gone from the first-class game but his first-class ability and modesty were still very much in evidence. He generously refrained from smashing me out of the attack and during one of my more testing spells (the ones when the ball occasionally hits the deck before getting to the batsman) even managed to give the odd spectator the impression he was not quite sure how to deal with me. Not true, obviously, but I am eternally grateful for the gesture.

I am delighted that Andrew Murtagh is herein paying tribute to this wonderful player, who has known great ups and downs in life, both off and on the pitch, but remains above all a sportsman and gentleman without bitterness and with few equals.

Preface

'It was as if Yehudi Menuhin had called into the Festival Hall of a morning, taken his fiddle on stage and reeled off faultless, unaccompanied Bach all day – just for the pleasure of the cleaners, box-office clerks, odd electricians or a carpenter who chanced to be there – without central heating, of course – without taking off his coat.'

Tony Lewis on Barry Richards's innings at an empty Lord's, 1974

IT just happened as it happened. No one had planned it, nothing had been scheduled, nothing organised. It was a day much like countless others in the life of a county cricketer. Net practice when no match is on the fixture list is not the way most professional cricketers would choose to spend a rare day off but the custom was almost *de rigueur*; it would be a brave captain who would say to his team, 'You deserve a rest, lads – go and play golf.'

And a captain who was brave enough to defy custom would only feel he could get away with it if his team were looking down on everyone else from the top of the championship. Sixteen other sides, of course, would be looking upwards, so 'naughty boy nets' would be ordered and everyone had to be there.

And that included the 'stars', the overseas players. In the 1970s, every county was allowed two overseas players on its books and a brief glance at the playing staffs of those days would reveal a glittering collection of the world's finest cricketers. Today, counties employ overseas players who are barely recognisable to the general public. Central contracts have put paid to county cricket being the finishing school for Test cricketers from other countries.

Even the England players now have little more than fleeting contact with their home county.

It was different then. The Hampshire side that gathered together at 10am by the nets at the county ground in Southampton one day in the 1974 season included two of the best cricketers on the planet – Barry Richards and Andy Roberts. Actually, there was a third – Gordon Greenidge – but owing to an oddity of the rules, he was registered as an Englishman, even though he had nailed his colours firmly to the West Indian mast.

He had come to this country from Barbados when he was 14 and was developing into one of the world's most powerful and destructive opening bats. England, West Indies, Reading, Mars…we didn't care where he came from as long as he was in our side. I say 'our' side because I was in that group of Hampshire players padding up or marking out their runs for the ensuing net practice. I was a fringe player, it has to be said, but though I was frustrated at my seeming inability to make much of an impact in the first team, I was nevertheless tickled pink to be rubbing shoulders with the best in the game.

For Hampshire were the best. The championship pennant fluttered proudly at the top of the flagpole and there was every hope, nay expectation, that the previous year's triumph would be repeated.

Especially now that the world's fastest bowler was registered to play for us. Those who had played with Roberts in the Second XI the season before, while he served his year's period of qualification, were only too aware of his raw pace and his deadly potential. There had been one match, against Gloucestershire at Bournemouth that had already acquired legendary status and had done much to promote his fearsome reputation. Gloucestershire were 30-odd for one, with numbers six and seven at the wicket. The missing batsmen were either back in the pavilion nursing painful bruises or on their way to hospital. He was fast all right and that winter he had already made his Test debut for the West Indies.

The other overseas player was Barry Richards, who, by contrast, had no need to make a name for himself. Among the county fraternity, to say nothing of the wider cricketing public, he was regarded as the most technically proficient and naturally talented of any batsman on earth. Even so, together with one or two others in the Hampshire team that summer's morning, he did not particularly relish the prospect of a morning in the nets; county cricket is a treadmill and he would rather have had the morning off, to relax and to catch up on his mail. But all were professionals and if nets had been ordered, then nets it must be. Everyone just got on with it.

Such practice sessions always followed a pattern, a routine. The batsmen would go in first, usually in the same order as on matchdays. There would be ten minutes in one net where the seamers were operating and then the coach would shout out, 'Change nets!' and a further ten minutes would be spent in the spinners' net, where the surface was a little bit worn. By the time it came for the bowlers to bat and the batsmen to bowl, everybody had had enough and things rapidly deteriorated. 'How do you expect me to hold my end up if the rest of you won't bowl to me?' would be the constant lament of the tail-enders to the retreating backs of his team-mates as they made their way back to the dressing room and a reviving cup of tea.

Richards strolled up the net, turned and took guard. He gave a little hollow laugh as someone gave him a guard several feet outside leg stump; it was an old trick and was becoming a little tiresome. He tugged at the blue Hampshire cap as he settled himself at the crease. It wasn't brightly sunny as it was back in his Natal homeland but he always wore a cap. It helped to keep the long, curly, blond hair from getting in his eyes. Round about, everything was proceeding as normal. There were raucous shouts for LBW from the bowlers, equally vociferous responses of 'not out!' from the victims and several fingers would shoot upwards from those in positions where they could not possibly tell one way or the other. In other words, it was just like a hundred net sessions that season up and down the country.

Roberts wasn't bowling. He was *lurking*. Fast bowling is physically demanding enough without having to strain nerve and sinew at a footling net practice. He didn't really know why he was there. He couldn't see the point. So he contented himself with lobbing down a few gentle off-spinners, which everybody, of course, treated with the utmost respect. But then we noticed that he had walked back as far as his normal run. Richards had noted it too and wondered what was going on. As a suitable gap presented itself in the bowling queue, Roberts came hurtling in, rocking from side to side in that familiar fashion, rather like a runaway express train, gathering his whole body in the delivery stride, to deliver the ball at full pace. Richards was ready for it and let it go but the bulge in the net behind him told him, as if he didn't know already, that Roberts meant business this morning. It would not be wholly true to say that anything like silence fell upon the Hampshire team at practice but everyone was keeping one eye on the duel that was unfolding in the top net.

The thought processes of a fast bowler are largely unknowable to other cricketers. Unpredictable, mercurial, malevolent and moody are some of the more repeatable adjectives used by colleagues and opponents alike. Roberts was no exception. His natural expression was guarded, impenetrable. You never knew what he was thinking. Except that right now he fancied having a dart at Richards. Richards recognised the signs immediately – after all he was an opening batsman – and, with an inward sigh, he wondered what it was that he had done or said that morning to upset the Antiguan. No time to ponder. He had to knuckle down and concentrate. Reputations were at stake here, bragging rights. He was damned if he was going to let anyone get the better of him. Time to forgo the expansive strokeplay and the fancy shots. He would play *properly*.

Besides which, if he didn't, there was every chance that he could get seriously hurt. Plenty had. Everyone clearly remembered the horrible injury – a smashed jaw – that Roberts had inflicted on the West Indian opener, Steve Camacho, the previous summer. As he was stretchered off, we were all kicking dirt on to the crease to soak up the blood before the next batsman came in. Oh yes, we all knew what damage a cricket ball could do when delivered at speeds in excess of 90mph.

Along with everybody else, I had been keeping one very interested eye on what was going on and I was not best pleased when someone had failed to spot the devilishly late swing of one of my deliveries and heaved the ball many a mile into the long grass. 'That'll take some finding,' I grumbled to myself as I went in search of it, 'and I shall miss all the fun.'

Chance would have it that I found my ball right away and, trudging back to my mark, I decided to make a detour around the back of the nets, the better to catch a close glimpse of the developing contest. There, you can stand a matter of feet behind the batsman and watch how he deals with whatever is bowled at him. It has been calculated that a batsman has 0.4 seconds to react to a ball delivered from 22 yards away at 90mph. The mathematics of the contest in that net escaped me at the time; all I know is that I flinched every time Richards let a ball go and it bulged the netting in front of my face. I remember thinking that I hoped to high heaven the groundsman had checked carefully that morning that the netting was safe and secure.

The following 15 minutes remained the most riveting piece of theatre I have ever witnessed on a cricket ground. And it was only a net practice! For some reason, the coach did not irately summon me back for cannon fodder duties. Probably, like me, he was engrossed in what was going on. Anyway, he forgot about me and I was able to take in the exhibition of a master craftsman at work. I should of course have said *two* master craftsmen for Roberts was no mindless slinger of a cricket ball. He was an intelligent bowler who worked batsmen out before he worked them over. That is what made the battle so intriguing.

To the uninitiated it might have seemed that not a lot was happening. Stumps did not cartwheel, balls did not disappear into the disused car park of the dilapidated bowling rink opposite. There was no shouting, no banter, no ironic cheers. But an intense struggle was taking place for supremacy and neither of them was minded to take a backward step.

I watched Richards closely as Roberts careered towards him. The most striking thing about him was his absolute stillness at the crease. Most of us – pretty well all of us, I would suggest – make an initial movement before the ball is bowled. With only a split second to react, the movement would be back and across, if only for the sake of self-preservation. Richards made no preliminary movement, forward or back. He remained motionless until the very moment the ball left the bowler's hand. And yet he seemed to have time to play his shots. How could this possibly be? Was the man possessed with superhuman reactions? So we would test him out in the nets, running in to bowl to him and following through without letting the ball go. There he would be standing, bat raised but head and feet stock still. Extraordinary.

The second noteworthy feature of his batting was the economy of movement. He did not lunge or jab at the ball, nor did he jerk his body one way or the other or jump out of the path of the ball. Calmly, and seemingly with all the time in the world, he went forward or back as required – unsurprisingly more back than forward as we're describing a genuine fast bowler here – or unhurriedly swayed out of the way of the bouncers. That is what separates the great players, of whatever sport, from the journeymen – *time*. Lionel Messi seems to have acres of space on the ball even when closely marked. Roger Federer moves like liquid and hits the ball effortlessly even when running at full tilt. Dan Carter makes room on a crowded pitch where none seems there. Richards appeared unhurried and relaxed at the crease, playing the correct shot – or no shot at all – to whatever ball was bowled at him. Relaxed? With someone trying to knock his head off? Well, that's how it seemed.

And thirdly, all his strokes were straight out of the MCC coaching manual. In a manner of speaking, that is. I've never read the MCC book of coaching. Nor do I know anyone who has. It's a bit of a cliché, really, used by cricketers, slightly tongue-in-cheek, to denote purity and orthodoxy of technique. Presumably Richards had been coached in the eternal verities of batsmanship from an early age but, even so, the technical perfection of each stroke was exceptional. Up and down the land, he had been constantly held up as a shining example of the correct way to bat and it was true. He had every stroke in the book and every one was a thing of elegance and refinement.

I had heard spectators purr with appreciation when he started to unfurl his cultured and polished shots – all round the wicket and all beautifully timed. When you watched him bat, you knew instinctively you were in the presence of greatness. Professional cricketers, by and large, are a hard-bitten lot, suspicious of anything flash, and not easily impressed. It takes something special to drag them away from a pack of cards in the dressing room to watch their colleagues batting. But whenever Richards took guard and played a few shots that indicated he was in the mood, all of us would be out there on the balcony watching in awe at the effortless manner in which he could dismantle a bowling attack.

That is not to say that he couldn't throw orthodoxy to the wind and improvise when he wanted to. There was one occasion in the nets when he turned his bat around and challenged us to get him out with his using only the edge. Needless to say, he wasn't playing Roberts on this occasion but even so, at the time, it seemed an outrageous proposal. We immediately took up the challenge. It would be exaggerating to say that he hit *every* ball in the middle – sorry, the edge – but we couldn't get him out. And practising with him in the minutes before play, bowling a few looseners at him on the outfield to get his eye in, he would hit the ball straight back at you, no matter where you pitched it.

Short outside his imaginary off stump? He would swipe at it cross-batted and the ball would land, on the bounce, in your hands. Short outside leg stump? Before anyone had even heard of the reverse sweep, he would hit a double-handed backhand, straight back at you. Full pitch outside off stump? Most of us would gratefully lean into it and drive it over to the other side of the ground. And that would be the end of the practice because no one could be bothered to go and fetch the ball. But not Richards. He would turn his wrists at the last moment and send it straight back to you, again. And, most remarkable of all would be the one pitched up well outside leg stump. He would do a little shimmy and turn it into a straight drive – straight back at you, of course. No wonder there was usually a tussle to bowl at him. It was easy. You hardly had to move.

So he could rip up the rulebook if he was of a mind to do so and the situation warranted it. There is a famous photo of him in a Gillette Cup match against Lancashire at Bournemouth. He is executing an imperious cover drive. But take another look. The wicketkeeper, Farokh Engineer, is standing up to the wicket but is several feet outside the leg stump. What is going on? The Lancashire spinners had been firing it in at his leg stump, or even outside, to a packed leg-side field, in an attempt to curb his run-making. To counteract this ploy, he was dancing to leg and hitting the ball through the vacant off side. Pure genius. To say nothing of the impudence of it and the complete faith that he had in his exceptional abilities. Bowlers thought he was taking the mickey. He wasn't. The bowler bowled the ball and he, the batsman, would hit it. Generally where he liked. He loved to bat. That was the essence of what he did, what had defined him since childhood.

There was no dancing to leg in this net practice, no extravagant shots, no experimentation or frivolousness. He was playing each ball on its merits. Occasionally he would push one into the covers off the back foot or steer it down through gully. Or he would lean on one whose line had strayed a fraction and ease it wide of mid-on. There were few front-foot drives. Roberts didn't pitch it up very often but there was the occasional square cut, not a savage one but carefully played with exquisite timing. Four runs, without a doubt. But it was how he dealt with the short ball that impressed me most and long stuck in my mind. If it was very short, too short in effect, he would simply sway out of the line. If it was aimed at his chest, he would get up on his toes and simply play it down. He was never rushed, never flustered. It was almost as if he knew when Roberts was going to bowl a bouncer. Later, he said it was all to do with where the bowler's head was going as he bowled the ball. If his head went low, it was because he was putting in that extra bit of effort needed to bowl the bouncer. So, it seemed he could look at the bowler's head as well as the ball. Sometimes you just have to accept that the gods apportion sporting talent inequitably.

Who won the duel? I suppose you could call it a score draw. Roberts had not got him out. But nor had Richards got on top of him and hit him out of the firing line. Honours had been shared, they both might have reflected with satisfaction as they sipped their tea back in the dressing room. It had been a fascinating quarter of an hour, a real tussle between two superstars of the game. And no one, apart from their team-mates and half a dozen interested bystanders, had witnessed it. It was unlikely ever to be repeated, not because they were both in the same side but because one was West Indian and the other was South African.

And therein lies the tragedy that runs like a thread through this book. By this time, South Africa's isolation from the international arena was, to all intents and purposes, complete and permanent. Barry Richards knew in his heart that he would never add to the pitifully small total of four Test matches that he had played for his country. For a year or two after bursting upon the world stage with a dazzling debut series against Australia in 1970, he had harboured hopes that the ban would be temporary and that his country would be welcomed back into the international fold. But slowly he had come to the dismal conclusion that it was never going to happen. He was condemned to the nomadic life of a professional cricketer, a hired hand wherever the money presented itself, without the excitement and glory of testing his skills against the world's best at the highest level. A 15-minute stint in the nets facing Andy Roberts was no consolation.

For a while, he had managed to keep alight the flames of his ambition by striving for success in the Currie Cup for his native Natal and in the championship for his adopted county Hampshire. And there had been rewards too. Under his captaincy, Natal had won two Currie Cups and of course there was that famous win the previous year for Hampshire in the County Championship. That was all well and good. But it wasn't Test cricket and Test cricket is what he craved. It was a bit like being perpetually on tour in provincial rep when all you want is to tread the boards in the West End. Great theatrical reputations are not made in little-known seaside resorts any more than cricket legends are forged in sleepy backwaters like Tunbridge Wells, Southend, Buxton and Basingstoke. 'Basingstoke! I've still got a splinter in my foot from that damned wooden floor in the dressing room,' he would complain, remembering his last visit to that outpost of Hampshire cricket. 'And Southampton,' he grumbled, 'it may be a bustling port and it may be the headquarters of this team but tell me, what is there to **do** in this dull, featureless city? It's by the sea but I haven't yet been able to find the beach.' He tried to hide his creeping dissatisfaction and despair from his team-mates but sometimes it was difficult.

Nothing could have reminded him more plainly of what he was missing than what had happened a couple of months earlier in the season. He had scored a big hundred at Lord's and in the eyes of those who witnessed it, including the long-suffering bowlers on the other side, it did not seem possible that anyone could have batted better that day. Even he had admitted that everything seemed to ping off the middle of the bat. And Old Father Time, up on top of the grandstand, was seen to nod his head in appreciation, and he had seen quite a few great innings on this famous old ground.

But it was no Test match, Lord's was not full, there were no television cameras, he did not return to the pavilion to a standing ovation, the MCC members did not cheer him as he passed through the Long Room on his way back to the dressing room. It was a bitterly cold day in late April, the ground was deserted and the crack of leather on willow had echoed eerily around the empty, ghostly stands. MCC were playing in the traditional pipe opener to the season against the champion county, who were of course Hampshire. And it had not been a powder puff attack that MCC had chosen. Richards had put to the sword bowlers of the calibre of Hendrick, Jackman, Knight, Edmonds and Acfield.

Despite the rawness of the day, the Hampshire players had huddled together for warmth on the dressing room balcony, determined not to miss something special, a world-class batsman in the form of his life. I was there. I didn't miss a ball. It was quite simply the greatest exhibition of batsmanship that I have ever seen. Mike Taylor, a team-mate and friend, turned to me as Richards executed yet another majestic stroke and said, 'This is sheer box office, bloody marvellous. *And no one's here!* It's a tragedy.'

And it was too. That was the tragedy of Barry Richards.

Acknowledgements

YES, but why Barry Richards? The question was posed to me on numerous occasions by friends and relatives, anxious to know what it was that had been absorbing my time these past 18 months. Most were satisfied by my answer that this was a story that deserved to be told, of a Test career cruelly cut short by an accident of birth and international politics. The fact that Barry's name is scarcely known by a younger generation of cricket lovers is an injustice which I felt ought to be put right; his genius deserves more than a footnote in the dusty annals of the game's history. And who better to tell the story than a former team-mate of his? Furthermore, if the account of his life needed a socio-political framework to interest more than just cricket buffs, then apartheid South Africa was as significant as most.

However, there was another reason, largely kept to myself, that impelled me to approach Barry, a trifle nervously, at our former Hampshire players' reunion on the 40th anniversary of the 1973 championship triumph. Would he be willing for me to write his biography? He was interested but wary. Ever a private man, he was no doubt weighing up in his mind the pleasure to be had in reliving great moments and reminiscing about happy times against his usual apprehension about becoming public property. 'Don't worry, I've grown up,' I assured him. 'So have I,' he smiled. 'I can write too,' I pressed him. 'Look – I've been published.' I flourished a copy of one of my books. He took it but did not open it to delve straight into chapter one. No, my academic credentials were fine, just dandy, he seemed to intimate. Something else was bothering him.

I could guess what it was. Some four years previously, his son, Mark, had taken his own life. We all knew but no one had brought up the subject with him, partly to save his feelings and partly to spare our own awkwardness. And therein lies the problem with mental health. It *still* remains an uncomfortable topic, in spite of recent, well-publicised cases of the terrible illness, even within the game of cricket itself. I took a deep breath and plunged in. I'm a sufferer myself, I told him, I've been hospitalised, I've been put on suicide watch, I've had numerous sessions of electro-convulsive therapy, I've been sent on counselling and therapy courses, I've been on heavy duty medication. In short, I know what it's like. I'm stable at the moment but those close to me still have to keep an eye on me.

Still he paused. And then he agreed to the project. Whether my words had reassured him, I do not know. We got cracking immediately and soon we were immersed in sepia memories of long ago. Incidentally, thank heavens for Skype. Barry lives in South Africa and I live in England. The thing wouldn't have been possible without the technology, even if I did have to suffer Barry's regular taunting by displaying to me the azure skies of the Western Cape while I sat huddled over my computer, the rain lashing the windows of the conservatory.

One of the great pleasures of writing this book has been getting to know my friend better this time. Team-mates are close but all too soon their careers come to an end and everybody goes his separate way. This project has brought us back together again and I hope these pages will reveal that my affection and respect for the man now extend far beyond his prowess with the bat. Nonetheless, we both knew that the fearsome fast bowler was girding his loins, so to speak, pawing at the dirt for one final burst before stumps.

We remained on our guard, fully aware that the tragedy that befell him, late in his life, sooner or later had to be confronted.

It wasn't easy, for either of us, but we knew that. I admired his honesty and I pitied his pain and guilt. I hope I have dealt with the dreadful affair with tact and compassion. It was a moot point whether we would mention it at all, wary of intruding on private grief. But it happened, even though Barry, with every fibre in his body, wished that it hadn't. It has fundamentally changed him, I believe. And if this is to be a true record of his life, it had to go in. For this, I take full responsibility. I know that Anne, Mark's mother, and Steve, his brother, desired not to have it included and I have done my very best to treat their feelings with sensitivity and due regard. My fervent wish is that the three of them, Barry, Anne and Steve, can somehow come to a point where they can grieve together for their lost son and brother, who was, by all accounts, a very special boy.

I am indebted to Tim Rice, a past president of the MCC and a long-standing friend and admirer of Barry, for his incisive and affectionate foreword to this book. He knows his cricket, Sir Tim, and he can recognise a star when he sees one. My thanks too go to Patrick Eagar, the doyen of cricket photographers, for his matchless portraits of Barry in action, capturing so well the artistry, beauty and technical perfection of his stroke play. Patrick's father, Desmond, who was our secretary at Hampshire when Barry and I were there, also appears in these pages.

The list of people to whom I am indebted for their help in the writing of this book is a long one. First and foremost, I am beholden to my personal editor, Ruth Sheppard, with whom I have worked before. 'Do you want this book to be the best?' demanded my wife, a trifle unnecessarily, I thought. I assured her that I did. 'Then I advise you to get hold of Ruth. Right now. The best deserves the best.' She was right of course and I duly surrendered my manuscript to Ruth's unflinching critical eye. 'Ruth – you're ruthless!' I cried as I surveyed the wreckage of my purple prose being dumped in the trash. In truth, every writer needs a Ruth, to curb the worst excesses of irrelevance, digression, flippancy and ostentation that we are prone to and I, as a former English teacher not averse to wielding the red pen myself, could hardly balk a tighter rein. In fact, I welcomed her stringency, admired her erudition and occasionally laughed out loud at her comments.

It is testament to the high regard in which Barry is held around the cricketing world that many of the people whom I have mentioned or quoted in the book have been unstinting of their time and help, providing anecdote, opinion, memory and background information. I list them in no particular order: Vintcent van der Bijl, Lee Irvine, Grayson Heath, Roger Tolchard, Bryan Richardson, Richard Gilliat, Keith Wheatley, Alan Castell, Neil Minnaar, Denis Gamsy, David Allen (RIP), John Mortimore (RIP), John Traicos, Tom Graveney OBE, Robin Jackman, Andre Bruyns, Dave Anderson, Graham McKenzie, Mushtaq Mohammed, Mike Taylor, Derek Underwood, Greg Chappell, Tim Murtagh, Martin Harrison, Bob Cottam, John Holder, Richard Lewis, Bill Buck, Mike Hill, Shelley Morris, Martin Tyler, Garth le Roux, Mark Nicholas, Wilfrid Weld, Darren Lehmann, Dennis Yagmich, Rev. Mike Vockins OBE, Colin Brydon, Bob Murrell, Ingrid Diesel and Di Charteris.

My grateful thanks go to Pitch Publishing for doing such a fine job producing the book and particularly to the director of the company, Paul Camillin, who has shown so much faith in me, Gareth Davis and Dean Rockett for their painstaking proof reading, and Graham Hales.

To conclude, let me say only this. The mistakes in this book – and there will be a few – are all mine and I apologise for them.

Andrew Murtagh
December 2014

Introduction

'S O,' said my dining companion opposite, fixing me with his eyes, 'who was the greatest batsman you ever played with or against?'

'Richards,' I replied, without a moment's hesitation.

He continued to chew while he gave this some thought.

'Fair enough,' he said, 'I don't think anyone could disagree with that. After all, *Wisden* named him as one of the five cricketers of the century, did they not? King Viv – surely the most...'

'Barry,' I corrected him, 'Barry Richards. Not Viv.'

His blank stare hinted that he didn't know whom I was talking about.

'Barry Richards?' came a voice from further down the table. 'The greatest batsman never to have played Test cricket!'

'Well, that's not entirely true,' I pointed out, 'He did actually play four Tests. Against Australia in 1970. He scored two hundreds and finished the series with an average of...74.86.' That last bit, about his average, was something of a stab in the dark. I couldn't remember exactly, not having a head for figures. In fact, I had not been that far off. His Test average was 72.57. Which puts him second only to the incomparable Bradman and above the greats of the game, such as Pollock, Headley, Sutcliffe, Hammond, Sobers, Hobbs, Hutton, Greg Chappell, Lara *et al*. But only four Tests is, statistically, too small a number to count.

And therein lies the problem and which probably accounted for my dining companion's look of puzzlement.

'Why did he only play four Tests?' piped up another voice.

'South Africa got banned, didn't they?' said someone else.

'That's right,' said another, 'they were isolated because of apartheid. A jolly good thing, as it turned out. Brought down the government, Mandela was released, paving the way for democracy and his election as president.'

'I'm not sure whether their cricket team being isolated was *entirely* responsible for the downfall of apartheid.'

'But banning their rugby team did.'

'It certainly helped to concentrate minds.'

And for the next quarter of an hour, the argument about apartheid and South African politics raged. The women looked bored. I was beside myself with frustration. 'Hang on!' I wanted to shout, 'You asked me who was the greatest batsman I ever played with or against. I've given you my answer and you won't let me say why.' But of course I didn't. Apartheid is one of those subjects, like the NHS or public schools or social benefits, that excite great passion and heated debate and nothing – not even the prematurely curtailed career of Barry Richards – can stop that person on his soapbox. I gave up and sipped my wine. Bloody politics, I thought, not for the first time either.

'Politics has been inextricably bound up with my life,' Barry said to me early on in the process of writing this book, 'It always has and so it remains.'

I pondered this for a while. It had been my intention to write the story of his life from a personal perspective, not ducking the controversies but not getting subsumed by them either, thus sabotaging the narrative flow. But the more I thought about it, the more I came to realise that he was right. It would be a bit like taking the reader through the unfolding events of the Second World War without mentioning Nazism. To be truthful, I had wanted to concentrate on his cricket career but I now saw that was impossible. Politics was at the heart of everything that happened to him.

My mind went back to an afternoon sometime in the mid-summer of 1970. I was a university undergraduate and was on a summer contract at Hampshire County Cricket Club. What better way was there to earn a bit of money to augment a meagre grant? Playing cricket every day of the long summer vacation hardly qualified as a job in my mind but there it was; I was paid £10 a week and I joyfully considered myself a professional cricketer.

There had been no match that day so we had been practising in the nets all morning. Following a lengthy session, we were refuelling in a local hostelry when in walked Barry Richards. All the others knew him because he was Hampshire's overseas player. There was no fawning or kowtowing to him; he was just one of the team, albeit one with a very special talent that had already attracted approving attention nationwide. Although I had attended pre-season training in early April and got to know everyone reasonably well, Barry had not been there. Overseas stars, by and large, didn't 'do' pre-season training – the English weather in spring is too inclement, so they normally pitched up just in time for the first match, much to the annoyance of the English players. So I had missed meeting him. As it happened, he was not in the Hampshire XI. He was playing for the Rest of the World.

No, this was not some make-believe series against Mars in which cricket enthusiasts indulge themselves by picking their World XI. It was a real series, hastily arranged by the Test and County Cricket Board, between England and the Rest of the World. That summer, South Africa had been scheduled to tour but following the D'Oliveira Affair and increasingly strident political opposition and violent public protest, the tour had been cancelled. Barry had been named in the South African touring party – he had even been issued with his tour blazer – but it gradually became clear that there was no way the matches could be played without the risk of serious disruption and the axe had inevitably fallen. It was a shame for the cricketing public who had been looking forward to watching the Pollocks, Barlow, Procter, Irvine, Lindsay and Richards in action. What a team they were! They had just walloped Australia 4-0 and were widely regarded as the most talented and most exciting Test team on the planet.

It was a shame for us cricket-lovers but never mind, the British public could lick their lips in anticipation of watching a team of all the talents. The Rest of the World had Sobers, Kanhai, Lloyd, Intikhab Alam, McKenzie, Gibbs, augmented by the South Africans, Barlow, Procter, Graeme and Peter Pollock and of course, Barry Richards; they would be a match for Mars, let alone England. For Barry, it provided some consolation for the abandonment of his country's tour of England. Did he sense that this would be it, the final flourish of his Test career barely before it had started?

It was difficult to tell on that summer's afternoon. It was clear, however, that he was relishing his days in the sun, notwithstanding the political clouds that were amassing on the horizon. The light of battle was in his eyes. He may even have bought us all a drink as he described with animation the progress of what was, I think, the third Test against England (in another fateful little twist of the knife in Barry's career, Test match status was retrospectively removed from these matches by the Test and County Cricket Board, a decision that seems as baffling today as it did at the time).

'This isn't Hampshire Second XI,' he told us, 'nor even,' turning to me, 'Southampton University. This is the *Rest of the World*!'

It might have sounded patronising but that was not his intention. It was almost as if he was reassuring himself that he was indeed dining at the top table of international cricket and that was where he belonged. And none of us could have disagreed or would have wanted to disagree. We all knew – it went without saying – that he was the best batsman in the world. And the best batsman in the world deserved the chance to parade his talents on the world stage.

Alas, that was it for him. South Africa were scheduled to tour Australia in 1971/72 but the possibility of it taking place became more and more unlikely as governments worldwide hardened in their opposition to that country's internal policy of apartheid. The team was picked, with Barry included, of course, but, as expected, the tour was cancelled and South Africa, as a cricketing nation, was effectively isolated. And not even the most optimistic dreamer could ever believe that their isolation would end anytime soon. Certainly Barry entertained no such hope. His Test career was over as soon as it had begun. All that was left was the peripatetic life as a hired mercenary in the professional game and the slow, sad descent into frustration and disillusionment. At the time, I had sympathy for his predicament. But now, many years later, I see that it was a tragedy, both personal and professional, and I wanted to tell his story before he becomes no more than a melancholy footnote in the history of the game. He deserves more than that.

Andrew Murtagh

1

A Singular Child

'Barry shows promise at cricket.'
An early school report

ON 21 July 1945, bowlers around the world gave an involuntary shiver. It was not the dawn of the atomic age – the bombing of Hiroshima took place a fortnight later – but the birth of Barry Richards that had given rise to their sense of foreboding. It was a nasty moment but it soon passed as suddenly as it presented itself. Not to worry, they reasoned, it won't be us who will suffer. That punishment awaits the next generation of bowlers.

They were right, of course. But they could not rest easy in their beds for long; ever impatient, Richards was ten when he made his first fifty, 11 when he was selected and made his first hundred for the Durban District Under-14 side – effectively the whole of Natal – and 18 when selected for his first tour overseas, to England as captain of the South African Schools. It was almost as if he somehow knew that his representative career was going to be brief so he had better get a move on.

It is a common misconception that all white South Africans during apartheid lived in grand mansions with a swimming pool, a tennis court, manicured gardens and a retinue of servants. And that all black South Africans lived cheek by jowl in ramshackle huts in crowded locations, without electricity, running water and even the basic sanitary facilities. This perception is not *entirely* accurate, it has to be said; not all members of the ruling whites enjoyed great wealth and gilded lifestyles any more than all blacks lived in abject poverty. There were poor whites too.

I am not sure that the Richards family could have called themselves poor, not in the sense that most inhabitants of the townships would have understood it. But they certainly did not have money to burn. They lived in a one-bedroom apartment in a block of 30 flats in Durban. Barry, their only child, slept on the balcony. *Whaat? Exposed to the elements? I know Durban has a sub-tropical climate but it's by the sea and the wind sometimes blows.* 'No Murt, you clown, it was an enclosed balcony.' Be that as it may, Barry was too young to be aware of financial difficulties; all he wanted to do was play rugby and cricket. With regular meals on the table and unstinting encouragement from his parents to embrace the outside lifestyle of a South African boy, there was little in his daily routine to spoil this idyll. But it was not a bed of roses for his parents; behind the scenes, they had to struggle to make ends meet. They were, I suppose, what used to be termed 'hard up'.

Both sets of grandparents were second-generation South Africans, his father and mother had been born there so the family were hardly newcomers to the continent.

In other words Barry belonged, and this of course informs us of his loyalty to, and love of, his country. He is firmly, resolutely, unashamedly South African. He did not cut and run, serve a qualification period and play for another country. At that time, it was unthinkable, he asserted. Players didn't even change clubs or provinces, let alone countries. That was completely off the agenda. *Well, what about Tony Greig? He was a contemporary of yours, was he not?* 'Greigy went because he had a Scottish mother and therefore had a closer association with England. And he knew he wasn't going to get in the Springbok team.' That tells you something about the strength of South African cricket at the time.

Was he a better all-rounder than Mike Procter? Without taking anything away from Greig's undoubted qualities of courage and leadership, I think it fair to say that Procter was the greater cricketer. Subsequent homegrown cricketers who did defect – Allan Lamb, Kepler Wessels, Chris and Robin Smith – were younger and the emotional ties not quite so strong, perhaps. For his own part, Barry wanted nothing more than to wear the Springbok colours and no one was more proud than he when that dream came to pass.

There was no history of cricket playing on either side of the family, as far as he knows. Certainly not on his mother's side; his father's antecedents remain a mystery. 'I knew nothing about them because my father never mentioned them,' Barry said. 'If anyone brought up the subject, he would immediately clam up.' So it would seem that Barry's special aptitude for the game truly was God-given. From the earliest age that he can remember, he always had a bat or a ball in his hand, which is, I firmly believe, another prerequisite for greatness. Nobody becomes predominant in the game if he doesn't eat, sleep and breathe it. That means hour upon hour of practice until it's too dark to play anymore.

But as a young boy, he had no idea that this was what he would have to do; he just played and played because he loved it. And if there was no one to play with, he would practise alone, by throwing a golf ball against the garage wall and hitting the rebound with a 12-inch bat. If he missed it, that would mean a long trek to fetch it. He soon learned not to miss. *That's what Bradman used to do when he was a kid.* 'But he used to hit it with a stump,' Barry corrected me, as if comparisons with the legendary Australian were entirely out of place.

At other times he would play with the three Morris boys, neighbours of theirs, on an old, disused tennis court at the bottom of the road. You could bowl – underarm – as fast as you liked from ten yards and no quarter was given. 'I was younger than all of them, so obviously I had to learn how to stay in.' All grist to the mill. *Did you ever have coaching lessons or were you entirely self-taught?* 'Well, we had a coach at school called Neil Fox. He encouraged me a lot but he didn't know much about cricket. What he did impart came straight out of a manual. He was Irish, you see.' *Steady on! There are plenty of good Irish cricketers, you know. I'm Irish, in case you've forgotten.* 'Which proves my point,' he countered.

He then went on to expand on one of his pet hobby horses. 'The current generation misses out on physical exercise, you know, climbing trees, playing games, running about. All that stuff is good for you when you're growing up.' Although he was encouraged by his parents to get outside and play, in truth Barry needed no such prompting. On his own admission, he was no bookworm.

Tell me about your parents. How was your relationship with your father? There was an intake of breath and a long pause. I suspected that this wasn't going to be easy for him. 'Well, they were very supportive,' he said, unconvincingly. And then he obviously decided to dive straight in; there was no point dilly-dallying on the edge of the diving board, staring down at the water below. His father had been made redundant in his mid-30s when, following a merger, a restructuring at the optical firm where he worked took place. He was forced to leave and seek another, lower post with the municipality with less pay. That experience would leave a sour taste in most men's mouths; in Les Richards's mouth, the bitterness never dissolved. 'He had a lot of anger in him,' said his son, 'and he just didn't know how to get it out.' Clearly, it put a strain on the marriage, which Barry all but tacitly admitted. 'There was no divorce in those days,' he pointed out. 'Marriage was for ever and they just got on with it.'

How did you get on with your mother? 'Mum was more forgiving,' he answered, intriguingly. Who, or what, needed forgiving? I did not ask because he was opening his heart here and it did not seem appropriate to interrupt. But I could read between the lines. 'She just got on with things,' he went on. 'It was tough for her. She was always…well, how shall we say, *overruled* by my father.' In the opinion of Vintcent van der Bijl, later a team-mate and good friend of Barry's, Doreen Richards was a 'wonderful, wonderful mother', who 'looked a bit like Barbara Bush' and who had, he felt, a soothing influence in the home. Barry was unsure about the allusion to a former First Lady of the United States but was in full agreement about his mother's selfless and compassionate influence on the family. 'Whereas my father…'

Added to the tensions in the relationship, there were obvious financial restraints on the family with less money coming in. Both parents had to work, his father for the municipality and his mother in a department store, and the hours were long. Barry's great friend and of course later team-mate, Lee Irvine, commented, 'Like my family, they were strapped for cash. As a result, I think, Barry always worried about money and where it was going to come from.' This would in time give rise to the popular notion that Barry Richards was a mercenary and would never do anything for nothing. Grossly unfair, when you examine the evidence; it's all very well for people to be baffled by perceived parsimony when they themselves have never known privation. 'I was a latch-key kid,' said Barry, with no hint of rancour. Nevertheless, in an ideal world you would want one parent to be there when you arrive home after a day at school, even if it is just to say hello, and did you have a nice day as you dash past to be first out in the street to be with your mates. Barry had no such stability in his early life. I gently probed the effects that this might have had on his upbringing but he was not going to wallow in self-pity. All he would own was that it toughened him up; it made him more self-reliant than he might otherwise have been.

There was Grandpa Percy, his mother's father. He took it upon himself, as all good grandfathers should do, to keep a devoted but protective eye on his grandson. Barry remembers him with nothing but extreme affection. If various items of kit or equipment were needed, somehow they were provided and it didn't need a detective's mind to know who was responsible. He came along to watch the young boy play and did his best to encourage him without ever allowing him to get cocky. After one particularly fine inning, Barry approached him, fully expecting congratulations and praise. Instead, he was given a fearful dressing down – for not raising his bat and touching his cap, as etiquette demanded, in acknowledgement of the spectators' applause. A lesson, incidentally, that Barry never forgot.

And of course, there were the madcap escapades that one normally gets into with one's grandfather. Percy felt that 11 years of age was time enough for the young Barry to be introduced to the internal combustion engine. Accordingly, he sat the boy down in the driver's seat of his Morris 1000 and went through the intricacies of gear and clutch with his pupil. 'Got all that?' Barry enthusiastically nodded. 'Right then,' instructed Grandpa, 'put it gently into reverse and ease out backwards on to the road.' Now those who have driven a Morris 1000 will know that that model had an unusually long gear stick and sometimes first gear and reverse were not easily told apart. Result? The car shot forwards and demolished the garage door. On another occasion, when presumably the callow driver had learned how to manipulate the long gear stick, the two of them were on their usual jaunt up along the coast road with Barry – still not yet a teenager – at the wheel. Rounding a bend, to their horror, they spied a parked police car. With commendable speed of thought and sleight of hand, Grandpa Percy whipped off his trilby and jammed it on Barry's head. The driver was blinded, the trilby being too large and covering his eyes, but 'we got away with it', he laughed.

He had no brothers or sisters so, apart from illicit driving lessons, he had to make his own entertainment. Of course, this meant that he had the stage to himself at Christmas and birthdays but it had the effect that he became 'a bit of a loner', he admitted. 'If you've always been on your own, it becomes a way of life. The only interaction I had was with neighbours in the flats or kids at school. As a kid growing up, when all you want to do is get outside and play cricket, you don't think about these things, do you?' Fair enough. I guess not. All I would say about his childhood is this; God may have put a golden bat in his hand but there was no silver spoon in his mouth.

I have a friend who was brought up in South Africa around the same time as Barry. He used to regale us with stories of walking to school for several miles, and in bare feet. It wasn't that his parents couldn't afford shoes; he said that it was nothing unusual. 'Everyone walked around barefoot where I lived. It's just the way it was. And there were no buses. Nor were we driven to school, like the kids today. It was a very safe environment. Nobody got lost. Nobody got run over. No one was abducted. Different world, I suppose.'

Barry was at pains not to paint too romantic a picture of the old South Africa, where everything seemed more organised, peaceful and assured. Although he was too young to appreciate it, the storm clouds were already gathering over the horizon and this idyllic world was about to be sundered forever, yet he will insist that growing up was 'more secure' back in those days. That could be said for anywhere, I dare say, but there was an unmistakeable note of wistfulness in his voice as he recalled to mind walking to school and boyhood tomfoolery and endless games of cricket.

Did you have a maid? There was just a second's hesitation. 'Yes, we did. She didn't live in, like some did. But you have to understand that everyone had a maid. The going rate to employ one was ridiculously cheap but if you didn't employ her, she would go without.' I understood the skewed logic here, of a social and fiscal system which forces the daily wage of those in the service industry to be so low, barely above subsistence level. Many South Africans that I have spoken to have pointed out to me the moral dilemma that confronted them, of living in an unequal and unfair society. A good proportion of them did what they could: giving their maids and gardeners extra food and clothing, paying for their children's school books, even sometimes paying the school fees and medical expenses. A drop in the ocean, perhaps, but what could they do? Some found the yawning chasm between the haves and the have-nots intolerable and emigrated. Many were in no position to do so, even if they had wanted to. 'South Africa is my home,' Barry said, 'It was where I was born and brought up. I am African. And there are many tribes in Africa. But it is just the case that our tribe is white.'

Were you aware of apartheid? Or rather I should ask, when did you become aware of apartheid? 'Well, you grew up with it,' he answered. 'So, in that sense, it was always there, in the background.' I can sympathise with that. What young boy, obsessed with sport and the outdoor life, bothers himself too much with the politics of the day? It wasn't until he went abroad for the first time, to England in 1963, on a cricket tour, that the painful realities of the unpopularity of his country and its racial policies hit home. 'There was no TV,' he reminded me. 'The only news we had was what we heard on the radio and read in the papers, both under government control. It was a very closed and protected environment. We were taught to be...' The right word, when it came, was obviously carefully selected. 'Compliant.'

More obvious to him was that there were actually two different groups of the *white* tribe and the social chasm between them seemed to be almost as wide as that between black and white. The earliest settlers in the Cape of Good Hope in the 17th century were mainly Dutch, later added to by Protestant French Huguenots, German missionaries and some Scandinavians. They spoke Afrikaans, sometimes scornfully referred to by English speakers as 'kitchen Dutch'. The British arrived later and seized control of the Cape as a colony in 1806, which led to the Great Trek northwards by the Afrikaners – known as Voortrekkers – in the 1830s to settle in Transvaal, Orange Free State and Natal, in order to escape British rule. The discovery of diamonds in 1867 and gold in 1887 brought turmoil to the country and friction between the two white peoples, which led directly to the Boer Wars at the tail end of the 19th century. The Union of South Africa, with Britain in control, was brought into being by an Act of Parliament in 1910, with the King its constitutional monarch. At the outbreak of the Second World War in 1939, the English speakers not unnaturally responded to the call to arms whereas the Afrikaners were firmly opposed. In 1948, the Afrikaners finally gained the majority they needed to win the election and South Africa was unswervingly set on its course to sunder all links with Britain and its King, leaving the Commonwealth and declaring itself a republic. It was under Afrikaner rule that Barry grew up, in a country whose government enthusiastically embraced the principle of apartheid, with the English-speaking community at best ambivalent about the policy.

Barry was as conscious of the divide between the two branches of the white tribe as anyone growing up in South Africa at that time. He had to learn Afrikaans at school as a second language, just as the Afrikaners had to learn English as their second language. *So, how good is your Afrikaans?* 'Pretty average. I suppose I can make myself understood. But as I've told you, I was pretty average at everything at school.' *Not cricket, though.* He had to admit as much. *Was there any social interaction between the two – the British and the Afrikaners?* 'You have to understand that Natal was one of the last outposts of the British Empire. The Afrikaners were not in the majority, as they were in other provinces.' *So there was an unmistakeable social divide?* He was not so sure about that but he did offer this interesting summation of the situation. 'I suppose you could say that the Afrikaners had the political clout whereas the English concentrated on trade, commerce and business.' Ah, 'twas ever thus. After all, what else drove the British Empire?

Did they play cricket? 'Traditionally, not much. It was seen very much as an English game. Rugby was their passion. But around the late 1960s, when the South African Test team were carrying all before them, they sat up and started to take a bit more notice. Now, of course, it's very different. There are plenty of Afrikaners in the Test team.' That, we both agreed, was a welcome state of affairs just as we both appreciate that it will take time before there are as many blacks in the team as whites. Cricket is complex, expensive and not easily accessible at the best of times. But it will happen.

Ali Bacher, former Springbok captain and influential administrator, had a dream that one day, South Africa would have a team of white batsmen, black fast bowlers and Indian spinners. Now that truly would be a gratifying advertisement for the new Rainbow Nation.

But we are getting ahead of ourselves – the poor boy is still at primary school and this political and moral web has yet to ensnare him. Probably, at this early stage of his life, he was too preoccupied with cricket even to dwell on whether he was happy or not. Then his father sent him away to boarding school and all equivocation about happiness evaporated. *How did you find boarding life?* 'Horrendous!' was his uncompromising reply. He was barely ten years old and Treverton School was 100 miles from Durban. *If your parents were not well off, how did they manage to find the fees?* 'Well, it wasn't a big school and they needed the pupils, I suppose. I don't think it was much.' The truth is that he was very unhappy there and felt very isolated. Quite why, he wasn't sure. What ten-year-old can analyse his feelings? Some boys love boarding life and thrive. Others are not suited, don't enjoy it and feel homesick. Barry was clearly in the latter category.

It was his appendix that rescued him. In great pain as it became inflamed, he was rushed to the nearest hospital, ten miles away, not in a well-equipped ambulance but in the back of a pick-up truck, driven at speed by the headmaster. The appendix was removed that night. After a few days of convalescence on the ward, he returned to the school where his parents came to see him. In answer to concerned enquiries about his wellbeing, Barry whipped out a phial from the bedside cupboard containing the aforementioned appendix and presented it to his horrified mother. 'There you are, mum,' he declared with commendable inventiveness, 'I told you they had little black things in their potatoes!'

Whether she was taken in by his story or whether, with a mother's instinct, she sensed that all was not well with her son, Barry was removed from the school at the end of the year – to his immense relief. But why, I wanted to know, had his father sent him away in the first place? Barry's answer took my breath away. 'To be brutally frank – now that he's gone – I think that he just didn't want to have me around.' How very sad. The consequences of not feeling wanted in childhood are incalculable and probably scarring for life. How much it affected Barry was not easy to determine. He is not one to wear his heart on his sleeve but I suspect it was more hurtful than he was prepared to let on.

In any event, he was mightily relieved to meet up once again with his old mates from primary school who had moved *en bloc* to Clifton Prep. This was a school whose fees were not inconsiderable. Whether it was guilt on his part or, for once, a tacit acquiescence to his wife's insistence that Barry had a good education, his father had to dig deep into his pockets to pay them. Was it money well spent? On his own admission, Barry did not set the world alight academically but of course he excelled at sport, as you might imagine, and his name is top of the published list of Clifton's famous alumni. He has even had the cricket pavilion named in his honour so the school evidently remains proud of him and his achievements. 'But not Kingsmead,' he told me. 'Nothing in my honour at my home ground.'

But most of all, the boy was content at his new school. And this manifested itself no more clearly than in his cricket. 'It was at Clifton when my batting started to kick off,' he said, though he might just as well have used the phrase 'to kick off' about his rugby too. It will come as no surprise to learn that he was a mighty good full-back, who could catch and kick and read the game in front of him. 'But I wasn't very fast over the ground, as you know well enough, Murt,' he reminded me, 'and when I started to have trouble with my ankles, I gave up and concentrated on my cricket.' When only 11, he was selected to play for Durban Schools Under-14s, the first in a long line of representative honours that stretched all the way to the South African Test side. Also selected was Lee Irvine, an experienced player all of one year older than Barry. As we shall see, Irvine features large in the Richards story.

Talking of age, how old were you when you began to realise you had a special talent, that you were better than everybody else? He screwed up his face. 'Difficult to say, really. You could tell straight away that some of the other boys weren't very good at hand-eye coordination but it didn't seem to me that I was particularly out of the ordinary. Obviously, when getting picked for Under-11 sides when I was nine and Under-14 sides when I was 11 hinted at some ability. But *special…?*' One trait of my subject's personality that I have always admired – something that has landed him in deep water more than once – is his willingness to speak his mind, frankly and unadorned. If he says that he was unaware of his exceptional gifts when he was a young boy, you can take it as read that that is the truth of the matter. By the same token, he won't pussyfoot around when he acknowledges that there did come a time 'when I would back myself against most opponents', as he wryly puts it.

When you were a kid, did you ever watch the Test matches? 'Yes, we were given half-day holidays to go to Kingsmead when the Test was on.' *Any game, any player, that stands out in your memory?* 'I can vividly picture John Reid, the New Zealander, batting. But touring sides visited once every three or four years so Test matches were few and far between.' He reminded me yet again that there was no television; the only sight they got of cricket elsewhere in the country or abroad was of a shaky, grainy, black and white clip in a newsreel at the cinema. *But there was the Currie Cup?* 'That's right. I remember watching two of the greats, Roy McLean and Jackie McGlew, little imagining that I would be playing with them in the Natal side when I was 18.' He then gave a little laugh. 'I also remember a chap called Gary Bartlett. My God, he was quick. But he chucked it!' *Would Kingsmead be one of your favourite grounds?* 'It wasn't the best appointed ground in the world. But you always have a special affinity with your home ground, don't you?' I could not but agree. I loved Northlands Road in Southampton, home to Hampshire cricket, now sadly a housing estate. 'I enjoyed playing at Dean Park in Bournemouth,' he said. 'It had such a beautiful and peaceful setting.'

And the best cheese rolls on the circuit. His stomach rumbles in agreement. He then cut short our wistfulness. 'The highlight of the year when at school was the Fathers v Boys match on the hallowed turf of Kingsmead. It was a great thrill. I can remember the excitement even now.' Barry doesn't do misty-eyed sentimentality but anyone who does not recollect with a little frisson of joy that special moment when he steps on to the grass for the first time at the theatre of his dreams cannot call himself a true cricketer.

In 1959, when he was 14, he moved on to Durban High School, the oldest and certainly one of the most highly regarded schools in Natal, with a list of notable alumni as long as your arm. In cricket alone, it boasts among its old boys: Trevor Goddard, Hugh Tayfield, Geoff Griffin, Denis Gamsy, Lee Irvine, Lance Klusener and Hashim Amla. There was little doubt that the young Barry Richards would flourish in that environment. On the sports field, that is; he is refreshingly candid about the mark he left on the school's academic status. 'I was lazy,' he admitted. 'I mean, I didn't want to dissect *anything!' Except a bowling attack.* He grinned. 'My speciality was blowing down a Bunsen burner, so that it wouldn't ignite when the teacher lit it.' He found himself in the B stream, and there he stayed. The teaching was, by and large, 'boring' and there seemed to be no continuity on the staff; rarely did they have the same teacher for one subject throughout the academic year. Furthermore, the way the curriculum was set up did him few favours. 'You had to choose between History and Biology, for example. And Latin and Geography. Where's the logic in that?' Indeed. *And Afrikaans?* 'That was compulsory. So we had to learn a language that we knew we would never use. Why not Spanish, or something more relevant to the world outside? No one speaks Afrikaans except the Afrikaners in South Africa. Surely it makes sense to have one national language and as practically everybody in the world speaks English, then…' Politics again.

What about the teachers outside the classroom? You know, when they met you in the corridor or on the stairs or down on the games fields? 'They were unapproachable and severe, very old school. Strict!' *The cane – was it still used?* 'Huh. The cane was no weapon of last resort.' *Did you get beaten?* 'Plenty! The prefects were allowed to cane as well, you know. That was hard! You can pull the wool over the masters' eyes but you can't fool your peers!' That was the way it was in those days. It was part of school life. Many petty rules and regulations were applied strictly and without favour. Minor infractions, such as not wearing your basher or not wearing the uniform correctly or bunking off compulsory watching of the First XV, were ruthlessly punished. That is why the trip to England with the South African schoolboys came as such an eye-opener for them all. *Is it true that every boy, when taking guard in a school game, before addressing the umpire, would have to take his cap off?* 'And call him Sir! In England, the umpires, who were deaf anyway, would go, "Eh, what did you say?" [As they were] not used to being addressed so.' In point of fact, he bore little or no resentment for the strict regime.

But it was through cricket that he felt he could express himself and cement his identity. His potential was evident to all. 'He was a small boy when he first came to DHS in 1959, aged 14,' Lee Irvine told me. 'He already had an immaculate defensive technique. No one could get him out!' Not strong enough to pierce the inner ring, his run scoring at this time was not prolific but his judgement of line and length was faultless and his determination to succeed unshakeable. This is what set him apart from other gifted players was Irvine's contention, no stranger himself to burning ambition. 'You could see straight away that he had been well taught.' *Not in the classroom though.* 'No, not in the classroom. But ask him about Alan Butler.' I did.

Barry's father, aware that his son had a special talent and needed proper coaching, engaged the services of a friend of his, Alan Butler, who was a reasonable club player and an experienced coach. 'He was a stickler for technique,' said Barry. 'He drummed into me the basics of an orthodox technique, you now, left elbow well up, lead with the top hand, point the left shoulder – all that sort of stuff.' He also insisted on the classic, but uncomfortable, grip that Barry used. His left hand had to be round the front of the handle, not further to the back, which is more comfortable and used by most players these days. In addition, he held the bat further up the handle than most.

Yes, I've noticed in the photos of you playing that there was a fair bit of the rubber grip visible below your bottom hand. 'In those days we had lighter bats, so I needed more leverage – a longer swing to hit the ball. I needed a flow to my strokes; now, all they need is a bunt,' he added, with a grin. Playing predominantly with the top hand in control did not feel entirely natural but that was the classical method and it gave him a textbook style of batting, especially on the off-side. I remember the purr of appreciation from the Hampshire members whenever Barry unfurled one of his off-side attacking strokes, off front foot or back, balanced, elegant, orthodox, perfectly timed – a thing of beauty. 'I can go home now and die a happy man,' said one old gentleman to no one in particular in the pavilion at Southampton and everybody knew precisely what he meant. 'He was inflexible about it,' said Barry of his mentor. 'I'm not exactly sure I would coach it to young boys now but it made me into a good off-side player.' Good? Well, I suppose you can say that perfection is good. 'It restricts you a bit on the on side though.' I was astonished. It never occurred to me, nor to any of the perspiring bowlers who toiled to get him out, that he was ever restricted in his strokes on the on side. He laughed at that. 'Well, I basically looked around and whichever side had fewer fielders, I would hit it there.' He was adamant, however, about Butler's influence on him and remains grateful to this day for the hours and hours of patient coaching that he bestowed on the young boy. 'He made me,' Barry said simply.

Another one who had more than a passing influence on the young Richards was Les Theobald, the master in charge of cricket at the school. In the words of Lee Irvine, 'Theo was the best schoolboy coach in the world – bar none!' Considering the precocious talent of the skinny 14-year-old whom he picked for the school First XI, it is probable that Theobald would have had to do no more than tinker with Barry's already secure technique. But it was in other ways that his clear direction was felt. 'He was a firm believer in the etiquette of the game, upholding all the traditions and manners,' said Barry. 'He expected you to turn up correctly dressed, with your kit immaculately clean and your equipment in perfect order.' In that sense, the discipline he instilled sank in; Barry's corner was ever an oasis of tidiness in the midst of the clutter and disarray of a dressing room. His kit and equipment were the tools of his trade and he meticulously looked after them. 'Theo – he was damn strict!' said Barry affectionately. 'Cricket's ethos was very important to him.'

He taught Latin, not that Barry ever met him in the classroom, and was, by all accounts, a pillar of the establishment at DHS; to the boys it seemed that he had been there forever. A conservative to his bootlaces – literally – he held no truck with modernity in any of its guises. 'Not a great humorist,' Barry commented wryly, 'No twinkle in his eye.' For all that, Barry had enormous respect for him. He did not coach him as such; Barry was, to all intents and purposes, already the finished article but he encouraged the boy and recognised immediately his rare talent. He was no great player himself but he was steeped in the game, its history, its spirit, its ethics; it totally absorbed him. 'A groupie!' said Barry cheerfully. *Before his time then – a trailblazer.* But we both recognised the type. The prim and proper Les Theobald may have been no trailblazer – despite his blazer being an essential component of his wardrobe – but he was to play a significant role in Barry's early career.

One other teacher at DHS whom Barry remembers with fondness is Grayson Heath, who taught Geography and who looked after 'the dregs who had little interest in academics but who had a disproportionate interest in rugby and cricket'. Heath was at the time playing in the Natal side and notwithstanding his modest assertions that he 'clung on' to his place in the team, Natal were a strong side at that time and Heath was certainly no mug. He related accounts of Geography lessons on a Monday morning following the weekend's cricket. 'It was almost impossible to get a discussion going on the country's climate zones when there were the weekend's cricket results to analyse,' he said. At one stage, he was going through a poor patch of low scores – and his class knew it. Loudly they demanded to know his score. When he admitted that he had not greatly bothered the scorer, the cry went up, 'Sir, Richards scored more than you.' The free-scoring and precociously talented Barry Richards was sitting smugly at the back of the class and, with his toothy grin, he confirmed his score.

And so it went on. Eventually it was time to turn the tables on his unsympathetic pupils. Every Monday, he would summon Barry to the front of the class. He was asked how many he had scored. If it was 37, he was berated for not scoring 50. If it was 52, he was admonished for not scoring 100. So to the following Monday…

'The lesson was as before except there was a heightened air of anticipation in the class, almost as if they were privy to something a bit special because in answer to my question about his score, Barry triumphantly blurted out, "I scored 101, Sir." My answer was that if he could score 100 then it should have been *not out!'* All good knockabout fun. But it was then that Heath – a provincial player, do not forget – realised 'what a batting genius Barry was.' Genius. That is a word you will hear frequently used by Barry's contemporaries to describe his batting.

The second story that Heath recounts deserves to be quoted in full:

'The tradition at the time was an annual cricket match between the school staff and the First XI. The year was 1962, which just happened to be the year of DHS's best cricket team of all time, boasting three South African Schools players in Barry Richards, Lee Irvine and Bruce Heath, my brother. Both Richards and Irvine went on to play Test cricket for South Africa. The Staff XI on the other hand was a collection of social cricketers, the odd has-been league cricketer and two current first-class players in Pat Schulz and me. Pat was a genuine quick with a dubious action that had him called out of the game for throwing in the wake of the Geoff Griffin throwing saga and I bowled offies that despite my best efforts refused to turn in from the off. The two of us were essentially the staff attack.

'My classroom was on the second floor of the school building looking straight down the wicket, providing a classic view for the cricket connoisseur. The fact that the windows were bulging with most of my class leaning out was no proof that they were all connoisseurs. The significance of their enthusiastic following of the match was not lost on me, as it was certain I was going to have to bowl to Barry. Sadly for me, the swimming pool was at long on and while every run that Barry scored off me was cheered by his classmates, there was a resounding roar when he lofted an effortless six off me into the pool.

'The die was cast! As soon as things had settled back into a sense of normality, there was this loud call from the classroom, "Barry – swimming pool!" to which he duly obliged by lofting me again majestically into the pool, to their collective glee. I lost count of the number of sixes all of which were delivered on cue after the call from the classroom.'

As Lee Irvine said of his friend, Barry could never resist a challenge.

As we're talking about swimming pools, were you any good at swimming? 'There was a time when I was going to give up cricket and become a lifesaver.' I don't think he could have said anything that would have astonished me more. 'As you know,' he went on to explain, 'Durban is a surfer's paradise and I really loved the life of sand, sea and sun. I got quite good at it.' That isn't surprising as Barry becomes accomplished at most sports that take his fancy. I remember once stepping on a squash court with him. He wiped the floor with me. Golf is his current passion. He plays off a handicap of five and he did not start playing seriously until he was 40. He was a good swimmer and was in the school swimming team and to him it seemed a wholly logical step, to leave school and to take up lifesaving. It was a job after all and his academic career was going nowhere. As for professional cricket – the possibility never entered his head. There was no professional cricket in South Africa. *How did your parents react?* 'They were horrified. But the impulse was short lived. It was just one of those crazy ideas that you get when you're a kid.'

So *Baywatch*'s loss was Durban High School's gain. By now, Lee Irvine was the captain of the cricket team and they swept all before them. Irvine explained, 'I opened with Bruce Heath, Barry was at number three, Dave Anderson at four and Harvey Wannenberg at five, all of us Natal Schools players. I think that year we had nine opening partnerships of 150-plus.' Barry spent a long time that summer with his pads on waiting to bat. His father complained to the school that he wasn't getting enough time at the crease! Pity, then, the poor boys in the middle order. 'One player, Des Daniel,' Irvine said, 'had already played for Border Schools and he was an excellent all-rounder but at number six, he scarcely had to strap on his pads, yet alone make a trip to the middle.' So Irvine dropped down the order towards the end of the year and Barry opened. For the new season in 1963, Irvine having left school, Barry took hold of the captain's reins, his first experience of responsibility. It was not something that he craved but he was sanguine enough when given the opportunity. 'Basically, the best player was always the captain,' he said matter of factly. He felt he was a reasonable tactician but the psychological details of the job, motivating his team and learning the art of man-management, did not greatly interest him, at least, not yet. 'To be perfectly honest, Murt,' he said, 'I've never been very good with players who are, shall we say...*average.*'

So the uncertain, unsettled days of school, misty and distant in the memory, came to an end. As with many people, he is ambivalent about its influence on his life; the effect was undoubtedly great and lifelong but quite in what ways is never easy to pin down. Of course, his cricket career was methodically assembled on its launch pad but did it provide the fuel for lift-off? Or was that already in the tank? Who can say?

There is a sad postscript to Barry's schooldays, a shocking occurrence that proved to be an augury to a dreadful event later in his life. A contemporary of his at DHS, a friend and a fellow team member of the Under-14 and Under-15 teams, hanged himself. The reasons remained unclear but Barry remembers vividly attending the funeral and filing past the open coffin. Then, he was bewildered by it all; now, with its uncomfortable echoes, the bewilderment is even more acute.

2

Nuffield Week

'He hadn't even got his honours blazer at school. And he'd just scored a
hundred against the full Western Province side!'

Lee Irvine

IT is a piquant fact that Barry Richards – as with countless other South African
cricketers – owed his chance to strut his stuff for the first time on a public stage to
a British philanthropist born in Worcester. William Richard Morris (1877–1963)
was a motor manufacturer and the founder of Morris Motors. He was ennobled as
Lord Nuffield in 1934 and became Viscount Nuffield in 1938. He had no children
so he donated much of his vast wealth to charities. Among numerous philanthropic
endeavours, he set up the Nuffield Foundation and Nuffield College, Oxford.

Anyone in South Africa with cricket in his blood will have heard of Nuffield
Week. The story goes that the good English lord was watching the third Test at
Durban between England and South Africa in January 1939 and was dismayed by the
pummelling suffered by the home side bowlers as England rattled up 469/4 declared,
Paynter scoring 243 and Hammond 120. After the second day's play, on the spur of
the moment, he decided to make a huge donation to South African cricket, provided
it was used to promote the game at school level. The match was duly lost by South
Africa, by an innings and 13 runs, but they acquitted themselves well enough for the
rest of the rubber, notwithstanding their new benefactor's concern, losing it solely
by this one English victory. The series is probably best known for the fifth Test, the
so-called Timeless Test, which was to be played to a finish, no matter how long it
took. In the event, it had to be abandoned as a draw at tea on the *tenth* day, with
England only 42 runs short of victory with five wickets left, otherwise the tourists
would have missed their boat home.

Consequently, a fund was established which was used to institute a cricket
tournament, known as the Nuffield Week, during which the representative school
team from all the provinces played each other and immediately after the event, the
South African Schools side was selected. Needless to say, the week loomed large in
any schoolboy's mind, who took his cricket seriously. Barry Richards was no different
and shared the same nerves and excitement of the occasion as many provincial and
Test players before and after him. The significance of Nuffield Week has lost some
of its lustre in recent years – it is now known as Coca-Cola Week and is just one of
several privately-sponsored cricket festivals – but back then, 'No one, but no one,
who had pretensions of playing first-class cricket would have come through the ranks
without attending Nuffield Week,' Barry announced unequivocally. It was the perfect

stage for him to exhibit his budding genius to the wider public. Influential people were there to impress and Barry seized the moment.

Barry explained that before Nuffield Week, it was necessary to make an impression during Offord Week when the Natal schools would play each other and during which the Natal Schoolboys XI would be selected. Barry was 16 and his exploits for DHS had already gone before him (on the cricket field, I hasten to add) so perhaps it would have come as less of a surprise to knowledgeable observers than it was to Barry that he was very much in the frame to be picked for the Natal side, even if he was still a colt. It may seem like just another plainly evident step in his career towards international honours but what 16-year-old looks far into the future and truly believes in his own destiny? He hoped, he wasn't sure, he bit his nails in anticipation and was thrilled when the team was announced and he was in the squad.

Interestingly enough, also included in the squad was a certain M.J. Procter. They knew each other well enough, having locked horns at prep school and at high school level. Their careers were to take remarkably parallel paths; one went on to play for Natal and Hampshire and the other for Rhodesia and Gloucestershire and of course they became team-mates for Natal Schools, South Africa Schools, the full South African Test side and the Rest of the World. So close was their cricketing association that it is generally assumed that they were joined at the hip. Not so, it would appear. 'Prockie was more social than me,' Barry said. 'I was an only child and as such, more of a loner. I would go out with the lads and have a meal and then go home. Prockie was more inclined to burn the midnight oil.' They had different interests outside cricket too. Barry played a lot of golf whereas Procter preferred the horses. Lee Irvine offered an interesting slant on the different personalities of the two. 'Prockie was easier socially and found making himself popular with team-mates, members, supporters a bit of a doddle. Barry was more reserved. He kept his own counsel and didn't trust people until he knew them well. That is partly why Barry got a reputation of being a mercenary and Prockie did not, even though they were both paid professionals.' The charge of acquisitiveness against Barry will be something we will be revisiting later in this story.

The venue for the festival that year was Johannesburg. They travelled overnight by train. It was the first time that Barry had been out of Natal and he was very much on his guard, determined to be as unobtrusive as possible and to toe the line, behaviour, he noted wryly, that was not common to the whole team. He kept close to the people he knew well, Lee Irvine and Harvey Wannenberg, both fellow DHS boys. They were billeted in boarding school accommodation and the games were of a traditional format, not limited overs, much like the Currie Cup.

The first match against Border, which Natal lost, was notable for an accomplished hundred from someone even younger than Barry. His name was Hylton Ackerman. Barry was hugely impressed by the mature and accomplished innings of the 14-year-old, knowing instinctively that this boy was destined for big things, and sure enough, their earlier careers were fated for similar stellar success and equal bitter disappointment. Barry may not have recognised genius in himself but he could see glimpses of it in one or two others. His own performances were good enough, if not outstanding, but he guessed, looking around at the talent on display, that he was in with a shout of being selected at the end of the week for the full national schools side. All the players from the competing teams were summoned on the Friday evening and as they stood awkwardly about, the team was announced. Barry was in, as was Ackerman, but there was no place for his friend, Lee Irvine. Why not, I wanted to know, especially in view of his undoubted talent and weight of runs at school. Irvine gave a rueful laugh when I asked him. 'I'd broken my arm during the previous rugby season and it hadn't fully recovered. So I had not even been considered for Offord Week, let alone this week in Joburg. But four or five senior boys had been banned for boozing, so they brought me back. I was short of cricket, not fully fit and missed out.'

The reward for selection was a full-on game against the Transvaal provincial side at The Wanderers. And these were schoolboys, let us not forget, sent into battle against experienced first-class cricketers and on what was traditionally one of the fastest and bounciest pitches in the world. It was no fairy tale introduction to the tough world of men's cricket for the youngsters; they were comfortably beaten. Barry was not yet an opener but the team was short of openers and he was sent in first to face the new ball. He remembers being dumped on his backside – for the first time in his fledgling career – by Slug Lodwick, a bowler considerably quicker than anyone he had faced before. He made only nine but was not put off by the occasion and has only buoyant memories of the whole week. 'We were playing against people whose names had been in the papers the previous week,' he said, in much the same awed tone of voice that others would convey when talking about him. But his first taste of the big time had only sharpened his appetite.

But first, it was back to Biology and the dissecting knife. If he could have cut through the boredom of never-ending lessons until the next cricket season, he would have. Mercifully, for him, as Joni Mitchell's lyrics sing to us, 'The seasons they go round and round', and it was not long before Durban High School were taking all before them on the cricket field. Apart from the majestic batting – 'crushing strokeplay', Barry called it – of the fully fit Lee Irvine, he has one particular memory that sticks in his mind. The famous England Test player, Denis Compton, came to the school and took what I suppose these days would be called a 'masterclass' with Barry and Harvey Wannenberg in the nets. By now, the great batsman, *bon viveur* and party animal was with his second wife, Valerie, a South African, and he was spending as much time as he could, cricket commitments aside, in the sunnier climes of southern Africa. *Did he pass on any momentous advice?* Barry admitted to being so awestruck that he took in very little of what the great man said to him. 'However, he must have been a little impressed for he publicly came out with his support for my inclusion as a 17-year-old in the South African touring party to Australia in 1963/64.' *Was that ever a feasible possibility?* 'No, of course not. But we did get on well whenever I met him later on.'

That tour, as it happens, was when another young prodigy burst on to the international scene. Graeme Pollock, lionised as a schoolboy cricketer even more than Barry, but one year older, had broken a number of records in South African cricket, including being picked for Eastern Province as a 16-year-old when still at school, the youngest to score a first-class century and the youngest to score a first-class double century. In the third Test during this tour, he scored 122, thus becoming the youngest South African to score a Test hundred, a record that still stands today. I remember listening to Ron Roberts on a tinny transistor radio under the bedclothes at night describing the precocious talent as a 'new star in the cricketing firmament'. I cannot be sure that those were the *exact* words used – it was, after all, 50 years ago – but the awe and excitement in his voice crackling over the airwaves from the other side of the world were unmistakeable.

Two questions cross the threshold of my mind at this point. Who was the greater batsman, Barry Richards or Graeme Pollock? It is a favourite conundrum of cricket lovers the world over and one that has been put to me and pondered on by the scores of people that I have spoken to in the course of writing this book. It is something

I have endlessly debated myself, having played with and against both, albeit only in passing. The answer is unattainable, I suppose, relying as it does on personal opinion and subjective analysis but the points of view of the great and the good of the game make interesting reading, as you will discover as this story unfolds. And the other question is: why do players from other countries seem to mature earlier than Englishmen? The answer to that is equally difficult to nail down but it is worth bearing in mind as we follow the early careers of both men.

For Barry, all was gearing up nicely for his second Nuffield Week in December 1962, taking place this time in Cape Town. A year older, Barry was no longer an *ingénue*; if not yet the finished article, his emerging talent was exciting the admiration of not just Denis Compton. The week was not only something of a triumph for the Natal side, who, with four DHS boys in the team, were unbeaten, but also for Barry personally. Consider his scores: 82 v Griqualand West, 50 v Rhodesia, 102 v Western Province, 101 v North East Transvaal. He has fond memories of sharing a partnership of 164 in 81 minutes with Mike Procter, who reached his hundred just before the declaration. I think it can safely be said that Barry was not chewing his fingernails in nervous anticipation as the team for the South African Schools was read out on the Friday evening. Sure enough, he was selected, with Lee Irvine as captain and another future Springbok, Mike Procter, in as well. Hylton Ackerman was also included and he would have brought up the total of later internationals in the side to four had the ill-fated tour to Australia in 1971/72 not been cancelled. In addition, several other members of the team were to go on to play first-class cricket so it was, in the words of Irvine, 'One hell of a strong side, perhaps the strongest South African Schools side ever assembled.'

The full Western Province team were experienced and battle-hardened, surely more than a match for schoolboys. It would appear not. Set 237 to win in 226 minutes, the Schools won by three wickets, with three-quarters of an hour to spare. Admittedly, the declaration was generous but you can bet your bottom dollar that the men had no wish to come off second best to a bunch of kids. The press were all agog, as you would expect, but the focus of their attention was not on the schoolboys' victory, newsworthy as that might have been, but on the new prodigy, Barry Richards. He had scored 106, his third century in successive days, only the fourth time a schoolboy had taken a hundred off a full provincial side.

In every successful sportsman's career there are defining moments when the rest of the world sit up and take notice. It might be defeating a leading seed at Wimbledon. It might be a sub-par round in treacherous conditions in The Open. It might be scoring a last-minute winner as an unknown in an FA Cup semi-final. This was Barry's moment and he had seized it eagerly, almost as if he sensed that destiny was calling. More than anything else, of course, he had convinced himself that he could cut the mustard at this exalted level. 'I never felt intimidated by the occasion or by the opposition,' he said. I wasn't sure whether he was referring to this match in particular or to the rest of his career. But clarification wasn't really needed.

And then, as if the fates were intent on bringing him down to earth after raising him so high, it was back to school and those dreaded lessons. 'He hadn't even got his honours blazer,' Irvine whistled in disbelief, who knew and understood the cachet of that privilege. That oversight was soon put right but the gold-braided blazer did little to affect Barry's preoccupation and rising excitement with the forthcoming South African Schoolboys tour of England in June and July of 1963.

3

England June/July 1963

Sexual intercourse began
In nineteen sixty-three
(Which was rather late for me)
Between the end of the Chatterley ban
And the Beatles' first LP.

Philip Larkin

APART from the beginning of sexual intercourse, what else of note happened in 1963? President Kennedy was assassinated, Martin Luther King made his great 'I have a dream' speech, a gang of thieves held up a Royal Mail train and made off with £2.5m and John Profumo first clapped his eyes on a pretty young girl called Christine Keeler swimming naked in a pool. These, however, were but side shows to the main event of that momentous year: the West Indian cricket team were in England. Shrewdly led by the charismatic Frank Worrell, their first black captain, the West Indies had recently toured Australia in one of the greatest series ever played, best known perhaps for the first tied Test match in history. Anticipation in England was at fever pitch at the prospect of seeing those joyful and talented Caribbean cricketers, who had done so much to reinvigorate Test cricket, displaying the same verve and dynamism that had earned them an open-top car, ticker-tape parade through the jam-packed streets of Melbourne on their departure. Furthermore, there had been an explosion of West Indian immigration in this country since the last time they toured in 1957 and the crowds were likely to be large, boisterous and partisan. Did the tour live up to expectations? The answer was a resounding yes.

Now, you may ask, why I am making a broad connection between Philip Larkin's witty verse on the permissive society and West Indian cricketers? These two themes, sex and race, would have been at the very forefront of the picture that a touring team of schoolboy cricketers from South Africa would have formed of England in 1963. To emerge, blinking furiously, out of the dark, censored world of apartheid and to step straight into the flamboyance and permissiveness of the Swinging Sixties must have been a considerable culture shock. 'We'd never seen a nude photo,' said Barry, 'and then we met the ladies of the night in Soho. Just imagine what an eye-opener that was for 16-year-olds.' *And the West Indians were about to be crowned in all but name as the world champions of cricket.* He saw my point. 'There were black people sharing buses, trains, public toilets, even mixing in the stands of the cricket grounds. We'd never seen anything like it.' *How did you cope? How did you marry what was in front of your faces with what you had been used to at home?* He shrugged. 'I guess we went along with the sort of brainwashing that we had grown up with – that "your" blacks were different to "our" blacks. Remember, Murt, there was no TV in South Africa at that time. The first time we saw a TV was at Heathrow.'

However, Soho was not on their minds when the team assembled at Jan Smuts Airport, Johannesburg, looking very neat in their tour blazers and ties. Or perhaps Soho was on their minds, or at least on the minds of a couple of them who were more worldly-wise than the young, unsophisticated captain. *Captain? You were the captain? I didn't know that.* 'It was a wholly unexpected honour, of course. But it didn't mean that they saw captaincy potential in me. At schoolboy level, the best player was always the captain. Simple as that.' *But what about Lee Irvine? He had captained the side in Nuffield Week. Why didn't they stick with him?* 'He'd left school by then. So he was ineligible.' The academic year ends at Christmas and the new one commences in January. Nuffield Week had taken place in the previous December, 1962, when Irvine was still a pupil at DHS. The tour of England was to take place during the English mid-summer of 1963, by which time Irvine had left. So it was Barry who had the privilege of leading the South African Schools on their first tour overseas.

No Irvine withstanding, it was an impressive side Barry had at his disposal. It is an astonishing fact that every boy in the touring party went on to play first-class cricket. In Barry's party, Mike Procter and Hylton Ackerman were friends; some of the others would have been not much more than vaguely familiar faces. But it doesn't take long for cricketers on tour to get to know each other. You can be assured that by the time they boarded the plane bound for London, they would have been laughing and joking as if they had been great mates for years. In fact, they had a couple of warm-up matches before they set out, both against men's teams and both of which they lost. They may be a bunch of talented schoolboys, you can almost hear their opponents muttering under their breath, but they've still got a lot to learn. And they would have been absolutely right, Barry admitted with a grin, both on and off the field. 'We were like rookies being sent to the front line.'

To keep them in line, at the front or at the rear, was Les Theobald, Barry's master in charge at DHS. This ensured that captain and manager had a strong working relationship from the outset and whatever might have been in the mind of others more inclined to devilment, it certainly wasn't in the mind of Barry. He respected 'Theo' too much. Besides, he had every intention of getting the most from this unique opportunity to learn and to improve. He was going to toe the line all right. Furthermore, he and his team were blessed to have in the capacity of assistant manager none other than the former captain of South Africa, Jackie McGlew. Theobald taking care of administrative duties, with his resolute insistence on good manners and proper etiquette and McGlew, a Test player of enormous experience, concentrating on the coaching and match tactics, were an ideal double act. All bases were covered. All was set.

Incidentally, who paid – the parents or the South African authorities? 'I'm not sure how the finances were broken down but I know someone paid for me. There was no way my father could have afforded it.' Quite right. On any tour overseas, you never leave your best player at home. By hook or by crook, the money was found. For the first visit to England of a South African Schools side was a huge deal. Press interest on departure and arrival was considerable; Barry remembers being greeted by MCC and ESCA bigwigs at Heathrow. 'But no sign of the Queen,' said Barry sadly. All the stops had been pulled out to prepare an itinerary befitting their guests. Of course, McGlew and Denis Compton, with his close contacts in both countries, had pulled a few strings and called in some favours and the hand of Wilfred Isaacs too, a noted and generous benefactor of South African cricket, was all over the planning.

A quick look at the boys' schedule clearly shows that much effort had been expended in providing the tourists with opposition in abundance, if not always of quality, to satisfy any cricketing visitor to these shores – 21 games in the space of five weeks. Most of the major public schools were on the fixture list: Bradfield, Charterhouse, Eton, Malvern, Radley, St Edward's, Tonbridge, Wellington and Winchester. Also lined up were the Second XIs from four counties: Hampshire, Lancashire, Warwickshire and Nottinghamshire. And in addition to those beautiful grounds of the public schools, the boys would be playing at famous Test venues: Old Trafford, Trent Bridge, the Oval and of course the home of cricket, Lord's.

This young team represented the future of South African cricket and the rest of the world sat up and took notice. A golden era was dawning. Graeme Pollock was about to erupt on to the world stage in the following winter in Australia. His brother, Peter, three years older, was already turning heads (actually, they were ducking) bowling for his country, and the nucleus of the side – Barlow, Lindsay, Bland, Bacher – that was to become undisputed world champions was already in place. How long this team of all the talents would have gone on to dominate Test cricket is anyone's guess.

This crop of youngsters was much too good for their English counterparts. Of the 21 games played, they won ten, drew nine and lost only two. *Wisden* records that the South Africans were a 'formidable side' and had a 'purposeful approach to the game'. It was a wretched summer and 'inclement weather was responsible for some of those draws'. They beat Tonbridge, Radley, Malvern, Wellington and Winchester, all reputable sides on the school circuit. Against the four Second XIs of counties, 'They were seen to good advantage, nearly winning all four, and the Canadian Schools were ruthlessly dispatched at Lord's.' The *Wisden* correspondent – nameless, but Barry has a shrewd idea that it was the respected cricket writer Michael Melford, because he had quite a bit to do with the planning of the tour – was particularly impressed by the tourists' performance against RJO Meyer's XI at Millfield. Founder and headmaster of Millfield School, Meyer had gathered together a formidable side, including the intimidating, not to say infamous, West Indian fast bowler, Roy Gilchrist.

Roy Gilchrist was an interesting, talented, notorious, ultimately tragic, character in the history of the game. Possessed of a fiery temper, he was rightly feared for the speed and hostility of his bowling. His Test career came to a premature end at the age of 24 when he was sent home in disgrace from India for bowling a succession of beamers from 18 yards. It is said that when he was informed of the decision to put him on the next flight out of town, he pulled a knife on the captain, Gerry Alexander. He moved into the Lancashire League where uncontrollable rage and controversy continued to stalk him. He once pulled a stump out of the ground and hit the opposition batsman over the head with it. He was also arrested, charged and found guilty of assaulting his wife. Not to put too fine a point on it, he was a loose cannon, liable to detonate at any moment.

Meyer had invited him to play for his side and secured his agreement – it was a long drive from Lancashire to Somerset – only by assuring the fast bowler that he would be used as a batsman. Gilchrist, in common with most fast bowlers, always reckoned he was undervalued as a batsman so he accordingly packed his pads in anticipation of slogging a few off these schoolboys. Meyer by reputation was never a man to stick to the script however and he declared just before Gilchrist was scheduled to bat. It didn't need a professor of human anthropology and body language to tell the schoolboys that Gilchrist was exceedingly disgruntled at this unexpected turn of events and when a fast bowler with a lack of self control has a fit of fury and he has the new cherry in his hand, the opening batsmen had better look out. Barry wasn't opening – he was not an accustomed opener at this stage of his career – but he was at number three, very much in the firing line. Gilchrist was an intimidating figure to even hardened Test players; he ran in from the sightscreen and had a terrifying leap into the crease, or sometimes well beyond. It was not long before Barry had to go out to face the music. In his own estimation, he coped 'reasonably well' after scampering down to the non-striker's end off the first ball he faced. In fact, the boys chased down the target of 226 with 25 minutes and four wickets to spare to take another prominent scalp on their travels.

Of the matches against the schools, Barry remembers only occasional incidents or places. What day is it? Oh, Tuesday…well, it must be Radley then. Or is it Winchester? Details merge into each other down the long corridors of time. He does call to mind the impressive buildings and the beautiful grounds that these public schools own. 'Most of our schools, even the really prestigious ones,' he pointed out, 'are in the cities, without boarding traditions like in England. All these were out in the *bundu*.' *I beg your pardon?* 'Sorry, a Bantu word. Out in the country. Very nice countryside, mind you.' One or two of their individual opponents, he remembers well, if only because he later played with them or against them in county cricket. Among their number, he would include Graham Roope, who was at Bradfield and later went on to represent Surrey and England. It was their first experience of strawberries and cream, which they could indulge in to their hearts' content as Bradfield had been dispatched before tea.

Another school team that was painfully whipped was Malvern College. In that side was a young player who, like Barry, was no stranger to the unwelcome burden of being tagged a schoolboy prodigy. And by a strange, uncanny quirk of fate, both of them were to play exactly the same number of Test matches – a wretchedly paltry four. The reasons were poles apart though. Roger Tolchard would surely have played more times for his country had his career not coincided with those of two of the finest wicketkeepers England has ever produced, Alan Knott and Bob Taylor. The scorecard of the match reveals that neither boy had a great bearing on the match, Richards dismissed for 20 (caught Tolchard) and Tolchard for seven. Nevertheless, the South Africans made a big impression on the young Tolchard. 'Bloody brilliant!' was his succinct verdict, 'They were immaculate too, both in manners and dress. We all remembered, with a mixture of amusement and grudging respect, their habit of removing their caps when taking guard and politely thanking the umpire, always referring to him as Sir, not Umpire.'

Malvern subsided to 73 all out and that in reply to the tourists' total of 222/8 declared. 'A chap called Ridley, a Rhodesian I think, bowled us out. Nifty little left-arm orthodox, he was,' Tolchard recalled. Ah yes, Giles Ridley. Not one cut from the same cloth as the rest of his team-mates. 'He was a studious type,' said Barry, 'He used to astonish us by visiting museums and art galleries when we were sightseeing in London, whereas the rest of us preferred the, ah, more interesting spots. Great at receptions,' Barry added with a laugh. 'He'd engage all these boring people in deep conversation and got us off the hook.'

The only other scorecard from the tour that I have been able to track down is for the match against Winchester. This ancient school has a proud cricketing tradition – one of its old boys was the controversial England captain, Douglas Jardine – but on this occasion, that reputation was torn to shreds. Winchester won the toss and batted.

I use the term loosely; their total of 36 suggests that not a lot of batting took place. Ridley again was the main destroyer. Rapidly, the visitors rattled up 200 (Ackerman 102 not out) and then immediately declared at the loss of their first wicket before the padded-up Richards could make it to the middle. *I thought you were the captain and could declare when you wanted.* 'Oh no,' he reminded me. 'All those decisions were taken by the management.' Winchester fared a little better in their second knock, managing 131, but the match was over well before stumps. And this was a two-day match! It tickled me to note that the scorer was M.J. Procter. Good for the soul, Prockie, good for the soul. History does not record what the boys did on their day off. I expect Barry joined Giles Ridley looking around the famous 11th-century cathedral. After all, as Ridley would have told him, Winchester Cathedral boasts the longest nave in Europe. 'Is that with a k?' enquired my subject.

Another match on the itinerary that stood out was the one against Warwickshire Second XI, if only for the slight amusement Barry felt when he looked at the scorecard and noted an opposing player had almost the same name – and initials – as he, B.A. Richardson. Bryan Richardson was, in the eyes of more than one knowledgeable observer, the most talented of the three Richardson brothers. The other two, Peter and Dick, had successful careers in the professional game and they remain, to this day, the only pair of brothers to have represented England in the same Test match. Bryan forsook the county game to pursue his entrepreneurial skills, later to take over the chairmanship of Coventry City FC. I sought Bryan's recollections of his first encounter with Barry. Of the actual game, he remembers little, except batting with the young Warwickshire legend, Dennis Amiss. But he does have this to say of the future South African star, 'I played a few matches with Barry for Derrick Robins, during the time of South Africa's isolation. Batting with him was *fantastic!* Just so good, and so much time. The other thing I remember about him was that he hardly moved at the crease. And not much in the field either!' If you're a slip fielder, the less you move, the better chance you have of catching it, was Barry's tart response. Besides, he had flat feet, he always said. That might have got him out of active service in an army but all this is really beside the point. Believe me, Barry Richards could move as quickly as anyone in the outfield when the situation demanded.

What about the Charterhouse match? You must remember playing against our old captain? Richard Gilliat, later captain of Hampshire, was at Charterhouse at the time, an extremely talented, all round games player – he played at Junior Wimbledon – and the captain of a cricket XI that was having a very good season. *Now I come to think of it, the pair of you must have walked out to the middle to toss, both of you suitably blazered.* We laughed. That would indeed have been a little cameo that Gilliat's future subordinates at Hampshire would have paid good money to watch. In fact, they were lucky to go out to toss at all. Rain had been all about, the wicket was wet and, had their visitors not been a touring side from overseas, the home side would probably have called off the game early that morning. Which made Barry's innings even more remarkable, in Gilliat's eyes. 'He got 50, on a very tricky wicket. And our attack, in schoolboy terms, was more than useful. He looked as if he had been playing on wet wickets all his life, rather than the hard, fast true wickets of a hot country.' *So you could see that he had a special talent, even then?* Gilliat nodded. 'We were all playing one game; Barry was playing another.' He went on to tell me another little anecdote of that day. 'At lunch, I was sitting next to Jackie McGlew, one of their managers. He told me, and I've never forgotten his exact words, that Barry was the best young player he'd ever seen.' Barry has other memories of that lunch. 'There was beer on the table! We'd never seen anything like it. We stuck to orange juice. Some of them batted as if they'd drunk a bit too much.' Whether alcohol or just good bowling was responsible, Charterhouse stumbled to ignominious defeat.

Tell me about Jackie McGlew, as we're on the subject. I had memories of McGlew being a brave, stubborn, obdurate opening batsman with an impenetrable defence that he used hour after strokeless hour to frustrate the England bowlers. It was said that his name symbolised his batting style. For all that, the English public came to respect his tenacity and his powers of concentration and his 'over my dead body' attitude. 'Known as "Buckets"!' said Barry. *Why?* 'He had massive hands, even though he wasn't a big bloke, and he caught everything.' *What was he like as a coach?* 'He was more of a mentor than a coach, full of little tips and advice, and always encouraging you to improve.' *Wisden* put it another way, 'McGlew provided the young team with shrewd counsel.' Barry continued, 'You see, he had to work hard at his own game, not being as naturally talented as, say, Roy McLean, in order to succeed.' *Did you get on with him?* 'Get on with him! We all hero-worshipped him. He was a South African legend.' *But you must have got to know him personally while you were on tour?* 'You have to understand, Murt, that it was much more formal in those days. At least it was for us. We noticed that the English boys seemed to have a friendlier, closer relationship with their masters than we ever did. We spoke when we were spoken to.' *Didn't you play together in the same Natal side when you were a bit older?* 'I was so nervous, I called him Mr McGlew. After a while, he called me aside and told me that he thought it was probably time for me to call him Jackie.'

Any other memories of the tour – the cricket side, I mean? Several, it would seem. One was being comprehensively 'done' by Richie Benaud. He wouldn't have been the first, I pointed out. 'I'd never seen a leg spinner. There weren't many around where I grew up. We were at Lord's playing against a strong Taverners side. I played Benaud reasonably comfortably for a while. Then he bowled me one a fraction shorter. I lay back to cut it and before I knew it, the ball had hurried through and castled me.' Benaud called it his 'flipper'. There is a lovely photo of the moment – though I doubt Barry would agree with my choice of adjective – with Barry, opened up like a can of beans, as the popular phrase goes, Benaud following through quickly, as if this was what he fully expected, and the wicketkeeper studying the wreckage of the stumps as if he'd seen it all before. Barry hadn't.

Although he was not to know it at the time, possibly his most significant innings of the tour was against Hampshire Second XI. Keith Wheatley, later to become a team-mate and friend at Hampshire, remembered the match very well. He was playing. 'Peter Haslop bowled the first ball of the match and got a wicket. In came Barry at number three. At the end of the over, the score was 20/1!' Alan Castell was also playing for Hampshire that day. 'During Barry's innings, the ball kept on disappearing into the orchard alongside the ground. Desmond Eagar, the club sec, was tearing his hair out – what was left of it – because the club were running out of balls,' he remembered. Barry scored a majestic 80 in only 76 minutes and left everyone, even these two sceptical and hardened pros, open-mouthed in admiration. The wicketkeeper standing behind Barry on that day, making a mental note of every perfectly executed stroke, was Leo Harrison, a stalwart of the county for umpteen years and now the team's coach. I remember him telling me much later that they all thought what a pity it was that Barry wasn't English. They'd never seen such natural talent and he would have signed him up on the spot had it been possible. The door to permit counties to employ overseas players was not yet even ajar.

So you had a good tour? 'I loved every minute of it.' *What I meant was did you think you had a successful tour?* 'I think I played pretty well. I scored a good hundred against

Eton and had quite a few respectable scores as well.' The tour figures tell a less modest story. Sitting astride the batting column was B.A. Richards with an average of 49.87, closely followed by M.J. Procter with 48.25 and then H.D. Ackerman with 36.49. *Wisden*'s assessment was this, 'Richards was in a class of his own. Procter is a batsman of high promise and a big future, at his best under pressure.' Barry told me about two of his friend's innings, both played 'when we were deep in the ****'. Against Radley, the tourists were reeling at 46/4. In strode Procter to smite 148, 100 of which were in boundaries. And against Nottinghamshire Second XI, they were in trouble again, 9/3. Procter came to the wicket to score 130. 'Such a clean striker of the ball,' Barry practically purred. *I note he only bowled 48 overs on the whole tour. Was he injured?* 'No. But don't forget he was only 16. He only started to bowl fast later on. I seem to remember that he kept wicket a few times. He was one of the finest all-round games players I've ever seen. Natal Schools rugby, talented at tennis…any game he played he was good at.' He continued to sing the praises of his brother-in-arms. 'People talk of the great all-rounders of that era, Botham, Hadlee, Imran, Kapil Dev, but no one mentions Prockie. He could have been the best of the lot, given the opportunity. And brave too. He had injury after injury and in the end he was only held together with Sellotape.'

The tour was deemed an overwhelming success. That the South Africans were strong surprised nobody – after all, you don't venture overseas with a weak side. But these boys were a notch or two above what English coaches and officials had ever seen. Some of the more percipient of observers must have looked at the future international itinerary and given a little shiver. That is if they left aside the niggling worries, already surfacing, over that country's racial policies. Which led me on neatly to my next enquiry. *Did the subject of apartheid ever rear its ugly head on tour?* Once again, Barry paused, as if measuring his words. I wasn't sure why any ambivalence – if that is what it was – should colour his answer. He was only a young lad, bear in mind, a bit naive perhaps, whose only thoughts were on cricket, one who had little interest in, and minimal understanding of, the murky world of politics. Besides, they had been warned, before setting off, not to get involved in contentious issues such as apartheid. He was sure that this instruction issued by the management was a genuine attempt to protect the youngsters, so they could concentrate on their cricket and savour the experience of a lifetime. There was no hint of government pressure or veiled threats from the police or anything like that. But it was a sensitive issue nonetheless and one that would have been raised much more often and much more forcefully a few years later.

'There was no great discussion about it,' he said, 'and we weren't greatly into politics, to be truthful. I suppose we were aware that it was a contentious issue but we were patriotic South Africans, proud of our country and supportive of our government. But we were only kids and …' It seems that their opponents weren't terribly interested either. There were many more interesting things for teenage boys to discuss than the rights and wrongs of one political system over another. I hope he enjoyed this period of blissful innocence, I ruminated, for it was not to last long. As he has said repeatedly, politics came to dominate his life.

Tell me about the story of Cassius Clay. Looking back on the incident, he finds it slightly humorous but at the time it did bring them up short, a sharp reminder that their country was possibly not the most popular on the planet. They were in Earls Court, close to the YMCA where they had been billeted. They became aware of busy activity on the other side of the road, with an excited crush of people swarming around a figure barely visible in the middle of the milling throng. Intrigued, they crossed the road to investigate. The object of attention was none other than Cassius Clay – who later called himself Muhammad Ali – the world champion heavyweight boxer, in London to fight Henry Cooper. The boys stood out in the crowd because they were all kitted out in their tour blazers, and not many teenagers were wearing blazers in London in 1963. The champ spotted them and wanted to know who they were and where they came from. Unwary, they told him. There was nothing to be ashamed of, nothing to hide. Ali's reaction disabused them of that conviction. 'Not very friendly,' said Barry. At that point, they were barely aware of the episode's significance in their lives and put down Ali's frostiness to his mood of the moment. Later events probably compelled them to reconsider.

What about the rest of the tour, sightseeing and all the rest? 'We did all the usual sights in London, all a bit boring, to be honest.' Who cannot look back on his own childhood memories of family holidays and groan at the recollection of yet another cathedral or chateau 'not to be missed'? Barry and the boys, with the exception of Giles Ridley, found the atmosphere and the buzz of 1960s London more interesting than the museums. 'We went on the Underground,' Barry marvelled, 'The hustle and bustle of the city with its diversity of people left us open-mouthed. And films with bare boobs! To say nothing of the magazines on sale. Leicester Square was amazing.' *And of course, Soho is just around the corner.* 'Is it?' he replied, wide-eyed. 'But we didn't get up to mischief,' he insisted. 'We were all too scared of getting caught. Or at least I was. Now, on later tours…'

Before we leave this tour, let me tell you of another, lasting memory he has of England. 'We were playing Lancashire Second XI at Old Trafford. The day before, I'd sent all my sweaters to be cleaned and they hadn't yet come back. And Old Trafford on a bleak, miserable day can be…well, you know what it's like. Jeez, it was cold! And I was in my shirtsleeves. No one would lend me theirs. Obviously.' Let me fast forward a few years and ask you to picture in your mind's eye a grumpy Barry Richards, heavily disguised as a Michelin Man wearing so many sweaters, being practically dragged from the fug and the warmth of the dressing room to take the field on a cold, blustery morning in early April at the start of the English cricket season. It was something he never got used to and always went to the most painstaking lengths to avoid. In retrospect, it probably would have been better for Hampshire to give him leave of absence until it warmed up. A century for each game he missed. He would have leapt at the challenge.

4

Natal 1964–70

*'This sunshine-faced, fair-haired, Natal opening
batsman is undoubtedly one of the most promising
youngsters I have ever played against.'*

Graeme Pollock

*A*FTER *the Lord Mayor's Show…comes the dust cart.* The very idea of Barry
sweeping the stands after a big match is not one that readily springs to mind
but as an expression of anti-climax, it does evocatively sum up Barry's mood
as he returned to school following his adventures in England. What was there to
look forward to? Further academic study was not high up on his agenda. Cricket
was all that Barry lived for but were the opportunities offered by Durban High
School sufficiently challenging? He had already been in the First XI for four years.
On his return, he was awarded his full colours blazer, which pleased him, but it was
no less than he deserved. What else? He could learn a musical instrument. Or join
the choir. Or audition for the school play. Or sit down at a chessboard. I'm guessing
that anyone who knows Barry would snort with laughter at the very idea. 'All I was
doing,' he admitted, 'was marking time, waiting for the cricket season.'

By now the routine was becoming familiar, Offord Week, followed by Nuffield
Week, with Barry as captain of the Natal side and Mike Procter as his second-in-
command. A score of 55 in the first match against Transvaal gave every hint that
normal service was being resumed. The cricket gods had other ideas, however.
His next three innings were: three, one and none. Not the sort of form that would
guarantee anyone, even Barry, a place in the full national schools side. But the
selectors stuck with him and he was confirmed as captain for the match against the
full North-Eastern Transvaal provincial side. Still the gods toyed with him; he made
only one. Some semblance of fluency returned with a fifty against a Western Province
Invitation XI but he felt he had been taken down a peg or two – probably a salutary
experience, he later felt. And that was that, as far as schools cricket was concerned.
Now it was time for the grown-up stuff.

What ambitions did you have at this time? 'To get into the Natal side and then have a
tilt at the Test team.' *No, I meant as far as a career was concerned. Presumably, the possibility
of playing for a living simply didn't exist at that time.* He agreed, explaining that there
was no such thing as a professional framework in the game in his country. All the
Test players, Barlow, Bland, Lindsay, Goddard, Bacher, the Pollock brothers *et al*,
had to find employment that was sympathetic to their cricket commitments. One or
two of the household names might be lucky enough to be engaged in some nominal,

commercial or promotional activity for a large company but the rest had to scrabble around as best they could. *Including you, I guess?* He smiled. 'Well, I didn't leave school with an impressive batch of qualifications, so my options were limited.' He pointed out that he was caught between two stools as far as getting a job was concerned. On one hand, the sponsorship of cricketers by the big multi-nationals was drying up, particularly the tobacco companies – the anti-smoking lobby was just beginning to stir. And on the other, full professionalism was a long way over the horizon.

So what did you do? 'A cricket loving chap by the name of Sean Ellis-Cole, who worked in insurance, gave me a job, a tea boy, really. But he was good to me and gave me plenty of time off to practise and play.' *And the pay?* He gave a sardonic laugh. 'R70 a month. Peanuts. Especially when my dad deducted R35 for board and lodging.' That last sentence was accompanied by a grimace. 'It took me ten months to save up to buy a car,' he exclaimed in indignation. Good grief. Barry Richards without wheels – the very thought. 'A 1950 Vauxhall it was. Cost me R50. Sold it a while later for R70, so I reckon I did a bit of good business there.' I had to stifle a laugh. Getting the best deal for his cars was an ongoing saga when he was at Hampshire and a source of amusement to his team-mates.

Thinking of Hampshire prompted my next question. *Was there even the merest hint at this time that you might be able to ply your trade in England?* Emphatically not, it would seem. 'The qualification period to play for an English county was four years. That is four years [of] continuous residency, which would have meant missing the cricket season in South Africa, and I would never have even contemplated that.' Indeed not. His ultimate goal was to get into the Test side. Once you joined an English county as a professional, you waved goodbye to any chance of playing for your country. Usually, it was financial necessity that persuaded these exiles to play for a county and set up home in England, where the game was fully professional. I am reminded of Hampshire's Roy Marshall, one of the most destructive opening batsmen in the 1960s, who abandoned his native Barbados to settle in England at the price of his Test career, a mere four caps for West Indies. That sacrifice Barry was unprepared to make. *And what's more, I just cannot imagine your surviving an English winter, let alone four.* 'Absolutely. Your summers are cold enough for me.'

So he was caught in a vicious circle. He needed to get into the Natal side to put himself in the public eye. Then, if successful – it's funny but Barry never seemed to doubt that he *would* be successful – he might catch the selectors' eyes for the full South African side. And then he might secure some sort of sponsorship or sympathetic employment to keep the wolves from the door. The trouble was that the Natal side was a strong one in an era when provincial cricket was highly competitive and richly supplied. Natal's pre-eminence in this period is reminiscent of another great team of a decade earlier. In the 1950s, Surrey won the County Championship seven times on the trot. In the 1960s, Natal, also packed with internationals, went one better and won the Currie Cup eight times consecutively. There was no youth policy, however. Veterans such as Jackie McGlew, Roy McLean, Trevor Goddard, and Pat Trimborn were unlikely to give up their places in the side willingly and they were canny enough – and good enough – to avoid any talk of being dropped. 'The thing was,' said Barry, 'they weren't doing anything wrong that put them under pressure. They were doing just enough to stay in the side.' Not exactly a closed shop but opportunities to break that stranglehold were few and far between. All he could do was to make his case for selection by sheer weight of runs in club cricket.

It is worth pointing out here that club cricket in South Africa at this time bore little or no resemblance to club cricket in England. I am not saying that there are not good players in the English club game but the picture conjured up in most people's mind of bucolic surroundings, arthritic fielding, rustic batting, enthusiastic but innocuous bowling, jam sandwiches and chocolate cake for tea, with the country vicar and the local squire looking on appreciatively, pint mugs in hand, would have been anathema to South African club players. They took their cricket *seriously*. And the standard was very good. Let me give you an illustration. Selection for an English club, such as it takes place at all, is often in the bar on a Friday night, telephone in hand, with desperate calls being made to secure the 11 players. Selection for the weekend's teams in a South African club would be made by a small group of gimlet-eyed and knowledgeable captains on a Thursday evening in front of the whole complement of players pouring sweat in the nets. A no-show at practice meant a Saturday in your shorts. Setting foot in the adult game was not a doddle for the young Barry Richards. Well, not for a little while anyway.

As night follows day, so did former cricketers of Durban High School transfer seamlessly to the Old Boys cricket club. But 'seamless' and Barry Richards do not always fit seamlessly, if you see what I mean. He joined Tech. *Tech? I didn't know you went to technical college.* 'I did not,' he explained patiently. 'Tech Cricket Club.' In so doing, Barry had defied custom and practice and it caused a bit of a rumpus. *So why did you do it?* He waggled his head as if once again weighing up the pros and cons of his decision. 'Well, Trevor Goddard played for them. But I think the main reason was that Alan Butler was there.' Alan Butler was the coach hired by his father all those years ago who drilled into the boy the virtues of a classically orthodox technique, one that would stand the test of time and a searching examination by the world's best bowlers. 'I was put under enormous pressure from DHS Old Boys, not least from my cricket master, Les Theobald. I did eventually go back there but I enjoyed my time at Tech.'

You said that you used to pester Alan Butler for a net until he must have been heartily sick of the sight of you. Now you were older, did you net just as assiduously? 'First in there, most Tuesdays and Thursdays.' The truth is had he *not* been the first in there, the likelihood was that he wouldn't have got a regular session, early or later. 'There were only two nets and everyone wanted a bat. With the light going quickly, there often wasn't time to fit everyone in. It's not like those long summer evenings in the UK. It gets dark in Durban at six.' Hello. Was that a compliment on the English climate from my South African friend? The reason that he was able to beat the crowd to the nets at the start time of 4.30pm was the kindness of his employer, Sean Ellis-Cole, who allowed him to shoot off from work early to beat the rush hour. *What were the nets like to bat in?* 'As you can imagine, there only being two of them, they got pretty worn. And the guys didn't let up. They wanted to impress as much as anyone.' *And I bet they bowled from 18 yards. Quick bowlers don't seem to worry about no-balling in the nets, do they?* Ruefully, he agreed. But I'm sure he coped well enough. He would no doubt have coped if they bowled from 12 yards.

He now warmed to his theme about nets. Facilities for practice in the first-class game are now streets ahead of what were on offer in the 1960s. The improvement in all-weather, synthetic surfaces has transformed net sessions and makes me wish... However, it is only fair to say that at some counties, at any rate, the grass nets were properly prepared and provided worthwhile batting practice. Not so at Kingsmead, the home of Natal cricket, Barry told me. 'They only had one net! And it faced into the sun!' He shook his head with incredulity. 'That's one thing I fixed when I came back to run the place later in my career.'

How was your social life? 'Pretty good!' he grinned. I was not intent on prying into what he got up to out of hours; I was merely enquiring what sort of entertainment and recreational opportunities there were for a young man in Durban at that time. A fatuous question, the more I thought about it. It really didn't take much of a leap of the imagination to presume what a single male in his late teens found to occupy himself in South Africa's second city, with its sub-tropical climate and beaches to die for. Especially as he now had wheels. I reminded him, as if there were any need, that there was a swimming pool adjoining the cricket pitch and on sunny days...I knew this because Grayson Heath, his former Geography teacher at school, the same Grayson Heath to whom Barry had already made plain his fondness for swimming pools, was the captain of the club's First XI and had one or two stories to tell me. Incongruously enough, swimming pools were at their heart. 'One or two stories!' said Barry. 'Knowing Grayson, there will be more than one or two. There won't be enough space in the book.' That was true. But they are amusing and in trying to distil some of their essence, I hope I do them justice. 'Ah, Grayson,' smiled Barry, not unkindly. 'He was such a cricket nut that he would still be playing in his wheelchair.'

Heath was the captain of the side and there is one game he particularly remembers. In the opposition that day was Pat Trimborn, the Springbok opening bowler, supported by a bevy of more than useful seamers. Their batting however was comparatively weak. So Heath's tactics were to win the toss and bat on an admittedly greenish pitch and hope his batters would score more runs on it than theirs. It was not an unrealistic hope. He had in his side the emerging genius and the talk of the town, Barry Richards, to say nothing of some experienced and capable batsmen around him. On a hot Durban day, Barry opened with Dennis Gamsy, a Natal regular and just the man to put into action the captain's ringing instruction to 'see off the new ball and carefully provide a decent platform to build the rest of the innings'. The best laid plans of mice and men. 'We lost our first wicket with the score on 50,' said Heath. 'Barry was caught at cover by the fielder who was essentially shielding his face from a cover drive that had the ball still climbing like a missile, knocking him over backwards. Barry had scored 45 of that total of 50. The new batsman had scarcely faced a couple of balls and Barry was already in the swimming pool. Dennis Gamsy's stunningly beautiful girlfriend, admired by Barry and the rest of us, was among the girls in the pool.' Barry was outraged by the slur. 'Gillian!' he cried. 'She's his wife.' Be that as it may, it did not go unnoticed that Gamsy got out soon after.

It is a curious fact that nobody – at least nobody to whom I have spoken – ever betrayed the slightest irritation or frustration at the extravagance and occasional carelessness of Barry's strokeplay. Not at this stage of his career, at least. I have to admit that there were occasions in the Hampshire dressing room years later when a scarcely audible sigh of vexation would emanate from some people's mouths as Barry got himself out in the 70s when a hundred and more were there for the taking. Another hour of this, was the unspoken admonishment, and we would have this lot by the throat. But the rebuke was rarely, if ever, verbalised when he came back into the dressing room and started to unbuckle his pads. The riposte from him would have been instant and cutting, something along the lines of, let's see if you can do any better when you get out there. But I don't think it was fear of Barry's tongue that stopped any direct criticism. There were some strong characters in that Hampshire dressing room and a timid concern for team-mates' finer feelings was not a hallmark of the professional game. I suspect all of us knew that we couldn't have done any better and in any case, a 70 from Barry Richards was a gift from the gods and we jolly well ought to appreciate it while we could. And later perhaps, when the heat of battle had died and participants started to reflect in retirement on their careers, they would have slowly come to an understanding of why Barry began to get bored and disillusioned when the challenges dried up.

In the meantime, the challenge was to play what was in front of him and hope that the Natal selectors would soon stir from their slumbers. He certainly did his best to ginger up the club scene in Durban. Listen to this from a boyhood admirer of Barry's, later a friend. 'I was 12 years of age,' Neil Minnaar said. 'Barry came in at number three and made 184. What made it such a standout knock was that it took him only about two hours 20 minutes. And he was only recently out of school. I was there that Saturday afternoon. It was like watching someone from another planet.' Or this, once again from Grayson Heath, 'Dennis Gamsy, a Springbok wicketkeeper-batsman, insisted on opening for us for three reasons. One, so that he could marvel at Barry's batting from only 22 yards away. Two, he could encourage/cajole Barry to play in the "V" because league cricket was hardly a challenge to him. And three, there was the lure of the swimming pool when he got out, with a bevy of beautiful girls escaping the Durban summer heat.'

That bevy of girls presumably included the future Mrs Gamsy. Heath explained that one ruse Gamsy employed to try and keep Barry's mind on the job in hand was play a game called 'nominations'. As the non-striker, he would nominate the stroke that Barry had to play the next ball. For a while, he would nominate safe shots, usually in the 'V'. When Barry's interest started to wane, he would introduce more risky shots, the cut, hook, lofted drive and so on. One day, when Barry was 50-odd not out, Dennis went a step further. 'Neil Govan, a tearaway fast bowler who had represented Natal B, was bowling and Dennis nominated the hook. As Govan walked past Dennis on his way back to his mark, Dennis whispered to him, "If you want to get him out, bowl a yorker."' Yes, you've guessed it. As Barry was halfway through his hook shot, Govan's yorker was hitting the base of the middle stump. 'He walked off muttering about being sold a dummy but his pace quickened as he neared the boundary and the beckoning sounds of the swimming pool area reached his ears.'

Gamsy has his own story to recount. On the second day of a club match, the Sunday afternoon, DHS Old Boys needed quick runs after tea to allow them the chance to declare and bowl the opposition out before stumps at 6pm. An unlikely scenario but they decided to give it a go. 'Barry and I opened to an 8-1 field, only one on the leg side with the bowlers instructed to bowl wide of the off stump. This was just the type of challenge that switched Barry on. After 35 minutes of running threes and sometimes fours, with Barry somehow sweeping, niggling and cajoling balls from outside off stump down to fine leg, an exhausted Richards got out when we were on 108. I had scored seven and he had scored 101!' The improbable win was not achieved but Gamsy had the privilege, he said, 'of witnessing from 22 yards away a genius at work'.

One further anecdote from Heath concerned a match played on a typical greentop at Kingsmead; fast, bouncy and distinctly capricious. The opposition, including five Natal players, were skittled for 129. Not much of a target it might seem but everyone knew that it was going to be difficult, given the state of the pitch. And so it proved. At number six, Heath walked in to bat with the score at 12/4. 'The stage was set,' he recounted, 'and Barry was in his element. The bowlers were seemingly able to make the ball talk but Barry was magnificent. Initially, he was uncharacteristically circumspect as he dealt with the challenge...I watched in awe, always ready of course to run his regular single off the last ball of the over, as he slowly negated, then began to dominate, the attack with a masterclass of batting brilliance.'

When the score had reached 90-odd, Barry clearly believed the match was as good as over as a contest and started to indulge himself with a few extravagant shots. But no captain ever really believes it is over until it actually *is* over and Heath went down the wicket to lecture Barry on this very point. 'He didn't say anything,' remembered Heath, 'but the perplexed look on his face said it all. He was caught on the extra cover boundary for 76 but by then we were only 20 runs short.' The only pity, according to Barry's former Geography teacher, was that 'there was only the proverbial man and his dog to bear witness to a vintage Richards innings'. Now, where have I heard that before?

What number were you batting? It seems you weren't a regular opener at this stage. 'Number three was my slot. That was where traditionally your best batsman played.' He went on to say that it was a little later, in 1966, he was encouraged to go in first. After all, the argument went, the score was invariably 10/1, so what was the difference? He might just as well go in first. Initially, he resisted the suggestion. He had been brought up in an era when the conventional wisdom was that the openers would grind it out to see off the shine on the ball and the strokemakers would come in later and make hay. 'Grinding out' was not in his vocabulary. Reluctantly, he assented to the plan and gave it a go. *How did you get on?* 'I got four hundreds in six innings,' he laughed, 'and that was that.' But he never compromised on his style of play, that was to attack whenever possible.

The club scene was the focal point of your life, I guess. 'Now, Murt, you know I was never a great clubber.' Actually, this was true. He enjoyed a night out as much as anybody but pubbing and clubbing was not really his cup of tea. I meant of course the cricket club. 'The cricket was of a pretty high standard,' he persisted in assuring me. 'All the best players played. If they weren't playing for Natal, they would turn out for their clubs at weekends. It was expected.' And at the close of play, everybody would repair to the bar and incidents would be replayed and stories would be told. He is of the firm belief that this competitive climate, playing with and against the best in the province, was essential experience for young players such as himself. 'There were no drink-drive laws then, so we would all have a few beers and then perhaps go out for a meal together.' He sounded almost wistful. 'Not like that now. All the kids are plugged into their earphones and no one talks to each other anymore.'

Being the impatient soul that he is, Barry was, by this stage, keenly anxious to test his mettle against better players. Well, *the* best, if the truth be known; South African cricket was as powerful as it had ever been, with people like Goddard, Barlow, Bland, the two Pollocks and Waite in the Test side and a new generation of young guns, including Barry, restlessly pacing about in the wings. 'Natal was the powerhouse in the Currie Cup,' he reminded me, 'and they did not exactly pursue an enlightened youth policy.' In other words, his way was barred by players not nearly as good as he was, even then. Barry doesn't do false modesty. He has always had a fiercely candid and honest opinion of a player's ability and he sees no reason not to put himself under the same intense spotlight. And if it means that he felt he was good enough, you can be sure he *was* good enough. Perhaps this searing frankness was what troubled his critics among the bureaucrats, officials and committee members in the English game when he first arrived on these shores as an overseas player. South Africans tell it as it is; Englishmen, by and large, do not. Barry knew he was good – damned good – and he believed he should be commensurately rewarded, and was not afraid to say so.

You believed, therefore, that you were waiting for dead men's shoes? He didn't answer directly but gave one of his ironic whistles. 'Varnals! He batted all day – you couldn't shift him.' He was referring to his debut for Natal. The call had come – at last – to play against Transvaal on 24 October 1964. He was 19 years of age. I did say he was impatient. A quick look at the scorecard of the match sheds light on what he meant. B.A. Richards was batting at number seven! The number three, the aforementioned Derek Varnals, had batted all day for his undefeated 102. You can bet your bottom dollar that had Barry batted for the same length of time, he would have scored more than 102. But in fact, he did not bat at all. McGlew declared with the score on 348/4. Barry may well have strapped on his pads but that was as far as it got. 'For the rest of the time, I spoke only when spoken to,' he said.

The aloofness of senior players towards the younger members of the team may seem surprising but those were very different times. Grayson Heath says this about the importance of hierarchy in the Natal dressing room in the early 1960s, 'My first match for Natal was against Western Province at Newlands. I was a 21-year-old and when I dared to venture an opinion in the changing room, I was greeted with a collective glare by the senior players, including Jack McGlew, Roy McLean, Neil Adcock and Trevor Goddard. I was instructed in no uncertain terms to "get some f****** service in". The message was clear – I was there to be seen and not heard.' Quaintly, he referred to this period as 'The Age of Aristocracy'.

You do not have to know Barry Richards well to hazard a guess that The Age of Aristocracy would not sit well with him. Things were to change, however, in a whirlwind manner that would bewilder more than those traditionalists in the Natal dressing room. Listen to Heath's description of the same scene several years later. 'The team had changed, with only Trevor Goddard of the illustrious group of Test players I mentioned earlier still there. The baton had been passed to an exciting new breed that included Barry Richards, Mike Procter, Lee Irvine, Hylton Ackerman and Vince van der Bijl. Compared to the changing room of the McGlew era, it was more like a crèche with this bunch of outrageously talented cricketers heading for stardom, dominating the banter and the discussion.' In a space of half a dozen years or so, the world had completely changed.

But not yet. For the time being, Barry held his breath to cool his porridge. The opportunity to test himself against international players was not long in coming. MCC were touring South Africa in the winter of 1964/65 and one of their warm-up matches before the Test series was against the South African Colts XI, for which Barry had been selected. Ted Dexter, who was the captain of the tourists that day – Mike Smith had been rested – lost the toss and the Colts opted to bat first. It was not long before a nervous Barry Richards was taking guard. He soon settled down, playing just as he would in a club game. Throughout his career he never believed that he should play himself in just for the sake of it. He played each ball, first or last, on its merits. Not quite on this occasion, it has to be said. Having reached a wholly satisfactory 63, he swept once too often at Fred Titmus and was LBW. He wouldn't have been the first, nor was he to be the last, to have been deceived by the off-spinner's ability to make the ball curve in the air before pitching and spinning.

A fortnight later, Barry was facing the tourists again, this time for Natal. He rather missed the boat but not the fielder when he holed out for 15 off Tom Cartwright in the first innings but played pretty well, he believed, in a second innings score of 29. It doesn't sound much but as ever with these things, you have to take into account the context in which it was played. It was a humid day, the ball swung prodigious distances and the Currie Cup champions were skittled out for 102. There were occasions in his innings that he missed the ball by a foot, so extravagant was the movement. He eventually fell LBW to another England off-spinner, David Allen. More of David Allen shortly.

Barry failed to establish himself in the Natal side that season, which was not surprising really, given the limited opportunities he was afforded. Despite his mediocre record, the jungle drums had been beating up and down the country with news of this precociously talented youngster from Durban. Accordingly, the national selectors took a punt on him and invited him to play in a Test trial, North versus South. The team to tour England in the summer of 1965 was being assembled and though the majority picked themselves, there were one or two places undecided. *Which side did you play for?* 'Eh?' *North or South?* 'The South, of course. The press, as usual, were jumping upon a possible story here – unknown youngster tipped for stardom included in touring party. Ridiculous. I hadn't even scored a fifty for Natal.' In the event, he did not exactly let himself down. Nor did he make a strong case for his inclusion. He hardly could have, batting at number seven, making 13 not out in the first innings and having the unsatisfying initials, DNB, against his name in the second. And that was as far as the selectors' gamble went. He was not selected for the tour. He knew he wasn't ready.

If he was denied his chance to make an early impression on English cricket, he did have one more opportunity to impress some Englishmen before MCC concluded their tour of the country, even if it was in a way that he could not possibly have imagined. The series was on a knife-edge. England, by virtue of their solitary victory in the first Test in Durban, were going into the final match in Cape Town needing only a draw to secure the series. As preparation for the showdown, they were scheduled to play against an Invitation XI. An invitation to size up some of our best young players, the generous South African Board might just as well have said, an act of altruism that would be unthinkable these days.

Both England's off-spinners, Fred Titmus and David Allen, were having an enjoyable and successful tour, and not only because they included the wicket of Barry Richards among their haul of scalps. Allen got him twice. 'I had heard about this young lad,' Allen told me. 'My great friend, Jackie McGlew, rated him very highly, so I was more than interested when he was picked to play against us. It was the last over before lunch. On the third ball, Barry ran down the wicket and was stumped by two yards, for none. We followed him off the field as he trooped disconsolately back to the dressing room.'

Normally, you would expect an experienced county player such as Allen, steeped in the ways and practices of the professional game, to click his tongue in disapproval at such a rash piece of misjudgement by a young batsman. In England, you were encouraged to 'play for lunch'. But Allen saw it differently. 'It takes a lot of courage to do that,' he said. 'It was as if he was saying, nobody's going to dominate me. I don't care what time it is or what state the match is in, I'm going to get on top here. I admired that.'

The South African selectors clearly did not think the same because, as I have said, Barry was not picked for the side to go to England; they saw no room in the side for a cocky, headstrong teenager who rather fancied himself. They would be forced to change their minds in due course but for the time being, Barry had no option but to contemplate another winter working in an office. David Allen, however, was thinking out of the box. He got in touch with the Gloucestershire committee back home, no easy task in the days before the revolution in instant communication and suggested that they might like to consider taking on this promising young player and offering him a contract to play in England the forthcoming summer. 'Dear old Gloucester,' he sighed. 'They never did make up their minds – on anything. Eventually, I heard back from them that I could proceed. I ran the idea past Jackie McGlew and he readily agreed that Barry was worth the gamble. And then he said that there was another young player whom I would not have heard of yet but that he was as good, if not potentially better, than Barry. His name was Mike Procter.' *And the rest is history, as they say*. 'Well, not quite. We still had the problem of the rules and regulations governing overseas players in the English game. How were we going to get over that?'

Rather like referring an umpire's decision to the interminable DRS, he left that to the officials and made his own appeal to the two South African prodigies. They needed little persuading. The experience would be invaluable and they didn't worry too much about their immediate futures as cricketing backpackers; all they wanted to do was *play*. And this time, unlike in 1963, they were no longer schoolboys. Bristol? It was a seaport, like Durban, wasn't it? Perhaps the surfing would be good.

If anybody is foolhardy enough to set foot in the cold waters of the Bristol Channel in search of a wave, a wetsuit would be the least that he would require to ward off hypothermia. A wetsuit might have come in useful for Barry when he took his first shower at Gloucestershire's county ground in Bristol. The club were so hard up that they turned off the heating when there wasn't a first team game. He remembers those showers with horror. 'Jeez! It was absolute agony. On a cold April day after a long session in the nets!' But the natural buoyancy and cheerful good spirits of the young saw them through these minor inconveniences. No, Bristol was nothing like Durban and their wages were meagre but the Second XI players were friendly and welcoming and the pair of them soon immersed themselves in the daily routine of a county cricketer. Practice was no chore for them; they practically lived in the nets. It is a sad irony, one that Barry readily accepts, that this boyish, unwavering love of the game contrasted so starkly with the dreary chore that it was to become ten years later. Pity the poor 12th man in the Hampshire dressing room during the 1975 season, or any other thereafter, who had forgotten to fill up the bath with hot water for Barry after a hard day in the field (and no, it wasn't me). In the summer of 1965, his destiny as one of the greatest batsmen of his era was in front of him; by 1975, he sensed that his future was probably behind him.

Having been instrumental in bringing Richards and Procter over to the West Country, David Allen took it upon himself to look out for them as best he could. 'I had a sort of paternal concern for them both,' he said. 'Although they were very young, everybody could see the latent talent there.' Barry revelled in the challenge of adapting to alien conditions, unseasonably cold and damp weather, seam bowling, green tracks – uncovered in those days, do not forget – and everything else that the life of a professional cricketer can throw at you. 'We *both* revelled in it,' he corrected me. 'Prockie was nuts about the game too.' He then went on to provide me with an interesting statistic. 'Funnily enough, I finished above Prockie in the Second XI bowling averages and he finished above me in the batting averages.' Supporters of Hampshire always saw Barry as an opening bat. Those who knew that he could bowl off-spinners, and quite tidily too, were always mystified why he let his bowling lapse. He could have been a genuine all-rounder. 'Too much like hard work,' he grins.

Hard work was not a problem for him that season. 'They were typical South Africans,' remarked Allen. 'They played hard on the pitch and they played hard off it too.' Barry claims a fading memory but Allen has firm recollections of their extra-curricular activities. 'The parties we had!' He was shaking his head almost in disbelief. 'I remember driving them home once with the two of them clinging on to the bonnet. Er, don't print that, will you.' Of course not, I lied.

But to return to the real reason Richards and Procter were there. John Mortimore, the other of Gloucestershire's fabled off-spinning duo, was the club captain at the time. He remembers them all right. 'Of course, we didn't see a lot of them because we were away playing for the First XI. And they were not qualified to play. But what we did see, in the nets and the like, it was obvious to everyone how good they were. We were able to pick them for the tourists' match though, because it wasn't a championship game.' The tourists were, as we know, South Africa. They knew who the tyros were and the tyros certainly knew them. 'It was a huge mistake to play Barry and Prockie in that match, you know,' said Mortimore. *Why on earth do you say that? I thought they acquitted themselves well.* 'That's just the point – they did! And thereby showed the South Africans that they had two future stars waiting impatiently for their chance.' *I still don't quite –* 'It put paid to any hope we had of signing them on. They wouldn't countenance qualifying by residence by staying in England. Not when Test cricket for their country was beckoning them.' Barry agreed. 'To spend a whole winter in the UK, with only cold showers! No way, buddy. Besides we both wanted to get back to play in the Currie Cup.'

Gloucestershire against the South Africans in July 1965 was a bit of a damp squib. In fact, rain washed out days two and three but there was time enough on the first day for Procter and Richards to show their own countrymen what they were missing and what they would assuredly get in the next year or two. In short order, Gloucestershire were reeling at 62/4 and the two friends found themselves together at the wicket, in a crisis and facing bowlers of international class on the rampage and smelling blood. But it was the wrong South Africans who went on the rampage. In the next hour and a half, they put on 116 runs in a thrilling exhibition of strokeplay that had the Gloucestershire supporters nudging each other and whispering the names of Hammond and Graveney in each other's ear. 'And they weren't given those runs,' Allen assured me. Generously, Barry reckoned Procter batted even better than he did. 'My God, he could hit it,' Allen said, the admiration still clear in his voice near on 50 years later. 'You ask me to compare the two as batsmen? Prockie would blast you out of the attack. Barry would clinically dissect you. He could bat with a walking stick.'

Back to the Second XI went the two boys, largely unaware of the avalanche of mail from members and supporters breaking over the club office, begging the committee to sign the pair of them. Both Allen and Mortimore, and others, knew it was a non-starter, even in spite of some generous terms on offer. Summer in Durban and an aching desire to make a strong case for themselves to be included in the Test side by performing well in the Currie Cup was more of a lure than any breaking surf in the Bristol Channel. The only wave of any note in those waters is the Severn Bore, well named, Barry said, as it only reaches a height of six feet, a mere tiddler compared to what was to be had offshore on Durban's beaches.

'But the story doesn't end there,' said Allen. In 1968, the rules in England governing the signing of overseas players were changed. Each county was allowed to sign two players; one could play immediately and the other would have to serve only one year's qualification. Immediately there was a stampede to get hold of the world's best players and the world's best players were only too happy to oblige, there being no organised professional cricket outside England and England being the only country (more or less) that played the game in the northern hemisphere during everybody else's winter. 'We tried to get the rules changed,' said Mortimore. 'We wanted to sign them both.' Allen was in complete agreement. 'Think what a batting line-up we could have had with those two and Graveney as well, if only the committee had handled Tom a bit better.' But a choice had to be made. Neither could be expected to spend another season languishing in the Second XI, not in 1968, when they had emphatically announced themselves on the world stage. 'In the end, we went for Prockie,' said Allen, 'solely because he was a fast bowler and we'd never had one, not someone of genuine pace. We felt it was about time we let off a few fireworks that had been coming our way for all those years.' Yet again, Mortimore was of the same opinion as his team-mate. 'We'd have settled for either. But we needed a fast bowler/batsman more than we needed an opener. And who can say we chose badly?' No one, not even Barry himself. Gloucestershire enjoyed a golden era of unfamiliar success and became known as 'Proctershire'.

Nonetheless, David Allen still had paternal concerns for Barry and his future in English cricket. He got in touch with his good friend, Jim Parks at Sussex, who had been, incidentally, the wicketkeeper who had stumped Barry off Allen for that nought against MCC. Parks nearly bit his hand off; Richards would be an ideal signing, he believed. But committees are the same the world over. They dilly and they dally and never seem to make a decision. By the time they did make a move, it was too late. Barry was already a Hampshire player. 'And it was all over a few bob!' Allen said incredulously. And this set off a train of thought in my mind. Would Barry have been happier and more socially content living in lively, not to say, hedonistic, London-by-the-Sea than in the busiest container port on the South Coast? As an answer, he directed me to the example of Imran Khan, who chose Sussex over Worcestershire. 'Worcester?' Imran is alleged to have said. 'What is there to do in Worcester?' Be that as it may, I and countless others were happy that the decision was taken out of Barry's hands and that he graced Northlands Road in Southampton more than he did Hove.

'You know we nearly didn't get Barry?' Richard Gilliat, our captain at Hampshire, said to me. 'Initially, we had agreed terms with Clive Lloyd. But we were gazumped by Lancashire who could offer more money than us. So he went to the Red Rose and Barry came to the White Rose.' Yorkshire are not the only county to sport a white rose as its emblem. 'And I think we got the better deal, don't you?' said Gilliat. I could do nothing but nod in hearty agreement. What a tangled web we weave! Let us go back to that duck: Richards st Parks b Allen 0. Has there ever been a more fateful duck in the game? Bradman bowled Hollies second ball in his final Test innings? I struggle to think of others.

Back home, Barry was relieved to discover that the showers in Durban were still hot. He was also relieved to be promoted in the Natal batting order to number three. He thought that was his best position. After all, your best player traditionally bats in that position and it did his confidence no end of good that others clearly thought so too. He played well enough in a season when Natal made a late surge to win once again the Currie Cup. His maiden first-class century still eluded him however but he was pleased with the fluency of his batting in scores of 68, 51 not out, 77, 67 and 61, interspersed with one or two failures. Good enough to get in the Test team? Who knows? There was no country touring that year (only England, New Zealand and Australia were prepared to come – for obvious reasons – and Test series were few and far between) so the question was academic.

But that was your ambition, wasn't it? 'Absolutely. One of the reasons I had turned down the chance to play professionally in England.' *Tell me, now we're talking of professionalism and money, were you ever paid by Natal?* 'Nah!' There is something about the expression of rebuttal uttered in a South African accent; it seems to stress even more strongly the repudiation in the word. Except that, curiously and paradoxically, it is frequently followed immediately by 'yah'. No, yes. I'm told it is an oddity that comes from Afrikaans. And I was expecting the qualification here too. After all, the English game at this time was riddled with 'shamateurism', players masquerading as amateurs but frequently being in receipt of more money than their professional counterparts, all done by various subtle and ever more devious means. 'No, the game in South Africa was 100 per cent amateur,' he averred, 'and run by amateurs too!' It is a shame that the etymological origin of that word (a derivative from Latin, via French, meaning 'to love' or 'lover') has been corrupted over the years to signify someone who is a bumbling and incompetent administrator rather than one with a simple but deep love of the game.

However, I was in no doubt what Barry meant. 'I lived in a deeply conservative country with deeply conservative values. It was deemed an *honou*r to play for your province.' *No backhanders? No money in your boot?* He shook his head. 'Many of the guys had to take unpaid leave to play. That is, if their employers were willing to let them off.' This would explain why some of their best players retired in their prime. At least it meant that, by and large, the arteries were not clogged up with timeservers and young blood could easily flow, which tended not to happen in the English game. 'So, if we were playing on Boxing Day, which we frequently did, all the guys had to practise on Christmas Day.' Not great for the married members of the team with young children. Another reason it was a young man's game in that country.

What was the routine like for a provincial game? Not a lot different to county cricket, it seemed. A day or two of practice then the match. *How were you informed you were playing?* 'Someone came up to you during nets and told you.' *What about travel? The distances are vast. Did you always fly?* 'Always by plane. We were at the back and the blazers were at the front. They were like schoolmasters. We were the kids and we had to do what we were told.' For a strong-willed and independently minded soul like Barry, that must have been torture.

In the meantime, a third visit to England was planned. *I thought you couldn't stand the weather and the cold showers.* 'Cold showers! Just what I needed when we stopped off in Amsterdam on the way over!' I wasn't going to delve too deeply – after all, what a grown man does once he has quit the field of play is entirely his own business – but his old friend, Lee Irvine, was more inclined to fill in the gaps. 'It was a Wilfred Isaacs tour to Holland and England. I bet you didn't know they played cricket in Holland,' he challenged me. Indeed I did. Cricket is popular in Holland and the Dutch are an associate member of the ICC. *Some good players who come from that part of the world.* 'Absolutely. Barry, Prockie and me, we were invited to go, all expenses paid. But we had an exceptionally strong side, with Adcock, McGlew, Tayfield, McLean, Goddard as senior players meant to look after us.' *On or off the pitch?* 'If it was meant to be off the pitch, they didn't do a very good job. Amsterdam is an *amazing* place. It certainly opened our eyes.' Barry was of the same mind. 'We came back more mature characters.' I'm sure they did.

This newfound maturity found its full expression in the 1966/67 Currie Cup season. 'It was the year when I announced myself on the world stage,' Barry said, and no greater current Test player than Graeme Pollock agreed, so much so that he was moved to write, 'This sunshine-faced, fair-haired, Natal opening batsman is undoubtedly one of the most promising youngsters I have ever played against.' Barry's avowed intent was to make a stack of runs for Natal and in so doing, making an irrefutable case to the selectors to pick him for the series against the visiting Australians. 'It was when I moved up from number three to open,' he said, 'but I didn't bat like an opener. Well, not like an opener was *supposed* to bat in those days.' Word soon spread that the young prodigy had finally come of age. But still that maiden first-class century eluded him. 'Aaagh! 96 against EP at Kingsmead. So near but so far. I kept on running myself out!' Eventually, the monkey was removed from his back when he scored 107 for a South African XI (not the Test side) against…Australia.

Richie Benaud, no longer playing and now a reporter, described it thus, 'Eleven Australian cricketers saw a new Test star born yesterday when 21-year-old Barry Richards carved a scintillating 107 off them.' For good measure, Barry took 38 and 75 off the same opponents a few days later, this time for Natal. And he didn't finish there. He scored 88 and 65 for a South African XI against Australia, again, just before the fifth and final Test in Cape Town. That season, he averaged 50.24. Only Hylton Ackerman, Graeme Pollock and Denis Lindsay of the Test team finished above him. What of the series itself? South Africa won 3-1 (it could so easily have been 4-1) in crushing style. That was in spite of a fallible top order. *Wisden* reported, 'Invariably, the Springboks made a disastrous start only for the wreck to be salvaged by the lower half of the order.' *So, you made all those runs against the Aussies. The South African side had a fallible top order. You were an opening bat. Why were you not in the team?* 'I kicked a flowerpot,' he answered simply.

Ah yes, the Flowerpot Incident. 'It all kicked off in East London,' said Barry's team-mate, Lee Irvine, with unconscious aptness. 'It was Hylton Ackerman's home town and we were trying to get into a disco. But Barry was refused entrance.' It was not many years later when Barry was allowed in, free of charge, at any disco, in England or his home country. But not yet. 'I wasn't wearing a tie,' Barry said, shaking his head as we might today if anyone insisted on formal dress for dinner. I know Barry hates ties. It was the devil's own job to tie one round his neck at formal functions when he was at Hampshire. But like his hair, which he had started to wear fashionably long, it was a symbol of his individuality at a time when conventions were being challenged and overturned all over the place. Even in conservative South Africa.

So, what happened? 'I kicked a flowerpot into the swimming pool.' I tried not to laugh. *Did it hurt?* He didn't answer but he went on to tell me that it certainly hurt his chances of playing against the Aussies that summer. 'The trouble was,' said Irvine, 'it was all over the papers.' Barry reckons he was lucky not to get arrested, so irate was the doorman, but to have his name splashed on the front, rather than the back, of the dailies, must have been galling for one so shy of public scrutiny. *I thought you said you'd matured.* 'But I repeat, it was a very old-fashioned and traditional place. You wore ties. You had short hair. You did as you were told. It was an honour to play for your province and you were at the mercy of men who were 30, 40 years older than you who ran the game. Anyone who didn't conform was a rebel.' I have a theory, which I shall develop later. Barry was born in the wrong era. If he had been of the following generation, no one would have turned a hair at his open neck collar or his thick, wavy, long blond hair or the fact that he was paid for playing cricket. And what's more, Nelson Mandela would be president, apartheid would have been swept away and the return to Test cricket for South Africa would have allowed him to display his genius on the world stage. And I would be 20 again. Ah well.

Nothing was said but neither was he picked. *What selector had it in for you?* 'Arthur Coy,' he replied unhesitatingly. 'Dunno why he was anti-me. But he was ultra-conservative and obviously felt I needed to be taught a lesson. Besides, he wanted Ali in the side.' Ali Bacher was later captain of the South African side, and a good one too, but a better batsman than Barry? *Was there no one on the selection panel who went into bat for you?* 'Each selector from each province was meant to put in a word for his players, if he thought they were good enough.' *And you weren't considered good enough?* 'Derek Dowling was the Natal representative. A nice enough man but he was weak and was easily overruled.' There was a pause. 'I should have played, you know.'

Kicking over a flowerpot is hardly the same as kicking over the traces. Why make such a fuss? Surely a stern word or two, an apology and some sort of recompense, such as buying a new flowerpot, should have sufficed. 'The flowerpot did not go in the swimming pool, as was reported,' said Barry, anxious to put the record straight. 'Only some dirt. Prockie was there too,' he added, a touch vexed, 'but he wasn't punished. Not that I blame him. I kicked the damn thing.' Procter, incidentally, was picked for the Springbok side, making his debut before Barry. He made little impression with the bat but his bowling made people sit up and take note. He took 15 wickets in the three Tests he played; only Goddard, with 26, took more. Barry would not have been human had he not felt, deep in his bones, a twinge of jealousy. How long would he have to wait to get his chance?

Now, what about this reputation he had unwillingly gained for himself? Barry felt aggrieved that he had been punished without anyone actually coming to him and telling him why he wasn't being picked. Was it for cricket reasons or was it because of that conversion kick into the pool? I sought the opinion of one or two others. 'Would he have been picked anyway?' mused Lee Irvine, who, as his friend, would have had no axe to grind. 'After all, it was a very strong Springbok side, they'd just demolished Australia, why change a winning side and, besides, he wasn't the only youngster scoring runs and desperate to get in that side.' I assume he was including himself in that number.

John Traicos, later a team-mate of Barry's in the Test side, was at Natal University when all this was going on. The university cricket coach was none other than Trevor Goddard. Goddard said to anyone with ears to listen that he regarded Barry as the most talented young batsman in the country. Jackie McGlew, a fellow Natal player, also spoke highly of him. He thought Barry had an exceptional talent as a schoolboy – as he had pointed out to the Charterhouse captain, Richard Gilliat, on the 1963 Schools Tour – and he believed that Barry was even better now. But…and there is always a 'but'. According to Traicos, 'Trevor Goddard seemed to be of the view that Barry at that time was a bit of a rebel, perhaps immature, who kept on throwing away his chances.' The overall view in Durban, and elsewhere, however, was that 'Barry had tremendous talent and should have played Test cricket earlier than he did, in other words against the 1966/67 Australians.'

There was nothing for it other than to score a stack of runs for Natal and make sure that he did seize his opportunity when England came on tour for the 1968/69 season. But one innings, played 5,000 miles away in England at the Oval in August 1968, put paid to all that and changed the face of international cricket for the next 30 years. *Were you aware of the political storm brewing?* 'I suppose so,' he answered unconvincingly. 'To be honest, I wasn't too interested in politics. All I wanted to do was play cricket.' Perhaps, this is understandable, cocooned as he was in a comfortable and tightly controlled world run by whites for whites. In England, the controversial subject of apartheid was beginning to take on the impetus of a moral crusade as well as proving to be a political hot potato for the governments. And by governments in the plural, I mean the one at St John's Wood as well as the one in Downing Street.

Anybody in the Test and County Cricket Board, the newly established governing body in England, who had half a brain – and subsequent events revealed that they were pretty thin on the ground – must have looked out of the committee room at Lord's and noticed the storm clouds gathering on the horizon. The thorny problem had been pricking them ever since Basil D'Oliveira made his debut for his adopted country in June 1966, two years previously, against the West Indies, as coincidence would have it. D'Oliveira, you see, was South African, born in Cape Town of Portuguese and Indian parents. As such, in his home country, under the laws of apartheid he was classified as 'Coloured' and therefore was barred from playing cricket either with or against whites. In order to further his career, following encouragement from notable figures in the English game such as John Arlott and Tom Graveney, who recognised his enormous talent, he emigrated to England, took out a British passport, scored heavily for his adopted county, Worcestershire, and was consequently selected for the Test team. So far, so good; a touching and inspirational story.

But a quick glance by the committee men at Lord's at the future tours programme for MCC would have disclosed the potential stumbling block. In the winter of 1968/69, MCC were scheduled to tour South Africa. Barry was not the only South African, player and enthusiast, licking his lips at the prospect of a visit from the Englishmen. But the strict interpretation of the laws set down by the Nationalist government in Pretoria would mean that D'Oliveira would not be welcome in his home country, even if he was a member of another country's touring team. Impasse. What to do?

Following a poor tour of the West Indies in 1968/69, D'Oliveira was dropped from the England team and the gin bottle at Lord's reached for with a huge sigh of relief. The South African tour was saved. If a week is a long time in politics, the same could be said about cricket. Regaining his form, D'Oliveira was recalled to the England team for the fifth and final Test of the summer against the Australians at the Oval. The pressure as D'Oliveira strode out to bat, with that familiar straight-backed and squared-shoulders walk of his, on that late August afternoon, was enormous. At 113/3, England were in trouble. Basil was playing for his team, his place in the team and a berth in the touring party that was shortly to set out for his home country. The stakes could not have been higher. Tom Graveney, his friend, mentor and team-mate at Worcestershire, watched in admiration from the other end as D'Oliveira played one of the most remarkable innings in Test cricket. 'He was majestic,' Tom told me. 'He had such powerful arms and struck the ball so cleanly that the ball just rocketed to the boundary. Basil always played better under pressure, you know – he was so excited about returning home and playing in front of his own people.'

By the time D'Oliveira had returned to the pavilion to a hero's welcome, having scored 158, you could say that the cat was well and truly in there, among the pigeons. That Test match, an enthralling contest from first to last, is probably best remembered for its final ball; all 11 Englishmen, the two Australian batsmen and the bowler's umpire are in shot of that famous photo as Underwood appeals for LBW against Inverarity and the umpire has his finger raised. In just 27 balls, Underwood had taken four wickets to secure England an unlikely victory with only six minutes left to play.

If that was dramatic, it was nothing compared with the events that unfolded afterwards. Graveney takes up the story, 'We were playing Sussex at Worcester and at six o'clock we all gathered round the radio in the dressing room to listen to the announcement of the touring party to South Africa. The room fell silent as we listened to the names being read out. Basil's name wasn't on it. I was stunned. For a moment, you could have heard a pin drop as the incredible news sunk in.' Then the air turned blue. It was Graveney swearing. 'I never thought they'd do this to you, Bas,' he said as his friend, in front of his team-mates, broke down and cried. D'Oliveira admitted later that he felt as if his world had caved in. 'The stomach had been kicked out of me,' he said.

Naturally enough, all hell broke loose, in the bars, in the newspapers, on the television, in the House of Commons even. Nobody believed the chairman of selectors when he tried to reassure the country that the decision had been taken 'on purely cricketing grounds'. Graveney scoffs at this. 'To score 158 and then get *dropped!* Nonsense. It was political.' The murky waters were further muddied when Barry Knight, one of the original touring party, dropped out through injury and bowing to public clamour, D'Oliveira was installed in his place. Now the political spotlight was turned glaringly on the South African government. This was just the opportunity that the prime minister of South Africa, John Vorster, had been waiting for. Angrily, he denounced the reinstatement of D'Oliveira into the MCC side. 'We are not prepared to receive a team thrust upon us by people whose interests are not in the game but to gain political advantages,' he thundered. 'The MCC team is not the team of the MCC but of the anti-apartheid party.'

At that point, all sensible observers in the UK knew that the tour was doomed. Accordingly, all contact between Lord's and the South African Cricket Board was sundered which inexorably led to South Africa's expulsion and isolation from all sporting contact with the rest of the world for the next 30 years or so. The D'Oliveira Affair, as it has become known, had a massive impact on political events way beyond the boundary, as it were, and it would not be fanciful to suggest that in the long run it must have indirectly contributed to the release of Nelson Mandela and his being sworn in as president in a truly democratic and peaceful election.

As all this was unfolding, Barry was in England, engaged in his debut season as Hampshire's new overseas signing and must have regarded developing events with mixed feelings. 'At the time, I thought it was no more than a temporary setback,' he said. 'I was only 22. Time was on my side. The political ramifications were lost on me. All I wanted to do was play cricket and I couldn't understand why sport and politics should be mixed.'

This was undoubtedly a naive point of view. But I find it difficult to be too critical here. I am only two or three years younger than Barry and at the time that these events were unfolding, I was in my first term at university. As with all cricket lovers in this country, I had been closely following the developing saga of the D'Oliveira Affair with a mixture of anger and dismay. Why had a political row prevented the opportunity of my seeing in the flesh the Pollocks, the Barlows, the Blands and the rest of this supremely talented side that I had heard so much about? Barry Richards, by the way, was unknown to me and the wider cricket community at that time. It seemed iniquitous and disproportionate. And what was all this fuss about Nelson Mandela? His name was unknown to me too. The first I had ever heard of him was when a fringe pressure group of fellow students attempted to get a motion passed that our common room should be renamed the Nelson Mandela JCR. What nonsense! What on earth had an obscure political activist in a faraway country got to do with a common room at a hall of residence at an English university? The motion was not carried, it has to be said.

You see, I too was naive. And so were a lot of other people who just could not get their heads round the fact that sport and politics had now become indissolubly intertwined. Time was to change our minds. Who can say now that sporting isolation of South Africa was not a good thing? We might have been piqued at being denied watching the South African team play. But there were millions of their disenfranchised countrymen who were more than piqued that they were forbidden, by law, from joining them in that team. Now that really was iniquitous and disproportionate.

For Barry and the others, it was back to provincial cricket and the Currie Cup. And all thoughts were bent up to the forthcoming tour by the Australians. The cancellation of the MCC tour was but a blip in their careers, they felt sure. Or at least Barry did. There may well have been some who smelled trouble and were not at all sanguine about the future but Barry was convinced, or had allowed himself to be convinced, that his career still had time to flower. He was only 22 after all. At that age, you feel that all things are possible. *Did you enjoy playing for Natal?* 'Loved it. We had a good side and we were successful. With only six matches a season and with Test matches few and far between, all the best players played and it was all pretty intense.' *How would you compare at that time the standard of the Currie Cup with the County Championship in England?* 'A notch or two higher, I thought. After all, there were only six provinces, whereas there were 17 counties. And just look at the players we had in the Natal side, let alone any of the others.' I made noises of assent. That had been my opinion too. 'I tell you what, Murt,' he said, warmly, 'without a shadow of a doubt, any of those provincial teams would have knocked the stuffing out of the Zimbabwe and Bangladesh sides of today.'

To evaluate his assertion, I followed a little detour of my own here and looked up the scorecard of a recent Test match between these two countries. I think you will find it interesting reading.

Zimbabwe: Marumba, Sibanda, Masakadza, Taylor, Waller, Chigumbura, Mutumbami, Cremer, Meth, Masakadza, Jarvis.

Bangladesh: Jahural Islam, Shakriar, Nafees, Mohammad Ashraful, Mahmudullah, Shakib Al Hasan, Mushfiqur Rahim, Nasir Hossain, Sohag Gazi, Enamul Haque jnr, Rubel Hossain, Robial Islam.

Have you heard of any of them? But there they all are, in the Test match records.

'Exactly,' said Barry, shaking his head sadly. I tried to reassure him that many cricket lovers would tend to agree with him. 'But they are the knowledgeable ones who understand the game. But what of the ordinary fan who looks at the records and doesn't realise that all those easy hundreds against moderate opposition help to inflate averages and make 'great' players out of those who are not?'

I said nothing and let his anger burn itself out, which it soon did. Bitterness at his lost years and proscribed chances of joining the 'greats' rarely surfaced in all our discussions and conversations but he would have had to possess the forbearance of a saint for his frustration not to flare up on the odd occasion. And he would not be alone in thinking that an asterisk ought to appear alongside any Test runs and wickets achieved against those teams.

Politically naive he may have been but the same could not be said of Barry's exploits on the cricket field. Even now, at a distance of 40-odd years, people still whistle in disbelief when they tell their stories and recount their memories. Grayson Heath was still playing for Natal and he remembers with absolute clarity a match against Western Province. This engine room of the domestic game was uncharacteristically languishing in the B section of the Currie Cup and that is a bit like Manchester United playing in the Championship. A match had been arranged, designated first-class, with Natal, in order to impress upon the authorities that it was high time they were returned to the top tier, where they felt they belonged. The match was played in Cape Town so it should not have come as a surprise to the visitors that the pitch at Newlands was tailor made for the Western Province spinners and likely to negate the Natal pace attack of Procter, Goddard, Trimborn and van der Bijl. According to Heath, there wasn't a blade of grass to be seen on it. And it was a baking hot day.

WP won the toss and 'gleefully batted first', he said. First ball, Procter came steaming in off his full run to deliver one of his thunderbolts. 'It was short of a length, there was a puff of dust and Gamsy, the wicketkeeper, caught it on the second bounce!' The Natal side's reaction was 'one of stunned disbelief'. For all that, they bowled WP out for 164. But then it was Natal's turn to bat on what cricketers popularly call a 'bunsen burner', though how much cricketers from other countries are familiar with Cockney rhyming slang – burner/turner – is open to debate. While others struggled, Barry gave a masterclass in how to play the turning ball. Heath called it 'an effortlessly efficient example of batting – the genius was in his element'. The upshot of his heroics was that Natal scored 215 and when WP themselves were bowled out for 175 in their second innings, the visitors had only to score 125 to secure victory.

'Only' is used loosely here; it was now the third day, the pitch if anything was more treacherous and a total of 125 was anything but a formality. And surely Richards could not do it all again. 'Well, he did,' said Heath. 'Even when we reached 100 without loss, had Barry gone then, we could still have lost. But we need not have worried such was his mastery of the conditions. We won by ten wickets, Goddard 43 not out and Richards undefeated on 81. This innings saw one world-class batsman near the end of his career – Goddard – being completely overshadowed by Barry at the beginning of his.'

There is another story of Barry's audacity at the crease, corroborated by two players on the field at the time. Robin Jackman, of Surrey, England and, at the time, Rhodesia, acts as our first raconteur. 'At our team meeting the night before, we were discussing how to deal with Barry Richards. Our captain, Andre Bruyns, unveiled his master plan. According to him, Barry hooked with his eyes closed.' I enquired of the said captain why he believed this to be so. 'I had seen a picture of Barry playing the hook shot,' confirmed Bruyns, 'and it looked as if his eyes were closed. So we plotted his downfall accordingly. You see,' he added, 'when he was focussed, it was almost impossible to get him out, for Barry had no weaknesses.' Their opening bowler, the fastest in the leagues the selectors could unearth, was instructed to test him with a few bouncers early on, with, not two, but three men back on the catch, a tactic which Bruyns ruefully likened to the bodyline, or leg side, theory of Larwood in days gone by. 'A big mistake,' Bruyns admitted, ' because Barry saw it as an insulting challenge and the focus showed in his eyes and the stance seemed more determined.'

The rapid short balls were duly delivered. 'Before Kingsmead was redeveloped,' said Jackman, 'there used to be a clock on the grass bank more or less at fine leg. Well, Barry, eyes closed or not, hit the ball out of the middle of the bat and it sailed right over the clock for six!' It did not end there. After four balls, the score was 20, including another six, after which Barry 'nonchalantly strolled a single to take the strike', an annoying habit that his batting partners came to know only too well.

Another plan to unsettle the great man, not wholly dissimilar to Rhodesia's, was hatched by Transvaal. Word had gone round that Barry had a weakness; if the ball was sharpish and aimed at his midriff, it would tuck him up in the course of trying to play it and he would lob a catch to leg slip or leg gully. The trap was duly laid. Four men were posted in readiness – two out on the boundary, a leg slip and another lurking close in, just forward of square. Mackay-Coghill was the bowler and it was felt that he would be especially effective in carrying out this tactic because he bowled quick left-arm and could therefore angle the ball at the batsman more awkwardly. Lee Irvine, Barry's team-mate in the Natal side, details the outcome of this devilish plan, 'Barry took guard a foot outside leg stump. If Mackay-Coghill bowled it at the stumps, Barry hit him through the covers for four. If he bowled it at him, he hit over square leg for six! He scored 120-odd that day, if my memory serves me. You see, Barry could never resist a challenge.' The only way to get him out, Irvine was convinced, was to make him bored.

Vintcent van der Bijl agrees. 'Barry hated defensive fields. So, in a sense, if you could cut off the boundary and give him one, he might get bored standing at the non-striker's end.' To counteract negative leg-side bowling, he would step outside leg and hit the ball on the off, a strategy that we at Hampshire would see for ourselves, particularly when the leg side was packed in limited overs games. Other players have since copied this of course but Barry was the first to try it and it was a measure of the genius of the man that he worked out how to do it, thus breaking the rules of orthodoxy, and then put it into practice. Mind you, this only underlines another truism of any artistic or creative activity: you can only break the rule, the norm, the established practice, once you have perfected how to do it properly first. Picasso could draw conventionally and accurately before he started to experiment with cubism. Barry could play through the on side in the orthodox style perfectly well until negative field placing compelled him to re-write the rulebook.

Here is another example of his flair and skill. 'I ran up to bowl to him on one occasion,' said van der Bijl, 'and delivered the perfect ball, which swung away late. Barry shaped to hit it away square on the off side. The ball then cut back sharply. Barry instantly adjusted his stroke and hit it to leg. Oh, and at the same time, he said, "Well bowled!"' The brazen cheek. The composed insouciance. The sheer genius of the man.

Andre Bruyns remembers another match, against Rhodesia, early in 1972. This time he was playing for Natal and opened the batting with Barry. Procter opened the bowling for Rhodesia and gave both batsmen a thorough going-over in a hostile spell, which they managed to negotiate safely. 'I got out before lunch,' said Bruyns, 'by which time Barry had about 80 not out. As he resumed his innings after lunch, I casually remarked that I had never seen a batsman bat for a whole day. He gave me a quizzical look but said nothing. He was not out at tea and as he went out for the last session, he turned to me and said, "Fill the plunge bath – see you later." At the close, he was 200 odd not out.' Bruyns did not seriously suggest that his casual remark had been the sole reason for Barry knuckling down for the day. He was generous enough to point out that the real motivating factor was the challenge posed by his old friend, Mike Procter. Bruyns was not the only contemporary of Barry's who noticed that throughout his career, Barry was usually 'at his best against the best'.

Rhodesia features in another Currie Cup story, though Barry would be the first to admit that on this occasion, unfolding events did not reflect so well on his reputation. On the third day, the match was petering out into a tame and inconsequential draw. Grayson Heath remembers what happened. 'Ray Gripper opened the innings for Rhodesia and had been in prolific form but it was widely acknowledged that many of his runs had been scored in meaningless second innings knocks when the pressure was off, which was precisely what he was doing on this occasion, having failed in the first innings.' Now, if I know Barry, this would have irked him no end – for two reasons. The first is that he would see such a situation as this in a *completely* different light to Gripper. If the match had become meaningless then so had his innings; I doubt he would have scored many runs or hung around for very long himself. And, in any case, he would have been bored by this stage and would have been thinking of plunge baths...or even swimming pools.

But there was a third reason, according to Heath, which added some extra spice to the pointed exchanges that were going on between the two opposing opening batsmen. 'Gripper would have been in contention for the same opening berth in the Test team that Barry was to fill.' Feelings got a bit heated; something was bound to give. Gripper continued to feast himself on some half-hearted bowling with Barry becoming increasingly hot under the collar. Heath recalled what happened next. 'Barry urged our captain, Barry Versveld, to give him a bowl, claiming he knew how to get him out. Eventually Versveld relented and gave him the ball. Halfway through his first over, with Gripper at the non-striker's end, Barry ran up to bowl but held on to the ball in his delivery stride and with Gripper barely a foot or two out of his crease as he backed up, Barry whipped off the bails and appealed for a run out.' Oh dear. That is not the done thing. The umpire of course has no option but to give the batsman out, though the captain can withdraw the appeal if he is so minded and wants to save a lot of aggravation, if not a full blown, angry confrontation.

It was significant that Natal's captain made no such concession but Barry cut a lonely figure as his team-mates shuffled away from him slightly embarrassed as the crowd erupted. Barry, somewhat shamefaced, put it down to youthful impetuosity and an unerring ability to upset the diplomatic apple cart, a trait that was to bedevil his early years. Mind you, at the end of the over, he did sidle up to his captain and say, 'Told you I knew how to get him out!'

I am not at all sure what it was about Rhodesia but that team seems to feature large in the many stories of Barry in the Currie Cup. I am indebted to Vintcent van der Bijl for this one. It was in the 1972/73 season. During an imperious innings of 197, Barry decided to have a bit of fun at the expense of one bowler whom he did not rate very highly. 'His name was Ricky Kaschula,' said van der Bijl. 'Barry sauntered down the wicket and said to his batting partner, 'I think I'll just hit him round the clock.' And this is precisely what he did – over mid-off, extra cover, cover, third man, then over to the other side, long leg, deep square leg, over mid-on. Incredible!' Indeed. How do you get the ball down to fine leg if it's a wide half-volley outside the off stump, I would like to know. With Barry, there was always a way.

Many of the stories about Barry have to do with his extraordinary talent with the bat and the more unorthodox ways that he chose to demonstrate it, especially on those occasions when he was bored, a not infrequent occurrence as we know. John Traicos had this one to share about an inter-city match between Durban and Pietermaritzburg. There was a fast bowler, brought in from the country – Hugh Saulez – who had been built up by Pat Trimborn, himself no slouch, and others as being quick enough to trouble even the great Richards. 'Barry carefully watched the first few balls from Saulez, who was really no more than medium-paced,' said Traicos, 'and then proceeded to play him with the edge of his bat, even cover driving him for four. Barry slaughtered the Maritzburg attack, getting a hundred in no time at all to wrap up the match.' And there were those of us at Hampshire who bowled to him in the nets and thought that we were the only bowlers whom he saw fit to entertain like this.

It is not often that anyone has the last word with our hero, who has a sharp tongue at times and is ever prepared to risk upsetting anyone whose bubble needs bursting. A typical example would be when Barry, to everybody's huge surprise, dropped a catch off the first ball of the innings. Van der Bijl is hazy in his mind what match it was but he remembers Barry rounding on his friend, Tich Smith, the wicketkeeper, and saying, 'I told you that you were standing too close!' However, van der Bijl can recall one occasion when even Barry was left speechless. 'There was a chap called Shaka Albers, a farmer who was desperate to play for Natal. The closest he got was when he was made 12th man for the match in Salisbury against Rhodesia. Barry instructed the 12th man not to forget to run the bath for him at the close of play because he intended to bat all day. Jackman had him dropped in the first over. After which, he helped himself to the inevitable hundred. At lunch, he called to Shaka to get him some fruit salad, without all the juice. When the fruit salad duly arrived, it was swimming in juice. "I said no juice," remonstrated Barry. Shaka took the bowl, poured the juice on to the floor and thrust if back at Barry. "Eat it!" he commanded. Barry was left open-mouthed.'

In point of fact, Barry was quite shy, especially early on in his life. Though he enjoyed the challenge of pitting his prodigious skills against the best in the world and relished the atmosphere of a big match and a large crowd, he actually disliked fame and all the unwelcome attention that it brought. He felt that the cricket fan could lay claim to his undivided attention and desire to entertain while he was out there, on the stage, so to speak. But once he had mounted the pavilion steps and entered the sanctuary of the dressing room, that was it as far as public scrutiny should go. And as for bothering him in private or when he was out, socialising with his friends, he could be quite brusque. He really didn't see that it was of anybody's interest or business.

That is why he had such trouble with autograph-hunters. For the life of him, he couldn't understand why anyone would want to collect scribbled signatures on a scruffy piece of paper or in a grubby, well-thumbed notebook. In England, during the first-class season, he came to understand that signing autographs was a long established custom, a ritual that everybody felt obliged to tolerate. You were a professional and it was part of your job. So he did it. But it still felt like his valuable time off duty was being infiltrated.

Even he found this incident amusing, however. I think it was at Lord's of all places. We had been waylaid by autograph hunters as we made our way across the car park after the close of play. I had got used to people idly crossing over to me to ask for my autograph, even though they hadn't a clue who I was. They were merely waiting for the queue for Barry to subside. After a while, I noticed a particularly scruffy urchin – I could hardly miss him – who had been up before me, on more than one occasion. 'I've just done you,' I pointed out. 'I know,' he replied, 'but I'm collecting you to swap. Ten Andy Murtaghs are worth one Barry Richards.' On reflection, I reckoned he had read the market just about right.

To continue the theme, Dennis Gamsy has his own story to tell. It was at this stage in his Natal career when fame was beginning to bump annoyingly against Barry's shoulder when he was out and about town in Durban. 'After a match,' Gamsy said, 'my wife Gillian and I, with Barry, decided to go to the Beach Hotel on Durban's beachfront. Two of Durban's great entertainers, Gary and Spider, were on stage.' I presumed Gamsy was not making this up and that there really was a singing duo by that name. Spider, it would appear, was an avid cricket fan and worshipped the very ground that Barry trod. 'As we entered the room,' Gamsy continued, 'it was clear that Spider realised that Barry had arrived. In those days, Barry was very self-conscious of his fame and was always under the impression, probably correctly, that everybody was watching him. He was, to say the least, unable then to handle the situation… Barry was angling to sit at a table near the back of the room but spotting a vacant table much closer to the front, it was there that I headed. Barry sat down reluctantly, head bowed. Spider then began his welcome. "Guys, I am absolutely delighted to welcome the newcomers to our audience this evening, among them one of the greatest batsmen you will ever wish to see. Ladies and gentlemen…" An interminable pause took place during which Barry was twisting and muttering in his seat. "Let's give a big welcome to…DENNIS GAMSY!" Even Barry had to laugh. Me, I took it seriously.'

What is it about fame, I ruminated, that makes ordinarily sensible people lose all inhibitions and lay claim shamelessly to someone else's privacy? I witnessed the phenomenon with brutal clarity at times when out with Barry socially in England

and I could see how much it irked him. But it was rapidly becoming, at this stage of his career, a fact of life. After all, it was now that 'I announced myself on the grand stage' – his own words. He meant as a cricketer but it could also be taken as a 'personality'. He was on the brink of stardom and if the prospect of international competition excited him, he might just have allowed himself a twinge of regret at the accompanying loss of privacy. From now on, he would be led to the table at the front; there would be no hiding place at the back.

But before we head for the bright lights of the West End, let us pause a moment and consider what his home environment meant to him. I rely here on the testimony of one of his closest friends, Dave Anderson. 'We played together for the DHS Old Boys team in the league,' said Anderson, 'and it is here that I feel he was at his most comfortable. He did not have to come down to nets every Tuesday and Thursday evening but he did, and it was here that he could socialise with his old school mates and guys from all age groups…. He got to know and mixed with all the club members and participated in all the club functions.'

When his Natal commitments permitted, Barry used to play for the club, 'choosing to be with his mates'. Anderson particularly remembers one day at net practice. 'He went into bat and said that he would run fielding practice from there, asking all the guys from all the teams to stand in the middle.' He then instructed the bowlers to bowl where they liked, and Anderson was keen to point out that these were reputable bowlers, not cannon fodder, most of whom were provincial players. Barry then proceeded to hit catches off the bowling to nominated fielders, never getting their names wrong. 'And the fact that he knew all their names tells you all you need to know about Barry,' Anderson assured me.

'He speaks to this day about the funny times we had there. He still giggles when we remember a guy called Sollo, who was a Third XI player, being sent on as our 12th man and taking this amazing catch.'

However, I cannot resist leaving you with this final comment of Anderson's about Barry before Test cricket beckoned, 'Depending on the weather and who was tanning at the club pool dictated how many runs he got that day!'

5

Annus Mirabilis 1970–71

'Don't fail to see this young man bat when he comes here.'

Sir Donald Bradman

A N *annus mirabilis* is a year of wonders. If it is stretching mathematics to refer to the period of Barry Richards's career from January 1970 to March 1971 as such, it certainly does not stretch the truth. His first-class career spanned the years from 1964 to 1983 but he was at his best, he believes, from 1968 to 1975, when his hunger was at its sharpest and his ambition burned brightest. In the months leading up to the greatly anticipated arrival of the Australians in the 1969/70 season, Barry was in the form of his life. He had returned to Durban on the back of two glittering seasons for Hampshire, scoring 2,314 runs at an average of 48.21 in 1968 and 1,440 runs the following year, curtailed by injury, at 57.60.

A year of dramatic change in the English first-class game had made up 1968. For the first time, each county had been allowed to sign one overseas player on immediate registration and in the scramble to secure the biggest names in the game, Hampshire's acquisition of the hitherto largely unknown Barry Richards had initially slipped below the radar. But not for long. After a quiet start for his new county, once the sun emerged from bleak, early summer clouds, he took the championship by storm. Promoted to open the innings, he scored 130 and 104 not out against Northamptonshire, followed by 206 against Nottinghamshire, and never looked back.

Wisden chose him as one of its five cricketers of the year. It was a hugely prestigious award with an accolade from the editor that must have been burning Barry's ears as the printing presses were whirring and clanking. *Wisden*'s citation belongs to a later chapter but it is as well to bring to mind the impact the young Richards was making on the game worldwide and how benignly the cricketing gods were smiling upon him during this period of his life. 'Garry Sobers apart, none of the new overseas players in county cricket made a greater impact than Barry Anderson Richards,' wrote the editor. He then went on to make two observations, one uncannily prescient and the other tragically mistaken. 'Keen as he is on the game, Richards shares the general opinion of overseas players that there is far too much cricket played in England.' He even quoted Barry's own words, 'I woke up on some mornings and said to myself, surely not another day's cricket!' You should have heard what he was saying by 1976 as he pulled back the curtains every morning.

The other pronouncement brings a lump to the throat as you read it, knowing how things subsequently turned out. 'Richards's horizons seem limitless and it will be fascinating to see how far his talents will take him. Few, anywhere in the world, have his possibilities.'

The only possibility that concerned him as he took guard once again for Natal at the start of the 1969/70 season was selection for the Test side against the visiting Australians. It was more of a probability than a possibility. There was scarcely a cricket follower in the country who did not expect that he would be in the team and if there was any vestige of doubt, it was swept aside by his form leading up to the Tests. It was nothing short of scintillating: 100 v Western Province, 41 v South African Universities XI, 110 not out v Eastern Province, 42 v Transvaal, 169 v Rhodesia. 'I was in pretty good nick. I scored four hundreds in six innings,' he said, reminding me of the one-day competition, the Gillette Cup, as well. *Be honest, what was your reaction when the team for the first Test was announced?* 'No great surprise really. Many people felt that I should have been picked in 1967 anyway.' And with the weight of runs supporting his inclusion, he would have had to have kicked something much bigger than a flowerpot to have been excluded again. No doubt with a broken foot to boot. Sensibly, he gave nightclubs a wide berth in the weeks leading up to the opening Test.

Was it an emotional moment when you were presented with your green Springbok cap? 'Obviously it was special to me. But there was no song and dance about it, no special ceremony. Don't forget there were three or four of us making our debuts that game. I think it was Trevor Goddard who gave it to me.' That would have been fitting: both team-mates for Natal but from different generations, the grizzled veteran passing the sword of battle on to the young warrior. Barry seized it eagerly. It was high time. The first clash took place in Cape Town. He travelled down several days beforehand for practice in the nets, which were good at Newlands. 'One side used them in the morning, the other in the afternoon,' he answered matter-of-factly to my query about the routine before a Test match.

How were you welcomed into the side? 'No problems at all. We all knew each other. We'd been colleagues and opponents in the Currie Cup, so I was no stranger.' *Ali Bacher was captain. How did you rate him?* 'An excellent man manager. He knew how to press all the right buttons for each different personality in the side.' Lee Irvine agreed wholeheartedly. 'There were one or two potential troublemakers in that team but he handled them well. Look, the Pollocks, Barlow, Goddard – a former captain – they were all experienced Test players and all had strong personalities. But he got all of us to gel.' In fact, Irvine went on to say that appointing Bacher as captain was a 'masterstroke' by the selectors because he was by no means the only candidate. By all accounts there had been much discussion before the decision was made. Goddard had the experience and Barlow the personality in most people's minds, including his own. 'Eddie was a great motivator of the youngsters,' Irvine believed, 'but how he was going to cope with the Pollocks, for example, was a moot point.' So, the right choice was made and all fell into line. 'Eddie was an outgoing, ebullient sort of character,' Irvine went on, 'Ali, by contrast, was very self-effacing, a bit of a loner, really. But that's no bad thing for a captain. He shouldn't just be one of the boys.'

But how was he tactically? Barry answered, 'Tactically very astute. But over the years I became more and more convinced that captaincy isn't really about setting fancy fields. Well, not at this level anyway. Everyone knew his job, what he had to do. What Ali was good at was creating the right atmosphere for all of us to have the confidence to go out there and show our talent.' Attention to detail is another quality of a good captain, Barry might have added. Bacher was meticulous in the manner in which he prepared his team. For example, he made sure that he roomed with one of the new boys and his vice-captain, Eddie Barlow, with another. Barry's turn for the prefectorial guardianship was in Durban during the second Test. Lee Irvine remembers being roomed with Barlow and getting the lowdown on Test cricket well into the night before the game. 'So much so,' said Irvine, 'I was so wired up that I couldn't sleep while Eddie was snoring away.'

The South African public had been starved of international cricket – the last series had been against Bobby Simpson's Australian side three years previously – and there was huge interest and anticipation before the first Test. 'The bottom line,' said Irvine, 'was that they came as world champions, in all but name, and had a reputation as a great team.' Their record in their last four series, against England, India, West Indies and India in that order, would seem to have borne out this view. Bill Lawry, their captain, was a seasoned and battle-hardened veteran, as tough as teak. He announced, on their arrival, that he had every confidence in his batting line-up of Stackpole, Walters, Redpath and Sheahan, as well as Ian Chappell, 'The best young batsman in the world.' Hmm, Barry might have wanted to have something to say about that. Lawry also pointed to Graham McKenzie, the youngest bowler ever to take 100 and 200 Test wickets, who would spearhead the attack, supported by the dependable Alan Connolly, a proven Test spinner in Ashley Mallett and of course the 'mystery bowler', John Gleeson, whose name was on everybody's lips. The South Africans were keen, naturally, but young, largely untried and short of Test match experience. The challenge was enormous.

Unlike Barry, Lee Irvine was not at all sure of his place in the team. An obvious rival was Colin Bland, who had an exceptional Test record and was of course the best fielder in the world of his era, some would argue of any era. But he had a dodgy knee. The selectors looked at the swollen joint with dismay after a long innings in the Currie Cup and there and then came to the judgement that he was not fit for a five-day match. So Irvine, Barry's friend and team-mate at Durban High, also received his green Springbok cap that morning.

Barry admitted to being nervous as he took guard at 11am on the first day at Newlands. As well he might. Every batsman battles with his nerves before an innings, especially one as significant as this. If you don't feel nervous, you don't care and Barry cared all right. He noticed that his opening partner, Trevor Goddard, playing in his 39th Test, was even more nervous. Test series came around infrequently for South Africans and much was at stake. Against the new ball attack of McKenzie and Connolly, Barry started with uncommon circumspection, taking 20 minutes to get off the mark. Eventually, a square drive for four off Connolly saw him on his way and he started to relax, believing that now the hard work had been done, he ought to settle in for a large score. But he had relaxed too early and a loose shot off Connolly took the inside edge and he was bowled for 29. 'I let my guard down,' he confessed. 'What is the pass mark for your first Test? Thirty-odd? Subconsciously, I guess I thought I'd made enough not to get dropped.'

All the other batsmen made good starts but only Eddie Barlow prospered. But not without controversy, it has to be said. Irvine was batting with him at the time. 'Eddie went on the hook, gloved it and was caught. But the umpire, Billy Wade, as nice a fellow as you could ever wish to meet, gave him not out. Of course, the Aussies went berserk. Lawry threw his cap on the ground and stamped on it and the rest of the Australians surrounded Eddie, all swearing at him. When Eddie "politely" suggested that it might not be a bad idea for them to get back to their positions to continue the game, the language became worse.' Eventually, the match did resume. Barlow, then on 66, went on to make 127, the backbone of a total of 382. Reasonable but not out of sight.

Australia's reply was disastrous and set the tone, in fact, for a series that seemed to go from bad to worse. The wicket at Newlands held no terrors, if being a little on the slow side, but their vaunted batting found different ways to get out and the total of 164 was patently inadequate. Chappell, for one, was unlucky, Irvine admitted. 'He hooked at a bouncer from Peter Pollock and really middled it. I was fielding at squarish leg gully and instinctively put up my hands and parried it up into the air. Chevalier, running behind me, caught it.' That was how it went, Test after Test, the South Africans taking miraculous catches and the Australians dropping even the simplest. Surely Bacher would enforce the follow-on and subject the visitors to more of the same. But no, the wicket had started to turn and with the 'mystery' spinner, Johnny Gleeson, proving to be something of a handful in the first innings, with no luck, it has to be said, Bacher sensibly avoided the possibility of having to chase a total, no matter how meagre, on a wearing wicket in the fourth innings. The instructions were clear – bat again, pile on the runs and destroy them psychologically.

In his second innings, Barry was more relaxed but again he fell foul of a moment's loss of concentration and was out caught behind off Connolly for 32. *Connolly got you twice in the match. Was there a problem facing him?* There was no problem facing Connolly, and later scores would seem to bear this out, but he was prepared to admit that he was a better bowler than given credit for and in fact was one of the very few in the Australian side to do himself justice on the tour. 'It was his change of pace that set him apart from the others. He bowled well throughout the series but really, I had only myself to blame for two cheap dismissals.' In their haste to make quick runs, several South Africans were equally carelessly dismissed but their total of 232 meant that Australia had to score a mammoth 440 to win on a wicket starting to take considerable turn.

In truth, all they could hope for was to grind it out for a draw but though the Aussies' resistance was stiffer than in the first innings, South Africa were not to be denied and Australia were dismissed 170 runs short. *I see you made a significant contribution in the charge for victory.* He laughed. 'My one and only Test wicket, Johnny Gleeson, poor fellow. He was deceived by my mystery ball and was yorked!' Delighted though they were by their victory in their first Test for three years, the South African team were not wholly satisfied by their performance. 'Prockie bowled well in the second innings and of course Barlow made the big score around which our first innings was built. But there had been apprehension in the team. We were a bit stiff, as if the wheels weren't properly oiled.' All one can say is that, come the second Test, the wheels had been given lashings of oil and were turning very smoothly.

How did the Aussies take their defeat? 'On the whole, they were a pretty decent bunch. We went into their dressing room afterwards, as you usually did, and Western Province put on a drinks party after the game.' He went on to record his surprise to discover that this was not custom and practice in the English game when he went over to play for Hampshire but he ascribed this to two reasons. The first was that the game was fully professional. 'It was your job, every day of the week. And at the close of play, you knocked off and went home.' And the second was that he felt that South Africans, with their colonial past, had much more in common with the Aussies than with the English. 'Enemies on the field and friends off it. Except perhaps for Barlow.'

How come? 'Bunter' Barlow? I always thought that he was a cheerful, no-nonsense sort of chap. 'He was really pumped for this game, on his home turf. He would go and have a beer with them but he remained guarded, not wanting to be too friendly. He wanted to keep up the pressure. The series wasn't yet won.' *Was there much sledging on the pitch?* Barry grinned. 'Plenty. Don't forget, there was no TV, no close-ups. And of course no stump microphones to pick up the unguarded comments.' *So what was said?* 'Obviously, the weakest or the most vulnerable would be targeted. And you'd get a lot of stick if you played a loose shot or didn't walk or something like that.' *Stick for not walking? Come on, the Aussies invented the innocent look and the crafty tap of the imaginary divot.* We both agreed on that one. Except that Lee Irvine recounted a story from the series that might perhaps put the Australians in a different light. And believe it or not, it featured Ian Chappell and might go a long way to explaining his subsequent abrasive attitude on the field to his opponents. 'I forget which innings but Chappell was caught by Lance in the gully. He asked Lance whether he had caught it. Lance said yes, so Chappell accepted his word and off he went. I was fielding at cover and I'd had a good sight of the ball. "Tiger," I said. "That was a bump ball." Tiger replied, "I know. But he didn't ask me whether it had bounced before I caught it, did he?"' I burst out laughing. 'Besides,' Barry added, 'it was much worse in the Currie Cup. We all knew each other and how to wind each other up.' While he was at Hampshire, I never remember Barry being wound up when he was at the crease. By then, I guess, everybody had worked out that it was a futile, not to say foolhardy, tactic anyway.

The anticipation and excitement before the second Test at Kingsmead was even more electric than it was at Cape Town, Barry reckoned. For him, it was always going to be a special occasion because it was at his home ground. *Were your parents at the match?* 'They were. But I didn't manage to see much of them during the game because I stayed in the team hotel with the rest of the lads. Ali shared a room with me.' All part of the best laid plans of a captain who left no stone unturned in his quest to keep the Australians on the back foot.

For some reason, Barry felt less nervous as he walked out to bat with Trevor Goddard than he had at Newlands. Perhaps it was because he was playing in familiar surroundings, in front of his home crowd. Perhaps he felt a little more settled in the side, now that he had experienced Test cricket for the first time and was confident he could, and would, cut the mustard at this level. Never mind 'this level', it was at a level more elevated than most had ever witnessed that he batted that morning. Nobody who was there has ever forgotten it. 'I started well and got on a roll,' was his bland assessment of how things went, as if the sheer majesty of his innings were an everyday occurrence. Even the bald facts give some clue as to the mastery he exerted over the Australian attack; he raced to 94 before lunch and was out later in the afternoon for 140 off only 164 balls.

Wisden preferred more vivid prose, calling it 'an exhibition of technical brilliance' in which 'the only false stroke in his three hour innings was his last.' Others remember it as a spectacle of outrageously brilliant strokeplay. Irvine called it 'awesome'. Barry very nearly made history by reaching his hundred before lunch. Only three players had performed the feat on the first day of a Test match and all were Australians, Trumper, Macartney and Bradman. No South African. 'And no Pommie,' Barry reminded me wryly, as if such a thing were unthinkable.

And to the present day, only Majid Khan of Pakistan has added his name to that illustrious list. So you can imagine the rising feverishness of a packed Kingsmead ground, on a gloriously sunny day, as Barry thumped and smashed his way closer to the landmark. Bacher was batting with him and it was ten minutes to one and lunch. 'He was six runs short,' Bacher recalled years later. 'So, in an attempt to give him the strike, I rushed out of the crease against Connolly and was duly bowled.' Around his legs. 'Barry should have got it,' John Traicos, whose debut this was while still a student at Natal University, 'and could easily have got it had not the Australians employed some outrageously slow tactics.' Indeed, they only bowled three overs in the last 20 minutes. 'Bill Lawry, the captain, was furious at what was happening,' said Barry, with more equanimity than he must have felt at the time. 'He didn't want to be the captain of the side that let a 24-year-old, playing in his second Test, score a hundred before lunch.' And just to make sure, Lawry suddenly discovered a problem with his bootlaces, bending down to do them up, then to undo them and to do them up again. The ploy succeeded. Barry was stranded on 94 as the umpires removed the bails and they all trooped off to have lunch. To this day, I have never encountered anyone from a country that does not play cricket who can get his head round the fact that the game stops so that the players can have lunch. Only in England, they say. Well, not quite – in South Africa too. *What did you have to eat, Barry? Was it a bowl of fruit without the juice?* 'The choice was salad or curry and rice. As I was batting, I had a bit of salad. No one squeezed out the lettuce, as I recall.'

If it was salad for lunch, his partner after the break, Graeme Pollock, must have had the same. It is difficult to describe adequately what took place that afternoon at Kingsmead. At the time, the headline 'The Golden Hour' was coined and later entered South African cricket folklore. If the crowd had thought that morning that they had been privileged to witness before lunch a display of batting the like of which they would be lucky to see again in their lifetime, they were mistaken. In fact, they had only to wait for 40 minutes. In one hour after lunch, Richards and Pollock put on 103 runs in an exhibition of inspired strokeplay that had everyone reaching for the thesaurus. I could reach for mine but I think I shall leave it to others to try to put into words what they had been watching. Lee Irvine said that it was 'unforgettable – one of the greatest partnerships of all time'.

John Traicos wrote to me in these words, 'Richards and Pollock thrashed the Australian bowling in what is often described as an hour of classic batsmanship, as the established maestro (Pollock) was determined not to be outdone by the young genius (Richards). The straight drives, all along the ground, were an exceptional feature of the partnership.' Ali Bacher, also watching from the players' balcony, reminisced in these words, 'I don't think this country has ever again seen batting like we saw that day.' *Wisden* recorded it as 'a glittering and technically perfect passage of batting.' Paul Sheahan, one of the helpless Australian fielders, took up this theme of the young gun and the older assassin, 'It was as if Pollock was saying, "You've seen the apprentice. Now look at the master."' Ian Chappell, a young firebrand in the Australian team at the time, put it more bluntly, 'I remember telling Stackie [Keith Stackpole], "We've got a problem here, mate. This bastard [Pollock] is going to see how many Barry gets and then he's going to double it." Prophetic words. That is precisely what Pollock did, but more of his innings later. The Australian captain, Bill Lawry, never one to give praise lightly, admitted afterwards, 'Never have I seen the ball hit with such power by two players at the same time.'

And what of Barry's recollection? 'It was just one of those days when everything clicked, you know, when everything hits the middle of the bat.' Then a thought struck me. Apart from their supreme skills with the bat, both Pollock and Richards were past masters at farming the strike. *How did you manage to avoid spending your time at the bowler's end?* He grinned. 'Getting on strike was a bit of an art form.' *How come there wasn't a run out then?* 'I think we both recognised that the other was playing just as well so we more or less took what was in front of us.'

Having hit 20 fours and one six, Barry had a slog at Freeman and was bowled for 140. 'Whatever you say about the Aussies,' Barry said, 'if you gained their respect, they were generous with their praise. Lawry, for example. He was a dour sod on the field but off it he was fair and complimentary – a very funny man, actually.' Lawry, together with the rest of his team, stood and applauded Barry all the way back to the pavilion. Barry sighed at the memory. 'I gave it away. A double century was there for the taking.'

Not for the first time, nor the last, in our protracted conversations, he lamented the number of times that he had given his wicket away in the course of his career. 'Staggering!' he sighed. As we shall see, even in this series, he was rarely dismissed by the bowler, more by his own carelessness and desire to entertain. 'I could never have batted like Boycott,' he said. Fair enough. It takes all sorts to make a batting line-up. If there were ten Boycotts in your side, you might build up a considerable score but it would be made in front of a sparse crowd. Kingsmead, packed to the rafters, stood as one to acclaim an innings of genius as Barry walked back to the pavilion, doffing his green cap, just as Grandpa Percy had told him all those years ago.

It needs to be put on record that the run feast did not cease once Richards had disappeared into the dressing room. As Chappell had predicted, Pollock did not give his wicket away. He carried on irresistibly, remorselessly, ruthlessly. Barry described Pollock's batting thus, 'GP was a wonderful player, one of the best. What I admired was his uncanny ability to miss the fielder. He never missed the gap.' Lee Irvine, who was watching from the other end, agreed. 'GP was hungrier. He never gave his wicket away. Never!' Pollock batted on for another six hours and was eventually out to a tired shot off the part-time leg spin of Keith Stackpole for 274, then a South African record.

During this day's cricket, it had passed almost unnoticed that the centurion from the first Test, Eddie Barlow, had been dismissed in short order for one. On his return to the home dressing room, he is alleged to have said, 'After the Lord Mayor's Show, there was no room for me out there. I was embarrassed. Those two have made a mockery of batting.'

And this from one of the finest all-rounders in South African cricket, whose top score in Tests was 201, finishing his career with a Test average of 45.74. To say nothing of his occasional inspired spells of bowling.

To add some colour, I think I shall quote at length the eyewitness accounts of two who were there. Ali Bacher first:

> 'Graeme had watched Barry bat supremely. He saw the centre stage was taken by an emerging, strong Barry Richards. Being a great batsman, he would never say it but I could sense him thinking aloud to himself, "That is great batting. I could do the same, if not better." So in many ways, Barry's performance motivated Graeme further. But he was very dignified. Great players compete against each other to raise their own performance. That is what happened at Kingsmead in that Test.'

And now let us hear from the great man himself. And for once I am not referring to Barry but to Graeme Pollock:

> 'I must agree that I was under pressure. Barry had not played in the 1966/67 series and he was a great player who should have played three or four years earlier. I told myself, "Look, the guy can play and I've got to be at my best to keep up with him." He had set it up and I had to play well when I came in to bat. Fortunately it worked out that way as Barry gave it away for 140 and I went on to finish the double century.'

Was this Pollock's greatest innings? 'I don't think so,' Barry answered. 'I think his 125 at Trent Bridge in 1965 was better.' *Was this 140 your best innings?* 'It's up there. But don't forget my 325 in one day at Perth.' Of course. How forgetful of me. 'Then there was the 120 at Port Elizabeth.' Yes, that was in the fourth Test but we haven't reached there yet. He started to think back in an abstracted manner. 'There was also 200 against Notts…and 70 against Yorkshire…oh, I don't know Murt. It was all a long time ago.'

You might be surprised to hear that a score of only 70 he rated as being one his best. But like all great batsmen, it is the level of difficulty, as well as the quality of the bowling, that he takes into consideration when assessing an innings. To satisfy my curiosity, I looked up the scorecard of this match. It was in early May in 1968 against Yorkshire at Harrogate. 'Jeez Murt, it was only my second match for Hampshire. I'd never seen a wicket like it.' Indeed. Harrogate is a charming spa town in north Yorkshire but the cricket ground is no more than a club ground and an ill-prepared greentop in one of the most northern outposts of first-class cricket in England was a world away, geographically, spiritually and environmentally, from southern Africa. I bet he did not lend out any sweaters on this occasion.

And look at the Yorkshire bowling attack – Trueman, Nicholson, Close, Illingworth, Wilson. They all knew a thing or two about exploiting local conditions. Keith Wheatley, a team-mate of Barry's at Hampshire, said this about it. 'Don't forget in those days we were playing on uncovered wickets. This one had been exposed to overnight rain and was a shocker, turning square and bouncing. Everybody was floundering but Barry would play this immaculate shot and cry, "Come two."' *Two? Why only two? He usually hit fours.* 'Outfield, mate. The ball would hit a puddle in the outfield and just stop. Illy was tearing his hair out.' Barry's score of 70 is put into sharp relief when you discover that only one other Hampshire batsman got into double figures, and that was a paltry 18. In runs scored, no, it was not Barry's most productive score but my word, he looks back on it with justifiable pride and satisfaction.

Did you celebrate that night? 'Not really. To be honest, I was too knackered.' *What about press interviews and all that?* 'Lots of people had been impressed. Reporters and radio people were milling about, all getting very excited. But I wasn't called to do a press conference or anything like that.' *Is there any TV footage in existence of your innings?* He looked at me as if asking himself how many times he was going to have to remind me that there was no television in South Africa. 'No footage at all. Well, there is some on 8mm film, but everyone looks a hundred miles away.' That is a crying shame. Who would not give his eye teeth to watch footage of that day's play?

He then went on to describe, in fascinating detail, his battle with Gleeson. Unlike any spinner before or since, with the possible exception of another Australian from an earlier era, Jack Iverson, Gleeson flicked the ball from his middle finger, and depending from which side of the finger it was flicked would determine whether it was an off break or a leg break. This is a fiendishly difficult trick to master; just try doing it with a tennis ball in your front room. You would expect such an unconventional delivery to be difficult to control but in fact Gleeson bowled with rare accuracy and troubled even the best players during his career. Certainly none of the South Africans could pick him and he was the subject of much discussion on how best to play him. Lee Irvine remembers those conversations before the match with great clarity. 'Gleeson mystified everyone,' he said. 'We all had an opinion on how best to play him. Barlow had one, Pollock had another, Bacher had a third. Barry announced to everyone his plan, "I'm not going to let it bounce." And that is precisely what he did!'

He then told me an amusing story against himself on this very subject. Pollock was 80 not out when Irvine, batting at number five, joined him in the middle. They had a little chat before Irvine took guard, the way you do, more for moral support than anything else. But Pollock had a theory on how to play Gleeson and told his partner he had worked out how to pick him. The unveiling of the mystery was good news so Irvine listened with all ears. If you could see the middle finger at the moment when Gleeson released the ball, reckoned Pollock, then it was the googly. If you couldn't, it was the leg-spinner. Irvine thanked his partner and resolved to take his advice; after all, Pollock appeared to be little troubled by the spinner and was now smashing the ball to all parts of the ground. *How did it go?* 'I watched the hand closely and saw that the finger was up. The googly! I played at it, missed and was bowled. Later, I asked Graeme, "What happened? You told me it would be the googly and it wasn't." "Oh, I just play him off the pitch," was his reply.' I suppose you can if you're a genius. They seem to see the ball so much quicker than the rest of us poor mortals.

Eddie Barlow's theory also failed empirical assessment. As we have seen, he was not at the crease long enough at Kingsmead to put it to the test but he was determined to do so in the next match. John Traicos takes up the story:

> 'Eddie disagreed with Barry's theory and said that he had already picked Gleeson's off-spinner but would not divulge his theory, saying that he would show us all how to play him in the middle. In the third Test, Eddie was batting at number five and Gleeson came on to bowl. Eddie nipped down the track to the second ball and, picking up the off-spinner, hit him through midwicket for four. As he strode back to the crease, chest protruding in typical "Bunter" style, sleeves rolled up high on his arms, he looked towards the changing room with a confident look as if to say, "I told you so." Two balls later, he charged down the wicket to hit what he thought was the off-spinner through midwicket, only to be stumped by three yards! Needless to say, he received several comments of "Well read, Eddie" when he returned to the dressing room.'

I wondered the theory Barry had come up with and trusted. 'Well Murt,' he said as if the answer was as plain as a pikestaff, 'If the ball doesn't bounce, it doesn't spin. Does it?' So Lee Irvine's comment was exactly right: Barry used his feet to combat Gleeson's mysteries. Successfully too, for Gleeson did not take Barry's wicket throughout the series, even though he bowled better than any of the Australians and to the end, none of the South Africans truly mastered him. 'He didn't spin it much,' was Barry's verdict. 'You'd allow a little bit of room to counter it if it was the leggie. And if it was the offie and you missed it, it would hit you on the pad. And no umpire's going to give you out if you're halfway down the wicket.'

I have seen the master batsman put this technique to the test on many an occasion. It is a tactic that tends to ruin the rhythm and the flight of even the best spinners. One of the most absorbing innings I saw him play was when he took on Bishan Bedi in a crucial match between Hampshire and Northamptonshire. The tussle between arguably the best spinner in the world and the best batsman was riveting stuff. Barry did not have it all his own way and always said afterwards that Bedi was the finest spin bowler he ever faced. That innings belongs in a later chapter but I refer to it because it needs to be pointed out that Barry *always* used his feet against the spinners. He seemed to be able to wait that fraction longer at the crease than most batsmen before making his move, so the bowler had no time to react. 'If you force him to adjust his length, he can't give it so much air, therefore reducing the amount of spin he can put on the ball.' As ever with Barry, it was a case of seizing the initiative, a refusal to be dominated. He rarely was.

Nor, it seemed, were the rest of the South African team in this golden summer, which was turning current international form and conventional wisdom on its head. It was not only in South Africa that this young, talented, exuberant team was catching the eye; *Wisden* marvelled at the scale of the humiliation heaped on their respected opponents in a series that 'rocked the cricketing world'. The home side's only possible enemy was complacency. They had made it all look so ridiculously easy. John Traicos takes up this theme. He said that Ali Bacher's concern was that this exceptionally talented, youthful team were *too* confident in their ability:

> 'Ali was so paranoid about over-confidence that before the third Test, he terminated the pre-match practice after half an hour because he felt that the batsmen, Barry and Lee Irvine in particular, were messing around in the nets. Ali called everyone together and lectured us on how the series was not yet won even though we were two up and he pointed out that South Africa had lost many series to Australia and that we could not ever be too confident. He then put us through a strenuous fielding session for an hour and a half.'

Shrewd reader of men that he was, Bacher had a point. Barry admits to carelessness being the cause of both his dismissals in this Test at The Wanderers in Johannesburg. 'I had a hundred in both innings there for the taking,' he said, 'but I got a bit carried away.' The lure of a century before lunch, denied him by Lawry's bootlaces in the previous Test, was understandably enticing. Graham McKenzie had been dropped – his figures so far in the series had represented a catastrophic loss of form for this tremendous bowler – and Mayne chosen in his stead. 'He was a bit sharper than the rest,' Barry said, 'so I took him on.' Not for the first time in his career, please note, it was the challenge that stirred his competitive juices. But once again, he gave it away. He was batting with supreme confidence, seemingly playing strokes at will, and it was a surprise when he was out for 65.

Looking back on this innings, and indeed on his batting throughout the series, he expresses wonder at the rapidity of the run rate. In those days, innings were measured by time at the crease rather than by the number of runs scored in relation to the number of balls faced. He was dismissed 40 minutes before lunch so the prospect of tucking into his salad with three figures to his name was not an unrealistic target. He was batting that well. He had faced only 74 balls, hitting 12 fours and a six, an extraordinary run rate for a Test match, for the first morning of a Test too. 'It wasn't really Test cricket,' he said, 'or at least how Test cricket was meant to be played.' By contrast, Pollock took 157 balls in scoring 52 but it must be stressed that for once, the great man had struggled to find his touch.

In the second innings, with South Africa holding an unexceptional lead of 77, Barry opened with Eddie Barlow, not Trevor Goddard, who had accompanied him to the middle on each occasion hitherto. He had been demoted to number nine in the order. In fact, this was to be Goddard's final Test. *Did he have an inkling that he was going to be dropped?* Those who accused Barry of being money-oriented and self-serving ought to listen to his response, uttered with real sadness and a touch of anger. 'There was no sentiment, no thought of allowing a great servant of South African cricket a public send-off at a time of his own choosing, like Tendulkar and Kallis.

I read, like he did, I guess, that he had been dropped in the paper!' Indeed, it does seem insensitive at best. The series had been won – South Africa won the match by the convincing margin of 307 runs – there was only one match left, Goddard was a legend in the game, his international career had spanned the years from 1955 to 1970 and he had been one of the great, if largely unacknowledged, all-rounders, a model of classical technique with bat and ball. Surely he deserved an appreciative farewell in front of his home crowd. 'I was very sad at what happened,' said Barry. 'He had been a great mentor to me; I owed him a lot. But that was how it was done in those days. Useless amateurs in charge.'

Talking of amateurism, may I ask how much you were paid per Test? He had to think about that, as if such a paltry sum was hardly worth remembering. 'I don't know… three or four hundred rand?' *Peanuts really, when you consider you were providing gripping entertainment to packed grounds.* He rather liked that word 'entertainment'. It lay at the heart of what it was all about, in his opinion. True, he could have scored more runs if he had been more run hungry. But it wasn't so much the number of runs that he scored but the manner in which he made them that gave him satisfaction in what he did. 'I was determined not to fit into the stereotype of an opener, cautious, safe, stodgy, whose job was to see off the new-ball bowlers by grinding them down. I wanted to play my normal attacking game.'

Today, aggressive opening bats are commonplace; back then, Barry was an innovator, the first of a new breed.

So where did all the money go? 'What money?' *The gate money. Sold-out matches. Huge revenue. Where did it all go?* 'To the individual provincial associations. So all those officials in blazers could sit in the front of the plane!' I laughed. So did he. Cynicism of the game's overlords in those days was not the sole preserve of one South African opening batsman. He then told me an amusing story of his time at Hampshire and seeing that we are currently on the topic, I raise it now, rather than later. When Barry first arrived at Southampton, he had no car, no means of getting around the country. He waited patiently for a few days but no car came rolling through the gates of the county ground. Nor did there seem any likelihood that one would. Eventually, after consultation with friends and advisors, among whom was numbered Richie Benaud, he went in to see the club secretary, Desmond Eagar. In point of fact, Barry quite liked the Sec, as Desmond was known, and he was not alone in this. The Sec had an old-fashioned courtesy about him that seemed to excuse the rarefied air of the conservative, even antiquated, world in which he had been brought up and lived. Barry explained what happened. 'I demanded a car. "A car!" spluttered Desmond. Yes, a car. You know, one with four wheels. And not any old, second-hand tin can. I mean a new car. "A *new* car!" Desmond choked. I thought he was going to have a heart attack.' *And did you get your new car?* Silly question. Of course he did. Not from the club but from a committee member who owned a garage. Barry then gave a sigh. 'I wasn't the most diplomatic in those days, was I?'

The South African team carried their aura of invincibility to Port Elizabeth for the fourth and final Test. Australia were mentally and physically spent. They had arrived in the country after an exacting tour of India. As amateurs, all of them had taken extended leave from their jobs and had now been away from home for five months. There was simmering tension between the players and the Australian Board about just about everything, a boil that was not to be lanced for a further seven years, when a certain Mr Packer flexed his considerable financial muscle. Their captain, Bill Lawry, was out of form and out of favour with several of his own players, most notably Ian Chappell, who wasted no time on his return home to effect a palace revolution, having Lawry removed and himself put in his place. They were a tired and dispirited team, ripe for the plucking, and Ali Bacher, the Springbok captain, was in the mood to complete a ruthless clean sweep.

A significant step towards his goal was taken when he won the toss for the fourth time in a row and out stepped Barry, with his new partner, Eddie Barlow, to torment the Australian bowlers once more. How heartily sick of the sight of him they must have been. 'We managed the only century opening partnership of the series,' Barry told me. I loved the use of that word 'managed', as if had been a struggle. In fact it was no struggle; it all seemed so ridiculously easy, aided as they were by dropped catches, an affliction that had plagued the Australians throughout all four matches. It is odd that the catching is often the first of the disciplines to fall apart when a team starts to implode. The South African catching, by contrast, was near faultless. Having been granted a life when the simplest of chances was muffed, Barry carved away merrily to score 81. 'Should have been a hundred,' he said ruefully. Connolly, who had got him, bowled well and was rewarded with six wickets for his toils. But it was no more than a futile counter attack from a tired and dispirited team who could already see the writing on the wall.

Armed with a lead of 100, Richards and Barlow were instructed in the second innings to deliver the *coup-de-grâce*. Barry needed no second bidding. It was at this point of my narrative that words started to fail me. How best to describe an innings of such sublime beauty and majesty when all my adjectives have been used up? Press into service the words of others, said a little voice in my ear, a whisper that became an insistent voice, a familiar one – down the phone, as it happened, belonging to an old friend and colleague of mine. Roger Tolchard, the former England and Leicestershire player, reminded me that he was in the Eastern Cape at that time, coaching in schools, and was at St George's Park to witness Barry's onslaught. 'It was a magnificent display,' enthused Tolchard and, believe me, Roger is not prone to hyperbole. 'He was the best orthodox right-hander I have ever seen.' And as a wicketkeeper who played 18 years of county cricket, he stood behind a few in his time. 'Barry read the length so well and the way he used his feet was…well, he played so beautifully.' And this was from one who was renowned for his nimble footwork. 'Tolchard,' remarked his cricket master, George Chesterton, 'He used to be up the wicket like a ferret up a trouser leg.' Roger said nothing about ferrets in his assessment of Barry's innings and many subsequent others. 'It was just an honour to play against him,' he said simply.

I guess honour was not at the forefront of the Australians' minds that day, though I am sure that they would have been honest enough to admit later that they had been in the presence of batting genius. Graham McKenzie, recalled for this match, was generous enough to say this of Barry, 'He was in my opinion the most gifted batsman I bowled to in my career.' In simple terms, Barry scored 126, with 16 fours and three sixes, which meant that 94 of his runs came in boundaries – Barry dealt predominantly in boundaries; the quick single and regular rotation of the strike were not to be found in his kit bag – and every one of which hit the boards must have sounded to the Australians like another nail being hammered into the coffin of a disastrous tour. My faithful *Wisden*, as you would expect, described it in less luminescent terms, 'Richards again played the dominant part and, after Barlow's dismissal, he ran amok and punished all the bowlers. He reached his second hundred out of 159 in three and a quarter hours and with his score at 118 brought his total for the series to 500. A quarter of an hour later, after four hours at the crease, he played a tired stroke to Mayne and was out for 126.'

How did you feel? 'I was walking on air,' Barry answered, 'with all the exuberance of youth.' Barry sauntered off to a standing ovation, doffing his cap – of course – before disappearing into the bowels of the main stand at St George's Park. And he never emerged again. His Test career was over, a brief, blinding streak across the cricketing firmament…and it was gone.

That team may not have known that it was all over – though one or two of them probably sensed that political trouble was afoot – but they certainly knew that the match was over and with it a thumping clean sweep of the series. *You'd won by 323 runs, you'd blown away the number one team in the world, you had been in magnificent form yourself…How did you celebrate?* 'We didn't have an open top bus parade to Trafalgar Square, if that's what you mean,' he commented archly. *Certainly not. I did think that was a bit over the top. But Port Elizabeth's finest hostelries must have thrown open their doors for you. After all, PE is known as the Friendly City.* He shook his head. 'No, not really. A few beers in the dressing room after the game. No official function or anything like that was laid on for us. We were soon on the plane and on our way home.' Somehow, it doesn't seem fitting, such a low key ending to a legendary series. That team of all the talents deserved more. But, as Barry said, the game was run by amateurs – what else can you expect?

Not only for Barry was this the end. The rest of his team-mates had just played their last Test match. Actually, this is not quite correct. In an interesting but little-known footnote of cricket history, John Traicos *did* play Test cricket again, 22 years and 222 days later, thus becoming the player with the longest interval between Test appearances. In 1992, when Zimbabwe – Traicos's birthplace – was granted Test match status, the country's inaugural match was against India in Harare and Traicos was selected. He could never have imagined that, needless to say, as he contemplated over a beer or two with others of the team in the St George's Park dressing room South Africa's uncertain future on the world's sporting stage, hoping for the best but fearing the worst. 'So that meant that two of us became the only South Africans – with the exception of some obscure guy in the 1930s – to have scored a hundred in our last Test,' said Barry. He was referring to his team-mate, Lee Irvine, who had scored 102 in South Africa's second innings, to follow Barry's 126, out of a total of 470/8 declared, leaving Australia a mammoth 569 to win. They had fallen agonisingly short, by 323 runs.

Irvine was proud of his innings, as well he might. 'The wicket at St George's was taking spin. Gleeson and Mallett were getting it to turn and Connolly was bowling his cutters.' We both agreed that the level of difficulty had put Barry's masterful innings into context. 'So that made *me* the last Springbok to score a hundred in his final Test.' *No longer, Lee, no longer. Jacques Kallis has just quit the international scene with a hundred in his last Test.* 'No, no, man,' Irvine sought to put me right, 'I am the last *Springbok* to do so. Kallis was a Protea, as they call themselves these days.' Politically, he is right of course and Lee was ever one to choose his words carefully.

So who was this 'obscure guy in the 1930s' to whom Barry was referring? I hate loose ends so I looked it up. It was none other than Pieter van der Bijl, the father of Barry's great friend and later colleague in the Natal side, Vintcent. The date was 1938, the match was the famous Timeless Test and van der Bijl scored 125 and 97, thus narrowly missing the distinction of being the first South African to score two tons in the same Test against England. The world war soon broke out, which put an end to the Test career of van der Bijl and that of many others. I spoke to Vintcent about this delightful coincidence. 'My dad would be flattered and amazed that he could be included with these great names,' said his son. 'He was a slow and resolute batsman. Barry would have had a heart attack at his run rate!' Never mind Barry's rocketing blood pressure at the defensive mindset of opening batsmen in those days, he nearly did have a heart attack when I revealed to him the identity of this 'obscure guy'.

Vince then went on to tell me an interesting little anecdote about that Timeless Test. 'Dad played before the days of arm guards, helmets and body armour and came back from his innings peppered black and blue by Farnes.' Ken Farnes, who was to die not long afterwards, killed on a night-flying exercise in the RAF plane he was piloting, was an exceedingly tall and fit fast bowler for England, who could generate surprising pace and lift from a short run. 'Dad was at Oxford at the same time Farnes was at Cambridge,' Vince continued, 'and they knew each other well. It was an era of tough gentlemen. "That's enough, Ken," said Dad after taking another body blow – that was all.'

And was it? 'No. Farnes continued to pepper him.' In another twist to the story, van der Bijl Snr later became a Test selector and though he was no longer on the panel when the team to play Australia in 1967 was announced, he went on record to say that in his opinion the young Barry Richards should be in the team. 'And he was not,' added Vince, 'much to Dad's annoyance.' And greatly to Barry's as well, let us remember, to say nothing of his sore foot. Van der Bijl's estimation of Barry's superlative talent had been vindicated in this series and he was pleased. According to his son, 'Dad saw Barry as the truly great classic exponent of batsmanship, the ideal model to emulate.'

But Richards was not the only great player in this team. The debate rages to this day where alongside the great teams since the Second World War the 1970 South Africans would have stood. In most people's minds, three teams vie for the accolade of the best ever – the 1948 Australians, the West Indies of the 1980s and the Australian side of the 2000s. Let us look at them in a little more detail. The Australian team that toured England in 1948 went through the summer unbeaten and were thus dubbed The Invincibles. Led by Bradman, they had, among others, Hassett, Harvey, Morris, Brown, Lindwall, Miller, Tallon, Johnson and Johnstone. The West Indian team which pulverised most opponents in the 80s was led by Lloyd and had in the side Richards, Greenidge, Haynes and an endless production line of fast bowlers: Roberts, Holding, Garner, Croft, Patterson, Clarke and Marshall (but no spinner, note, though they hardly needed one). The Australians who carried all before them in the 2000s were captained by Steve Waugh and called upon Mark Waugh, Hayden, Langer, Ponting, Gilchrist, Warne, Gillespie, McGrath and Lee (and they did have a spinner!).

Now, how would the South African team of 1970 have compared? Shrewdly led by the good doctor, Ali Bacher, the team comprised Richards, Barlow, Graeme Pollock, Irvine, Lindsay, Lance, Procter, Peter Pollock, Trimborn and Traicos (Procter at number eight!). It seems to me that all bases have been covered, allied to which electric fielding and entertainment value would have cemented their popularity in the public's eyes. It is a melancholy thought that this team were to disband, depart and never convene again on or off the field of play. How it would have competed over a period of time is anybody's guess but it is diverting to imagine. It goes without saying that the greater good brought about – partly – by South Africa's banishment was effective and worthwhile but it is difficult not to weep at so much forfeited talent. It is Irvine's opinion that they would have dominated the international scene for the next decade.

'Look at the ages of that team,' he said. 'We were all in our 20s with our best years ahead of us. It was heartbreaking, to be truthful.' Then Barry interjected with this conviction. 'A year or two later, it would have been an even better side, with van der Bijl, Rice, Hobson, le Roux.' Perhaps so but how much better it might have been if apartheid had not existed and players of colour could have joined them. There were plenty more D'Oliveiras where he came from. And that came from Basil himself. 'Politics, politics,' Barry said. 'Politics have dominated my life.'

They have indeed. In 1970, politics, specifically the politics of apartheid, were dominating just about every newspaper, TV current affairs programme, public forum, debating chamber, legislative assembly, even the dinner table, pretty well throughout the world. As the victorious South African team celebrated with their beers in the St George's Park pavilion, they needed only to have stuck their heads out of the door to appreciate the problem. The teeming throng that hailed them as they left the field was exclusively white. There were coloured spectators but they were segregated in another, shabbier part of the stadium. Actually, the series had been of great interest to the non-white population and they had flocked in their thousands to watch – particularly in Durban and Cape Town – but it had become apparent that most of them were cheering for the Australians.

This is not to accuse any of the South African team of political naivety or moral blindness; far from it. Some of them had long been harbouring genuine misgivings and real fears about the future, not just of cricket in the country but also of the very fabric of South African society. Lee Irvine, for one, strenuously rejects any claims that they were complacent or immobile in the face of the gathering storm, rather like those farmers who heedlessly continued to till their land on the slopes of Mount Vesuvius as the volcano erupted. 'What irritated us most,' he said, 'was that we, coming largely from English backgrounds, were far more liberal than the rugby players, who were mainly Afrikaans and supported apartheid.'

Ah yes, the Springbok rugby team. While their countrymen were annihilating the Australians on the cricket field, the national rugby team were undergoing – there is no other word for it – a tour of the British Isles and Ireland. It was beset by violent demonstrations and acts of sabotage and their progress around the country took on a nasty and dangerous edge. I well remember Peter Hain, the chairman of the Stop The Seventy Tour campaign, hectoring the British public through a loudhailer in front of vociferous and increasingly unruly crowds. The rugby tour had gone ahead, in spite of massed protests, but now Hain and his supporters had the impending tour that summer by the South African cricket team firmly in their sights. At the time, I was appalled by the ferocity of the protestors' anger and the extreme lengths they were prepared to go to to force the issue. I abhorred the principle of apartheid as much as the next man but to scupper games of *cricket*…well, that was going too far. Time and subsequent events were to bring me to my senses.

My lack of worldliness was not at all excusable – after all, there was plenty of hot air being expended around my university campus at that time – but what of our friends basking in the glow of their 4-0 whitewash of Australia? Had they got their heads firmly buried in the sand too? First, I think it's important to understand the mental attitude of the professional sportsman. To be successful, you have to possess extraordinary powers of concentration, able to block out of your mind any extraneous distraction, focussing sharply on the task in hand, so much so that you appear to be in a bubble of absorption. All that counts in your life at that moment is the 4.25-inch diameter of the hole as you line up your putt, the 24-foot width of the goal in front of you as you step up to put that penalty away, the ten-foot height of the crossbar that you must clear for a conversion, the 100m of rubberised track stretching out in front of you as you crouch in readiness for the gun.

A friend of mine who was an international squash player said to me that when he was on court and the door was closed, he felt as if the rest of the world had been shut out. Cricketers are no different; their business concerns exclusively the cut and rolled 22-yard stretch of turf. The travails assailing the national rugby team in Britain could not have escaped their notice but they couldn't afford to worry about that; they had a series to win. So Barry's decision to sidestep the issue for the time being, hoping against hope that things would sort themselves out, is more understandable, given the context of his personal situation. After all, he had just been catapulted into the stratosphere of cricketing fame and it would take a bit of getting used to.

Barry had already returned to England for the start of the cricket season with Hampshire when the touring party to England was announced and for the record it comprised: Bacher (captain), Barlow, G. Pollock, Irvine, Lindsay, Lance, Procter, P. Pollock, Richards, Trimborn, Traicos, Short, Watson and Chevalier. A team to whet any cricket lover's appetite and there were plenty in England, in spite of the demonstrations, who were eagerly looking forward to their arrival. And it seemed, for a while anyway, that they *would* come. But Barry smelt trouble. 'I started to realise it would never happen,' he said, 'Peter Hain was gathering his troops and I could sense the public mood was against it, something I had been unaware of back home.'

Yet the cricket authorities in both countries were adamant that the protestors would not win the day and that the tour would go ahead, come what may. They must have been blind. And deaf. The rugby tour was staggering on, the matches played behind police cordons and in an atmosphere that was becoming increasingly ugly. The Springbok coach was even hijacked on its way to Twickenham for the international against England. Lord's was forced to protect the playing area behind barbed wire. Weed killer had been poured on to the outfield at Worcester, traditionally the venue for the first match of the tour. In total, 12 county grounds were vandalised by protestors. Even I could see that you could never fully protect a cricket match from disruption. If one dozy spectator can bring the game to a halt by carelessly walking in front of the sightscreen, just think what an army of violent protestors could do. It was not as if there was no precedent.

Only recently, MCC had had a salutary experience. Following the cancellation of the tour to South Africa in the wake of the D'Oliveira Affair, they had sent the England side to Pakistan. Not the most insightful of judgements. The country was in the throes of a civil war and the team had to flee for their lives in the middle of a Test match in Karachi. It is said that when their plane cleared Pakistani air space, a great cheer went up in the cabin. No, the tour was never a feasible proposition; when passions are aroused and tempers flare, cricket is very vulnerable. Lee Irvine, who was also in the country plying his trade with Essex, clearly saw the futility of the whole thing. 'No way could that tour ever have taken place,' he stated emphatically.

As if manna from heaven, a fortuitous, if shocking, piece of propaganda had fallen into the laps of the campaign to stop the tour. In February 1971, Arthur Ashe, the US Open champion, was refused entry into South Africa because of his colour. Whatever the morals of the conflict between the two sides, the PR battle was being won by the protestors. When the politicians got involved, the game was all but over. A general election in Britain was but a month away and Harold Wilson, the prime minister, was fearful of racial unrest and the unpopularity to the government that continued unrest would cause. The tour was shortened, the first month abandoned. Finally a strong and official letter of warning from the home secretary, James Callaghan, forced the issue. In late May 1970, the tour was officially called off. MCC regretted the decision, stating that it was their firm belief that sport and politics should not mix. But they might as well have been howling at the moon. In the end, it was the politicians who made the call.

'For me personally,' Irvine told me, 'it was heartbreaking. We'd even sewed the name tags on all our official kit. Having played on what were no more than club pitches for Essex, I was looking forward to batting on decent Test wickets.' He also had his eye on the batsman/wicketkeeping role. 'That was my ambition anyway. It would have allowed us to play another bowler.' Perhaps he would have been a forerunner of the modern Adam Gilchrist. Perhaps, perhaps. This story is full of perhaps. And what of Barry's reaction? More a resigned submission to the inevitable than anything else. 'Almost unbelievably, I still believed that it was not the end. There was still the 1971/72 tour to Australia to look forward to and prepare for.' His preparation could not have been more meticulously planned and executed. But then politics stuck its nose in again and after that, it really was all over.

In the meantime, the Test and County Cricket Board, having turned down the South African tourists, found themselves with a large hole to fill at very short notice. A collection of overseas stars was hastily assembled to play five Test matches against England during the summer, a team which was to be called the Rest of the World. No lack of aspiration there. In all fairness, the *ad hoc* team had a decent sprinkling of stardust over it. The irony of ironies was that five of the original South African party – the two Pollocks, Barlow, Procter and Richards – were invited to play, and no one turned a hair. In a sense, that was perfectly understandable as they were not representing their country but were playing as individuals in an invitation XI. The rest, if you will pardon the pun, were employed by English counties and were already in the country. They were: McKenzie (Australia), Engineer (India), Intikhab, Mushtaq (Pakistan), Gibbs, Kanhai, Lloyd, Murray, Sobers (West Indies). Without doubt, this was a team fit to set before the British public.

But the series never really took off. For the true aficionados of the game, it proved to be a sumptuous banquet of varied and mouthwatering dishes but it lacked the true edge of international competition. Not that any of the players on either side took the games lightly; they had their reputations to protect and we all know how jealously sportsmen guard their reputations. It was no different for Graeme Pollock, for example. He knew that the eyes of the cricketing world were upon him, comparing him to that other great left-hander at the other end, Garry Sobers. He could not afford to let his guard down any more than Sobers could. And they didn't.

For all that, they weren't the South Africans, whom everybody had heard about and everybody wanted to see, leaving aside political and moral misgivings. From a purely cricketing point of view, it had been a beguiling prospect and the decision to cancel had been met with huge disappointment, if philosophical acceptance of the reasons. The explanation that the British public were slow to warm to the replacement series, interesting and competitive though it was, can probably be put down to the fact that the Rest of the World were *not* South Africa, even if South Africans were playing. Some years later, I talked to Mushtaq Mohammed about it all. It had been a marvellous experience, he said, and the cricket had been hugely enjoyable. 'But after it was all finished, I was left with a funny feeling because we weren't playing under a flag, as it was when I was winning with Pakistan.' Barry agreed. 'We weren't really a team but a collection of highly talented individuals.'

How did you all get on? 'Fine, absolutely fine. Most of us knew each other because we had all been playing county cricket. No one was a stranger.' *How did the black players get on with the white South Africans?* He shook his head. There had been no reason for my asking the question really. Cricketers of all nationalities and races have traditionally got on well. Social or professional acceptance has never been a problem in the dressing room. Respect has always been gained by performance on the field, not by colour or class. 'Look Murt,' Barry said, 'when I came to Hampshire, we had three West Indians in the team, Roy Marshall, Danny Livingstone and John Holder, and a bit later, of course, my opening partner, Gordon Greenidge. You know we all got on okay and happily integrated as a team.' That was no less than the truth. Let me leave the last word on the subject to Clive Lloyd; 'The whole situation seemed so silly. We weren't allowed to take on South Africa but here I was playing alongside half of their team in a Test match.'

There was another reason for the initial sluggish start before the series started to warm up, Barry contended. 'Because it was so hastily arranged, there wasn't much marketing or publicity that had gone on. The crowds weren't great, at least not to start with.' *Were you paid handsomely?* 'No, not much. We were playing for our reputation, not for the money.' *Did you train, practise, have nets?* He laughed. 'We didn't take it *that* seriously. We just went from one ground to another, rocked up, had a chat and next day we went out and played.' *Was there a sense of* esprit de corps, *team spirit, bonding and all that?* 'Oh, we all had a great time. Ho-hum, let's have fun!' He drew a telling contrast with World Series Cricket during the Packer Revolution eight years later. 'Now those game *were* taken seriously. The pressure was immense. If you didn't perform you were *out*, man, no messing about. Packer wanted red-blooded competition and entertainment and what Packer wanted, Packer usually got.'

Perhaps the lack of true edge to the games, which can only be guaranteed by representing your country, goes some way to explaining Barry's mediocre form during the series, in this year of all years. 'I played all right,' he said unconvinced, 'but I never hit the heights.' Surprisingly true. He played in all five Tests, scoring 257 runs at an average of 36.71. His highest score was 64. Graeme Pollock had a relatively lean time too. He scored 250 runs at an average of 31.25 but he did hit the heights at last with his masterful 114 at the Oval in the final match sharing in an unforgettable partnership of 165 with Sobers, the world's two best left-handers slugging it out, side by side. Who can say how adversely Richards and Pollock were affected by the disappointment of the tour's cancellation. Perhaps they did find it difficult to summon up that fierce patriotic fervour that only manifested itself when playing for their country. Eddie Barlow seemed to have no such qualms. He had an excellent series, scoring 353 runs at 39.22 and taking 20 wickets at 19.80. But there, as everybody to whom I have spoken about this ebullient man said, 'Bunter' would fight and scrap to beat his own grandmother at cards. The Ballon d'Or, if such an award existed in cricket, went to the undisputed greatest cricketer in history, Garry Sobers. He scored 588 runs at 73.50 and took 21 wickets at 21.52. Oh, and he captained the side too. In his own inimitable way, as ever. Mushtaq again, 'How do you tell the best players in the world how to play? So it always ended up being a party. Garry would say, "Do your best and enjoy it." And then he would say, "Let's have a drink!"'

The first Test at Lord's only served to reinforce the popularly held view that the series would be a mismatch. By lunch on the first day, England had been reduced to 44/7 and never really recovered. Sobers, bowling seam-up, was at his masterful best, taking 6-21 to bowl England out for 127. 'He was a wonderful swinger of the ball,' said Barry. 'He would run in and bowl quickly.' There is an interesting comment about Sobers from Mike Taylor at Hampshire. Before Nottinghamshire ill-advisedly let him go to play for Hampshire, Taylor had played a lot with Sobers in the Notts side. 'As a new-ball bowler,' Taylor said, 'Garry was without equal, swinging it both ways, at pace too. But his slow stuff was pretty ordinary, to be truthful.' Judged by the lofty standards of his faster variety, that could possibly be accepted as a fair comment but Sobers could, and did, still get useful wickets when he switched to his slower varieties. The Rest of the World piled on the runs. *Wisden* noted, 'Sixty-nine for the first wicket, with Richards, all ease and elegance, seemingly untroubled until he was out for 35.' The total of 546, owing much to a scorching innings of 183 from Sobers, was far too much for England and though they fared better in the second innings, they still lost by an innings and 80 runs. The match attendance was only 35,000 and the sponsors must have had a few sleepless nights as the prospect of a humiliating, not to say financially ruinous, whitewash loomed.

'Perhaps we did take it a little too easy,' admitted Barry, 'for we certainly caught a cold in the second match.' To everybody's relief and considerable surprise, England won the match, comfortably in the end, by eight wickets. It was Tony Greig's debut for England and as ever with this handsome, blond, controversial giant of a showman, it was no muted launch to his international career. He did not feature with the bat but he did take seven wickets, one of which was Barry's. In cold and damp conditions which greatly favoured the seam bowlers, Barry had batted resourcefully for two and a half hours – no thought here of a hundred before lunch – battling against extravagant seam and swing, before falling to Greig, caught behind for 64. 'Aaagh – Greigy. Another one of his strangles, caught down the leg side by Knotty.'

Greig had what was known on the circuit as a 'golden arm'. Ian Botham, too, cast the same sort of spell over batsmen, especially in the latter stages of his career, when he seemed to take wickets with rubbish balls, almost by the sheer force of his personality. Greig exerted the same jinx on Barry in the second innings as well, bowling him for 30. Hereafter, Greig's story is well known – captain of England, leading light in the Packer Revolution, criticised for his naked commercialism, ostracised by the English hierarchy, respected in later life as a TV commentator in Australia – and he will of course reappear in an important role a little later in this narrative. Even today, following his premature death in 2012, he divides opinion. Whatever you may have thought of him as a player and as a man, it cannot be denied that he was one of the game's fiercest competitors. It is no coincidence that his Test average with the bat (40.43) far exceeds his first-class average (31.19). Like Barry, he relished a challenge and thrived on the grand stage. 'Look, Greigy was Greigy,' Barry commented. 'A larger than life character. Aggressive and combative.'

Had he come to your notice back in South Africa? 'He'd played a few games for Eastern Province but he'd made up his mind that he had no future as a Test player in his homeland so he had gone quite early in his career.' There is no doubt that Tony Greig yearned for the limelight and in England he found it. He also found the daily grind of county cricket tedious. Hove on a chilly morning in early May was just as unappealing a prospect for him as was Portsmouth for Barry, playing in front of a handful of spectators, shrouded in overcoats to combat the biting wind blowing in from the Solent.

In spite of England's sterling fightback, the Nottingham crowd remained lukewarm about the match; there were more than a handful of spectators but a gate of only 16,000 is slim pickings for a Test match. The cricket fans of Birmingham came out in reasonable numbers, thankfully, for the third Test at Edgbaston. They were rewarded by a typically robust century from D'Oliveira, who alone withstood the fast bowling of Procter, who took five wickets. 'Prockie wasn't really fit, you know during this series,' Barry interjected. *No, I didn't know. It didn't seem to affect him. He bowled and batted with great skill and purpose throughout, did he not?* 'Just shows what a tremendous athlete he was. He always had a niggle somewhere but he still ran in and bowled quick.'

Barry, out for 47, felt that he had missed out 'big time' as the Rest amassed a huge score, with Sobers and Lloyd outdoing each other with the savagery of their strokeplay. *Wisden* described it as 'a blistering attack on the bowling'. England batted better in their second dig but the Rest's target of 141 seemed a formality. In fact it wasn't. Barlow, Richards, Kanhai, Sobers and Lloyd all fell cheaply and with Pollock injured and unlikely to bat, the alarm bells were set off before Procter knocked off the runs and victory was achieved by five wickets.

England were making a better fist of this than many people thought. What was your opinion of the team? 'England? It was a well-balanced side. Useful spinners, Illingworth and Underwood. Good pace attack too – Snowy, always a handful. And actually, I thought Alan Ward at Lord's bowled quicker than anyone. But he was a bit delicate physically and always seemed to get injured.' *Talking of getting injured...you didn't bat in the fourth Test. How come?* 'I injured my back trying to catch Basil. Actually, I did bat in the second innings but only because I had to.' Indeed. A closely-fought encounter had led up to this thrilling finale. Snow in an inspired, hostile spell, presaging his Ashes-winning feats in Australia the following winter, had the Rest reeling at 75/5, still 148 short of their target, with Barry, now joined by Kanhai, injured in the pavilion. Injured or not, Barry had to strap on his pads – or perhaps he got someone to do that for him – to make his way gingerly to the middle at number ten to join his mate Procter. Forty-three to win, Barry injured, only the hapless Gibbs to come, Snow's nostrils flaring and the new ball due – territory unfamiliar to both batsmen. I leave it to *Wisden* to describe how it ended, 'The new ball was taken but the England bowlers could do no more and with ice cool batting the two young Springboks settled the match and the series.'

And a hefty win bonus? 'You're joking. Our remuneration was...moderate. And what's more, we were docked our pay from our counties for the matches we missed.' And once again, he made telling comparisons with the highly organised, fiercely competitive and financially rewarding World Series Cricket. 'That was much, much tougher. No slacking. Look, in my side were Ian Chappell, Tony Greig and Clive Lloyd, international captains all and fiercely competitive down to their bootlaces.' *But this series wasn't just a jolly, was it?* 'Some of the guys took it more seriously than the others. I guess the older ones were a bit more focussed.' Barry was only 23 and certainly not one of the older ones.

You suffered from a bad back from time to time, didn't you? It was never a serious problem, he said, but as with many bowlers, it occasionally stiffened up. I presumed he was joking about his status as a bowler – when he did bowl, he had the shortest run-up in the world, even for a spinner – but it is true that few professional sportsmen escape discomfort from the stresses and strains on the lower back. 'It's often a question of how to manage the pain,' he maintained. 'Nowadays, with better medical knowledge, experienced physiotherapists and all the latest equipment...well, it's light years away from what we were used to.' And then we both started to laugh, calling to mind the prehistoric first aid facilities available at Hampshire. The physio's room was no more than a converted cupboard beneath the dressing room steps. The physio, however, was no physiotherapist at all. He was what Mike Taylor humorously referred to as 'a rub man on the *QE2*'.

Dear old Jim Ratchford. He had apparently worked as a masseur on cruise liners and massaged more than a few aches and pains of ladies of a certain age. He was a nice man and would do anything for you but he was unqualified, his diagnoses questionable and his treatment limited to a vigorous rub in the vague vicinity of the injury. He had a bag full of unidentified pills stored in suspiciously anonymous phials and his only piece of equipment was a lamp that bathed the room, sorry, shed, in an iridescent red glow, not unlike a darkroom in a photographer's studio. I doubt he did much harm; indeed, it could be argued that he lent a sympathetic ear – and all professional cricketers need mollycoddling from time to time – and a bolthole for tired players in need of 'urgent' attention.

To return to the series…the Yorkshire faithful had turned out in their droves for the fourth Test at Headingley, which brought a smile back to the faces of the sponsors, though the more cynical of observers might have pointed to the fact that attendances were boosted by the return to the England side of one who had the nearest standing to deity of anybody in this white rose county, namely Geoffrey Boycott. By the time of the final match at The Oval it could be safely said that the contest had fired the public's interest at last and the crowds, 53,000 in total, were treated to an exhibition of batting that was as sublime as it was poignant. The two mighty left-handers, Sobers and Pollock, one a West Indian and the other a South African, doomed never to take the field as opponents in a Test match, shared a partnership of 135 in the last two hours of the second day. It was, as *Wisden* records, 'A batting spectacle which will live long in the minds of those privileged to see it.'

Mushtaq, watching from the players' balcony, remembered hearing someone shout, 'Lads, come and watch – you'll not see this again.' Pollock, who had uncharacteristically struggled for form throughout the series, now regained his touch as the ball scorched the grass in his innings of 114. 'He'd been experimenting with glasses,' Barry reminded me. 'It's okay if you've been wearing glasses all your life – you're used to them. But trying to adjust to them halfway through your career is a different matter altogether.'

It was fitting that Sobers should hit the winning runs to bring the crowd on to the field, thus wrapping up the series 4-1. It had been a closer-fought contest than many predicted and certainly closer than the winning margin suggested. Illingworth, soon to lead his team to Ashes triumph in Australia, said this about his opponents, 'They were good. There'd never been a side like it.' Praise indeed from a Yorkshireman. Clive Lloyd, not a Yorkshireman, agreed, 'We had an excellent side – the near-perfect team. Spin and pace, great batsmen and two fine wicketkeepers.' One and all were unanimous in their judgement of the dominant personality of the summer, Garfield Sobers. The abiding memory of the series would ever be the sight of Pollock and Sobers gracing the late summer evening at the Oval, batting together in the cause of international cricket. Black and white – the game of cricket was colour blind and hope burned, if not brightly then at least fitfully, that nothing could possibly wreck that ideal.

As we shall see, politics had not yet done with cricket, not by a long chalk. Another of many body blows was delivered by the International Cricket Conference (later Council) three years later, a glaring instance of a foul punch being dealt long after the bell had sounded. Having originally agreed that the series would be afforded Test match status, the ICC later rescinded this in order to lay down a principle that Test matches can only be played between countries. To the ordinary cricket supporter, the decision seemed crass. To the participants, it was no less than an insult. To poor Alan Jones, who was selected to play in one match, it was a tragedy. He remains the only first-class cricketer to be awarded his country's cap only to have it taken away from him. Barry's comment on it all cannot be put down in words; it consisted of no more than a snort of contempt. Mike Denness, a member of the England side, said this, 'Why? It wasn't as if it was a mickey-mouse set-up.' Derek Underwood went further, 'When they took away Test status, that was a blow…And another thing – if the games had been official, I would have taken 300 Test wickets!' Which just goes to show that if a first-class cricketer ever claims he is not interested in figures, he is a liar.

Back to Hampshire then, Barry? He nodded. *Tell me how it came about that you spent the winter in Australia, not South Africa.* 'Murray Sergeant, convenor of the South Australian selectors, was on the lookout for an overseas player. They'd had Sobers, obviously a popular choice, and the previous year – I don't know why – Younis Ahmed, who hadn't been so much of a success. So he made me a generous offer that I couldn't refuse.' *What was that, if I may ask?* 'One hundred dollars a week, plus $1 a run. Not a fortune but more than I was getting anywhere else.' *But what about Natal?* He shrugged. 'I heard nothing. Had they made a counter offer, or any sort of offer for that matter, I would have gone back.' But the concept of professionalism simply hadn't yet taken hold in South Africa. He would have been expected to return and play for Natal for nothing – indeed, it would have been considered a duty for him to do so, one that he ought to have been honoured to fulfil – and hoped that someone would take pity on him and offer him suitable, temporary employment. Thus, add up the possible and set it against the definite and what you have is, as they say, a 'no brainer'. He was now a professional cricketer and a professional in any walk of life expects to be paid for his services. He went where the money was.

And it was here, I guess, that the whispered charges of 'mercenary' started to take hold – Barry Richards follows the money. I should like to turn that around and put it another way. The money follows Barry Richards. And is that not as it should be? Representing your country should be about more than money, I think everybody would agree on that, even though today's Test players are paid a fortune. But it should still be an honour to wear your country's cap. However the day job, as it were, should be the free choice of the individual. It is every person's right to seek employment where he wishes and to expect a fair and reasonable wage for a day's work. As South Africa had no Test series that winter and as the South Australia offer was so attractive, he took the plane bound for Adelaide, not Durban.

There was another reason for accepting. South Africa were scheduled to tour Australia the following winter, 1971/72, and Barry wanted to familiarise himself with the playing conditions in that country. He has always liked to be prepared and any professional worth his salt should make the necessary provisions to be ready and equipped for the challenges ahead. The concept of mental and physical preparation for a sporting encounter is *de rigueur* today, not disparaged. I bet the South African Cricket Board would have lauded Barry to the heavens for his foresight if he had broken all records during the tour, had it ever taken place.

South Australia pushed the boat out then, when you landed, said I, mixing my metaphors. 'Actually I was sponsored by Coca-Cola.' *Did you have to ask for a car?* He grinned. 'No one hit the roof, like Desmond Eagar at Hampshire. It was a big brown one, as I remember – the make escapes me.' *What were your duties?* 'I had to do a bit of coaching in schools during the week and turn out for Prospect Cricket Club at the weekend. And of course represent South Australia in Sheffield Shield matches.'

The Chappell brothers were Adelaidians and both Ian and Greg were in the state side, Ian having just been appointed captain. During their season together, Barry got to know, and became friends with them. It was Greg who met him at the airport and took him to pick up his car. 'It was now quite late in the day and getting dark,' remembered Greg, 'and Barry didn't know the way. Follow me, I said.' Barry has memories too of what happened next. 'Greg was tanking it and I was struggling to keep up as it was dark and the roads were unfamiliar.' Greg did admit that he took a backstreet route to Barry's apartment. 'When we re-joined the main road, there was a set of lights. I made it on green. Barry didn't.' In order to hold on to Greg's fast disappearing coat tails, Barry put his foot down and almost inevitably he was caught on camera by a police car lying in wait. Barry desperately pleaded, if not his innocence, then his case. 'Look, I'm Barry Richards,' he said, 'and up there is Greg Chappell.' Chappell was indeed 'up there', he had pulled in further up the road and 'he was laughing' said Barry, 'but he did nothing.'

As to the outcome, here memories diverge and historical accuracy is impossible to determine. 'They didn't bat an eyelid,' said Barry, 'and did me anyway, even though I said I was a friend of Greg Chappell.' 'They let him off!' claimed Greg, perhaps unwilling to admit that his fame, and therefore his influence over the local constabulary, had yet to ignite the country.

Chappell's ability as a batsman, honed by a two-year apprenticeship at Somerset, was clear to everyone at this point, including the Australian selectors, but inconsistency had hitherto held him back. He maintains that spending a season with Barry in the South Australian side was instructive and hugely influential in his development. Barry was (still is!) a couple of years older and when they played against each other in England, Hampshire v Somerset, Greg was naturally drawn as a player to the South African. 'He was obviously massively talented,' he said. 'Tall, upright, assured, mature. When we played Hampshire, I studied him closely. It was a revelation.' As a naturally leg-sided player, he marvelled at the way Barry hit through and over the off side. 'Not many do that, you know. He seemed so confident, as if it all came naturally and easy to him. Quite unlike me.'

I gulped. This was Greg Chappell talking to me here, in anybody's book one of the most elegant and illustrious batsmen of his era, and he was telling me he lacked confidence. One or two bowlers of the 1970s and 80s might be a bit startled to hear that. 'I was fortunate to be able to study him at close quarters, often from the non-striker's end,' Greg continued, 'the way he played each ball.' One particular technical detail he noted was Barry's grip. Remember the hours and hours in the nets, with Alan Butler exhorting the young Barry to get his left shoulder round and his elbow up? This classically accepted off-side shot can only be played with the left hand around the front of the handle. At first it had felt uncomfortable but gradually it became embedded in Barry's technique and Greg believed that, to become a better off-side player, he had better copy it. 'It's an odd way to hold a bat,' he confessed. 'Most people have their wrist a little further round the back of the handle because it feels more comfortable, more natural. But I persevered.' And who is going to deny that the perseverance paid off?

For Prospect CC, Barry broke all club records. But not before being put firmly in his place 'in true Aussie style' by his team-mates. There were two Test spinners in the side, Terry Jenner and Ashley Mallett, apart from Barry, and there was a fourth international there as well, Eric Freeman – no wonder Prospect carried all before them. Although Barry bowled occasional off spin, and not badly either, he was never going to get a smell of the ball, as Australia's finest informed him. 'I bowl one end,' Jenner told him, 'and Rowdy the other.' I don't think Barry was too bothered about the banning order. Having said that, he was mightily concerned by his first look at the Prospect ground. The Aussie Rules season had just been completed (to the average uninformed Englishman, 'rules' seems a loose concept in that game). 'The whole playing area had been top-dressed,' he said. 'Basically it was covered in sand.' *Slow outfield then?* 'Huh. I scored a hundred and only managed two fours.' That certainly would not have impressed South Australia's latest overseas signing – the reason you have fours, and sixes, is to save running between the wickets.

Club cricket, coaching and the odd promotional appearance for his sponsors aside, Barry's true purpose was to win the Sheffield Shield for South Australia. No one man can win a cricket game but if anyone dominated the Shield in Australia during the 1970/71 season it was Barry Richards. In 16 innings, he hit 1,538 runs at an average of 109.86. Positively Bradmanesque, you might say. The comparison with The Don is not by the by; South Australia was his home state and he alone, among many other records to his name, had scored a century against all opponents in one season. That was until Barry's *annus mirabilis*. Barry scored a century against each state, plus two against the touring Englishmen for good measure. These six hundreds comprised four singles, one double and one triple. That is why Bradman, having watched one of Barry's early-season centuries in Adelaide, told the rest of Australia, 'Don't fail to see this young man bat when he comes here.'

Barry's first appearance in the red cap of South Australia was in a limited overs match against Victoria. He scored a duck. That concerned him less than the strange sight of Bill Lawry doing a jig on the pitch following Barry's dismissal. Perhaps, if you had been in Lawry's shoes, you too might have done the same. Barry, possibly more than anyone in that South African team, had knocked the stuffing out of the Australians the previous winter and left Lawry, the captain, feeling as powerless as a general who's run out of ammunition.

The dam did not burst on that occasion, nor did it in Barry's Shield debut against Western Australia. He was dismissed for seven, by McKenzie of all people, whose reputation he had almost destroyed in his onslaught in that previous series. *Just a minute, Barry. I see you bowled ten overs and took 3-29. You were picked for South Australia as a spinner but you couldn't get a bowl for your club side. Grade cricket must have been very strong back then.* He laughed ruefully. 'So it seemed. And I got reminded about it too.' He did score 44 not out in the second innings as the match petered out in a draw but it hardly merited more than a chime from one of the 749 bell towers in Adelaide, the city of churches.

That was saved for a few days later, against the touring MCC. The English team, under Illingworth, went on to reclaim the Ashes that season, their first win on Australian soil since Hutton's side of 1954/55. That was a considerable achievement and Illingworth justifiably earned much praise for the way in which he instilled discipline and a hunger for success in a disparate band of talented mavericks, including John Snow and Geoff Boycott. But they played an attritional brand of cricket that did not meet with universal approval by the Australian media and public. Illingworth didn't care one jot. He was a Yorkshireman and they don't do frivolity and entertainment; they just get the job done, whatever it takes.

Now, as it happens, Barry's approach to the game was the antithetical opposite to Illingworth's; his lips would curl at the safety first mindset of the professional English cricketer. Barry *did* do frivolity and entertainment, as we already know. He could knuckle down and grind it out if the situation demanded but his natural inclination was to attack. 'I played my shots,' he always said. And ironically – for Boycott always admired Barry's technical skill and dazzling genius – it is Boycott that Barry always holds up as the type of batsman he could *never* have been. 'I wasn't really a stats man, like Boycs,' he said. 'Run-gathering was never my motivation. I always looked on batting as an entertainment rather than a numbers game.' *You would have scored a hundred hundreds if you had.* He sighed. 'When I look back and consider the times I gave it away in the 70s and 80s...'

When you consider his innings for South Australia against MCC – he scored 224 – you have to say that on this occasion, he did not give it away. 'Oh yes I did! I was out on the last ball of the innings, having a slog. We were going to declare so a four would have been more important to the team than a dot ball and a not out to my name.' And then, as an afterthought, he pointed out that his season's enormous average of 109.86 would have been boosted even more had he blocked that last ball from D'Oliveira, which slightly undermines his claim that he had little interest in figures. Let's just say that he was less obsessed by his average than most top-class players and certainly a great deal less than Boycott. Boycott had batted all day for 173 after MCC had won the toss. It had been a typical Boycott innings, marked by patience, determination, courage and technical skill, one such that his country had come to be hugely grateful for on many occasions. But it was not a Richards innings.

After play had ended that day, Barry was surprised, and not a little indignant, to see Boycott, who was not out overnight, drag some net bowlers – what we would have called club and ground bowlers – into the nets for some practice. He's been out there all day boring the pants off us, thought Barry, and now he's going to smack a few club players around. I'll show him how to bat. Incidentally, Boycott was out first thing the next morning without adding to his score. And Barry did show everyone, including Boycott, how to bat. He was 100 not out at the close of play and yes, his innings had been quite different. 'I played a few shots,' he said, a trifle unnecessarily, 'and it just went on from there the next day.' The local paper put it more colourfully, "One hundred degrees in the shade and climbing and 200 for Richards in the middle and climbing!"'

What does he make of his scores of 51 and 42 against Victoria, relative failures in this season of plenty? 'Stupid shots at stupid times,' was his uncompromising verdict. *Thomson got you in the first innings. Now, he was a strange bowler, wasn't he?* 'Froggy Thomson, not Jeff Thomson.' His nickname stemmed from his peculiar hop and a jump as he bowled off the wrong foot. Most batsmen who faced him found him awkward and difficult to work out. Not Barry. 'I had a bit of an advantage over the others. I was used to facing Prockie and though he didn't actually bowl off the wrong foot, as many people believed, he did have a similar funny jump to Froggy as he got into his delivery stride.'

Thomson tended to blow hot and cold that summer. He is better known for bowling an over of bouncers at Illingworth in one of the Tests and giving the same treatment to John Snow. This did not impress England's poet and paceman, not so much that Froggy had let him have a few but that he got no warning from the umpire, whereas Snow had been repeatedly warned for short-pitched bowling throughout the series. Thereafter, Froggy slowly receded from view on the international scene.

Barry was not going to recede from anyone's view. As the team flew into Perth, he felt happy with his focus and form and believed he was more than justifying the faith and confidence that had been invested in him. At that time, Perth (usually referred to as the WACA) had the reputation of preparing the fastest and bounciest pitch in the world. When he first cast his eyes on the wicket, Barry knew straight away that the pitch's reputation for pace would be wholly merited. It was hard and shiny, so much so that conventional studs did not do the trick; sometimes you would slip as if you were playing on glass, he recalled. The most effective boots for those conditions were the light, cut-down ones with moulded studs that were spiky and sharp, more so than the conventional ankle-high boots with screw-in studs. At practice in the nets the day before, his eyes were opened – literally – by the way the ball flew off the pitch. 'But the thing was,' he said, 'the bounce was entirely true. Once you got used to it, you could trust your judgement and play your shots.'

The following day witnessed one of the most glorious exhibitions of classical strokeplay in the history of the game. It is to be admitted that such a claim is a brave one. We can all bring to mind great innings that deserve that accolade for different reasons – the state of the game, the quality of the bowling, the vagaries of the wicket, the importance of the contest, even the emotional pull of the occasion. But for sheer technical perfection and total mastery of the bowlers and the conditions, it is doubtful that this innings has ever been bettered. A few statistics first: his first hundred came after 125 minutes, his second after 209 and his third after 317, comprising 39 fours and a six. At close of play on the first day, South Australia were 513/3, Richards 325 not out. Incredible. And yet again, we have to make do with the fact that innings in those days were measured in time spent at the crease, not the number of balls faced. We do know that no one had ever scored so many runs in one day, not even Bradman. This record was broken by Brian Lara in 1994 in the process of amassing his famous 501 not out for Warwickshire. He made 390 that day but it should be borne in mind that rain had ruined the match as a contest and the Durham attack had been weakened by injury. Let me state immediately that the Western Australian attack was most certainly *not* weak; they had bowlers of the calibre of McKenzie, Lillee, Mann and Lock. They all finished with three figures against their name for runs conceded, a statistic that all bowlers dread.

Funnily enough, it very nearly didn't happen. Graham McKenzie wrote to me about that day, 'I bowled the first ball to him in that innings. The ball swung away and he played and missed. I remember Ian Brayshaw at mid-on asking me how it looked, to which I replied that it looked like a good day to bowl! That was the first and last ball to beat the bat all day. It was the most memorable long innings I was to see in all my days playing cricket.' For the record, McKenzie played in 60 Tests, so he witnessed quite a few in his career. Rodney Marsh, the wicketkeeper, later admitted that after that first ball, he turned to John Inverarity at slip and remarked, 'Hello, this fellow isn't as good as they're all saying he is.'

However, he had to eat his words; Marsh always said that he kept immaculately that day, the reason being that he took the ball behind the stumps on very few occasions throughout all three sessions. Greg Chappell's recollections were this, 'Either Barry hit them for four or he pushed the ball back to the bowler as if to say, hurry up and bowl me another one that I can hit for four.' His brother, Ian, scored 129 at the other end 'and his innings was hardly noticed'. Tony Mann, the Western Australian leg-spinner, wrote in an article later, 'Richards placed the ball magnificently – minimal footwork, brilliant eye, very strong wrists. He just caressed the ball to the boundary rope, no big hitting at all. That was his trademark, finding the gaps.' Inverarity simply said this, 'It was the only occasion in my life where I began to enjoy an opposition batsman making a lot of runs. It was just sublime. He was toying with the bowlers.' The last words of the admiring Australians ought to go to Barry's friend and team-mate, Greg Chappell. 'Barry looked like a man batting against boys.'

Even in the tranquillity of recollection, Barry cannot spell out the reasons for his great innings; why, at this time and in this place, for a short period in his career, he played like a god. All he can say is that once he had got used to the bounce, he felt secure enough with his technique to play his shots. And as it was a fast outfield, the ball flew to the boundary – 39 times. Strangely, he cleared the ropes only once. *How come, Barry? After all, you were never afraid to go the aerial route.* 'Long boundaries, buddy.' Fair enough. Much better to hit the gaps. Sometimes, when someone is playing on a different plane to the rest of you, there just doesn't seem to be enough fielders out there.

I've never seen any footage of the innings. Were there any cameras there? 'Only a couple of minutes taken on one of those old 8mm home cameras.' A shame, but I don't need celluloid evidence; I can see, in my mind's eye, the last ball of the day, as described by the batsman himself. Many times I've seen the stroke, the follow through, the confident stride back to the pavilion. 'As Lillee bowled the last ball of the day, I walked down the wicket, drove the ball down the wicket past him for four and carried on walking towards the pavilion.' And as he did so and the Western Australian team followed, Inverarity turned to Marsh and, mindful of the wicketkeeper's initial judgement that morning after McKenzie's first ball, said, 'I suppose he can play a bit!'

The following day, Barry batted for a further 42 minutes and who knows what records he had in his sights before the fickle finger of fate, namely the umpire's raised digit, put the Western Australian side out of their misery. 'It was a shocking decision,' said Barry, the indignation still raw. 'Mann bowled me a googly. I knew it was a googly, I saw it. I missed it sweeping and it hit me on the boot. It was clearly going down the leg side. But the umpire gave me out. Probably sick and tired of the sight of me.' Tony Mann later became a good friend and to this day they both laugh about it. But there it is in the book: B.A. Richards lbw b Mann 356.

It is not unknown for a batsman in a run glut to suffer a drought after a major innings such as that. But Barry was not made of ordinary stuff. MCC made a return visit to the Adelaide Oval and it was a further opportunity to parade his skills against a team of Test players. Yet again, he played as if an international attack comprising Lever, Shuttleworth, Willis, D'Oliveira and Underwood were club bowlers. His hundred came off 131 balls. There was no double hundred this time. He was stumped by Taylor off Underwood for 146. 'I had a slog at Deadly in the last over of the day and paid the price.' Many have, and paid the price too, I told him, but still he was cross with himself. He was less cross for getting out for 35 in the next match against Queensland. 'The struggle is to get from nought to 50,' he said.

During the Christmas period, Barry took a well-earned break from run-making. You note I use the idiom 'run-making', not 'run-gathering'. His scores so far during this remarkable season may have resembled those of an insatiable run machine such as Bradman, Hanif, Tendulkar, Lara, Kallis and Cook but Richards and a machine are two concepts as contrasting as papist and puritan. He needed a bit of a holiday. People do not realise that cricket is a draining physical and mental activity. In England, where the game is played daily for the best part of six months, without a break, it can be gruelling and eventually enervating, as Barry was slowly to discover playing for Hampshire. But in the southern hemisphere, there is the opportunity for a rest over the Christmas holiday. *Time for a few braais, eh?* 'I never did manage to convert them to use the word braai instead of barbie,' he confessed sadly.

It being the school holidays, it was also a rest from coaching, which can get a bit monotonous, no matter how talented are the boys you have in the nets. And on his own admission, Barry preferred the fine-tuning of a sound technique and a special talent to merely supervising a gaggle of bored kids. The tedium of long car journeys between towns was alleviated by the company of Greg Chappell who was engaged on a similar contract with Coca-Cola. Greg's memories of these months together are warm and affectionate. There was one occasion when he and Barry were driving from one school to the next on the schedule. It was not just an hour or two on the road. We're talking about Australia here, where distances are vast. They were in fact travelling out of New South Wales and into the adjoining state of Victoria. Furthermore, whoever had arranged the visit had neglected to take into consideration that there is a time change of half an hour between the two states. Once they realised, Greg had to put his foot down to try and make up the lost time.

Barry was not best pleased. In fact, he was disgruntled, mightily cheesed off, you might say. 'Barry was complaining about how hard they had made it for us,' recounted Greg. 'And then we noticed two railway workers on a cart on the railway line running parallel with the road. It was one of those carts that has a hand generated mechanism, much like a see-saw, which the guys were pumping like mad to move this thing along the track at good speed. Barry completed his outburst. I pointed to the two guys on the hand trolley and said which would you rather be – us or them? We both laughed and decided that life wasn't so bad after all.' *And did Barry complain again?* 'Nope.'

It didn't stop with humorous conversation in the car. Barry is a serious student of the game and a knowledgeable conduit of information and advice – for those prepared to listen. Greg Chappell was prepared to listen all right, 'To be able to spend hours together talking cricket, mainly batting, I was able to get a different perspective from someone other than my father and brother. Barry was a tall and upright, driving batsman like me as opposed to the back foot, cross-bat player Ian was. Because we were coaching young cricketers, I had to think about why I did certain things and whether they could be done differently. To listen to Barry explaining batting each day was very educational for me as a player and budding coach.'

Chappell's words set me thinking. For whatever reason, Barry was definitely under-utilised at Hampshire in the nets. I do not mean that he should have been designated an official coach – he would never have wanted that role anyway – but his advice and his help could have been sought on a much more regular basis. Perhaps this was our fault for not asking. Perhaps it was the club's fault for not demanding (with more pay, of course!). Or perhaps, with the busy schedule and relentless travelling of a county cricketer, Barry simply cherished his intermittent periods 'off duty'. One of the joys of playing in those days was the opportunity to chat to, and to pick the brains of, great players over a drink in the bar after the close of play, much as Greg Chappell was doing during those hours together in the car.

Barry rarely stayed for long after a game and if he did, the last thing he wanted to talk about was cricket. Of course we all had eyes in our head and could watch the master batsman go about his daily business but still, some of us to this day kick ourselves for not being more questioning and probing. Barry was – is – a fine analyst of the technical side of the game; he was a craftsman as well as a genius. In fact it is my contention that you cannot be one without having the basic framework of the other. You have to know the rules before you can break them. Picasso could draw according to classical principles before he went off on his journey through abstract impressionism, surrealism and ultimately cubism. To illustrate my point, Barry Richards, the very exemplification of orthodoxy, was playing the ramp shot, the reverse sweep and the paddle long before they were 'invented'. He was an improviser as well as a purist.

Let me furnish you with an example. It was a long time ago and the details of the occasion are a little blurry around the edges. It was a charity game. Barry opened the batting. The crowd had come to see him. Opening the bowling was a chap known to us; he had played in a few Second XI matches. His name was Bell. We had no idea whether he had a Christian name; he was known to one and all as Dinger. Now Dinger rather fancied himself as a fast bowler. He had all the necessary accoutrements of a fast bowler, piratical beard, long run up, malevolent glare, dictionary of swear words, but he lacked one crucial weapon in his armoury, namely pace. He thought he was fast, and in club cricket he probably was considered to be a bit sharpish. But there is a world of difference between a club quickie and the real thing.

First ball, he gave Barry a bouncer, not a terrifying one but at least it got up high enough for Barry to sway out of the way. Dinger gave Barry the stare. Barry opened his eyes wide, in astonishment or for the first time that day, it was not possible to say. Predictably, the next ball was a bouncer. Barry stepped inside the line and flicked – there is no other word for it – the ball over his shoulder, over the wicketkeeper's head and over the boundary. That shot today is known as the 'ramp' but no one had ever heard of that word back then. But Barry was playing shots like that long before T20.

On the resumption of the Sheffield Shield, it soon became clear that any Christmas indulgence had not dulled Barry's appetite for Australian bowling. The Gabba in Brisbane had a reputation for being a little 'fiery', as he described it, certainly early on. It could have been ablaze for all the difference it made to his form; he scored 155. Interestingly enough, he did not have it entirely his own way. Tony Dell – born in Lymington, a beautiful, Georgian market town on the edge of the New Forest in Hampshire of all counties – was an awkward, left-arm fast bowler, 'useful' in Barry's lexicon. Of all the bowlers he faced in that season, Dell gave Barry the most trouble. I have this from the mouth of Greg Chappell. 'Dell was the only one whom I saw make Barry change his initial footwork. Barry always expected and looked for the full ball and was ready to launch forward at it but Tony's angle, left-arm over, and his good bouncer, made Barry hang back more. He never got him out but he did make him more uncomfortable than anyone else.' Barry still made 155, his century coming up in only 130 balls.

There was another sad end during this match. Or rather funny – it depends on your viewpoint. Barry takes up the story, 'We were having fielding practice. Someone called for a bat to hit catches so Eric Freeman went into the dressing room and grabbed the first bat he could lay his hands on. After six hits, the bat broke in half. It was my bat!' *No! Not the…the…* 'Yup. My 356 bat.' *Oh dear, that's tragic.* 'They managed to glue it together and now it's in a glass case in the museum.' *Well, we all end up in a box, don't we?* When I had stopped laughing, my mind went off at a tangent.

How far can I go in comparing a cricket bat with a musical instrument, say a violin? Both, wielded by a virtuoso, can produce a performance of distinction and grandeur. Both are made from wood, not any old branch fallen from a tree in the garden but from special timber, willow and cane for a bat, maple and spruce for a violin. Both are fashioned with great care and attention to detail by skilled craftsmen and when finished are perfectly balanced, exquisitely carved and elegantly shaped artefacts of rare beauty, to the eye and to the touch. Both, at the top end of the range, are fabulously expensive, though it has to be said that the hole in your pocket after you have purchased the most expensive bat on the market, a £1,000 Newbery Cenkos, is as nothing to the cavern in your bank account if you want to get your hands on the priceless 'Lady Blunt' Stradivarius. In actual fact, it does have a price; in 2011, it was bought for a staggering £10m. In America. Where else?

Are these costly pieces of equipment worth it? Probably not. After all, it is said that Denis Compton, awakened from his slumbers in the dressing room, would grab hold of any bat from the nearest kit bag and go out there to play the most magical of innings. And I daresay Nicola Benedetti could produce a half decent tune on a dusty old instrument from the cupboard in the school music department. But that is not really the point. Great performers need the finest implements, the better to lay on an exhibition of their special talent before the public. And what's more, they become used to their favourite tool; it becomes like an old friend, familiar, comfortable and perfectly proportioned, almost an extension of the arm. Of course, the inescapable dissimilarity is that a bat comes into frequent contact with a hard ball – sometimes windows, balustrades and dressing room doors as well – and its lifespan is perforce limited. Just imagine a virtuoso smashing his violin in fury over the conductor's podium because he had hit a bum note. But the demise of a favourite bat can result in wretchedness and desolation for a batsman, even to the extent that it ruins his recent run of good form.

Did the expiry of the 356 bat affect Barry's form? Not a bit of it. I reckon he could have picked up any discarded plank, left behind in the nets at one of the schools where he coached, and still scored a ton. He was in that sort of form and that sort of mood. He placed his trust in a replacement Gray Nicholls and a few days later, the New South Wales bowlers became better acquainted than they would have wished with the bat's distinct logo. Of his team's total of 316, he made 178. The next highest score was 48. His memories of the match have little to do with his innings. He was greatly impressed by the new boots the NSW captain, John Benaud (brother of Richie), was wearing. 'They were these new Adidas, low cut ones, with moulded soles and those sharp spikes rather than studs.' Remembering how he had difficulties in keeping his balance on the shiny, rock hard surface at the WACA, he thought these were ideal. It was not long before he too was wearing them.

New bat. New boots. Same old outcome. Against Victoria, it was 105 in the first innings and 72 in the second. He made nothing of the historical significance of the century. He had now joined The Don as the only batsman to score a hundred against all opposing teams in the same season. He had scored six, one a double and another a triple, but a noteworthy fact of the feat was that five of the six were among the ten fastest centuries of the season. In other words, he had not simply ground out the runs with machine-like efficiency. He had held true to his credo of entertainment throughout all the abundance of runs and records.

Notwithstanding the hullabaloo surrounding his extraordinary feats, it has to be remembered that cricket is a team game and South Australia had a shield to win. It all boiled down to the final match against New South Wales in Adelaide. For once, Barry did not carry all before him, single-handedly hauling his team over the line. It was a marvellous, sustained performance with the ball by Eric Freeman (13 wickets in the match), which secured the match and the Sheffield Shield for the home side. In his first innings, Barry had been struck a painful blow on the finger by a ball that reared off a length. He carried on batting but with increasing discomfort. Not surprising really, because later investigation revealed that the finger had been broken.

He wasn't supposed to bat in the second innings. However, Ian Chappell wanted quick runs to make a declaration with the purpose of giving his side sufficient time to bowl the other side out but his strategy was being derailed by a leg-spinner called Geoff Davies, who had taken five quick wickets. Needs must, so Barry, with his hand heavily strapped, emerged from the pavilion at number nine, a unique experience, as far as he can remember. He played one-handed, the left hand, the top hand. You could say that those countless hours in the nets as a boy, with Alan Butler beseeching him to play the correct way, with the top hand in control, now paid off. Somehow he managed to hit a few fours through the covers before ruthlessness was restored. Dave Renneberg, the fast bowler, was recalled to the attack and promptly hit Barry on the broken finger. Common sense prevailed and he retired hurt, the necessary quick runs having been garnered. Freeman bowled them out and victory and celebration was secured.

Statistics can tell a story but as with any story, it's all about how you tell 'em. Here is a detail, however, that is incontrovertible. Barry's aggregate for the season was 1,538 runs at an average of 109.86. I have already described that feat as Bradmanesque, and not idly so either. The record for the number of runs scored in a Sheffield Shield season is 1,690 by, yes, you have guessed it, Don Bradman, in 1928/29. Barry merely said that it was 'an honour' to be even mentioned in the same breath as The Don. As it happens, the respect between the two men was mutual. Bradman made no secret of his admiration. Adelaide was his home and at the time he was chairman of the Australian Cricket Board, much involved in the administration of the game and well acquainted with the modern player. He was a firm believer in brighter cricket and a tireless champion of the attacking, positive player who would entertain the paying public.

Barry, therefore, was right up his street. So much so that he said this of him, 'Barry Richards is the world's best right-hand opening batsman.' And he put his money where his mouth was, so to speak, by naming Barry in his world's best ever team. As he had included seven Australians, one of whom was himself, which I doubt anyone could disagree with, there wasn't much room for other nationalities. Barry is South African and had only played four Tests, so this was indeed an accolade of the highest order. Bradman wasn't finished there. 'Richards,' he said, 'was one of the best players of the short ball, opener or otherwise, *ever.*'

This is a question whose answer I can probably guess but I shall ask it nonetheless. Did you enjoy your time in Australia? 'Loved it!' Australia is not unlike South Africa climatically and Australians are not unlike South Africans socially so his Adelaide adventure was no journey into the unknown. He didn't need two sweaters for a start and Sheffield Shield cricket was similar in standard and intensity to the Currie Cup. Furthermore, his girlfriend, Lorna, had joined him from home. He could not have been more contented. Not for the first time, an identifiable connection between a sportsman's equanimity in his personal life and his performances on the field of play could be contended. Life was good. And he would be back the next season, this time playing for South Africa.

Or would he? Those in the country with more finely tuned political antennae than Barry were beginning to doubt that the tour could possibly take place, despite assurances from Bradman and the ACB that it must go ahead because 'politics should not come into sport'. Many Australians agreed with him though an increasingly vociferous and militant number did not. So, as Barry prepared to leave Adelaide, the decision was still in the balance. 'Strange though it may seem,' he said, 'I *still* believed that it would take place. It's not as if we had sat on our backsides and did nothing.'

A grateful South Australian Cricket Association, together with his sponsor, Coca-Cola, put on a celebratory dinner at which Barry was presented with awards and mementoes and listened with crimson ears to some laudatory comments in a speech from The Don. On a more personal level, he had made a good friend of Greg Chappell. 'I look back on that season with much fondness,' Chappell said, 'I learnt a lot from working and playing with Barry and we formed a lifelong friendship that endures to this day.' When Australia toured England in 1975 and the tourists played Hampshire at Southampton, the warmth of the greeting and the firmness of the handshake – even if Barry was wearing those trendy boxing gloves that masqueraded as batting gloves – between the two of them was unmistakeably genuine. 'We're still in touch,' Barry assured me, 'and just take off from where we last left off. Loves his golf. He's a good guy.'

How did you find his brother, Ian? 'Tough as nails. He wouldn't entertain any talk of a nightwatchman, a principle that still holds firm in the Aussie Test teams of today. If a recognised batsman is due in, that's when he should go in. That's his job. That was Ian's view. Mind you, as a captain, he would never ask you to do something that he wasn't prepared to do himself. He spoke his mind, Ian, and was prepared to take on the Australian cricket authorities, leading right up to the Packer confrontation.' Barry, too, it would seem, was not afraid to give his opinion in the dressing room, and forcefully too, on occasions. 'But we didn't mind that,' said Greg. 'How could we? After all, I had a brother who was the same and he was the captain of the side! No, Barry got on well with all his team-mates.'

And it seemed that the impression he had made on the South Australian public was equally positive. After the Shield had been won and Barry was on his way, the *Adelaide Advertiser* printed a whole page with the simple banner headline: 'Thank you, Barry'.

Back to England and the vagaries of early season weather? No, it seemed there was an important matter to attend to in South Africa first. When he arrived home, he found a sporting fraternity submerged in gloom. The very real prospect of sporting isolation was beginning to take root in everybody's mind. As it happened, the Springbok rugby team were in Australia at the time and suffering the same sort of unfriendly welcome and violent protest that they had encountered on their tour of the British Isles two years earlier. Grounds had to be protected with six foot barbed wire barricades, police were struggling to protect the visitors as they made their way around the country, a near riot in Melbourne had only been averted by a baton charge, the cost of security was rocketing and even the rugby players were becoming dispirited by the hostile environment enveloping them. 'Pox on the Boks' was one of the more printable placards that greeted them wherever they went.

To most people, the facts were starkly apparent; if it took this much trouble to ensure a rugby match of 80 minutes took place, what chance was there of securing a five-day Test match? But still, the South African Cricket Association were insistent that the 1971/72 tour of Australia would go ahead. Were they out of their minds? Something had to be done. And it was the players themselves who took it upon themselves to make some sort of demonstration.

Transvaal, the current Currie Cup champions, were scheduled to play a match against the Rest. This was now in early April 1971 and was intended as part celebration for the ten years since the republic had been formed and part trial for the touring party. Barry had been selected for Transvaal. *But you were a Natalian. What were you doing playing for a rival province?* 'I know. But I was only a guest player. It was only a trial really. I'd just flown in the day before. I was knackered.' Both teams discussed the worsening political situation before the match. 'Trouble had been brewing for a while,' said Vintcent van der Bijl, who was playing for the Rest. 'After the Sharpeville Massacre, we knew that it could only end in tears.' At a political demonstration in 1960, police had opened fire and killed 69 blacks. It was a watershed moment in the history of apartheid. It signalled a hardening of the government policy of separate development and the banning of organisations such as the African National Congress. Consequently, the strategy of passive resistance among the black population moved towards armed protest. And the liberals among the white population – the group from which cricketers largely came – were caught between a rock and a hard place.

'Before the match,' said van der Bijl, 'we knew that the tour to Australia was in jeopardy.' He remembers everybody meeting in a pub to discuss what to do. 'We all knew the system was unjust,' said Lee Irvine, 'but we didn't know about the worst excesses. The truth was hidden from us. But we had to do *something*.' Barry believed it all boiled down to the tensions between the Afrikaners and the English. 'The government was Afrikaans. They didn't much care for cricket. Rugby was their thing. If the cricket tour was called off, all they would have done was shrug their shoulders.' There was not total agreement among the players what form their protest should take. Some were all for boycotting the match altogether but Charles Fortune, a broadcaster known as the voice of South African cricket, dissuaded them from taking such drastic action.

'Think of the paying customer,' he urged. 'A lot of people have paid a lot of money to watch you fellows tomorrow.' So they all came to the decision that they would walk off after one ball and hand a letter of protest to the authorities. And then they would resume playing. 'Look,' said Fred Goldstein, another of the players, 'if this is just about getting to Australia, I want no part of it. If it's a genuine protest, count me in.'

When you read the content of the open letter, I don't think there could be any doubt that it *was* a genuine protest, 'We cricketers feel that the time has come for an expression of our views. We fully support the South African Cricket Association's application to invite non-whites to tour Australia if they are good enough and further subscribe to merit being the only criterion on the cricket field.'

Barry does not want to take any of the credit but Graeme Pollock, captain of the Rest, said afterwards that the protest was led, in the main, by Barry Richards and Mike Procter. Significantly, both players were currently engaged by English counties and played daily with and against black cricketers.

Transvaal won the toss and Barry walked out to bat and his old friend Mike Procter marked out his run. Procter charged in and Barry nudged him for a single. Procter stood in the middle of the wicket with a look of surprise and disgust on his face. 'What did you do that for?' he demanded as Barry sauntered past. 'I thought we'd agreed to walk off after one ball.' 'I'm on a rand a run, buddy,' grinned Barry. 'Every one counts!'

Then, to the astonishment of the crowd, all the players trooped off the field. The manager of the Rest handed the statement, signed by all the players, to an official of SACA. After a few minutes, the players returned and the match resumed. *What sort of stir did it cause?* 'Massive, man, *massive*. All the press were there and soon the place was humming.' *What were the immediate consequences?* 'Well, we knew we weren't very popular. A reception that evening, to be hosted by the minister for sport, was immediately cancelled.' *Did it make any difference?* He gave that some thought. 'I suppose it changed nothing. But it gave everybody something to chew over. The politicians hammered us.' Irvine went further. 'We were accused of being complacent. We weren't. We *did* protest and it was a brave thing to do in a police state. We did what we could. Not enough perhaps but those bleating about half-measures weren't in our shoes.'

Did it save the tour? No. Most knew that the tour was probably doomed. But SACA carried on as if oblivious to political reality. Bradman, and the ACB were still, at this stage, frantically negotiating with the South African government and SACA to see whether anything could be salvaged from the mess. The tour team was announced and caps and blazers issued – 'those distinctive green stripy ones' said Barry. 'I'd love to know what happened to them.' Bacher was to lead the side, with Barlow as his vice-captain, with the usual suspects in attendance, the Pollocks, Lindsay, Richards, Procter, Irvine, Lance, but even arguably stronger this time with the inclusion of the new, young fast bowlers Clive Rice and Vintcent van der Bijl. It was a team to excite the imagination of any cricketing public but no one seriously believed that it would ever assemble.

The tipping point came during a diplomatic mission to South Africa by Don Bradman himself. A meeting was arranged between him and John Vorster, the South African prime minister. The meeting swiftly became tense, then sour. Bradman asked some fairly blunt questions about blacks being denied the opportunity to represent their country. When Vorster replied that was because blacks were intellectually inferior and couldn't be expected to cope with the intricacies of the game, Bradman replied grimly, 'Have you never heard of Garry Sobers?' Apparently, that one bitter exchange convinced Bradman that he was spitting into the wind and his mind was made up, there and then. On his return to Australia, it was but a short meeting with his colleagues before he issued publicly this one-sentence statement, 'We will not play South Africa until they choose a team on a non-racist basis.' The door on future sporting connections with South Africa had finally been slammed shut and was not to be opened again for another 21 years.

What was your reaction this time around? 'No great surprise. We all had to deal with our crushing disappointment individually and in our own way. I hoped against hope that something could be saved but as one year went by, then another, then another, the realisation sank in that it was never going to happen.' Barry found the international isolation very hard to bear and it took him years to reach any sort of acceptance or inner peace about what had befallen him. Others found it easier to rationalise the situation. Van der Bijl is in no doubt that isolation was good for the country and hastened the dismantling of apartheid, which would lead to total integration in sport. Irvine continued the good fight, to explore any loopholes in the law to make some sort of difference to inter-racial cricket but, in the end, after he found his phone had been tapped and he was beginning to receive non-specific threats from shadowy authority figures, he decided the safety of his family was more important, so he was forced to sit it out and wait for better days. 'Was the ban worth it? Yes! Otherwise the government would never have listened. I had my personal regrets, of course, but the bigger picture was more important.'

Barry has never doubted for one moment that the ban was morally right and changed things for the better in the long run. But he seemed to suffer from the effects more than most, in his spirit and in his heart. Gradually, he became more and more demoralised and the game of cricket, which defined him, slowly lost its allure until, in the end, he no longer wanted to play. Why was he hit particularly hard, I wondered. I have a theory, one that Barry might well shoot down, but like others in the Hampshire dressing room, I needed to understand the mood of despondency that seemed to envelop him in the dressing room. Yes, an hour or two of Richards batting like a god was a privilege to witness but if he wasn't enjoying it, then what was the point? It wasn't until I finished playing professionally that I began to understand. Like a lot of players who used to play for a living, I found it difficult to adjust to the lower tier of the game. Some club cricket is of a pretty high standard and there are some good teams out there but it wasn't the *same*. I found the excitement and the motivation had gone and it was not long before I was looking around for other outlets for my competitive instincts.

In many ways, I envied my brother who did not play at such a high level as me but he found his niche and continued to enjoy playing for his club until well into his fifties. Barry missed the stimulation of Test cricket, the challenge, the thrill, the elation, the sense of fulfilment. When that was snatched away from him, everything else seemed so banal and run of the mill. But unlike his contemporaries in that South

African team, who were amateurs and had careers to pursue, he was a professional. He had to carry on playing. It was his job. He had no other. And with the bright lights of the West End fading from view, he had to make do with lesser roles touring the provinces – Basingstoke, Ebbw Vale, Glastonbury, Southport, Harrogate, Darley Dale, Guildford, Westcliffe on Sea, Kidderminster, Dover…for all he cared, they might just as well have nipped across the Channel and played in Calais. And through all this, he was expected to smile and smile and smile again, all the time grinding out the big scores and pretending that he was enjoying it. And Barry has always been hopeless at pretending. Yes, we must weep also for the lost generations of black cricketers in his country but it would be churlish not to weep too for the lost genius of one man.

By the way, Barry's scores in the 'protest' match were 140 and 67. Truly, this had been an *annus mirabilis*. Don Bradman was distraught over the cancellation of the tour. He was in no doubt of the ramifications of the decision, necessary though it was. 'It was one of the saddest days of my life,' he later said. 'It meant the end of Barry Richards's Test career.'

6

Happy Hants
Hampshire 1968–1973

*'Richards's horizons seem limitless, and it will be fascinating
to see how far his talents will take him. Few, anywhere in the
world, have his possibilities.'*

**Wisden, 1969, announcing Barry as one
of its five Cricketers of the Year**

MANY and varied are the forms of greeting around the world. In Japan, they bow from the waist. In Thailand, they press their palms together. In Tibet, they poke out their tongue. The Masai in Kenya perform a jumping dance. In New Zealand, the Maoris rub noses. The Arabs hug and kiss both cheeks. West Indians touch knuckles, followed by a complicated routine of shakes, slaps and snaps. The Russians try to crush your knuckles. The French kiss twice. Or three times. Or four.

The Hampshire greeting for Barry Richards when he first arrived as their new overseas player, as delivered by Butch White, was *five* bouncers. In succession. And in the gloom of the indoor school. Accompanied, as you would expect from Butch, by an offer for Barry to pick the bones out of that – or words to that effect. It was early April in 1968 and it was cold. Barry had been to England before – with the South African Schools and Wilfred Isaacs's team – but never in the winter. For, as far as he was concerned, this was winter. 'Jeez, I've never felt so cold in my life. It was *sleeting!* I put on every article of kit I had and it still wasn't enough.'

This would explain why they were practising in the indoor school. At this point, it were best if I put the title 'indoor school' into context. In fact, to call it a building at all is being unfair to buildings.

It more resembled a long shed, not unlike those at marshalling yards that contain rolling stock for the railways. Inside, the amenities were basic, the lighting dingy, the acoustics deafening, the run-ups inadequate and the matting in one net fast and skiddy and in the other net more fast and more skiddy. I can guess which net Butch was bowling in that day.

Even then I was astounded that a professional club did not have better indoor facilities. And from my conversations with colleagues from other counties, it seemed that Hampshire were not alone in the substandard provisions made for practice on rainy days.

What Barry felt as Butch White followed through so that he was practically underneath the nose that the ball had just whistled past can only be imagined. 'Good morning, Butch. Nice to meet you, buddy. My name's Barry Richards. I'm the new boy from South Africa. I'm sure we shall get along fine as team-mates.' No, I cannot hear Barry saying that. The city, the culture, the weather, the conditions, the welcome, the atmosphere, the undercurrents – all were alien to him. He must have wondered what he had let himself in for. Durban it most certainly wasn't.

Yet, despite the unpromising beginning, it could be said – and many have – that Barry Richards's career with Hampshire was one of almost unqualified success. By any yardstick, Barry's value to the county was immense. Number of runs? 15,270, a hefty haul. Consistency? There was only one year, 1977, his last, when he did not score 1,000 runs and even then, he fell only 73 short. He often scored many more in one season than the benchmark 1,000. His average fluctuated from 44.53 to 61.13 – ranging from the merely very good to the exceptional. And let us not forget the 261 catches, most at first slip and most made to look ridiculously easy.

Team successes? Hampshire won the County Championship in 1973, for only the second time in their history, and would have repeated the triumph the following year had not rain cruelly robbed them. They also won the Sunday League in 1975, though a Lord's final continued to elude them. In fact, it is no exaggeration to claim that for a spell in the early and mid-1970s, Hampshire were the most complete and feared side in England. Value for money? Just remember the words of Richard Gilliat, the captain, who remarked that the failure to land Clive Lloyd as their overseas player and the signing of the young, virtually unknown South African was a blessing. 'No one can deny that we greatly profited by missing out on Lloyd,' he said. 'And Clive was no slouch at Lancashire, was he?' Indeed not. So the favourable comparison between the two was a ringing endorsement of Barry's prestige in the county game, and that from somebody who should know.

But what about lasting impressions? Does the memory of the Hampshire supporter glow with a nostalgic hue when a Richards innings is called to mind? Let me try to answer this by painting a picture in words as best I can. The fine Victorian pavilion at Hampshire's headquarters in Northlands Road, Southampton, was just about full, if not quite packed to the rickety old rafters as it would have been if the match had been a one-dayer. My job on match days was to guard the entrance to the members' enclosure. I was supposed to demand sight of the match day pass but I rarely did.

You could tell who was a member and who wasn't without much difficulty. A few you recognised by sight, most of the rest wore the club tie and the one or two dodgy ones who were thirsty and had their eyes on the bar I would wave through. I was a university undergraduate and at the time I had a rather skew-whiffed perspective on privilege and entitlement.

Or maybe I was just lazy. After all, I reasoned, the more money taken at the bar the better for the club and some of these chaps bore the ruddy features and the uncertain gait of the dedicated daytime drinker. All of my colleagues in the Second XI had much the same slack attitude to the guardianship of the holy places of the cricket ground but they were more militant than me in voicing their displeasure at our menial role; I was just happy to sit there quietly watching the cricket without interruption. As far as I was concerned, a rampaging mob of hooligans could have passed without let or hindrance, though, to be truthful, the level of animation of an average Northlands Road crowd rarely rose above the slumberous. But they knew their cricket all right, to the extent that they occasionally recognised me and exhorted me, in those hybrid tones of the Hampshire supporter, to 'get out there, lad, and show 'em how it's done'.

I think not. And I did not fool myself either. There were some mighty fine players in the Hampshire side and I was fascinated by the way they went about their business. Take Roy Marshall. I had heard about him and knew that he was one of the finest attacking opening batsmen in the country. But when I first saw him bat I was completely taken aback. I had expected a player of silky skill, delicate strokeplay and supreme timing. But not a bit of it. He stood tall at the crease and *smashed* it. There is no other way to describe the onslaught. It wasn't elegant, it wasn't handsome, sometimes it wasn't textbook. But it was breathtaking in its power and ferocity, quite magnificent really.

And watching Butch White thundering in to bowl was exhilarating, all pounding hooves, flaring nostrils and solid frame generating the same sense of panic and impending havoc as a runaway horse. When the great beast ruptured his Achilles tendon as his front foot thudded into the popping crease at the moment of delivery, the scream of agony haunted those who were there for many a day. There was also the peerless fielding of Barry Reed in the covers, whose example and encouragement inspired me to take fielding seriously. Oh yes, there were much more serious things to concern me at the entrance to the members' enclosure than checking match credentials.

And there was Barry Richards. It is often said of great players that they empty bars. Barry didn't empty bars because everybody was already outside, pint in hand, watching and waiting. Perhaps this was because he was an opening batsman and his appearance on the stage could be timed, either at the start of play or between the innings, a hiatus of ten minutes, sufficient time to slip in that last order and resume the vantage point. The crowd were in good spirits, Hampshire were doing well and Richards was on song. The sun was out, the pitch was a good 'un – or so Barry made it seem – and the old ground was just the most perfect place to be on a summer's afternoon. Barry played a back foot drive and the ball raced to the boundary in front of the pavilion. Even before it had reached the rope, the umpire was signalling four.

I've seen many fours struck in my lifetime, a good number of them coming off my bowling. So what was so memorable about this one? First, there was the sound. You can always tell when a ball has been cleanly struck, by the satisfying thwack of the ball on willow. But it wasn't that, although we could all hear it as distinctly as the chimes of the ice-cream van in the car park. It was the sound of a thousand onlookers simultaneously sighing. The best way I can describe it is to compare it with an expression of unarticulated pleasure at the first draught of a particularly good Chablis, suitably chilled. Or better still, the unmistakeable expression of delight from the congregation as the bride makes her way down the aisle. It is an utterance, restrained but genuine, of pleasure, a feeling that it is good to be alive, at this place and at this time.

And why had a back foot drive elicited such a response? It was a delightful stroke, perfectly timed, flawlessly executed. If a video of it had been made and used as the model of how a back foot drive should be played, the authors of the MCC coaching manual would have nodded their heads appreciatively. Barry played in the classical style – unless he wanted to improvise, that is – and there it was, demonstrated exactly how it should be played. But wait a minute. There were plenty of batsmen up and down the country, including one or two in that same Hampshire side, who could play the back foot drive correctly and effectively. So what prompted this collective expression of approval? Because it was a thing of beauty. A moment of supreme skill on a cricket field is difficult to describe and to pin down but as plain as a pikestaff when you see it. It is the moment when spectators of any sport turn to each other and say, 'Did you see *that*?'

We've all heard the cliché 'worth the entrance fee just to have witnessed it' uttered often enough but it sums up that response. Like the rest of the crowd that day, I had been left in no doubt that I had been privileged to be in the presence of greatness. Unforgettable. Barry Richards had this effect on cricket watchers.

And yet…there was a niggardly minority of Hampshire members who continually voiced their reservations. Did Hampshire's overseas player fully justify the huge salary he was paid? Did he provide value for money? Barry had set himself up as a professional cricketer, the first in his country, so he would have appreciated and understood the concept of a fair wage for a day's work. His first response to the charge that he was paid a fortune elicited nothing more than a hollow laugh.

I persisted. *So, how much were you paid that first year?* 'Nine hundred pounds. So work out what that's worth in today's money.' I couldn't. Numbers and me are total strangers. But it didn't seem an awful lot. My nephew, Tim Murtagh, opens the bowling for Middlesex so I asked him, without the need for him to go into detail, what a professional with similar seniority and experience to Barry's would be likely to earn today. His estimation was something in the region of £80,000 a year. Barry's £900 for the 1968 season would today equate to around £13,000. *That's a pittance!* Barry shrugged. There was no need for him to comment. And forget not that Barry was Hampshire's overseas signing, the best of the best, a superstar. 'That was why the Packer Revolution was the biggest thing in cricket history since…' *Just a minute Barry, I know, I know. But keep your powder dry until that chapter.* Not that for one second does Barry, or anyone else of that generation, begrudge the modern day players' substantial remuneration; it's just hard for them not to wish that the revolution had come earlier.

Incidentally, and not unrelated, how come you ended up at Hampshire? Jim Parks told me that Sussex were initially in the hunt. 'They offered me £750. Hampshire offered me £900. No contest.' Fair enough. Barry was after all a professional and was entitled to go for the highest bidder. A mischievous thought crossed my mind at that point. How much happier would Barry have been, living on the south coast in the fashionable resort of Brighton? Southampton is also on the south coast but there the similarity ends. Richards playing for Sussex? It doesn't bear thinking about.

I came back to my original point. Did he give value for money? 'I think I did,' he responded. 'Look at my figures. I scored over 1,000 runs each season. I believe I did right for Hampshire.' Indisputably. *But could you have scored more?* 'Of course I could. Look at the number of times I threw it away in the 1970s and 80s.' The charge that he often got bored out there in the middle, especially when he wasn't being challenged, and was dismissed trying to do something outrageous, is one hard to shake off. And, to be fair, he made no attempt to do so. 'I could, I should, have got my head down a bit more. I would have scored a hundred hundreds.' I don't think there can be any doubt about that. But really, is that proof positive of a career squandered? He was never a run gatherer. Averages, statistics, weight of runs did not truly interest him. If he had a yearning for statistical immortality, he would not have been half the player he was. Remember his stated philosophy that he was in the entertainment business. And did he entertain? You bet he did.

As an example of his disdain for the massaging of his average, listen to this. 'You'll note that after my first year, I didn't play much against the universities.' He had no need to say more. There was a time when Oxford and Cambridge could boast a wealth of fine cricketers, which more than justified their first-class status in games against the counties. Their heyday was arguably in the 1950s when players such as May, Cowdrey, Dexter, Sheppard, M.J.K. Smith, Lewis, Nawab of Pataudi, Brearley and others all went on to play Test cricket. But in the more egalitarian era of which we are talking, the reputation and prestige of Oxbridge cricket had begun to fade. They still hung on to their first-class status but this was beginning to be queried by many. Some thought it was a nonsense. To be candid, there were some very weak sides put out under that distinguished umbrella and not a few county players would make sure they were on the team sheet to fill their boots and boost their averages.

'So they could go to the committee at the end of the season and say, look how many runs I've scored – you can't sack me, surely,' said Barry, a little caustically but no less truthfully for that. He may have been a professional cricketer but he did not share the narrow, parochial and self-serving attitude of what he came to see as the typical pro. So, yes, he could have scored a few more runs. But so could we all.

Hampshire did not provide him with accommodation when he landed on these shores; he had to shift for himself. For his first year, he was taken in by Leo Harrison, the club coach, and lived with his family in Mudeford. 'Oh dear,' Barry grimaced. 'I don't think I was too popular with the Bird.' 'Bird' was Leo's pet name for his wife. *Why was that?* 'Well, I wasn't the tidiest of house guests.' *Barry, I have yet to meet a tidy South African.* He laughed and owned that it was probably true.

I happen to know someone well who can confirm this. Leo's son, Martin, a contemporary of mine at Southampton University and, incidentally, my cricket captain, remembers Barry's time with his family very well. 'Barry expected pretty well everything to be done for him. Understandable really, when you realised the sort of privileged background he came from.' Not *that* privileged, of course, for a white South African but nonetheless all families had a maid, even Barry's. 'You must remember where I came from,' Barry pointed out. 'We had maids who cleaned and did all our washing.'

He was not extolling the virtues of a system that fostered social inequality in his country, providing maids for white families; he was merely stating a fact. He was 22, he had to fend for himself in a totally different environment, he had no idea how to cook or to clean or to wash and iron kit. In short, apart from on the cricket field, he was ill equipped to look after himself. It was, as they say, a steep learning curve. 'We used to have long conversations about apartheid,' said Martin, 'and though he defended his country, I got the impression that he wasn't convinced about South Africa's racial policy and didn't defend apartheid at all vigorously.'

Martin also remembers having throw-downs with Barry in the garden. 'Barry's drives were hit with such power and timing that I swear they scorched the lawn. I also recall one drive that did not get one millimetre off the ground and broke a picket of the wooden fence.' It is extraordinary that everyone who ever saw Barry bat seems to have one shot that sticks in the mind, a stroke of elegance, correctness, power, beauty, genius or even outrageous improvisation. 'I knew then,' said Martin, 'what a prodigious talent we had on our hands.'

So did Hampshire. Not that Barry could detect much in the way of pecuniary recognition, not at first anyway, until he began to speak up. For the second year, Charlie Knott, the chairman of the cricket committee, put him in touch with a landlady who provided digs, of the most basic kind. 'No heating,' he remembered with displeasure. 'Jeez, I froze my nuts off in that place.' *Still, you had the sponsored Jag, didn't you?* 'Huh! No car. I had to walk in to the ground every day. And then I went in to see the Sec and told him, in no uncertain terms, that things were going to change. I thought the poor old boy was going to have a heart attack, the way the colour drained from his face.' Barry got his car. A Ford Capri, number plate BAR 777 J.

No one, not even the hard-bitten sceptics, can deny that he proved that he was worth it all, even with the Capri. That is why he struggled to understand this simmering resentment that certain players had for his prestige and his remuneration. Back home in Durban, his Natal team-mates, all amateurs it has to be said, were only too pleased to have arguably the best batsman in the world in their team. 'So why the jealousy, Murt?' I shrugged. It did smack a little of pettiness. Perhaps that is a trait of the English. Perhaps that is the nature of professional sport – you are always eyeing up a colleague and wondering if he's getting paid more than you. Whatever the reason, he had a funny feeling that complete integration within the Hampshire dressing room was not going to be seamless and immediate.

But should not the star player in any sport be paid more than anybody else? Barry was the new overseas star. With the pressure and the expectation came a commensurate salary. That is only fair, surely. I know times have changed but can you imagine what Ronaldo would have said if a new Lamborghini had not been waiting for him at the gates of the Bernabeu when he signed for Real Madrid? It seems almost antediluvian, looking back on it, how Barry was treated by Hampshire, at first, at any rate. I'm not suggesting that he was in any way ill-treated or neglected by the club but the perception that the red carpet was rolled out for him was an erroneous one.

There was the famous claim of yours that you were going to score 2,000 runs in your first season. Did you actually say that? 'Ach no, man. I was quoted out of context. As usual. When I arrived, I was asked on Southern TV what my ambitions were for the season. I replied that my aim was to score 2,000 runs. I didn't say I *would* score 2,000 runs.' Newspapers however don't do nuance. 'Richards boasts he will score 2,000 runs' screamed the headlines, and he was stuck with the prediction, a hostage to fortune.

He made his debut on 1 May against Sussex. The weather, as it can so often be at that time of year, was cold and blustery, the threat of showers ever present. Sussex batted first and found the going tough. Hove on a cloudy day is a haven for seamers, especially when the tide rolls in (and this is not a myth) and sure enough Shackleton and Cottam were in the ascendant. During the 65 overs it took his team to dismiss their opponents for 135, Barry was seen to have his hands in his pockets throughout, except for the moment of delivery. This was not casual arrogance on his part; he was just trying to keep his hands warm. In the evening session, it was Hampshire's turn to see what they could do on this green wicket. Barry did not open the innings. The tried and tested pair, Marshall and Reed, were the first to emerge from the pavilion. Barry was down to bat at number four.

When did you start to open, for Hampshire, I mean? 'After four matches, I think. I swapped with Roy Marshall.' In any event, he might just as well have opened; it was not long before he was out there in the middle. The score was 15/2 and John Snow had his tail up. Unsurprising really. He bowled down the slope, sometimes terrifyingly fast, and on a wicket that helped him, he was always a handful. And there taking guard was a young whippersnapper of a South African who had said that he was going to take apart county bowling. If he ever needed motivation – and sometimes he did – then this was it. The Hove crowd, not known for their animation, leant forward expectantly. The journalists in the press box looked up, took note and licked their pencils in anticipation. The Hampshire team were all out there in the seats reserved, there being no view of the middle from the dressing room, to see how their new overseas signing was going to fare.

It was inevitable really. In short order, the score was 15/3 and Barry was trudging back disconsolately to the pavilion, having been bowled by Snow for nought. On his way, he passed Tony Buss, not known for the tact and courtesy of his on-field observations. 'Only 2,000 to go,' he offered by way of a send-off. 'Ah, but I got 50 in the second innings,' said Barry, keen to put the record straight. Fifty-three not out actually. 'So that was all right then. Only 1,947 to go.' Well, nobody said it was going to be easy.

In point of fact, there was an uncomfortable few minutes during the three days when some of his team-mates feared that their overseas star would never score another run, let alone 1,947. 'That first night, back at the hotel, we got him p*****,' Alan Castell told me. *But Barry hardly drinks!* 'That's why he got p*****. Anyway, we were larking around late at night, the way you do. I hit him with a lavatory brush,' said another team-mate, Keith Wheatley. *With a what?* 'A lavatory brush. It bloody hurt him and his eye immediately swelled up. We were panicking, I can tell you. Next morning he came down to breakfast with the biggest black eye you've ever seen.' *Why did you hit him with a lavatory brush?* But I got no answer on that from either of them, or at least anything that was intelligible through their howls of laughter.

And the reason for this rare disclosure of confidential information? It gives the lie to a common misconception, one among so many, that Barry was aloof and antisocial at Hampshire. 'Absolute rubbish!' Bob Cottam assured me. 'And I should know. I was his "roomie" on away trips. He was a great bloke. I won't hear a word said against him.' Castell and Wheatley were vehement in their agreement. 'Great guy,' they chorused, 'One of the lads.' Cottam elaborated, 'Barry mixed in well with us younger players. He wasn't in any way arrogant or stand-offish. It was immediately apparent to all of us that he was a magnificent player but he never threw his weight around in the dressing room.' *What about the South African bit? How did he cope with all the adverse publicity over apartheid and white supremacy?* Cottam shook his head. 'There were no problems at all. In any case, you know what it's like – cricket is like one big family, wherever you come from. He was very uncontroversial. He didn't get involved in any heated discussion or anything. In fact, I thought he was a bit shy – certainly not arrogant.' *Except with a bat in his hand!* 'Ah well, he had every right, didn't he?'

On this potentially vexatious question of colour, I sought the opinion of John Holder who was in the team at the time. Barry Richards and John Holder, you might say, came from two different planets. One was a white South African opening batsman who did not always agree with umpires; the other was a black West Indian opening bowler who later *became* an umpire. 'How did I get on with Barry?' answered Holder. 'Well, initially I had reservations about how he and I would get on, given his country's policy of apartheid and all the horror stories about how blacks were treated over there. But my fears were groundless. He was extremely friendly and at no stage were there any displays of white superiority from him.'

He went on to say that Barry later admitted to him that Garry Sobers had the same worries before he met Barry and wondered what it would be like sharing a dressing room with him when they both played for The Rest of the World. 'Garry's a really nice guy,' Barry said to me. 'Friendly, approachable, great fun, easy, man, easy!'

Cottam was anxious to get his point across, fulsome in his praise of Barry, not just as a player, but also as a man. And, believe me, Bob Cottam is not one to 'spread the lurve'. He was an opening bowler, after all. 'We might not see each other for a couple of years or so,' he said. 'And then, when we do, it's just as if all the years have fallen away and we're exactly the same as we were before.' Holder is in total agreement. 'We were good friends. And to this day, that friendship has lasted.' I have struggled to find anyone in that Hampshire dressing room who openly disliked Barry. One or two of the older ones didn't really get to know him well and sometimes disapproved of his antics but all were united in their admiration of his batting and if there were the odd occasion when he didn't take things quite as seriously as he might, well, that's the price you have to pay sometimes to walk in the shadow of greatness. 'As a player,' said Holder, speaking for all of us, 'he was the nearest thing to genius I have ever seen.'

'One look at him in the nets,' said Richard Lewis, who was to open with Barry a number of times, 'convinced us all that we had a special one here. He came as a superstar and a number of us were quite sceptical at first. Hello, who's this upstart? But it didn't take him long to win us round.' The very next game, in fact. It was against Yorkshire which Barry has stated as being one of his most memorable innings. But before he could take guard, he had to get there. 'Hove to Harrogate. Work that one out.' I had no need. Southampton to Scarborough was the worst journey for an away match I have ever done. 'And no motorways!' He's not absolutely correct on this score; the M1 was opened in 1959. But I do accept that most of the motorway network in England was built later, in the 1970s. The journey, on a Friday evening, along clogged A roads, was a nightmare. 'We arrived at our hotel at 3am.'

And you had to play the next, sorry, the same morning. 'Worse than that, it was a Temperance Hotel! Completely dry. You can imagine what Butch White said about that!' *Yes I can. And I suppose it gave you an early glimpse into the life of a professional cricketer continually on the road.* He shook his head in bewilderment to how he had lasted on the treadmill for as long as he had. Back home, there would be weeks between Currie Cup games.

The next morning, as the Hampshire players inspected the wicket, they were seen to be rubbing their eyes. It was not so much owing to their lack of sleep, though that would certainly be true, but in disbelief at what confronted them. Harrogate, a very pleasant spa town, often known as the Cheltenham of the north, was one of those outposts of Yorkshire cricket that was in truth no more than a club ground, with a wicket to match. Barry had never seen anything like it. It was as green as the outfield and wet at one end. These were the days of uncovered wickets but only during the match. Why on earth it was wet at one end before play started, no one could explain. Or would explain.

County cricketers have ever been a cynical old bunch and conspiracy theories did not take long to surface. One look at the Yorkshire attack confirmed the Hampshire team of their worst fears. Trueman, Nicholson, Close, Illingworth and Wilson had all been round the block a few times and would surely make short work of any batting side on that strip. Which is precisely what they did. Hampshire were dismissed for 122 in 75 overs. Only two batsmen reached double figures. Peter Sainsbury scored 18. Barry Richards made 70, unforgettable runs to those who were there. Sometimes great things come in small packages.

All the necessary components of a great performance were in evidence that day: the wicket was atrocious, the opposition formidable and the situation desperate. And somehow, when everybody else was floundering, none of them a mug, Barry made it look easy. 'It was Trueman's last season,' he reminded me, 'and he could still bowl.' By now, Trueman was no longer the tearaway fast bowler of his youth. He had cut down his pace but was just as effective – some said more so – moving the ball both ways, even running his fingers down the seam to bowl cutters, when the conditions suited. And Harrogate on a wet morning in early May was tailor made for him. Both openers, Marshall and Reed, fell to him cheaply and Barry barely had time to rub the sleep from his eyes before he found himself at the crease, the score 5/2. If he thought that seeing off Trueman, who only bowled in short spells these days, was the route towards safety and ultimate prosperity, he was quickly disabused of that notion.

Illingworth on this track was just as deadly, with Wilson bowling his left-arm spinners not far behind. According to Keith Wheatley, Illingworth was 'unplayable'. You might be forgiven for responding that he would say that, wouldn't he, seeing as Illingworth got him out for three but on this occasion there was no exaggeration. 'It was unbelievable,' he said. 'Illy was bowling sharply turning offies. Barry was stepping *inside* the line and hitting him into the gaps on the off side. Illy was standing there, in the middle of the wicket, scratching his head in bemusement as this young South African was toying with him.'

Many people in this book have remarked on Barry's uncanny knack of missing the fielder. We've all done it – hit a magnificent shot but straight at a fielder. Barry never wasted a good shot. But on this occasion, his genius touched new heights. 'Not only did he know exactly where all the fielders were,' continued. Wheatley. 'He knew where all the puddles were too! He'd play a shot worth four on any other ground and shout, "Two!" as he hit it between the puddles.' I said that Harrogate was a long way from Hove. It was a world away from Durban. 'Jeez,' said Barry, 'A helluva wicket. And on top of that it was so *cold*!' He had never before been in a dressing room with heaters. He remembers standing in front of one of them and noticing a burning smell. The hairs on the back of his bare legs were singeing.

Illingworth, a Yorkshireman to his boots, was never one to give praise lightly. He rated Barry up there with the best that he had ever bowled to. But Raymond being Raymond, he always believed, he said, that Barry gave him a chance because he would play the turning ball 'inside out', in much the same way that Keith Wheatley has described above. 'Only a top player can do that,' said Illy, 'hit the off-spinner through the covers on a turner.' Notwithstanding these flashes of genius and improvisation, Barry possessed excellent balance, Illy maintained, with a thoroughly orthodox technique. 'And 'e makes it all look so bluidy easy,' he muttered admiringly. He drew favourable comparisons with the young, languid left-hander, with blond curls, at the crease at the very moment he was talking, leaning effortlessly into a cover drive for four. 'Mark my words,' he said, 'that boy Gower's got the same sort of God-given talent.'

While we're on the topic of wickets, Barry, many games in those days were played on 'out grounds'. What was your opinion of them? He paused in order to frame a diplomatic answer, not something he was known for in his younger days. 'Well. Some of them were quite pretty!' That is true. The attractive ones that stick in the mind were Tunbridge Wells, Bath, Eastbourne, Dover, Cheltenham and…'Dean Park', we both said simultaneously. 'Yes, I liked playing at Bournemouth,' he said, 'with the trees and the marquees…' He sounded almost nostalgic. But mention of the more spartan of the county outposts – Ponypridd, Lydney, Ilford, Kidderminster, Blackheath, Glastonbury, Ilkestone, Westcliff, Dudley, Burton, Southend, Middlesbrough, Bradford, to name but a few – elicited this damning praise. 'They were no more than club grounds, very popular with the locals, but hardly up to scratch.'

These days, the festivals at these smaller venues have become uneconomic and all but disappeared. That is to the regret of some traditionalists who liked to see the game spread around the counties but most of the players – batsmen, in the main – always preferred to play at county headquarters. It is often said, a little unkindly perhaps, that Derek Underwood, for one, would not have taken the wickets he did if he had not bowled so often on helpful pitches all over Kent, at Gravesend, Blackheath, Maidstone, Dover, Folkestone and Tunbridge Wells (for all the lovely rhododendrons surrounding the ground).

Although the County Ground at Northampton never won prizes for charm, it was their headquarters and it was the scene of Barry's first hundred for Hampshire. 'And my second!' he piped up. True enough. He scored a hundred in both innings. 'Well, you might as well cash in when you can,' he offered drily. He also remembered a run-in with Sarfraz Nawaz. 'You know what he was like, always mouthing off. So I gave it back with both barrels. I think it shocked some of the older members of the side.' *Did you kiss and make up afterwards?* 'With my team-mates?' *No, Sarfraz.* 'Oh, he was fine. After all, it was no worse than what went on all the time in the Currie Cup.'

Therein lay a difference between county cricket, as it was then, and the domestic game played overseas. The Englishmen saw themselves as professionals, doing a job on a daily basis, and respect towards a fellow professional had its unwritten and unspoken parameters. Swearing at each other was considered a breach of these parameters, without doubt bad form. No such restraints inhibited cricketers overseas. They were, shall we say, a little more forthright and plain spoken in their observations on how the game was unfolding.

I notice Hylton Ackerman was playing for Northants. You must have known him well. 'Ah, lovely guy. I think he was the youngest ever, 14, to have played for South African Schools. He died recently. So sad. Liver failure, I think. He never did enjoy the best of health.' And then Barry laughed. 'Loved a party, that guy!' Barry was never a party animal himself but there is no puritanical streak running through his body; he had no problem with people enjoying life to the full. Though he did draw the line at foul play with lavatory brushes.

By this stage of the season and with the sun at last warming his back, the runs had started to flow and the full extent of his talent was beginning to unfold in front of the British public. The Hampshire team had already cottoned on to the fact that they had someone special in their midst. Against Warwickshire at Basingstoke, he pretty well won the game with one brush, as it were. Just a minute, I hear Bob Cottam interjecting, bowlers win matches, batsmen merely put the team into a position where they can win it. That is a fair point and I should record that Cottam took ten wickets in the match to secure a six-wicket win for the home team. But take note of this. In Hampshire's first innings, Barry scored 133 out of 272. 'You do the maths, Murt,' he told me, 'but that is a pretty high proportion of the runs.' Only two players from either side, Timms for Hampshire and Amiss for Warwickshire, managed a fifty. 'The wicket had some uneven bounce,' Barry recollected, 'and don't forget, I was not yet a Test player. So batting against someone like Lance Gibbs on that track was a bit daunting.'

So, what about Underwood? Facing him on an unprepared club wicket at Gillingham must have been a bit daunting too? He laughed at the memory. 'We were bowled out for 58 in the second innings. What were Deadly's figures? Seven for 17 or something. The wonder of it was how on earth we managed to score 17 runs off him. One ball he bowled to Barry Reed...Barry played forward and the ball hit him smack in the face.' The passing comment about Derek Underwood and favourable pitches was not intended by either of us as any sort of disparagement of his skill. Yes, he was unplayable on pitches such as this but he knew how best to exploit them. And let us not forget what a fine Test bowler he was, on all types of wickets and in all sorts of conditions. His tally of 297 Test wickets tells its own story (it would have been 300, he wryly reminds everyone, had not the ICC removed Test status from that Rest of the World series).

Later on in that month of July, Hampshire were back on another of England's beaches, Westcliff-on-Sea this time. Barry's great friend, Lee Irvine, was playing for

Essex and he has already told us how much he was looking forward to playing Test matches on proper wickets, rather than the cabbage patches he was used to at Essex. The home side managed only 95 in their first innings, Irvine dismissed by Cottam for nine. For the rest of the day and some of the next, Barry gave a masterclass in batsmanship. It seemed that he was playing a different game to everybody else. Keith Boyce, for some time the great hope of West Indies cricket to fill the large boots of Garry Sobers as a fast-bowling all-rounder, went for the dreaded hundred in his analysis, and one or two other Essex bowlers might well have suffered the same fate had they bowled more overs. And on that wicket!

Essex fared a little better in their second innings (Irvine, caught guess who, bowled White for 51) but they still suffered an innings defeat. Once again, had there been a man of the match award, a certain bowler would assuredly have pushed his way forward, complaining that it's a batters' game and bowlers get 'owt. On this occasion, Derek Shackleton might have had a point. His figures in the rout of Essex's first inning were 20-13-17-5. Compare that with Boyce's figures on the same pitch: 21-1-100-1.

Barry's opinions on Derek Shackleton's bowling mirror exactly his opinions on the depth of his pockets. 'He gave nothing away, nothing.' Admirable in many ways and mightily effective too. 'But he would have been destroyed in today's game,' was Barry's uncompromising verdict. 'With covered, properly prepared wickets, bigger bats, smaller boundaries and a completely different mindset of the modern batsman, he wouldn't have stood a chance bowling those little seamers.' But he was scrupulous enough to admit that in those days and in those conditions Shack was often a handful. 'I stood at slip and I could see how he would gently hit the seam and the ball would nibble a bit this way or that. Tricky.' Tricky enough for 2,857 first-class victims.

I notice in the return match against Sussex at Portsmouth, you gave Tony Buss a fair riposte to his earlier comment. 'Eh?' *That you only had 2,000 to go after your debut duck.* He really didn't seem to think Tony Buss was worthy of further comment so just let me put the record straight. Barry scored two 80s in the match to help Hampshire to a seven-wicket win. Perhaps the only man who held a candle to Barry in this first experiment with overseas players during the 1968 season was the incomparable Garry Sobers. He went on to score 1,590 runs and take 84 wickets and his impact on the county game, to say nothing of his Nottinghamshire team, was as dynamic as Barry's. The difference was that Sobers was well known to the British public – he had been on the Test scene since 1954 and as long ago as 1958 had made his world record score of 365 not out – whereas Barry was not. Although, it has to be said that by this stage of the summer, cricket lovers up and down the country were beginning to sit up and take notice.

How did you get on with the great man? 'Garry? He was a lovely, lovely man. What do I mean "was"? He still is. One of the good guys in this world.' He might have added that Sobers was also, without question, the greatest cricketer ever to have laced up his boots. Was that why Barry seemed to reserve some of his finest innings for when Sobers was in opposition? He doesn't deny the suggestion. 'It always raised your game if one of your peers was around and publicity was to be had.' I do not hint in any way that there were occasions when he did not try. I leave aside benefit games, exhibition matches, charity bashes and the like; they were opportunities to show off for a few overs to entertain the crowd before seeking the sanctuary of the dressing room. In first-class matches, he always tried. It's just that sometimes the spirit was weak and the inspiration lacking. Not so when someone like Sobers was in attendance. And Sobers was definitely lurking that day at Portsmouth at the end of August.

Barry's finest, certainly his most glittering, innings that golden summer very nearly didn't come to pass. Everybody remembers the 'incident of the bail'. Mike Taylor, later a stalwart of the Hampshire XI in the 1970s and a future team-mate of Barry's, was playing for Nottinghamshire that day and takes up the story. 'Carlton Forbes, a West Indian fast bowler – now sadly no longer with us – was bowling. Barry got an inside edge, it hit the leg bail, Deryck Murray, the keeper, dropped the catch and the ball rattled down to the boundary. Everyone stood about, open-mouthed in astonishment. The bails had not been dislodged. Arthur Fagg, the square leg umpire, sidled up and had a look at the wicket. The ball had hit the bail but the groove on the top of the stump was too tight so the bail had not been knocked out!'

Richards had been reprieved with a slice of luck that most cricketers never experience in their lifetime. Needless to say, another set of bails was immediately called for. 'But too late!' Taylor laughed with an acute sense of the ridiculous that he certainly did not feel at the time. Barry remembered it well enough too. 'Lucky twice because Murray could have caught it.' *Deryck Murray – what did you think of him?* 'I played with him for the Rest of the World. Quiet guy but really pleasant.'

You don't give Barry second chances. And sure enough, Mike Taylor's worst fears were realised; Barry took his due to the tune of 206 runs. 'Oddly enough,' Taylor's mind was jogged, 'Sobers, in his first over, took a chunk out of the wicket. Uh-oh, we all thought, this'll be interesting. Well, it wasn't. That is unless you were a Hampshire supporter. Not a single ball misbehaved for the rest of the day. Barry hit it everywhere.' Barry himself doesn't quite remember it like this. He hit the ball everywhere – he certainly agreed with that – but he thought the wicket wasn't very good at all. It just shows how great players can make a very difficult game look easy.

'Whenever Garry was around, there was plenty of press and media people there and that definitely gave me…well, reason to concentrate,' he added. The press were most certainly in evidence and following Sobers around the country. Their perseverance and devotion to their calling paid off handsomely; three days later, in Nottinghamshire's next match against Glamorgan at Swansea, Sobers hit six sixes in one over off Malcolm Nash, immediately wiping Barry off the back pages of the newspapers. It was, after all, the first time six sixes in one over had been scored. If he had to bend the knee to anyone on a cricket field, Barry would do it gladly for Garry Sobers. Oh, and Graeme Pollock too.

That extraordinary feat by an extraordinary cricketer did not rub any of the gloss off Barry's imperious innings for those who witnessed it. John Holder was watching from the home dressing room. 'When Notts took the second new ball,' he said, 'Barry was running down the wicket and hitting it back over the bowler's head. He was doing it again and again. And then, when the short one came, as it surely would, he rocked back and smacked it off the back foot. It was almost as if he was taking the p***! That was the genius of the man.' Hampshire declared at 411/6 and yet again, Barry had scored half of his team's runs. Notts in reply ground their way to 331 in 20 more overs – without any fireworks from Sobers – and the game petered out, notwithstanding hopeful declarations. Let me allow Mike Taylor the final word, delivered in his characteristic half sardonic, half reverential tone of voice. 'Barry? Huh – he *loved* Notts!'

And that was pretty well that for the 1968 season, apart from a fluent 87 against Surrey at the Oval. There were a couple of matches for the International Cavaliers, which was just what Barry wanted at the end of the season, before he was on the plane back home to South Africa and Natal's Currie Cup campaign. *Before we put this season to bed, I notice that you played two matches for the Rest of the World earlier on in the summer*. 'Not quite true. In one of those matches, I was playing *against* them, for Hampshire.' *So you were. But why? What was the background for those games?* He searched his memory but could come up with no answer. He would only say this about them, a familiar beef with him and a valid one too, when you think about it. 'Whatever they were, they weren't taken very seriously. How can those exhibition matches be classified as first-class when World Series Cricket got no such official recognition…?' His voice tailed off but his sentiments were clear enough.

'Did you see my seven wickets?' he suddenly asked. No, I had not. Quickly I scanned the scorecard. And there it was, third change for Hampshire in the Rest of the World's second innings: B.A. Richards 24-6-63-7. *Good God! You bowled them out to win the match by 68 runs. The same number of runs that you scored in the first innings.* 'It was at Dean Park,' he said by way of slightly embarrassed explanation. That was true; Bournemouth did favour the spinners. That was why Bob Cottam had taught himself to bowl off cutters in the nets. He told me that he had got fed up with being left out of the side whenever they played at Bournemouth because his seamers were deemed ineffective on those tracks. I well remember those net sessions with Cottam. A big man, he was bowling medium pace off-spinners which were hitting me in the chest. It must have been galling for Cottam, a regular bowler, to flog himself for 24 overs for little reward while a part-time spinner was cleaning up at the other end. I looked again at the scorecard, scarcely believing the evidence of my own eyes. Barry's victims that day were Barlow, Nurse, Butcher, Lloyd, Saeed Ahmed, Graeme Pollock and Wes Hall.

Now, be honest with me Barry. Everybody knew that you could bowl. So why didn't you? 'I did, from time to time, when a breakthrough or a change was needed.' *No. I mean, why didn't you take it seriously and bowl regularly?* He hummed and hawed. In the end, he admitted that he really wasn't that interested in bowling; all he wanted to do was bat. And he concentrated on that. I was reminded of a story John Holder told me. During a casual conversation with Barry one evening, he asked him why he didn't bowl more. 'Come on – you've got long fingers and everyone knows you can bowl more than useful off-spinners.' 'Hod, Hampshire pay me to bat,' was Barry's uncompromising reply. 'If they want me to bowl, they'll have to pay me more money!' I doubt that Barry was being completely serious here but there was probably a smidgen of truth in his answer. He wasn't being paid a king's ransom and he wanted to keep himself mentally fresh for the challenges ahead.

As if to underline his point about his relatively paltry salary, he told me about a club award at the end of the season, for the player of the year. *Well, with over 2,000 runs, you were the obvious choice.* 'Yes and no. I shared it with Cotters.' And on reflection, that seemed fair enough. Cottam had had just as good a season as Barry. 128 wickets could arguably be equated with 2,314 runs. But no, it was not the sharing of the award that rankled; Barry had no problem with that. He felt that his 'roomie' more than deserved the honour. It was the amount. 'One hundred pounds,' he laughed. 'Fifty quid each!' *More than enough for a round at the Cowherds Inn.* 'Huh.'

There is no pecuniary reward for being named as one of *Wisden*'s five Cricketers of the Year but the distinction is praiseworthy. When the 1969 edition hit the bookstalls, Barry Richards was included in the roll of honour. Not a huge surprise or controversial in any way, considering the outstanding season he had just had, but one that was gratifying nonetheless. 'Yes, it was a great tribute,' he said. 'Don't forget I had yet to make my Test debut and many more illustrious players than me had been chosen over the years.'

The article that accompanied his selection is worth quoting at length:

'Garry Sobers apart – and as ever he set his own standards – none of the new overseas players in county cricket made a greater impact than Barry Anderson Richards, of Hampshire, who was born in Durban, Natal, on July 21, 1945. The arithmetic of his achievements was convincing enough. In his first English season, and a wet one at that, he scored 2,395 runs, the highest aggregate, with an average of 47.90, bettered only by the infinitely more experienced Boycott.

'Yet it was the composed manner and assurance and the maturity of technique for one so young, which impressed the responsible critics, and friend and foe alike. His off and cover driving were frequently compared with the great Walter Hammond and Sir Leonard Hutton.

'When Richards took 206 off Nottinghamshire, E.D.R. Eagar, secretary and former captain of Hampshire, commented, "I have never seen better driving since Hammond." There could be no higher praise. And as many a bowler found to his cost, a shorter length ball, designed to avoid punishment, produced a savage square cut.

'Richards denies that he has based his style and methods on any player in particular, but Hutton seems to have consciously influenced him. "When I was at Durban High School," recalls Richards, "I remember studying action pictures of Hutton with immense interest. I think his technique was the best I have ever seen."

'Tall and athletic in appearance, Richards benefited much from the individual encouragement, which is possible for the talented white cricketer in South Africa to enjoy. He never lacked help and his own considerable ability has always been supported by the vein of dedication and single-minded purpose which threads through the story of most top-line players...'

The citation goes on to outline the meteoric rise of his career to date, already chronicled in earlier chapters, as well as the complaint of Barry's, sympathetically regarded by the writer, that too much cricket is played in an English county season. The article ends thus, 'Nevertheless, Richards, who is a first-rate slip fielder, retained his concentration until the very end. He emerged a better batsman for his 33 matches and his 55 innings. His selection and placing improved match by match and belied his years. Moreover, he started to collect runs on the leg side, which had largely been forsaken territory for him.'

And then comes that unintended sad and poignant denouement that is hard to read without feeling that a beautiful young plant is about to be pulled out of the ground, 'Richards's horizons seem limitless and it will be fascinating to see how far his talents will take him. Few, anywhere in the world, have his possibilities.'

As Barry, and the countless cricket lovers who had unwrapped their annual Christmas present, read this, the MCC tour to South Africa of 1968/69 had already, in the wake of the D'Oliveira Affair, been cancelled.

It was said that Barry's second year in county cricket did not match his first. If that were true, it would be hardly surprising; to reach such heights of endeavour and success on a regular basis would be uncommon. But Barry was uncommon, so why not? A total of 1,440 runs in the season represent a considerable drop from 2,395. What had happened? First, owing to the introduction of the new Sunday League, the number of three-day games had been reduced from 32 to 24. Also, he suffered a number of injuries, which further limited his appearances to 20. And his average actually went up from 47.90 to 57.60. A poor season in comparison? I think not.

Was there a grain of truth in the claim that he was not quite as ambitious and focussed as he had been in his debut season? 'I had a few injuries,' he contended. *What were they?* 'Oh, this and that,' he replied vaguely. *I note that one of them coincided with Wimbledon.* Then he started to chuckle. 'Well, you could say that there were a few furfies among them.' *What?* 'Furfies. Have you never heard of furfies?' I had not. Furfies was an unknown disease to me. 'A furfy is a non-existent injury. Or at least an injury that has been, how shall we say, slightly exaggerated.' So the rumours were true. It was always noted, with some scepticism, that Barry's injuries would coincide with Wimbledon fortnight.

'Yes, but you must understand that I had been playing cricket non-stop since 1964. I was knackered, mentally shot. I needed a break and I could see no way of getting one.' In his defence, it ought to be pointed out that, as well as the seven-day-a-week treadmill that was county cricket in England, even on days when not involved in playing for Natal and Durban High School Old Boys, he was coaching at clubs or schools. He was beginning to feel a little stale. To put the record right, he did suffer one or two injuries that season – when he was at Wimbledon, he had split the webbing between two of his fingers – but he did not, it has to be admitted, rush back to duty. *What were you doing playing for the Second XI in May?* 'What game was that?' *Middlesex.* 'Where?' *At Lord's.* ''Spect I wanted to get up to London and the bright lights. Ah yes, I caught up with a couple of mates, Mike Milton and Norman Featherstone.' Already, Barry was beginning to find the provincial character of life in a featureless, south coast, container port dull and restrictive.

That said, there were several outstanding innings that he played that summer to keep the Hampshire faithful happy. He found the fledgling John Player League to his taste. The crowds were large, the games were televised and the 40-over format set some new, exciting challenges. 'No fielding restrictions, no circle, no power play. The captain could put his fielders where he wanted – nine on the boundary if necessary.' One way to combat a far-flung outfield was to hit the ball gently into open spaces and run like hell to take two. And then the opposing captain would be forced to bring in a couple of sweepers and gaps would start to appear. Challenges like this appealed to Barry; he could manufacture shots and improvise and play off the cuff. And some of his strokes took the breath away.

In the three-day game, he tended to shine if the opposing attack was mettlesome or if the conditions meant that everybody else struggled. Against Worcestershire in mid-July at New Road, he scored 103, the next highest score being 32, out of a total of 275, which set up the win by 60 runs. *Tell me about Basil. This was not long after the D'Oliveira Affair, you were both South Africans yet of different colour. Were there any tensions between you?* 'You have to hand it to Basil, the way he coped with a very difficult situation. He was fine with me, both on and off the field. That is, until he had a few toots. Then he was dynamite!'

A toot is a drink in South Africa, and certainly not of the soft variety. Apparently, Basil D'Oliveira had never touched alcohol until he set foot in these shores but then he more than made up for it. According to Tom Graveney, Basil did not actually drink that much but he obviously had little tolerance for it because he would get roaring drunk on only a few pints. But he was such a decent fellow and such a fine player that his friends, of whom he had many, would keep an attentive eye on him.

Another galvanising influence on Barry's motivation was the arrival of the tourists in town. He only partly agrees with my premise here. Yes, he enjoyed pitting his wits against the game's best and yes, there was always a decent following and coverage by the nation's press so an outstanding performance would be bound to get a good airing in the following day's papers. 'But they weren't Test matches,' he reminded me. 'Often the tourists were using these games as a warm-up. And often, one or two of our own team would be rested.' Nonetheless, against the West Indians, the first of the split tourists that summer, he showed who was boss, with 86 in the first innings and a matchless 120 in the second, out of a total of 215/4 declared. Barry was in the mood, clearly. Garfield St Aubrun Sobers, the West Indies captain, evidently was not. He bowled a mere ten overs in the first innings, only two in the second, and batted on both occasions at number seven. 'Even Garry sometimes found it difficult to motivate himself,' Barry said.

Later that season, it was the New Zealander's turn to visit the county ground in Southampton. Barry scored 132 in Hampshire's only innings – and has no recollection of the knock at all. John Holder, who was playing, suffers from no such failure of the memory. 'I remember Collinge, their left-arm quickie, bowling to Barry and Barry treating him with the utmost contempt. He was just hitting him wherever he liked. He was coming down the wicket and driving Collinge through the covers for four. Next ball, he made as if to charge again, whereupon Collinge bounced him. Barry stepped back and hooked him nonchalantly to the square leg boundary.' I do not believe that Barry set out to humiliate bowlers, not consciously anyway. It may have looked like that, such was his dominance when on song. But the ball was there to be hit, whoever had delivered it, and if he had the ability and the confidence to find the gaps, wherever they were, and if he had a choice, sometimes three or four, which shot to play then why not use that skill? It would be a sin not to.

While we are on historical figures, let me introduce you to another, if only briefly. *Do you remember the composition of Hampshire's opening attack in that New Zealand match?* Barry rubbed the side of his nose, a characteristic gesture of his when deep in thought. 'Well, there was Hod…and…oh yes, Bill "Never Bowled A Bad Ball" Buck!' He was right, John Holder and Bill Buck. The latter occupies a unique and little known footnote in cricket history. He is the only person to have played against two different touring sides for two different counties – in the same season! How come? Bill was in his last term at St Luke's College in Devon that year. He was a useful fast-medium swing bowler ('Much too good for you, Murtagh!') and as Somerset at that time were struggling for opening bowlers, they decided to give the student a trial. Against the West Indies!

As it happened, Bill did not acquit himself badly. Once term had finished, he returned to his home town of Southampton and some eagle-eyed member of the Hampshire committee expressed his displeasure at Somerset poaching one of their 'future stars'. Future star or not, Bill was unceremoniously pitched in against the New Zealanders later the same summer. He did not set any houses alight but he bowled well enough. The match was spoilt by rain but the wet underfoot conditions did provide a moment of pure comedy, much enjoyed by Bill's team-mates, both at the time and at numerous recounts. 'Hod [John Holder] bowled the first ball of their innings,' remembered Buck, 'and it was steered down to third man, where I was stationed. Speeding round to pick up the ball – in true Buck style – my feet kept sliding and I ended up on my a***! Great merriment from Stephenson, Richards, Wheatley, Castell and all the others in the slip cordon.'

To say nothing of the crowd. But a career patrolling the third man boundary was not in Buck's life plan; he wanted to become a schoolmaster, which he did, successfully. There was a standing joke at the time, which became a sort of legendary catchphrase at the club. Bournemouth, as we know, and as Bob Cottam has eloquently expressed in these pages, did not suit the quicker bowlers. Roy Marshall, the Hampshire captain and one of the shrewdest cricket brains around, knew this fact only too well and when it was suggested to him that Bill perhaps ought to be included in the 12 for the forthcoming match in that pleasant seaside town, he was heard to exclaim in that odd, high-pitched tone of his, 'Bowl Bill Buck at Bournemouth? Oooh.' Apparently, he was quite exercised at the prospect. We all laugh at the phrase even now, and Barry chuckled too, when reminded of it.

Although that was Bill Buck's solitary game for Hampshire, he did play for a number of years in the Second XI and bowled plenty of overs to Barry in the nets. His views on the master batsman are distinct. 'Barry had that innate, sublime talent – and remains the best batsman I have ever seen. His dismissal of county bowling seemed to some to have the hallmarks of arrogance but I was privileged to be around to see him conquer unfamiliar, extreme conditions, so different to the wickets in South Africa, in his first few years at Hampshire. Once the challenge of mastering new pitches and new opponents had passed, then the grind of the county round started to depress him.'

Buck remembers a conversation with Barry on the boundary once. 'Barry was bemoaning the overblown fixture list with so many journeymen intent only on preserving their averages to prolong their careers. He seemed a complex chap and… troubled.' Barry agrees. 'Even now, at this early stage, I was beginning to suffer from the first signs of burn out.' Quite possibly. But if he had voiced his dissatisfaction, or, at the very least, his reservations about the workload, he would have got short shrift in the dressing room. The run-of-the-mill county player – what Buck called a journeyman – regarded the daily routine as work, much like any other job. That was what he did. Some days were a struggle, some days were a joy, but whatever came up, he simply got on with it. Barry however was cut from different cloth. He believed that more meant less, that a surfeit of cricket promoted mediocrity. However, for the time being, he kept his own counsel.

Notwithstanding, a few of his innings that summer were far from mediocre. There was the 155 he scored against Lancashire whose attack comprised Shuttleworth, Higgs, Simmons, Hughes, Wood, Sullivan and even a few tidy overs from Clive Lloyd. Another was the 127 not out against Northamptonshire out of the team's total of 192, the next highest score being 17. *Your old friend from South Africa, Fred Goldstein, was playing.* 'That's true. We got on well. But it has to be said that he and I did not speak the same language.' *He was Afrikaans?* 'No. He spoke intelligent! He went to Oxford. Just like another former team-mate, Giles Ridley, who I'd played against earlier in the season. Both were seriously bright.'

There was another gem, other than the glittering intellects of Goldstein and Ridley, to admire that summer. I am grateful to Bill Buck for his memory of the match, though he was not playing on this occasion. Hampshire were playing Surrey at Northlands Road in the quarter-final of the Gillette Cup. Surrey had a strong attack, suited to this format of the game, comprising Arnold, Cumbes, Intikhab, Gibson and Storey. 'At the time,' said Buck, 'Geoff Arnold was the premier England seamer. In his opening overs – an experienced Test bowler, don't forget – he placed a third man and a cover, as well as a deep backward cover, square of the wicket and a deep point. Then, for extra protection, he put another man in between those two.' *Pretty obvious what line of attack he was going to pursue then.* 'Precisely. But it made no difference to Barry. He placed successive fours – timed effortlessly but rocketing to the fence – bisecting every man as he was moved. They were classic cuts and shots square of the wicket, dismissing the England man as if he was playing with a stick of rhubarb. Quite brilliant!' Sadly, it was in a losing cause. But Barry's imperious 78 earned him the man of the match award. And how often is that ever awarded to a player on the losing side?

Before we turned our backs on the 1969 season, I was curious to hear the inside story of one of the most bizarre episodes of that season. *What happened in that abandoned match against Glamorgan?* Barry snorted with laughter. 'It was at Dean Park. It had hosed down all day and the game was dead in the water. Come on, we said to the umpires, call it off so we can all go home. So they did. We all loaded up the cars and left. I was in the car with Jets [Trevor Jesty] and we turned on the radio when we were somewhere in the middle of the New Forest to listen to the cricket scores from around the country. Sensation at Bournemouth, they were saying, Glamorgan win match in extraordinary circumstances! Er, haven't we just been playing in Bournemouth, said Jets, a bit puzzled, and I don't remember Glamorgan winning. Yes, I agreed, and I don't remember anything out of the ordinary that happened.'

Those of us not in the team had already got wind of the unfolding drama, back at HQ in Southampton. Apparently, as soon as the Hampshire team had left the ground, it stopped raining and, improbably, the sun came out. The umpires, in the finicky way that only umpires can be, told the groundsman to mop up in the hope that a few overs could be completed before stumps at 6.30pm, even though the game was dead and – nearly – buried. The Glamorgan players were intercepted as they were leaving the ground and told to prepare for play. When the umpires decided that play was possible, out they went, followed by a straggle of half-dressed Glamorgan players, as bemused as anyone else at what was happening. The statutory two minutes elapsed, there was no sign of any Hampshire batsmen and the game was awarded to Glamorgan.

Richard Gilliat, the vice-captain, was by this time halfway to Eastbourne to play in an invitation XI for Derrick Robbins. 'We got there before most of the others, obviously as we had left Bournemouth early – that was Danny Livingstone, David Turner and myself. As we entered the hotel bar, Ray Illingworth, the captain, said in his blunt way, "You've lost!" Of course we didn't believe him. But when we woke up the next morning and read the papers, we found out that it was all too true.'

So what happened in that dressing room? Had the umpires called it off before you left? 'Yes!' he insisted, 'Lloyd Budd, an ex-Hampshire man and liked by us all, came in and said that was it for the day. But he was only the junior of the two. Peter Wight was the senior umpire and when he saw the Glamorgan boys getting on to their coach, he called them back and told them that he'd not called off play. I think it was just Peter being officious and letting everyone know that he was in charge.' *What happened then?* 'I remember listening to Roy Marshall, our captain, being interviewed on the radio. He was apoplectic!' Unsurprisingly, Hampshire put in a formal complaint, the matter was referred to Lord's and on appeal the result was rescinded. *So all was well in the end?* 'Yes,' said Gilliat, 'I don't know whether Peter Wight had his knuckles rapped. I presumed so. But Peter could be a bit like that – fussy.' It was, all things considered, a funny old chapter in Hampshire's history.

In 1970 we saw the disbanding of The Beatles, the near disaster of the Apollo 13 moon mission, the dissolution of Rhodesia's ties with the UK to become a republic, and Brazil's dismemberment of Italy in the World Cup Final in Mexico. Happily there was no 'dis' in the headway of Barry's cricket career; as we have alluded to in the chapter *Annus Mirabilis*, it was going from strength to strength. He returned to Hampshire in April of that year a Test player for the first time. And, as he freely admits now, he still believed, against all common sense really, that his international career was in its infancy, not in its death throes. In point of fact, his season for his club was a little in and out, if I can put it like that, not helped by the fact that he was frequently absent on Rest of the World duty.

The figures pale a little in comparison with his herculean feats in sunnier climes during this 16-month period but in his own words, 'They weren't too shabby, all things considered, were they?' In 25 innings for Hampshire, he compiled 1,410 runs at an average of 58.75. I'm inclined to agree – not too shabby at all. But I am not sure of the verb I have chosen. His runs might have piled up but they were not really compiled, assembled, gathered, in the same way that Samuel Johnson put together his *Dictionary of the English Language*. Or, as Barry would have put it, 'like one of Boycott's innings'. *You're not a great fan of Boycott, are you?* 'Oh, Boycs is fine, not a bad guy at all. I only use him as a means of comparing his dedication to the business of run-gathering – at which he was very good – to my approach to batting.'

There were, as you would expect, innings of quality and virtuosity, one or two of which came in the 40-over Sunday League, a competition which allowed him the full expression of his all-round strokeplay. Both knocks almost single-handedly won the points for his side. The Circle in Hull was not the most congenial of cricket grounds and became less so over the years once Yorkshire discontinued playing there in 1974. Sadly, no denizen of Hull can now take his grandson to the cricket ground to show him where he saw one of Barry Richards's most sparkling innings. Barry scored 155 not out in a total of 215/2…in 40 overs!

There is no need, I hope, for me to reiterate how extraordinary that knock was in the infancy of limited overs cricket. The next highest score for either side was 18. Yorkshire were despatched for 74, by the way; there is no hiding place for a team coming off second best in those contests.

Another one was at Bournemouth at the end of the season against Kent. This time it was 132 not out chasing down a target of 221. The task was completed in a mere 32 overs. Barry remembers hitting the sound dish of the BBC outside broadcast apparatus alongside the wooden commentary box behind the bowler's arm. The bowler happened to be John Dye. 'The viewers' ears were ringing up and down the country,' Barry chortled. He was in a hurry that day. He had a plane to catch back to South Africa.

In between, there were innings of true substance in the three-day game. One came at Chesterfield, the town of the wonky church spire (apparently because the devil sat on it) and a pitch like greased lightning. To face a Derbyshire attack of Hendrick and Ward on that wicket might have put the fear of the devil into any batsman's stomach but not Barry's. He dismissed any talk of the long-tailed one with a score of 153, helping his side to declare at 302/6. Early on in the innings, he nicked one to Bob Taylor behind the wicket. Taylor claimed the catch but Barry was not at all sure that it had carried. So he stood his ground – as he was fully entitled to do – and the umpire found in his favour. The bowler, Alan Ward, was 'not best pleased' and as one of the quickest bowlers around, he let Barry know what he thought of the decision in the way that fast bowlers do. It made little difference.

'There was a bit of chuntering from Bob,' Barry admitted, 'and we would talk about it and laugh about it for many years afterwards.' The next highest score wa s by his opening partner, Barry Reed, with 47. The opening partnership, by the way, was worth 180. It tells its own story. The same story is repeated later at Southampton against Worcestershire. He shared an opening partnership with Reed of 136 before he departed for 94. And it was the same in the second innings; they put on 94 together before Barry departed for 66. This is not in any way to belittle Barry Reed, a fine county player and an outstanding cover point but Barry (Reed, that is) would be the first to accept that his namesake batted on a different planet to most players.

There was also an imperious 150 against Leicestershire at Grace Road. 'We were playing on one side of the square, so the boundary was quite short on that side. Of course, Illingworth put himself on at the end with the long boundary on the leg side while poor old Jack Birkenshaw had to bowl with the short square leg boundary.' If you realise that both bowlers were off-spinners who would naturally prefer the safety net of a long boundary on the leg side, you will understand Birkenshaw's dismay at his captain's choice of ends. Not that he could, or would, do anything about it; it was a standing joke on the playing circuit that Birkenshaw spent his career thus hamstrung by his captain's choice of ends or his preferred time to bowl. Or indeed whether he fancied a bowl at all.

It made no difference to Barry. He simply hit Illingworth 'inside out' as it is called, steering the ball on the off side – the shorter boundary – wherever the England captain pitched it. My old friend Roger Tolchard purred at the memory of the audacity of it, having, as he did, a front row seat, as it were, immediately behind the great man, not that Roger, the original jack-in-the-box, ever sat down. 'And what's more,' added Roger, 'he flayed us again in the return match at Southampton.' This time he only scored 124.

There was another significant occurrence in this season, for Barry, Hampshire and the West Indies. I refer to the county debut of Gordon Greenidge, against Glamorgan in the middle of August. He scored 65 and it seemed with that knock, the axis of world cricket shifted, slightly but perceptibly. A famous opening partnership, possibly the most famous in county cricket (I can only think of Hobbs and Hayward of Surrey before the First World War that might equal them) had been forged and the association, close but uneasy at times, was to have a profound effect on both players. At first, it was a classic exemplification of the sorcerer and his apprentice. Gordon, in years and experience, was patently the junior partner and for a year or two, that was a role he was prepared, eager even, to play. After all, who better to observe and to study from such close range than the premier opening batsman in the world?

And Gordon was eager to learn. A fierce, inner fire burned behind those hooded eyes, seldom verbalised but unmistakeably present. Like Barry, he had had a difficult upbringing. Born in Barbados, he had come to England when he was 14 and was immediately picked up by Hampshire as a raw but immensely promising hard-hitting batsman. To some of us who knew him as a young lad on the staff, it didn't seem that he was wholly at ease with himself. Brooding, temperamental and mercurial, the only way that he felt he could define himself as a person was to hit the ball harder, further and more frequently than anyone else. Many a time I had to trudge into the far distance to retrieve my ball when bowling to him in the nets. Sometimes, the ball would sail out of the ground into the disused car park of the derelict skating rink opposite, a prodigious distance. It was nothing personal; lots of others suffered the same fate. But it was obvious that he had a point to prove, if only to himself.

It is astonishing to reflect, and it struck more than a few people as astonishing at the time, that Gordon was very nearly let go in the early stage of his career. There was a perception that he was impulsive, intransigent and unwilling to learn; his talent was obvious but he couldn't restrain himself from trying to hit the leather off the ball, whatever the circumstances. His future was discussed at a cricket committee meeting and by a single vote, it was agreed to re-engage him. Can there ever have been a more momentous majority of one in the history of cricket committee meetings? But

Gordon was more shrewd and canny than he was given credit for. He did learn, he did curb his impetuosity and without ever for one moment suppressing his aggressive instincts, he transformed himself into one of the finest Test players of his generation. If there was a point to be made, I think we can safely assume that we all got it.

Did you help him in any way? 'Who, Gordon? No, not directly. I don't think he was one who readily sought advice. Not from me, anyway. But he looked and he learned and he developed rapidly.' *I know you weren't bosom buddies but you got along all right as partners, didn't you?* 'Oh yah. No problems at all. I think he respected me as a player even if he did have secret misgivings, I guess, about me being South African and all that. I don't know how much he was influenced later on by the guys in the West Indies dressing room but as pros, we made the partnership work. But he was definitely wary of me.'

Barry then went on to recount a story, which only goes to show how language and its misuse, no matter how innocent, can cause offence. 'When I was playing in Oz,' he said, 'we got in the habit of using the phrase, "Bullshit, boy!" whenever anybody said anything stupid or half-baked, which you must admit is not unknown in a dressing room. I think it was Ian Chappell who started it. It became a stock phrase, a cliché. Anyway, one day, I said it to Gordy when I disagreed with something or other that he said. No malice or insult intended at all. I was immediately pinned against the wall and yours truly was playing a few defensive shots, I can tell you, buddy!'

Gordon's temper was notorious. But to his credit, this too he learned to control. In short, he grew up and though he never managed, or perhaps bothered, to penetrate Barry's protective carapace of reserve and steeliness, he grew to trust and respect him as a player and an equal partner, both in the slips and out in the middle. The development of this relationship was a crucial component of the later success of the Hampshire team. There was no more playing second fiddle, content to count to six and then run like crazy, for Barry's opening partner. Except, that is, when Gordon was away on Test duty with the West Indies, and this, as we shall see, presented Barry with a troublesome and dispiriting complication to deal with.

On his return to England in 1971, following his remarkable exploits in Australia, Barry found that there had been a changing of the guard. Roy Marshall had been replaced as captain by Richard Gilliat. *Were you aware that anything was afoot towards the end of the previous season?* Barry shook his head. It had taken everyone by surprise including Marshall himself. It was an open secret at the club that the outgoing captain was not best pleased at the decision. He still had two years left of his contract and I guessed his long-faced presence in the side would not have been very helpful to the new captain. I sought the opinion of Gilliat himself. He agreed that it wasn't the ideal situation and that it took a lot of careful handling. 'Roy took it badly,' he said, 'but the decision to replace him wasn't mine. There was no palace revolution. The committee had got wind of the fact that Roy's captaincy was not meeting with universal approval in the dressing room and decided that it was time for a change. I'd captained the side whenever he was absent so it wasn't such a big deal, really.'

The problem had been that Roy Marshall, one of the most attacking and destructive batsmen of his era, was paradoxically the most defensive of captains. No thought of victory was ever entertained until the possibility of defeat had been eliminated. There were a lot of games that meandered along towards a tedious stalemate, which could have been enlivened by more aggressive bowling, more attacking field-placing and more challenging declarations. Furthermore, he never forgot or forgave perceived slights from, or disputes with, opposing captains; games with Kent were often like uncontested scrums in rugby because he and his opposite number, Colin Cowdrey, had had a disagreement so long in the past that no one could remember its origin. 'Roy was such a tremendous batsman, a great cricketer and so knowledgeable about the game,' said Gilliat, 'but he was no communicator, no captain. And he found the arrival of the young upstart from South Africa difficult to deal with, especially when he discovered that Barry was earning more than he – the captain! At first, the two of them, Barry and Roy, tried to out-do each other with the bat before Roy caved in to the inevitable and put himself down to number four.'

Strangely enough, Roy Marshall, once he was relieved of the burdens of captaincy, became much more approachable, friendly and helpful to us younger players on the staff. Hitherto, he had always been taciturn and remote. Once he took his place in the ranks again, he was expansive and gregarious and we all hung on to his every word of advice and encouragement. Cricket was like an extended family in those days, with all its attendant squabbles and alliances, its favourite uncles and its hated nephews.

As far as Barry was concerned, the change of captain suited him well enough though he took no part in any of the political infighting, such as it was, before or after. He saw the move as inevitable, a broom sweeping away the old and replacing it with the new, a necessary revitalisation of the team in preparation for its future success. Butch White was on his last legs, Bob Cottam soon sought pastures new, Derek Shackleton was about to retire and both Danny Livingstone and Roy Marshall would not stay long. 'Out with the old,' Barry put it, a little bluntly, if true. If ever the cliché 'a period of transition' were apposite then this season was it.

There not being a great deal to excite him in the County Championship and his dream of continuing with his Test career fading by the day, Barry found it difficult to motivate himself as much as he, together with his team-mates, would have wished. During the course of the season, he made 22 scores in excess of 50 but only one hundred, 141 not out against Kent out of a total of 211/2. 'Payback time!' Barry announced. *Why?* 'Because it was at Southampton, not one of those p***-poor out grounds in deepest Kent, where wickets were tailor made for Deadly.'

I looked up Underwood's figures for the match: 30-14-51-2 in the first innings. Economical but far from deadly. In the second innings, Barry had put him to the sword: 10-1-54-0. And that didn't happen very often to Derek Underwood. But this was a brief flourish. Barry had a point to make there. For the rest, his poor conversion rate from 50 to 100 told its own story. He got bored. Frequently, he would do the hard work by seeing off the opening attack and then he would try to take the bowling apart or he would try some extravagant shot or he would fall foul of a moment's lack of attention and he would get out. And then everybody else would struggle and curse him for having his feet up in the dressing room instead of battling it out with them in the middle.

You can see both sides of the discord. 'Come on,' Barry would say, 'I've broken the back of our opponents; now you get on and take charge for once. You can't expect me to do it for you all the time.' 'Ah yes,' would be the retort, 'but think how much easier it would have been if you had not been so careless. This is a team game, you know.' Barry might then have made a pointed reference to his season's aggregate of 1,938 runs at an average of 47.26 – match that, he might have said. Both sides were right of course, a fact more readily accepted by both parties as the years slip inexorably by. 'The number of times I threw it away!' Barry often sighed. 'Richo – he could have scored 120 first-class hundreds, instead of the 80 he did,' was Mike Taylor's lament, 'if only he had wanted to.' All of us who played with him, and many who played against him, were unanimous in this conviction – the sky was his limit. All that was lacking was the desire.

In 1972 there was little hint that the rebuilding of the Hampshire team was anything other than a work in progress. Just four wins in the County Championship was not the form of potential champions. The batting would look after itself; there was little doubt about that. Marshall was in his final year and enjoyed something of an Indian summer, finishing with over 1,000 runs for the season, but there was still plenty of firepower at the top of the order – Richards, Greenidge, Turner, Jesty, Gilliat and the ever-dependable Sainsbury. No, runs were never going to be a problem. But where were the wicket-takers? Who was going to bowl sides out?

In order to win matches, you have to take 20 wickets, leaving aside the occasional interesting declaration and run chase. You only have to surprise another team by winning that run chase, usually against the odds, for captains around the country to make a mental note never to be as generous to Hampshire as those idiots had been. *Did you at any stage believe that this team had the potential to upset the odds and go all the way?* Barry shook his head. Like everybody else, he thought the bowling cupboard was worryingly bare. So, for him, there was nothing else to do for his wages – considerably more now that he had put his foot down, but hardly a fortune – than knuckle down, do his best, strive to stave off the debilitating onset of *ennui* and enjoy the big moments when they came. The stimulus of fighting for a championship pennant was far from his mind.

What about the Aussies, who were in town that year? You must have wanted to put one over them, surely? He rubbed his nose. 'Er, yah,' he answered unconvincingly, 'but touring sides were using these games as practice for the Tests, so the intensity levels were not that high. Besides, there were no performance or win bonuses on offer.' Coming as he did from a less privileged background, Barry was ceaselessly concerned about his financial future, judging by the number of references he would make to the insecure nature of his calling. 'What was I going to do when I stopped playing? How was I going to live?' It clearly preyed on his mind.

As for his personal contributions to Hampshire's cause in the County Championship, his figures remained remarkably consistent: 1,424 runs at an average of 44.53. No one could say that he wasn't giving value for money, if that was what he was being judged by. But an anomaly begins to emerge when you compare this and other summers in England with what he was achieving in the winters (their summers, of course) for Natal in the Currie Cup. In the 1971/72 season, he averaged 77.78! 'I think what you must understand, Murt,' he tried to explain when challenged on this, 'was that I don't really believe I was ever cut out to play cricket seven days a week.'

That is manifestly true. There were only eight Currie Cup matches a season. He had a mere 15 innings that season, but he still amassed 1,089 runs to earn that average of 77.78. 'I just couldn't gee myself up when you seemed to go to the crease almost every day. You'd make a low score and sit down in the dressing room unbuckling your pads and you'd think, well, never mind, there's always another chance tomorrow. Not in the Currie Cup there wasn't! You might have weeks before your next serious innings.' The unspoken suggestion was that a match for Natal inevitably assumed a greater importance than one for Hampshire because of its infrequency.

There were days when he got out of the right side of the bed and his roomie had made the early morning cup of tea to his satisfaction. Against Essex at Chelmsford, when tasked to set up a declaration target, he and Richard Lewis put on an unbroken opening stand of 185, Barry's contribution being 104 not out. If Lewis was opening with him, where was his usual partner, Greenidge? Exhausted it seemed, asleep in the dressing room, following his explosive century in the first innings. As I have said, Hampshire's batting resources were the envy of other counties around the circuit.

Mike Taylor's sardonic observation that Barry was partial to his, Nottinghamshire's, bowling attack received more in the way of needless confirmation with another large score, 118, in a rain-ruined match. And how about this, taking into account what was to happen the following season?

Warwickshire won the championship that summer and in their match against their successors, they played like champions. Hampshire did not. They were bowled out for 79. Barry made a duck and the pitch was not so bad. In the second innings, he and Greenidge put on 128 for the first wicket before Gordon was out for 64. The days when Barry was able, indeed even encouraged, to hog the strike were at an end as the West Indian's career curved ever more steeply upwards. But Barry was not to be outdone. He went on to make 105. It was not enough to save his side however from a heavy defeat by five wickets. Worse still, despite a healthy lead of 138 runs in the first innings against Kent at Folkestone later that summer, largely down to Barry's 101, Hampshire still contrived to lose the match by five wickets. And no Underwood; he was away on international duty for his country. Hampshire potential champions in the making? It hardly seemed so.

Yet there were hints. It was John Holder's final season for Hampshire and his first-class career – not that he had an inkling of these two unpalatable facts – so there is a certain irony that he chose the match against Northamptonshire, a team that was going to feature large in Hampshire's success the following season, to remind me of Barry's genius and the potential flowering of a championship-winning side. 'Probably the most astonishing innings I saw Barry play was against Northamptonshire at Northampton late on in May on a raging "bunsen",' he told me, 'and in that side were two Test spinners in Bishan Bedi and Mushtaq Mohammed.' In the fourth innings (Barry had already top scored with 77 in his side's first), Hampshire had been set 228 to win, a near impossible task on that wicket. 'Barry told us that the only way to play the spinners was not to let the ball land,' said Holder. Now, where have I heard that before? 'He then proceeded to do just that, massacring the Northants attack.' Would 'massacring' be perhaps too robust a term? It seems not. 'Watching him run down the pitch to the spinners to catch the ball on the full or get back deep in the crease to smash it off the back foot had to be seen to be believed. It seemed he was able to score runs wherever he wanted.' Hampshire won by five wickets.

There was always the stimulus of the one-day games, with their larger crowds, to stir the blood. Barry played three marvellous, breathtaking innings in the limited overs format, one in the Gillette Cup and two in the John Player League. His 129 against Lancashire was a magnificent innings, according to those who witnessed it, either at Dean Park or on the television, but it was in a losing cause.

Was that one of your best? 'It was good, yes, but not particularly great.' Many people remember it for the famous photo of Barry steering the ball delicately square on the off side. What is remarkable about the shot is that the wicketkeeper, Farokh Engineer, is shaping to take the ball down the leg side. Clearly the bowler, David Hughes, a left-arm spinner, is firing it in at, or just outside, leg stump, a favoured tactic at the time. Today, the umpires are much more strict about negative bowling outside leg but then it was considered a legitimate ploy to restrict the areas of the field where the batsman could hit the ball. Barry's riposte was to step outside leg stump and hit the ball into the vacant gaps on the off side.

Sounds easy but it is not. It demands nimble footwork, a quick eye, perfect timing – and nerve. Barry was by nature deficient in none of these attributes. He was a trailblazer in improvisation, much like Ranjitsinhji at the turn of the century was largely attributed to have invented – or, at the very least, popularised – the leg glance. Hitherto, batsmen had scored their runs primarily on the off side. BB, as opposed to BC, (Before Barry, that is), batsmen tended not to play 'inside out'. Barry showed to everyone that it could be done.

The home dressing room at Northlands Road in Southampton was an unremarkable spot, more like a boat shed or a wooden outbuilding, just about fit for purpose you could say, though a little cramped and totally lacking in any of the routine amenities and accessories that any modern changing area would boast. The only thing going for it was its raised location with a balcony reached only by a flight of wooden steps, according a certain amount of privacy and an uninterrupted view of the play, albeit from over slog man's corner. Nevertheless, it held a special place in the players' affection; it was, after all, 'home', so much so that family squabbles would break out over the bragging rights to the table, which could artfully be converted to a comfortable spot for a snooze. It could just about accommodate 12 players with their 'coffins', each spilling out the abundant detritus of any cricketer's equipment and clothing but it was a tight squeeze – you had to fight for your pegs.

There was a vague air of the *sanctum sanctorum* about it, hugely ironic really when you consider it was populated by a group of individuals not ordinarily distinguished by their godly behaviour, and interlopers and uninvited guests were given short shrift. Even uncapped players were expected to knock before entering, a minor irritation to Second XI players who would attempt to perfect the tricky manoeuvre of simultaneously rapping the door with their knuckle with turning the door handle and pushing inwards, sometimes resulting in painful smacks to the forehead when the door was jammed.

However, for an all too brief period during pre-season practice, egalitarianism prevailed. My first season as a full-time professional at the club was 1973 and as I looked around the dressing room during a reviving tea break, 20 of us crammed into that poky space, the first team pretty well picked itself, it seemed to me. Many faces were familiar – I had been around the club for four years previously as a part-timer – though two were unknown to me. Mike Taylor was a surprise and, as subsequent events proved, an invaluable transfer from Nottinghamshire. The other one was an unfamiliar face from Antigua, a fast bowler with the unlikely name of Anderson Montgomery Everton Roberts. His face was to become swiftly better known to all of us, mostly from 22 yards away in the nets. He was an overseas signing and as such not available for county duty until his season's qualification period had been served. 'That is, if he's good enough,' muttered a team-mate in my ear in what must rank as one of the worst predictions of future success since Churchill's teacher wrote in his school report, 'He has no ambition.'

Richards and Greenidge to open, followed by Turner, Jesty and Gilliat, the captain. That was the batting sorted out. Bolstering the middle order would be the evergreen Sainsbury, a left-arm slow bowler and obdurate bat, the aforesaid Taylor, then the wicketkeeper, Stephenson, another left-armer O'Sullivan, the swing bowler Herman and…well, who? What a pity I'm not a fast bowler, I mused, because we are certainly short of someone to take the new ball with Bob Herman. And waiting in the wings was Richard Lewis, a batsman of great, if as yet unfulfilled, talent and very useful reserves such as John Rice, Larry Worrell and Nigel Cowley.

It was a good side, there could be no doubt about that. But good enough to challenge for the championship pennant? The odds offered at the start of the season for Hampshire to win the title were 66/1, and that seemed to tell you all you needed to know about pre-season optimism. 'Jeez, I wish I'd had a little dart with those odds,' said Barry wistfully, a full 40 years since the cashier in the local bookies slammed shut his grille and announced that all bets were now off.

When did you begin to sniff a chance that you might win it? 'Not until August was it ever really on,' Barry replied, 'and even then we thought it was more of a fluke than anything else.' The problem, he believed, and he was not alone in this, was that there was no strike bowler. Herman and Jesty swung the ball effectively and bowled a tight line. Taylor bowled straight and nibbled it around when the conditions suited. And Sainsbury could always be relied upon to tie up one end. Furthermore, it was a dry August, the pitches took spin and the New Zealander, David O'Sullivan, would come into his own to bowl sides out with his fiercely spun left-armers. But in the meantime? 'And then, charging over the brow of the hill,' Barry announced, the amusement in his voice hard to conceal, 'came the Pink Panther!'

The Pink Panther was our affectionate nickname for Tom Mottram, possibly the most unlikely opening bowler in the County Championship's history and a legend at the club. Although it has to be stressed that he was no legend at the start of the 1973 season. In fact he was hardly known. As he walked through the gates of the county ground in Southampton, his kit bag – no one could ever describe it as a bona fide cricket coffin – spilling out creased and untidy pieces of white clothing, he could easily have been mistaken, with his tall, gangling figure, plodding gait and patrician air, for the club doctor or accountant or legal advisor or architect (which, in fact, he was). But a fast bowler to send shivers of fear down opposing team's spines? Well, quite frankly, no.

However, you underestimated him at your peril – and many did. I had played with him in university cricket and I knew he could bowl. And what's more, he had a bottomless pit of unshakeable confidence in his abilities, something that others thought of as overweening arrogance but I actually admired. He delivered the ball at a pace slightly above medium, from the full extent of his height, and he moved the ball a little way, but enough, off the seam. He was the missing link, our own Pink Panther, and we would delight in humming those famous opening bars of Henry Mancini's theme tune whenever Tom unexpectedly, but frequently, took a wicket.

'I'm not sure that Barry rated Tom all that highly,' Richard Gilliat told me, with a little smile. 'He'd come up to me and say, "Take him off, captain," and I'd have to explain to him that there's more than one way to skin a cat. Sometimes you need to bore a batsman out, which went against Barry's natural attacking instincts. And then Motters would take a wicket and Barry would throw up his hands in mock horror.'

This happened on 57 occasions, I reminded Barry, in case his memory had failed him. He laughed. 'The Pink Panther! How did he do it?' Well, I have my own theory. Tom, an intelligent man with an analytical brain, looked upon his year as a professional cricketer (he was only ever going to play full-time for one season; his architect career could only be put on hold for that short period) as an academic exercise in maximising potential, using all methods, physical and psychological, to prove his point. He was a good bowler, he knew that, if few others did, and he believed all batsmen, even the best, had weaknesses which could be exploited. So he studied the opposition, he hatched his plans, he marked out his run and he executed his stratagems with discipline and self-belief. And he stayed fit, always a prerequisite for a bowler.

Gilliat explained his success thus, 'I think Tom got so many wickets for two reasons. First, batsmen did not "rate" him and thus took undue risks. And secondly and more importantly, I don't think Barry took into account the fact that Tom, on account of his height, bowled with a different trajectory to others and the bounce that he obtained, allied to his accuracy, got him a lot of wickets.' As for his fielding… that was for others to take in hand. He believed firmly in the old-fashioned concept that fast bowlers wore heavy-duty boots for a purpose, and it wasn't to run after a ball. He never possessed a bat. 'I borrowed one of Trevor Jesty's,' he said, 'and never gave it back!' Of course, he would probably have been found out had he stayed for any length of time within the game. If he analysed opposing batsmen, you can take it as read that opposing batsmen would have wasted little time in analysing him. As it transpired, however, he had his '15 minutes of fame', as Andy Warhol once memorably put it, and then largely disappeared from the scene, content to design and create buildings 'at the cutting edge of my profession', he told me. Of course, Tom, what else? He remains a cult figure at the club, if elusive – rather like his bowling, I always thought.

Barry always felt that there were two seasons in an English summer, the first wet and cold and usually seamer-friendly and the second when the sun came out, the wickets hardened up and the spinners came more into their own. It goes without saying which time of the year he preferred but as we know, he could score runs on any surface, providing the challenge was there and his appetite was not dull. Usually, it has to be said, he took a while to get going in the County Championship; there were times when you got the impression, especially watching him stand at slip with his hands in his pockets – he still caught the nicks, though – that it was just too damn cold for him to perk up. He shared a first-wicket partnership of 135 – the first of six over 100 that summer – with Greenidge in the first match against Leicestershire and watched from the dressing room with increasing admiration as his young apprentice amassed 196 not out to help secure a win against Yorkshire a week later. 'Gordy had not yet been selected for the West Indies,' Barry said, 'and by now he had worked out that people sat up and took notice when you made big scores, big hundreds, I mean.'

Up until this point, notwithstanding his undoubted talent, he had always been accused of being too aggressive, too impatient, too eager to hit the leather off the ball. Was this fair? 'Not really. He was a strokeplayer. We both were. And if you look to attack, sometimes you will choose the wrong ball. Or the wrong shot. I did it often enough. But it is true that he became a bit more selective, content to wait for the right ball to open those huge shoulders of his.' My impression was that Gordon had muscles where the rest of us only dreamed; no wonder he spent so long on the masseur's table.

Talking of injuries reminded me that one to Barry's back forced him to miss the match against Gloucestershire – and no, it was not Wimbledon time, it was far too early for that – which enabled me to make my first-class debut, although it was not an auspicious beginning, nought and two. We were definitely outplayed but avoided defeat – just – and the captain was in a hurry to get Barry back in the side. No wonder. On his return, Barry topped his highest score in England with an awesome innings of 240, out of a total of 396/7 declared, condemning Warwickshire, the current champions forget not, to a thumping seven-wicket defeat.

Did you believe, then? 'Believe? That I could bat?' *Ha ha. No. That you were on the glory trail?* 'Nah. It was only the sixth game of the season. And the season in England, as you know Murt, is a long one.' *I don't know the Courtaulds Ground in Coventry. Not one of cricket's high spots, was it?* 'Like many of those old company grounds, it was a cut above some of the club grounds where we played. The facilities were all right and the wicket was a good one.' Incidentally, Richard Gilliat is not wholly in agreement with him over the magnitude of this win. 'That 240 was quite simply a great innings,' he said, 'and it certainly set us on our way. Possibly it was our best performance of the season, to beat the champions so comprehensively. We were now top of the

The young Barry Richards. I am not alone in thinking that the toothy schoolboy with the mop of curly hair resembles a putative US president – John Kennedy. (BAR personal collection)

Natal Schools 1962. Three future Test cricketers here. Mike Procter is on the far right, top row. Barry is seated, second from left. On his left is the captain, Lee Irvine. In fact, most of this team went on to play first-class cricket. "It was a helluva side," said Irvine. Do regard Barry's immaculately creased flannels and his sparklingly white boots. Grandpa Percy would have nodded his head in approval. (Lee Irvine personal collection)

Barry Richards on the sweep for Hampshire against Middlesex at Lord's in 1968. John Murray is the wicketkeeper and Peter Parfitt is at slip. Barry's unusually high grip on the bat handle can be clearly seen here. "Bats were much thinner then and not so springy," he explained, "so I needed a longer pendulum to get some leverage on the ball." He promised he would score 2,000 runs in this, his first season in English cricket. And he did.

The South African XI at Kingsmead, Durban for the second Test against Australia in 1970. Top l-r: Mike Procter, Dennis Gamsy, Barry Richards, John Traicos, Lee Irvine, Pat Trimborn. Seated l-r: Tiger Lance, Graeme Pollock, Eddie Barlow, Bob Williams (manager), Ali Bacher (capt), Trevor Goddard, Peter Pollock. This was the scene of Barry's maiden Test hundred. Perhaps the description of him as the golden boy of South African cricket was not that far wrong – just look at the bright halo illuminating his hair! (John Traicos personal collection)

Barry square cuts during his innings of 140 v Australia at Kingsmead, Durban in 1970. The Springbok emblem is clearly visible on his cap. Where is it now? Sadly, Barry has no idea.
(BAR personal collection)

The Australian captain, Bill Lawry, congratulates Barry on completing his century at Kingsmead. Barry had been denied reaching his hundred before lunch on the first day of the second Test by some outrageous time wasting by Lawry, who seemed to be inordinately concerned by the state of his bootlaces. No matter. Three figures were reached shortly after the break. (George Byron personal collection)

The sorcerer and his apprentice. Barry Richards and Graeme Pollock in discussion after their famous partnership of 103 in 60 minutes' play after lunch on the first day of the second Test against Australia at Kingsmead in 1970. It was immediately dubbed The Golden Hour by the press and has gone down in South African folklore. Barry scored 140; Pollock went on to score 274. "I don't think this country has ever again seen batting like we saw that day," said Ali Bacher, their captain.
(George Byron personal collection)

s.a. SPORTS illustrated

BARRY RICHARDS – MAN WITH THE GOLDEN FUTURE

FEBRUARY 1970 20 Cents

Barry Richards – The Man with a Golden Future. The year is 1970 and *Sports Illustrated* could be forgiven for their enthusiastic headline. In fact, Barry's golden future in Test cricket had just one month to run. (George Byron personal collection)

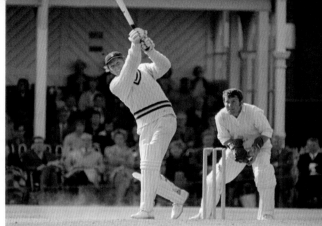

Barry hooks Alan Connolly of Australia during his innings of 126 at Port Elizabeth in the fourth Test of the 1970 series. It was to be his final innings in Test cricket. He had played four matches and scored 508 runs at an average of 72.57. "The bona fide great who never was," Telford Vice poignantly observed.

Barry plays a classical, lofted on drive, a shot of majesty, power and elegance, for Hampshire against Glamorgan at Northlands Road, Southampton, in 1970. "That went for six," he informed me. (Patrick Eagar)

Barry batting for The Rest of the World v England at Lord's in June 1970. "I played all right," said Barry of his performances during the five match series, "but I never hit the heights." Surprisingly true during this year of all years, his annus mirabilis. That said, do admire the balletic poise and perfect balance as he hits the ball, perched on tiptoe, away on the off side.

Hampshire v Northamptonshire at Northlands Road in August 1973. This was taken during Barry's unforgettable tussle with Bishan Bedi, the world's premier batsman taking on the world's best slow left-armer. Whoever won the duel won the match. And whoever won the match won the championship. The stakes were that high. This drive off the back foot is straight out of the text-book, with the top hand in control, the left elbow high, the head perfectly aligned, heels off the ground to stand tall and the bottom hand following through to add power. The technique had been perfected after endless hours in the nets as a young boy. (Patrick Eagar)

Hampshire County Champions 1973. Taken at their home ground at Northlands Road, Southampton. Top l-r: Richard Lewis, David O'Sullivan, Mike Taylor, Tom Mottram, Bob Herman, Gordon Greenidge, the author, Trevor Jesty. Seated l-r: David Turner, Peter Sainsbury, Richard Gilliat (capt), Barry Richards, Bob Stephenson. (Patrick Eagar)

Gordon Greenidge and Barry Richards open the batting for Hampshire at Northlands Road in 1973. Has there ever been a better opening partnership in the history of county cricket? (Patrick Eagar)

Barry clips the ball away on the leg side batting for Natal against Eastern Province in the Currie Cup at St George's Park in Port Elizabeth, March 1974. He scored 106 but bad weather prevented Natal from winning the match. However they secured sufficient bonus points to allow them to claim the Currie Cup that season. Note the flimsy protective equipment worn in those days: the lightweight pads, thin thigh pad on one leg, insubstantial gloves, no arm guard, no chest protector….and no helmet! Not that he would have needed one when I bowled to him. (George Byron personal collection)

A faultless stroke by Barry during his innings of 189 at a deserted Lord's in April 1974. We all thought that he had put on a bit of weight over the winter. In fact, he had donned every sweater that he could lay his hands on, it was that cold. It didn't stop him however from putting a strong MCC attack to the sword. This innings prompted the famous analogy drawn by Tony Lewis, in which he compared Barry to Yehudi Menuhin reeling off a perfect piece of Bach in front of an empty Albert Hall. In my eyes, it was simply the greatest exhibition of batsmanship I have ever witnessed. (Patrick Eagar)

Currie Cup action. Natal v Transvaal. Barry is batting, Lee Irvine is behind the stumps and Donald Mackay-Coghill is fielding (rather deep!) at backward short leg. Barry here looks a little cramped as he plays the shot but he is still in control and on top of the ball. His head remains balanced and he has rolled his wrists at the moment of impact to keep the ball down. Incidentally, I never thought the beard suited him. (Lee Irvine personal collection)

Old friends reunited. Barry meets up with Greg Chappell before the start of the Hampshire v Australia match in 1975. The warmth of their handshake bore testimony to the regard in which each held the other. It is a friendship that remains close to this day. (Patrick Eagar)

Hampshire v Lancashire in the Gillette Cup at Bournemouth in August 1972. In many ways, this can be regarded as the most famous photo of Barry at the crease. He scored 129 that day and displayed the genius – and there is no other word for it – for which his batting was becoming renowned. The Lancashire spinners, Jack Simmonds and David Hughes, were firing the ball down the leg side, protected by a packed leg side field. The Lancashire spinners were firing the ball down the leg side – look how far across to leg the wicket keeper, Farokh Engineer, has gone – protected by a packed leg side field. Yet Barry has stepped away to leg and played a cover drive! (Patrick Eagar)

Hampshire v Australia at Northlands Road in 1975. Barry relished the opportunity of playing against the tourists, many of whom were his friends. He certainly relished this powerful stroke off the back foot during his innings of 96. Max Walker is at short leg. (The ball's over there, Max!) (Patrick Eagar)

Hampshire v Middlesex in the Sunday League at Lord's in June 1977. Ian Gould is the wicketkeeper. Barry scored 102 out of his side's total of 178. It was another of those masterful innings that we all crowded onto the small dressing room balcony to watch. John Emburey was the luckless bowler, I believe. (Patrick Eagar)

There is so much to admire in this photo of Patrick Eagar's. The light is perfect, the late afternoon sun at Northlands Road casting an almost ethereal glow on Barry's sweater and the stumps. The stroke too is a thing of beauty – balanced, elegant, orthodox and perfectly timed. And the face is a picture of fierce concentration. Perfection takes hard work. (Patrick Eagar)

Mike Procter and Barry Richards, schoolboy friends, in opposition. It was a Benson and Hedges semi-final in 1977 at Northlands Road between Hampshire and Gloucestershire. Yes, that match! Procter won it for Gloucestershire practically single-handed, taking 6-13, including a game changing hat-trick. I was not one of his hat-trick victims, though perhaps I should have been. I was otherwise engaged in the lavatory. And we never did get to a Lord's final. (Patrick Eagar)

Don Bradman's Dream Team (digitally created). Top l-r: Ray Lindwall, Barry Richards, Dennis Lillee, Bill O'Reilly, Don Tallon. Seated l-r: Clarrie Grimmett, Alec Bedser, Sachin Tendulkar, Don Bradman (capt), Garry Sobers, Arthur Morris, Wally Hammond. Bradman described Barry as "the world's greatest ever right-handed opener." When the South African tour to Australia in 1971 was finally called off and South Africa's isolation from international competition was confirmed for another 22 years, Bradman said that it was the saddest day of his life because "it meant the end of Barry Richards' Test career."

Nobody ever claimed that the 1970s was a halcyon era of fashion. For all that, this delightfully informal shot of Barry shows him in a rare relaxed mood in the midst of the hectic schedule of a professional cricketer, one with which he became increasingly disenchanted. (George Byron personal collection)

World Series Cricket. WSC World XI v WSC Australia in Perth 1978. Barry scored 208. Here is one of four sixes he hit that day in an exhibition of strokeplay that left everyone, including wicketkeeper Rodney Marsh, open mouthed in admiration. WSC had given Barry a belated chance in his career to test himself in the international arena again. But by now, he was 34, not 24. "My eyes had gone," he later admitted, "so it wasn't the carefree approach of days gone by. I had to fashion my innings." He wanted to prove to himself, not the rest of the world, that he could still do it. And he did, with skill, courage and determination. He topped the averages in Supertests of all the teams. "Believe it or not," he told me, "if they had counted those Supertests as Test matches, I would have played enough matches to be included in the official list and my average would have gone up from 72 to 79!" Second only to the incomparable Bradman. Is there any more that needs to be said? (Patrick Eagar)

The two Richards, Barry and Viv. Who was the greater batsman? The jury's still out on that one. Here they are in the same team for once, the World XI in Kerry Packer's World Series Cricket. Barry looks as if he has had some attention given to his finger by those West Indian fast bowlers in the nets. (BAR personal collection)

The two legends of South African cricket, Graeme Pollock and Barry Richards, in The Kingsmead Mynahs Room inside the stadium in Durban. I expect both could have made runs with those miniature bats too.

Barry as TV commentator. The occasion is the ICC World Cup in April 2007, South Africa v England at Bridgetown, Barbados. Graeme Smith, the SA captain, is tossing the coin and his England opposite number, Michael Vaughan, clearly trusts him because he is not watching. Probably, he realises that the match referee, Ranjan Madugalle, will ensure that no monkey business takes place. (Getty)

Happier times. Barry is flanked by his two sons, Mark on the left and Steve on the right. Mark's suicide in 2009 devastated the family. Barry remains deeply affected. "You just don't get over something like that," he told me. "The nightmares have diminished but I still get sleepless nights." (BAR personal collection)

Gary Player introduces Barry to Nelson Mandela on the occasion of the Gary Player Golf Tournament to raise money for Mandela's children's charity. Like all South Africans, and indeed most people on the planet, Barry greatly admired his nation's father figure. (BAR personal collection)

Barry with his partner Ingrid Diesel. "You know, Murt," he said to me, "I've always punched above my weight with women." This delightful photo seems to underline that very fact. Barry reckons Ingrid saved him "from a very dark place" following the death of his son. For that, and her many other qualities, he remains deeply grateful. (BAR personal collection)

championship and if nobody thought we'd stay there, it certainly gave us confidence that we could beat anyone.'

For another opinion of Barry's innings, I sought the views of Mike Taylor. 'Every ball they bowled to him was either a half-volley or a long hop,' he chuckled, tickled pink at the way opponents have been put to flight. What he meant of course was that every ball the champions bowled to Barry was made to *seem* a half-volley or a long hop by the genius of his batting. Mostly, hard-bitten old pros such as Taylor mete out praise grudgingly, even within their own dressing room, let alone the opposition's, so when the respect is unequivocal, you can be sure something special is going on. 'He made them look very ordinary,' Taylor added, for good measure.

Barry now had the bit between his teeth and Surrey were the next to suffer. He and Greenidge put on 207 for the first wicket before Gordon fell for 99 and Barry went on to score 116. 'It wasn't an easy track,' he recalled. 'One end bounced more than the other.' There are two interesting points to be made here. The first is a little known fact, except to the protagonist of course, who delights to this day, if a trifle ironically, in his footnote of cricketing fame. The scorecard reads: B.A. Richards c Long b Jackman 116. 'Yes it's true,' grins Robin Jackman, 'I am credited with having dismissed Barry Richards more times than anyone else in his career.' The pause is always perfectly timed. 'But listen to the facts. Jackman v Richards: 25 matches, 41 innings, three not outs, 2,279 runs, average 59.97, with eight hundreds, nine fifties and a highest score of 197. The stats speak for themselves, don't you think?'

Barry is also amused by the piece of information. 'Well, we did play against each other a lot, both in England and South Africa. One of the game's great triers, Jackers, roared in all day and gave it 100 per cent every time – and a genial bloke, too. We always got on well. Couldn't say that about all the Surrey boys. Oh, apart from Geoff Howarth – he was a good friend.'

The other topic that this encounter with the Brown Caps, as the Surrey team were, not always affectionately, termed was the significance of the Richards–Greenidge axis at the top of the order. Not everyone was fully convinced that it was a sensible use of precious resources, rather like putting all your eggs in one basket. In another of my conversations with Ray Illingworth on the balcony of the dressing room at Grace Road, Leicestershire, he postulated firmly and confidently that 'I would never open with those two!' *Why not, Raymond?* 'Because they try and out-do each other. I'd have one of them coming in at number four.' *Which one?* 'Whichever one I bluidy told!'

Many years later, I put this point of view to Richard Gilliat. 'No, no,' he answered with rare passion, 'They were magnificent together. Look how many opening stands of over a hundred we had that season.' Six, in case you've forgotten. 'But even more importantly, they got those runs *quickly*. They wrested the initiative away from the opposition attack from the word go. This had two benefits. One, it was a damn sight easier for the rest of us coming in later. And two, because we scored our runs so quickly, that gave us longer to bowl sides out. Which we did.' *Quod erat demonstrandum,* I should say.

But how did they bat together? I mean were they genuine partners or were they really trying to out-muscle each other? 'There was great respect between them,' Gilliat replied, 'but little love. I think Barry inspired Gordon to become a better player. He watched him and learnt from him and of course went on to become the world-class player he did. There was never any animosity between them but their relationship was purely professional. From our point of view, of course, their partnerships were like gold dust.' The sad thing for Barry was that he could see an emerging Gordon Greenidge at the other end getting the headlines, getting picked for the West Indies and then getting the opportunity of parading his skills on the grand stage. Would you agree? Gilliat nodded sympathetically. 'I think Barry missed Test cricket,' he said in his understated way.

It may not have been Test cricket but there was a championship to be won. Having said that, no sooner had Hampshire hit the top spot than a collective wobble seemed to go through the team. The loss of form, loss of confidence, loss of nerve, call it what you will, proved temporary; winning ways were re-established at Southport against Lancashire after a fallow spell of six consecutive draws. At least these draws, one or two achieved by the skin of the teeth, meant that no one team was able to take advantage and surge ahead. By late July, Hampshire were still in the hunt. What was needed was a clear, unequivocal and compelling statement of intent and this was provided in the most emphatic manner imaginable. Illingworth is a fine strategist and tactician, Gilliat might well have said (to himself, of course, being the polite and well-bred Carthusian that he was), but this is why I put the two finest strokemakers in the world together at the top of the order.

Richards and Greenidge put on exactly 200 together and Lancashire reeled. Barry was out for 128 and Gordon for 153. Interestingly, Barry's hundred came in only 169 minutes. Gordon's took a little longer, 240 minutes. He clearly had one eye on a possible (more and more probable, it seemed, as each day passed) place in the West Indies side. Both he and Barry passed 1,000 runs for the season in this match, and we were not yet in August. It remained only for Jesty, 5-24, to bowl out Lancashire for 100 to secure victory by an innings and 74 runs and send Hampshire back to the top of the table. If nobody had taken them seriously up until this point – and that included Barry – they did now.

Enter, stage left, at a crucial point in the season, Hampshire's unlikely man of the hour, Palmerston North's finest ('Where's Palmerston South?' we demanded to know; his answer was unprintable), David O'Sullivan, our left-arm spinner from New Zealand. Peter Sainsbury always took issue with this description as he was a left-armer and he did bowl slow but even his supporters, of whom there were many, admitted that it was not often he got it off the straight and narrow. 'Sains!' laughed Barry, 'Ach, he never spun a ball in his life!' That said, he and everybody else in that team had cause often enough to give thanks to Sainsbury for his vital, usually obdurate, performances with bat and ball. Sully, however, was a completely different kettle of fish.

No one is quite sure how Sully came to Hampshire's notice. He had already made his mark in the domestic first-class game in his native New Zealand but had come over to England to try his luck, ending up playing club cricket for Finchley in north London. Knowing Sully and his sense of direction, it seemed quite possible that he had just got lost and strolled through the gates of Northlands Road and, realising that it was a cricket ground, he thought he might just as well ask someone for a game. Relaxed, imperturbable, laconic, humorous, slapdash, chaotic, a bit of a roughneck but with a heart of gold, he soon became a popular figure within the dressing room.

Of course, he would not have gained everybody's high regard had he not been a more than useful cricketer. He was an attacking left-arm spinner, who gave the ball a real rip at times and he proved to be the perfect foil for the more defensively minded Sainsbury at the other end. Sully also had a wickedly deceptive arm ball, delivered at such a pace that many a batsman had barely brought his bat down before the stumps were shattered. This delivery, a match-winner, or probably more accurately a match-turner, caused a few mutterings that swelled into veiled accusations, followed by dark insinuations that eventually burst out into a full-blown controversy. Did he throw it? His quicker ball became a *cause celebre* and in the end, sadly for all of us and distressingly for him, it probably did for him and curtailed his career.

I vividly remember one afternoon during a Second XI match at Southampton a crew of technicians arriving from Lord's to film him in an attempt to prove one way or the other whether he 'chucked' it. The banter, as you can imagine, was merciless, though never unkindly meant. But humour can sometimes puncture the seriousness of the situation and offer solace of a kind. 'Smile, Sully, you're on camera.' 'Sully – your trousers are undone.' 'Have you discussed a fee yet, Sully?' 'This one's for the missus back home, Sully.' These were some of the more repeatable comments that were flying about. And, as he came in to bowl, 'Lights. Camera. Action!' – the final command barked at the very moment of delivery. How the poor batsman, who hadn't a clue what was going on, kept his composure, I shall never know. How Sully kept his composure, none of us knew. For he did; he was very cool, carried on as if it was his grandmother whirring at the camera for the folks back home, restricting himself only to a few, choice, Antipodean oaths. It passed nobody's notice that he bowled no arm balls that afternoon.

It seemed a natural fit, Barry and Sully, the two 'colonials' if I can call them that – which we did – and sure enough they became good friends. In fact, they got on like a house on fire. That metaphor is not at all far-fetched; they were housemates, neither had much culinary experience or expertise and both were notoriously slapdash in front of a stove. Thankfully for their neighbours where they lived, both were on the road a great deal and few barbecues were lit that summer. 'A braai – in England!' cried Barry, horrified. 'You must be joking, pal!' The lighting of fires was saved for the cricket grounds of England as Hampshire cut a swathe through the counties in that hot, dry August of 1973. 'Once the wickets became parched,' said Barry, 'we needed another spinner to bowl sides out. Cue Sully!'

Yes indeed. It was David O'Sullivan's moment and he seized it eagerly. When he was selected to play against Essex at Portsmouth at the beginning of August, his total of wickets was a meagre ten at 35 each but he finished the season with 47 wickets at 21.10. It was a remarkable transformation and though it cannot be said that he won the championship single-handedly – it was much more of a team effort than that – Sully's intervention was crucial. No one was to begrudge his brief days in the sun – this was to be his final month at the club – for there was no more popular member of the side. Barry was particularly sorry to see him go for he believed that, at last, he had found a true companion in arms, someone who shared his philosophy – on the game and on life.

It is not without resonance in his cricket career that Barry's personal contentment was often bound up with what was happening on the field of play. The prospect of Test cricket was slowly disappearing over the horizon. That was a vexation constantly at the back of his mind, especially when the dailies splashed Gordon's name across the back pages the following day. Of course they would. Gordon was an up and coming young star and it was obvious to all and sundry that international stardom was beckoning. Barry was not up and coming. His days on the grand stage were done. 'Jeez!' he exclaimed in a rare moment when he let his guard down. 'I was 28, at the top of my game, my physical and mental peak. You can understand how frustrating it was not to be playing for your country in front of packed stands at Lord's, Trent Bridge, Old Trafford, the Oval, not to mention Sydney, Adelaide, Culcutta, Bombay, Bridgetown, Sabina Park and the grounds back home.'

Not that he begrudged for one moment the swelling reputation of his young West Indian partner; it was just difficult for him not to feel twinges of envy. After all, no matter how good, possibly great, a player Gordon was to become, he was better. And he would never be able to prove it. I wonder how many Test matches between South Africa and West Indies were played at this time in cricket lovers' dreams, with Gordon facing up to Vince van der Bijl and Clive Rice at a febrile Kensington Oval in Barbados or Barry taking on Andy Roberts and Michael Holding in front of his home crowd at Kingsmead. Who won? We shall never know. I can only speak for myself but I always frustratingly woke up before the game had finished. Whether Barry ever allowed his imagination full rein like this, he is not saying. He bit his lip, said nothing and suffered in silence.

But it wasn't all gloom and doom. When he first arrived, as a wide-eyed *ingénue*, promising, a little naively, 2,000 runs for the season, he was met with suspicion and no little resentment by the senior players, a barrier that was never completely dismantled in spite of the grudging respect he was accorded for fulfilling his promise and scoring those 2,000 runs – and many more in subsequent seasons. But all of those senior players, save Sainsbury, had now gone, there was a new captain and he was surrounded by a younger generation of team-mates who accorded him unqualified respect – how could we not? – among whom he felt more at home and more socially at ease. And he had his co-driver, David O'Sullivan, alongside him. 'Sully was not the best driver,' Barry said, laughing at the memory. 'I once lent him my car. He had to pick it up from the ground at Northlands Road. Later, he rang me. 'Nose,' he said, 'I've got good news and bad news for you.' I sighed. 'Okay, give me the bad news.' 'Your car's a write-off.' I sighed more deeply. 'And the good news?' 'Don't worry, Master – you can get another one!' He hadn't even got it on to the road! He'd crashed it coming out of the entrance to the ground.'

Stories of Sully abound, most of them unrepeatable. I think Barry got on with him so well because they shared a streak of rebelliousness, one that Barry only occasionally revealed, such as refusing to wear a tie at official functions, but one to which Sully had no qualms about giving full rein. What continually surprised Barry, and certainly amazed us all, giggling at his latest escapade, was that Sully always seemed to get away with it. Perhaps it was his aptitude for feigning innocence or his ability to keep a straight face or his essential humanity underpinning it all but he usually emerged unscathed from his scrapes. If not, he would simply pick himself up, dust himself down and carry on as if nothing had happened.

On one occasion, in the middle of an over, he doubled up and was copiously sick on the side of the pitch. The game happened to be televised and the camera zoomed in close to discover the cause of the break in play. We all knew the real cause and it had nothing to do with what he had eaten for lunch. When the scene was revealed in all its glorious technicolour on the screens of the watching British public, John Arlott, with commendable *sang froid*, offered this commentary to the viewers, 'Oh dear, it seems that O'Sullivan is having a bilious attack.' The camera diplomatically panned away, Sully kicked a load of dirt to cover the offending evidence, took hold of the ball and resumed his over. He bowled well. Nothing was said. The game was won and no action was taken.

Sometimes, Richard Gilliat did not get the credit he deserved for the tactful but effective way he handled his troops. Later, Sully remained unperturbed, in spite of our best efforts to goad him. 'Whaddya on about? I got him out, didn't I?' Exactly. Mavericks are tolerated so long as they bring home the bacon. And that glorious August in 1973, Sully brought home the entire pig. Barry admired him for his inspirational bowling and held him dear for his uncomplicated temperament and his wry sense of humour. Sometimes, Barry felt that the English could be a little too insular, cautious, conservative, too much bound by tradition that often found its expression in the defensive mindset of the average county player. 'It's as if the cork's in too tight,' he once said. Sully would have put it in another way altogether.

I make no apology for emphasising the relationship between the two because it worked well for both of them and it worked well for their team. Who knows how much longer Barry's onset of disillusionment with county cricket could have been staved off if his buddy had remained at his side, both on the field and back at Barry's house in Chandlers Ford? Certainly, Barry was saddened by O'Sullivan's departure. We all were but I fancy Barry felt it more keenly than most. Thereafter, the fun started to seep away from playing for Hampshire and the daily grind began to take its toll. Incidentally, we often used to amuse ourselves by picking a team for Chandlers Ford, a suburb of Southampton where a lot of us lived, to play in the National Village Cup: Richards, O'Sullivan, Hill, Jesty, Rice, Taylor, Lewis and Murtagh, together with the bloke behind the counter at Lloyds Bank, who reckoned he had a couple of mates who could play a bit. A team for all seasons.

However Barry was nothing if not a realist and he knew that the oxygen of ambition was the desire to win, especially if the prize were worth the struggle. Hampshire were top of the table coming into the final furlong, with Northamptonshire hot on their tail. Intriguingly, neither county had been fancied as title contenders at the start of the season. In fact, it could be argued that neither county has *ever* really been fancied, in comparison to the bigger, wealthier clubs. Hampshire had only won the championship once in their history, in 1961; Northants had never won it (and still haven't at the time of writing). That Hampshire were still challenging strongly as the season neared its exciting climax owed a lot to another unlikely source. The captain had scored two centuries in successive games, vital ones. This might seem to be damning Gilliat with faint praise, referring to his contributions with the bat as coming from 'an unlikely source'.

Gilliat was a fine, attacking batsman, albeit with an unorthodox style, but he had always subjugated his personal ambition to the good of the side, usually in the pursuit of quick runs after the explosive starts provided by his openers. On these two occasions, he rescued the batting single-handedly and relied on his bowlers to do the rest, which they did. 'It was a feature of that summer,' he said, 'but whenever the big guns failed to fire, there was always someone who would take responsibility and put in a big performance.' Barry shook his head in wonder at the memory. 'We just kept going. The bowlers bowled straight, we took some incredible catches, dropped nothing and the bandwagon rolled on.'

The title decider – for that was what it was in all but name – was at Southampton. Northamptonshire were a capable side; they were not in such a good position in the table by accident. They had experienced batting, Roy Virgin, Colin Milburn, David Steele, Mushtaq Mohammed and Geoff Cook. Their pace attack was spearheaded by someone well known to the Hampshire faithful, Bob Cottam, and greatly respected for that. And they also possessed arguably the best spinner in the world at the time, Bishan Bedi. 'So, what did we do, as the home side?' cried Barry, the incredulity in his voice still echoing down the years. 'We prepared a wicket that turned square! Thank you Ernie, for that welcome present.' Ernie was our quirky, irascible and totally unbiddable groundsman. It may have been true that he had prepared a bunsen but it provided the foundation for a riveting, at times nail-biting, contest that lives long in the memory of those who witnessed it, even if it did not live long in actuality. The game was over in two days. I wasn't playing – once again the vital, onerous duties of 12th man had been entrusted to me. In fact, so vital and so onerous were the duties deemed to be that two 12th men had been assigned. Richard Lewis joined me as a white liveried manservant. 'No, Murt,' said Lewis, putting me firmly in my place as the junior player, '*I* was 12th man. You were 13th!' Whatever, I still had a close, ringside seat as the drama unfolded.

The capacity of the old ground at Northlands Road was alleged to be 7,000 but that always seemed to be a bit of a nebulous figure, especially when lax stewards such as me were on duty. But there was no doubt that the place was packed to its ancient, dusty rafters as Northamptonshire won the toss and chose to bat. I wonder what was going through their minds about that decision when they chewed mournfully on their ham salad at lunch, avoiding any eye contact with the scoreboard outside which read 60/8. The ball swung and seamed all over the place. Nobody realised that it was actually a turning wicket; neither of the two spinners, Sainsbury and O'Sullivan, got a look in. Led by Taylor (4-30), the Hampshire attack disposed of their opponents for 108.

Above everything that was going on that eventful morning, there was a moment of pure theatre that seemed to encapsulate the improbability of Hampshire's charge to the title. Richard Gilliat always ascribed the success of his team to three factors, 'We scored our runs quickly, which gave us longer to bowl sides out. Our fielding was outstanding, which allowed the bowlers to keep up the pressure. And our bowling was greatly underestimated.' Barry has already paid tribute to the support he had all around him and down the order. 'The batting was good,' he enthused, 'Turner was touted for a while as a possible England player before he got hit on the head. Jesty was good enough to play for England too, if only he could have converted those majestic fifties into hundreds.'

Did I just hear you say that, Barry, he who gave away more hundreds than anyone? He laughed. 'I know I should have got 100 hundreds but I did get 80 of them,' he reminded me. 'Jets didn't get his first first-class hundred until he was 28!' That is true – Barry scored his when he was 18 – and it is one of the great anomalies of that era that such a talented batsman as Trevor Jesty did not score more runs than he did. Mind you, he could bowl a bit too and that point of Gilliat's, that the Hampshire bowling was underestimated, is well made. There was no star, no match-winner, but they operated highly effectively as a unit.

The fielding, all knowledgeable observers, was indeed something else. The ground fielding was athletic and predatory. No runs were given away and many saved. 'The captain!' cried Mike Taylor. 'He was the best mid-off in the country!' Before anyone feels tempted to scoff at this assessment – after all, mid-off is not where you would ordinarily station your finest and lithest – it needs to be emphasised that Gilliat did indeed take some valuable catches in that position. But apart from being at the ideal station to advise and encourage his bowlers, Taylor went on, 'Gillers seemed to know exactly when to go back or to come in a few paces. Instinctive really. All good games players have that sixth sense.'

That old adage, catches win matches, was never better served by Hampshire's record that season. In all, 160 catches were taken behind or close to the wicket, some of them phenomenal. It is remarkable what a transformative effect a brilliant catch can have on a team's morale. Throughout 1973, brilliant catches were being pouched for a pastime.

Which brings me back to that dramatic incident before lunch. Yet another brilliant catch was taken, one that brought the crowd to their feet with a roar of disbelief. Wait a minute…not from Stephenson, Richards, Greenidge, Jesty, Taylor, Sainsbury, Gilliat…but from Mottram! *Mottram?* Let me quote from John Arlott's account, 'Tom Mottram, whose height and leanness are hardly the physical attributes of an outstanding fieldsman, was bowling to Roy Virgin, the main opposing batsman. Virgin had taken no chances but seeing a full length ball, he leant into it and drove it, characteristically hard and low – no more than four or five inches off the ground – towards mid-on. Mottram, checking his follow-through and pull-away, changed direction, dived far more than the width of the wicket and scooped up the all but impossible catch.'

Tom Mottram was not the only Hampshire player sprawled across the Northlands Road grass at that moment. All of his team-mates were prone with laughter and disbelief. And if no one could believe that example of wizardry, then Northamptonshire's second innings provided another, also involving Mottram. 'The Pink Panther,' smiled Barry. 'Who would've believed it?' Mike Taylor went further. 'Motters! D'you remember how thin his shins were?' I said I did, not at all sure where this was leading. 'Well, whenever the ball missed his hands, it always seemed to smash into them!' It is hard for any of us to recall the Pink Panther without a huge, warm grin splitting our features.

For a while, with Richards and Greenidge seemingly in muscular control and the score at 76 without loss, the possibility of a rapid overhauling of Northamptonshire's total and the building of a substantial lead was very much on the cards. Certainly the Hampshire faithful believed and were in fine voice as the afternoon wore on. But we in the dressing room were not so sanguine. In point of fact, a fascinating duel was unfolding and in the middle of it was the Sultan of Spin, as Bedi was called. Barry and Gordon were running down the pitch and attempting to hit him off his length. When he was nailed and a four was hit, Bedi would stand there in the middle of the pitch and applaud the stroke. An act of sportsmanship? Or a clever ploy by the beguiling Indian magician?

We winced every time that the ball squeezed past the bat or just eluded a catcher in close. It couldn't last. It was as if Bedi was luring them into a trap. The way he kept on tossing up juicy deliveries to be greedily devoured put one in mind of Eve tempting Adam with a red sphere similar in size. With the same disastrous consequences. Both openers chased one too many and were dismissed from the Garden of Eden, stumped. I remember Barry coming back into the dressing room, sitting down and shaking his head in bewilderment bordering on admiration. 'That guy is a *seriously* good bowler,' he said. And none of us had ever heard him say that. A position of 111/1 quickly deteriorated into 167 all out, Bedi 6-69. A slender lead of 59, with the prospect of facing Bedi in the fourth innings on a wicket already turning sharply, had not been in the script. One way or another, the championship was going to be decided on the outcome of this match. And it was on a knife-edge.

Once again, the Hampshire bowlers performed gallantly to put the home side within touching distance of the pennant. Some could already see it fluttering from the club's flagpole. Yet something had happened in the Northamptonshire innings, so uncommon, so bizarre, so lucky really, that it seemed the gods were smiling on this Hampshire side and that they were destined to win, whatever happened. Stephenson stumped David Steele. What's so unusual about that, you might ask. After all, his opposite number, George Sharp, had stumped Richards and Greenidge the day before. Ah, but this was off Mottram, the opening bowler. Well, unusual perhaps but not unheard of; Stephenson was good enough to stand up to the seamers when the situation or conditions demanded. But he was standing back – look, you can see it in the photograph. What had happened was this. Mottram had lumbered in and bowled an innocuous ball or a rip-snorter of a delivery, depending on whose word you take. Steele had played forward and missed. Stephenson had taken the ball and there was no appeal. Why should there be? He had missed it by miles, or possibly an inch anyway.

For a second, everybody stood still. Nothing happened. Mottram would turn on his heels, Stephenson would throw the ball to Greenidge at second slip. Richards at first slip would intercept it, much to the annoyance of his team-mate, and chuck it to Turner at cover to make its circuitous way back to the bowler. Steele, having glanced behind him to check that the ball was indeed on its way back and was therefore 'dead', would have sauntered out of his crease for a spot of gardening and a lot of introspection as to how he had missed such a harmless delivery.

But Stephenson had noticed something. Steele had 'held his pose', as the saying goes; that is, he had not moved a muscle after the completion of his shot. His back foot, his toe, in point of fact, was resting on the popping crease. The popping crease belonged to the bowler; technically Steele was out of his ground. Carefully, deliberately, unobtrusively, Stephenson took aim, much like a bowls player, and rolled the ball back towards the stumps. He hit. To be honest, 'hit' is too strong a word. The ball caressed the stumps and a bail was dislodged. Steele was out.

There is a wonderful photo by Patrick Eagar, one of many pivotal moments in important matches over the years, at the very second that the bail has popped out of its groove. It reminds me of a mediaeval painting, of a biblical scene perhaps, where clearly something momentous is happening but the artist's eye is yet naive and has little sense of movement or perspective. Thus all the participants are frozen, motionless, two-dimensional and seemingly posed. All is still, except for the bail in the air. The umpire has not yet straightened up from his crouching position. Virgin, the non-striker, has half turned to wander back to his crease. Mottram is standing stock still, a faint look of bewilderment on his face. Barry is standing with his back to us, long, curly blond hair spilling over his upturned collar, having just removed his hands from their usual home in his pockets. Only Stephenson seems energised, with both hands raised in appeal, though the appeal looks a little half-hearted. And Steele, an inanimate statue, has his eyes on the offending piece of turf where the ball had pitched. His toe is clearly on the line – out!

Richard Lewis, sitting with me on the players' balcony, turned to me and muttered, 'There's no way we're going to lose this now.' 'The gods have spoken,' I agreed. We had to speak out of the corner of our mouths because we were surrounded by the Northamptonshire team. There was no viewing space for opposing players; they had to invade our dressing room. That was fine. Everybody was friendly and the banter usually good-humoured and if anything was ever spoken out of turn, it was forgivable – this is professional sport we are talking about here and it would be very odd if sometimes emotions were not stirred. On this occasion, Steele's team-mates were apoplectic, not at Stephenson and his sharp thinking, but at their senior batsman for making such a crass, silly, dozy mistake. 'Larry the Lunger, we called him,' said Barry at the memory. 'He was always doing that.' Mike Taylor recalled the incident with total clarity. He was fielding in the gully and being pretty square on, had a perfect view of what happened. 'Steeley – when he heard the death rattle, he instinctively moved his toe behind the line. But too late – he was gone!'

The stuffing appeared to have been knocked out of their opponents and they were dismissed for 148, leaving the home side a mere 90 to win. I quote from the report of the match in the official *Hampshire Handbook*, 'They did it with ease by 6.16pm and earned themselves a day's rest.' To the outside observer, that may have seemed to be the case. But for those inside that dressing room, nothing could have been further from the truth. For a start, a small target is sometimes inordinately difficult to achieve. There must be something psychological in this – so near but so far, and all that. Furthermore, the wicket was now a brute to bat on. Bedi was a master at exploiting those conditions, only Underwood in the game at the time could be considered his equal, and he knew exactly how to prey on the insecurities and technical flaws of batsmen nervous of the occasion and the proximity of the prize. It was going to be a struggle, we all knew that.

None more so than Barry. In the first innings, his instinct had been to attack. Remember his words during discussions on how to play Gleeson, 'If it doesn't pitch, it can't spin.' That had always been his *modus operandi* against the spinners, use his feet and hit them off a length. Now, he adapted his technique. He would play Bedi from the crease. *Why?* 'Because it was going through the top. And because Bedi was such a fine bowler. He could adjust his length wherever you played him from. It was bloody difficult, I tell you.' That much was obvious, even without the corroborative evidence furnished by those batsmen who had been and gone.

'Basically, Barry blocked us to victory,' said Taylor. 'It wasn't very pretty, it wasn't a triumphant charge towards the finishing tape, but it got us there and that was all that counted.' There were plenty of chewed fingernails in that dressing room. One or two just couldn't watch and only emerged into the daylight once the end had become inevitable. 'I just couldn't afford to get out,' said Barry. 'If I had, the whole innings could have collapsed like a stack of cards.'

It was the most riveting passage of play that I have ever witnessed on a cricket field. The battle of wits between the world's best spinner and the world's best batsman was totally absorbing and it was a privilege to have been there, so closely involved. Hampshire got those 90 runs for the loss of four wickets. Barry had scored 37 not out. It had taken him 30 overs to do so. In runs scored it was the least productive of his great innings, for make no mistake, it *was* a great innings, but it was one of his most valuable. And it had not, most definitely not, been achieved 'with ease'.

Even the most pessimistic of Hampshire supporters at last began to believe that their team's momentum was now unstoppable. Nottinghamshire were dispatched comfortably in the first of the two fixtures during the Bournemouth Festival week – O'Sullivan with match figures of 11-41 – and the necessary bonus points for outright victory in the championship secured in the second against Gloucestershire. Two ironies surface here. One was that his friend and long-time ally, Mike Procter, was on the other side. And the other was that winning the game, aside from the relevant bonus points, was the first that Hampshire had secured that season by means of a declaration. Gloucestershire were in the hunt for a place in the top four and of course the prize money was of considerable interest to them. A draw doing their cause no good at all, they declared to leave Hampshire to score 187 in just under two hours. Thanks mainly to Greenidge, they did, to post their tenth victory of this special summer. I mention this because it had been said that the 1961 side had won the championship owing to generous opponents who had set them targets by declaring. That may have been so but it could equally be argued that winning possibilities had often been set up by a captain, Colin Ingleby-Mackenzie, who had risked defeat in several skilfully managed, close run chases. By contrast, the 1973 side had to bowl sides out twice in all but one of their ten victories. Unfancied champions they may have been, but lucky? 'Good teams make their own luck!' scoffed Mike Taylor at the very suggestion.

It remained only for them to sign off with style in their final match of the season against Kent. It was drawn but Hampshire amassed their highest total of the campaign, 471/8 declared. Richards and Greenidge put on 334 for the first wicket. 'That's not correct,' Barry put me right. 'Actually, it was only 200-odd.' Bemused, I looked again at the scorecard, Richards 143, Greenidge 118. Surely my mental arithmetic...*Ah, I see now that you were retired hurt. What happened?* 'Richard Elms hit me in the face when I missed a hook. Fractured my cheekbone. It made for a very uncomfortable flight home to South Africa a couple of days later.'

Uncomfortable it may have been. But it cannot have been without a certain amount of satisfaction as he reflected on a crazy, enjoyable and gloriously successful season. 'Job well done,' was his terse summation. There was satisfaction that, yet again, he had earned his corn and made significant contributions and it is always more agreeable to play in a winning side. But he had other fish to fry, in another hemisphere, captaining Natal while his team-mates were enjoying liquid celebration and a reception at Buckingham Palace. Two days later, he was strapping on his pads, broken cheek and all, at The Wanderers in Johannesburg, turning out for Derrick Robbins, that tireless benefactor of South African cricket, to whom nobody said no. Not even Barry.

Two other significant events took place that summer, neither of which concerned Barry directly but both of which were to affect him significantly. The reputation of Andy Roberts, serving his year's qualification in the professional game and therefore unavailable for county matches, had been spreading around the country like an uncontrollable bush fire. It is important to separate fact from fiction here, or at any rate to keep in mind the true story that was rapidly being embellished to mythical status. Yes, Roberts was fast, seriously so. We knew, we played with him every day in the Second XI. Yes, he did practise bowling bouncers to us in the nets until we persuaded him it was far better to conserve his energies and bowl gentle off-spinners instead. Yes it was true his spinners were rubbish and yes it was also true that we treated those off-spinners with respect bordering on reverence. And yes it was true that he had started hitting inexperienced batsmen some sickening blows.

But it was not true that Gloucestershire were at 60-odd for two in their first innings with numbers seven and eight at the wicket, the rest having been carted off to Accident and Emergency at the Royal Bournemouth Hospital. But it was certainly true that Roberts had terrified them out of their wits and they had been dismissed for 69, admittedly with two retired hurt and on their way to hospital. I remember their opener, Jim Foat, a good player and a popular opponent, losing his presence of mind and giving Roberts the charge. It almost goes without saying that he was one of those hospitalised. 'Why did you do that?' we asked Jim, incredulous. 'Well, if I was going to die,' he answered, 'I thought I may as well die on the front foot.'

There was an element of gallows humour in his reply but the prospect of death was not that fanciful. In an age before helmets, a blow on the head, worst of all, the temple, from a cricket ball delivered at 90mph was a serious business. The recent tragic death of Phillip Hughes, hit on the head by a bouncer, even with wearing a helmet, puts this into even sharper perspective. Take note of this. Roberts was selected for the tourists' match, against the West Indies. It was not a county game, so he was eligible to play. It was against his countrymen and as an up and coming fast bowler, who was being touted as the next Wes Hall, he was anxious to make an impression. Barry was not playing. He needed a rest, he said. 'What!' cried Desmond Eagar, the secretary, aghast, 'But you can't. The members want to see you play.' Barry said something about the members that is unrepeatable and was adamant that he needed to step off from the daily treadmill to recharge his batteries.

It was Wimbledon fortnight, I notice. 'The dates were entirely coincidental, Murt,' he grinned. If he helped us win the championship, who could begrudge him some time off was my opinion but his absence was not received with unanimous endorsement in the committee room.

Roberts was fired up and tore in like a madman. He was still raw and had yet to develop into the shrewd, cold-eyed assassin he later became. He was quick, very quick, but erratic and took only one wicket in the match. But he bowled one ball, I would contend, that sealed his fate and his career. Steve Camacho, the Guyanese opening bat who had already played 11 Tests and was expected to open with Roy Fredericks in the forthcoming series against England, was hit a sickening blow in the face by a Roberts bouncer. I was 15 yards or so away at cover point. I heard the crack of splintering bone. He crumpled in a heap and was immediately surrounded by concerned players. Medical help was summoned and soon he was stretchered off the field. Roberts, I noted, had gone back to the end of his run, impassively waiting for play to resume.

Lest you take issue with this lack of solicitude and criticise him for insensitivity, you have to understand that fast bowlers are warriors and no warrior stops to enquire after the health of an enemy whom he has just struck down. I also remember, together with Richard Lewis, kicking dirt over the popping crease to soak up the puddle of blood before the next batsman made an appearance. The immediate upshot of this unfortunate occurrence was that Camacho, following an operation to rebuild his shattered jaw, took no further part in the tour and never played for the West Indies again. Within the year, Roberts had become a fixture in the side as part of the most fearsome fast bowling attack – four-pronged – that international cricket has ever seen.

Now Barry had never seen Roberts bowl but had heard enough about him from his housemate, Mike Hill, the reserve wicketkeeper. 'All Hillers went on about all summer was how his hands were in a state of permanent bruising from keeping to Fruity.' Many of the nicknames in the Hampshire dressing room were as transparently obvious as a clue in *The Sun*'s crossword but the moniker accorded to Roberts of 'Fruity' has always escaped me. Some said that it was because he was teetotal and only ever drank fruit juice. But his beverage of choice was coke, and coke alone. In fact, in all the years he was at the club, that one word 'coke' was all we got out of him. Either he was taciturn to a remarkable degree or he adhered religiously to the theory of method acting as a mean and moody fast bowler or simply his English wasn't very good. None of us ever really got to know him. Occasionally he would say to me 'Joseph' (my middle name) and his shoulders would shake in a little silent giggle but that was as close as I got. And I never knew what had tickled him. Probably it was because he knew only too well I was relieved he was on our side and not the other.

For Barry though, the explosion on the scene of the West Indian had presented him with an enormous, personal dilemma. The regulations of the game in England stated clearly that each county was only allowed to field two overseas players. Three – Richards, Roberts and O'Sullivan – did not go into two. The following season, one of them would have to go. Effectively, it was a straight choice between Roberts and O'Sullivan. At a recent 40th anniversary lunch for the 1973 team, when this predicament was remembered by Richard Gilliat in his speech, Sully shouted out, 'Well, you could have sacked Barry!' which brought the house down but that, of course, was never a realistic option.

Before Barry departed for South Africa, he was approached by Gilliat for his opinion. He replied that as he had never seen Roberts bowl, it would be unfair of him to comment. In fact, he was riven with misgivings. He had seen this coming and desperately wanted his friend to stay. And what's more, Sully's haul of wickets in the last month of the season had gone a long way to securing Hampshire's title success. But every side craves a fast bowler, a genuinely fast bowler, who will lead the attack and blast sides out, especially the tail-enders. Furthermore, there were the persistent, damaging rumours about Sully's action, in particular his arm ball. Mike Taylor laughed in cynical amusement when I reminded him of the controversy. 'I've just been watching a certain Sri Lankan spinner on the box in the Indian IPL,' he snorted. 'Compared to him, Sully's action was as pure as the driven snow!' That may be so but a lot of political blood has flown under the bridge since the 1970s and things, for better or worse, are different now. Back then, could Hampshire take the risk of Sully being 'called' and effectively banned?

To those of us who had seen Roberts close up, there was no argument. Such a talent comes along once in a blue moon and Hampshire would have been mad to let him go. Hampshire were not mad – well, not on this occasion – and Roberts was given the nod. O'Sullivan walked through the gates and out of Northlands Road for the last time and he never returned. He was not signed by another county, his career fizzled out and he took up insurance work in his native New Zealand. We were very sorry to see him go. We were all very fond of him; he was a character, an amusing and cheerful presence, and he was a fine bowler. Barry's sadness was more acute. He had lost a soul mate as well as a house-mate and life for him in England was going to be the poorer for Sully's absence. His heart hardened a little, not helped by the fact that he knew, in his bones, that the decision was the right one.

7

Not So Happy Hants
Hampshire 1974–78

*'I don't really believe I was ever cut out to play
cricket seven days a week.'*

Barry Richards

'HOW we didn't win it again next year beats me,' Barry said. That is one of the great puzzles that has racked the brains of Hampshire players, officials and supporters ever since. 'What points system that man has ever devised could be more unjust than the one that denied us the championship in 1974?' bemoaned Mike Taylor. 'I mean, we were on top of the table from mid-May until the last afternoon of the season! How did that happen?'

How indeed? History records that it happened because Hampshire were holed up in their dressing room at Bournemouth for four solid days (the final day of the match against Somerset when they were poised for victory and the full three days of the last match against Yorkshire) while it rained. And rained. And rained. All they needed were a few bonus points while Worcestershire, on the other side of the country, bowled Essex out on a wet wicket to secure victory and win the title, by two points. It remains, in my mind and the minds of many others, not all Hampshire followers incidentally, one of the great injustices in County Championship history.

A sense of grievance not soothed, I have to say, by the fact that for the last 30 years, I have lived and worked in Worcestershire and have had to bite my tongue on many an occasion, particularly in the year of writing this book, the 40th anniversary of their victory, with all its attendant celebrations, many of which I had been invited to attend. I tried, but I am not at all sure that I succeeded, to emulate Richard Gilliat's generous and sportsmanlike public utterances at the time and on all occasions since. 'Perhaps the disappointment was not so acute because we had won it the previous year,' he told me, 'but there was no doubt we were the best side in the country by far.' Indeed! Only one month earlier, Hampshire had dispatched Worcestershire by an innings and 44 runs, in only two days. They had been bowled out for 94 and 98! Worthy champions?

The traditional pipe opener to the cricket season was the MCC v Champion County at Lord's. It was still April and the weather was…inclement, shall we say. Barry had just arrived in the country and had not had much in the way of practice. Had he put on a bit of weight, we wondered, as he picked up his bat, put on his cap and together with Gordon Greenidge, exited the dressing room to make their way down the stairs, through the Long Room and out on to the grass at Lord's. Or was it muscle? Had he been spending the winter beefing up in the gym?

As the two openers walked towards the middle, it was noticeable that Barry's bulk was not a great deal less than the Incredible Hulk beside him. But the appearance was deceptive. Barry had put on every possible article of clothing he could lay his hands on, including two sweaters. His profanities about the English spring weather were familiar to us by now but on this occasion we were wholeheartedly in agreement – that wind that was swirling around the empty stands was biting. When I say 'empty', that is not in a manner of speaking. There was not a soul to be seen. The English public had not been enthused by this fixture, the football season was nearing its climax and cricket supporters had given St John's Wood a wide berth. We were reliably informed that there were a few loyal, hardy MCC members downstairs in the comfort of the Long Room but that was about it. I have heard footballers trying to describe the weird, surreal, echoing atmosphere of playing a competitive match behind closed doors, for whatever reason, and I can imagine it must have been similar that day at Lord's. 'I see that the great and the good have flocked in their droves to watch the champions,' was Mike Taylor's caustic observation, as we settled down to watch the opening exchanges.

I have already recorded my memories of Barry's innings of 189 that day in the preamble to this book. It remains quite simply the greatest innings I have ever witnessed. But don't take my word for it; how about those of Tony Lewis, writing in the *Sunday Telegraph*, 'Swathed in many layers of Hampshire sweaters, Barry Richards today defied the biting cold, and swung his bat freely to score 189 unforgettable runs. A most reputable MCC attack of Hendrick, Jackman, Knight, Acfield and Edmonds appeared to be sending down half-volleys and long hops all day. It was not so but sadistic flashes by Richards even put third man in danger. There were persuasions to fine leg and lofted golf shots over long-on. The MCC captain tinkered with his field all day but concluded that he must have taken the field four or five men short!'

The captain was Tony Lewis, no less. He too remembered the forbidding weather, the bitter wind and the empty stands, 'a chill, cheerless theatre' he described it. And then he went on to make a memorable comparison, appropriate for its imagery as well as for the fact that Lewis was no mean practitioner of the fiddler's art himself, 'It was just as if Yehudi Menuhin had called into the Festival Hall of a morning, taken his fiddle on stage and reeled off faultless, unaccompanied Bach all day – just for the pleasure of the cleaners, box-office clerks, odd electricians or a carpenter who chanced to be there – without central heating of course – without taking his coat off.'

When Barry came back into the dressing room after he had been dismissed, with his coat still on, sorry, the two sweaters he was wearing, he sat down for a while without removing his pads, wordlessly acknowledging our muted congratulations, seemingly lost in thought. Why were our congratulations less than effusive? Why were we not surrounding him, slapping him on the back and loudly lauding him to the heavens? Individually, I think, we came up to him and murmured, slightly embarrassed, our appreciation and admiration, but there was no outbreak of joyous celebration. What was there to say? We all knew that we had been in the presence of greatness and it felt humbling, to be honest. An unplayable delivery, an astonishing catch, a towering six – all those can send team-mates into a paroxysm of delight and jubilation. But an innings like that takes away the breath and with it the power of speech. He knew – or at least, I jolly well hope that he knew – what we thought about what we had just witnessed. In the bar, later that evening, there was no other subject of discussion, among players from both sides.

But I was struck by Barry's five minutes of introspection before he eventually stirred himself to unbuckle his pads. No one can choose his moment when form strikes and he plays out of his skin. But if he is playing at the highest level, in the international arena, there is a chance, a good chance if he is a seasoned Test player that his day in the sun will be at one of the major grounds in front of a large crowd and televised nationwide. Barry had been fortunate, you might say; he had played one of the great innings at Lord's, the home of cricket, the Mecca for all players and supporters the world over. What more could he want? Well, to play it in front of more than one man and his dog, for a start. Was the realisation seeping into his bones, as he slowly got changed, that he would never play these majestic innings in front of a full house in games that really *mattered*, that is, for his country? Hereafter, it would be touring repertory, never the West End. To the rest of us, retaining the County Championship pennant was stimulus enough. Barry was beginning to think he was not so sure.

The germ of disenchantment, obvious to no one and probably not even sensed by Barry himself, had nothing to do with the team for which he was playing. The tag of underdogs had long since been discarded; Hampshire were now the real deal. In point of fact, in many experienced eyes, they were the favourites to retain their crown, an opinion that quickly grew into a conviction after Roberts had routed a series of counties, by an innings and within two days on several occasions. You could say that the impact Andy Roberts made on the English county game in 1974 was every bit as dramatic as Barry's had been in 1968. He took 119 wickets at an average of 13.62. He took a good many wickets at the other end in addition, if that doesn't sound too Irish. He was fast, he was hostile, he was ruthless and he was cunning. No one, not even the best and the bravest in the land, fancied facing him. Those of us who had played with him in the Second XI the previous year greatly enjoyed our spell of *schadenfreude*. We had been banging on all that summer about how lightning quick he was and few took us seriously. Now we watched as experienced campaigners ducked and weaved, and were sometimes hit, and returned to the dressing room ashen-faced.

Let us take as one example of the intimidating, unnerving way that a genuinely quick bowler can scramble the brains of a batsman. Colin Cowdrey was as brave and as experienced a player of fast bowling as anyone in the country. Who was it the England selectors turned to as a replacement to be flown out to Australia the following winter to come to the rescue of an injury-riven and shell-shocked touring team suffering at the hands of Lillee and Thomson? Apparently the players had asked for Cowdrey, despite the fact he was 41 and in the autumn of his career. They knew he could handle pace. 'Well, he couldn't handle Fruity,' laughed Mike Taylor.

It was at Basingstoke and I remember the moment, and the preamble leading up to it, with complete clarity, watching from my usual spot on the players' balcony as 12th man. 'Fruity had two bouncers,' said Barry. 'It was what fighters would call the sucker punch.' We had seen the ploy often enough. For the unwary, it usually ended in disaster. First would come the slow, looping bouncer that often ballooned harmlessly over the batsman's head. Well, if that's the measure of the fearsome Andy Roberts bouncer, then bring it on, would be the tacit reaction of the unsuspecting victim in the cross-hairs of Roberts's viewfinder. The killer ball, the rapid bouncer, the one that reared up at the throat, did not always come the next ball but it always came from nowhere. Sure enough, Roberts tempted England's veteran with his slower bouncer.

'Kipper started to act the fool!' said Mike Taylor, the incredulity in his voice still there 40 years later. 'He pretended he hadn't seen it, that it had been too fast for him, looking around theatrically as if he'd lost it in the clouds or something.' The crowd loved it, of course, the old entertainer having a joke with his adoring audience. Barry muttered to Bob Stephenson, keeping wicket alongside him, 'Here we go – red rag to a bull.' Richard Gilliat was at mid-off and as he returned the ball to his fast bowler, he looked at him. 'There was no need for me to say anything,' he said. 'Andy's face was expressionless, as usual. But we all knew what was coming.' Richard Lewis was positioned at short-leg, directly square on, where you do not look at the bowler charging in, you do not see the ball delivered, you just concentrate on the front pad of the batsman, waiting for the possible bat-pad ricochet. Of course there was no likelihood of a bat-pad catch on this occasion.

'I knew it was coming,' said Lewis. 'All I can remember was Colin falling like a sack of potatoes and noticing that in so doing he had knocked over his stumps. He was out, hit wicket.' There is another of Patrick Eagar's wonderful photos that captures the moment. Lewis is bending over the stricken Cowdrey, lying face down with his head buried in his gloved hands, with a concerned hand on the batsman's back and the other seemingly signalling to the pavilion for help. 'Second time I was first on the scene.' Lewis pulled a face. 'Remember Camacho the year before?'

Apart from Richard Elms in the last match of the previous season, which was a bit of a fluke, do you remember ever being caught out like that? Barry pondered for a second or two. 'That was when I top-edged a hook into my face, so that doesn't count.' *Well, the stitches did, but let's not quibble.* 'It was Alan Hurst from Australia in an SA Invitation XI versus the International Wanderers at Kingsmead. I'd smashed him for a few fours and he let me have a couple of bouncers. I wasn't expecting three in a row and this one didn't get up like the other two. It skidded, I turned my head and it hit me behind the ear.' *Retired hurt?* 'It affected my balance. I couldn't stand upright.'

To be fair to Cowdrey, he eventually picked himself up and after some medical assistance, put it about that he was willing to continue. Somewhat embarrassed, the Hampshire fielders pointed out that he was in fact out – he had fallen on his wicket. He turned to Gilliat to remonstrate. 'He said to me that he wasn't out and that he wanted to carry on,' said Gilliat, 'and I just shrugged and said, but you're out, Colin, you knocked over your stumps. Then David Constant, the umpire, bustled over and said, of course you're out, Colin. And he had to go. He didn't want to, you know, and muttered something about the spirit of the game. And he never spoke to me again.' *Do you mean for the rest of the match? Or the season?* 'No, never. And what's more, he avoided playing against Andy after that. If Andy was in our side, he'd find a way of excusing himself from Kent duty.' How very strange. Two of the true gentlemen of the game, two nicer men you could not wish to meet, Cowdrey and Gilliat, Tonbridge and Charterhouse, Oxford, Kent and Hampshire, born to lead and lead they did, captains of every team they played in, having a spat that festered for years.

I hate to disagree with a legend of cricket and a man of Hampshire but a comment by John Arlott in his review of the 1974 season is, if not entirely wide of the mark, certainly missing the stumps. He maintained that Barry and Gordon, potentially the most destructive of openers in the country had an 'inconsistent season'. That could be said of Greenidge, who had already made his debut for the West Indies that winter against India, who *did* have an in-and-out season, an early blip in a glorious career that was to extend to 107 Tests. But Barry finished the season with an average of 61.76! Admittedly his aggregate of 1,297 runs was fewer than his fans would have wished but still…those are figures mere mortals dream of. 'Look,' said Barry, 'I only once failed to top the averages and get 1,000 runs and that was in my final season, when I'd pretty well shot my bolt. So I think they got their money's worth.'

There were plenty of fine innings in this season and one indisputably great one. I find myself at this stage of the narrative becoming a bit vague about how many innings of Barry's I have decreed to be 'great'. A dozen perhaps? The thing is that with most of the finest players I can remember or about whom I have read, I can immediately pin down one of their knocks that can be deemed great. Perhaps two or three. Immediately coming to mind is Geoff Boycott's 146 in the Gillette Cup Final against Surrey at Lord's in 1965. Oh, that he had unveiled the full range of his shots more often in a career where shot-making was subsumed to the principle of run gathering as he did that day. Dennis Amiss, who had widely recognised problems against extreme pace, conquered his demons in Jamaica in 1974 against the full force of the West Indian quick bowlers and made an unforgettable 262 not out. Then there was Mark Butcher, who batted as if in a dream to carry his bat and win the match for his country against the Australians in 2001 at Headingley, scoring 173. His opponents said that every shot had come off the middle of the bat; earlier that season, out of form and out of favour, he had been languishing in Surrey's Second XI. And I am always reminded of Stan McCabe's peerless knock of 232 for Australia at Trent Bridge in 1938.

Don Bradman called his team out on to the balcony to watch because, he later said, 'they would never see anything like it again'. On McCabe's return to the dressing room, Bradman shook his hand and said, 'I wish I could bat like that, Stan.' And it is alleged that the pair did not even get on that well.

I have little doubt numerous other such innings could be quickly reeled off by lots of people. But my point is that in my account of every season of Barry's career, there seems to be a moment when I have had to pause, to examine and to marvel at a wondrous innings that no one else on either side could possibly have played. And here was another. Yet when I quizzed him about it, all he could remember was Mike Taylor's all-round contribution to a crushing defeat of Nottinghamshire at Trent Bridge by an innings and 101 runs. Paradoxically, Taylor had been released by Notts two years previously and his 5-29 in the home side's miserable first innings total of 98 must have been doubly pleasing. 'Tay was a useful bowler,' said Barry. 'He bowled a good line and moved the ball around if conditions suited.' However, it was not his contribution with the ball that Barry remembered. 'Didn't we share in a big stand together?' *Yes you did, 202 to be exact.*

By this stage of the season, at the end of May, Hampshire were carrying all before them; there seemed to be no team in the land that could live with them. When it was Hampshire's turn to bat, quick runs, a decent lead and bowl 'em out again cheaply would have been at the forefront of their minds – confidence was that high. But it didn't quite turn out like that. Well, it did, in fact, but the means by which a commanding, ultimately victorious, lead was attained was not so straightforward. Greenidge was run out for 14. Thereafter, nobody reached double figures. Barry was batting serenely at one end while at the other all manner of strange things were going on as wicket after wicket went down. When Taylor joined Barry, Hampshire were perilously placed at 113/6 and a commanding lead was a long way over the horizon. 'It was a pretty crucial partnership,' said Taylor. 'Just a few runs ahead and not much to come after me.'

How was Barry playing? 'Like a dream. Honestly, it was a magnificent innings.' *So, Barry, how did you think you played?* 'Pretty well, I reckon.' Pretty well meant carrying his bat for 225, out of a total of 344, 140 of which came in boundaries. That sounds suspiciously as if he scored, single-handedly, about two-thirds of his team's runs. Had it not been for Taylor's brave 68 in support, the percentage would have been even higher. *You must have batted pretty well, Tay.* He laughed that sardonic laugh of his. 'Well, Murt, let's just put it like this. I had a good elementary grounding in arithmetic at school. I could count as well as the next boy up to six!' The lead of 246 was too much for Nottinghamshire. They subsided to 146 all out, Taylor capturing two more wickets to round off a thoroughly satisfying personal performance. *Did you enjoy exacting revenge over your previous employers for sacking you?* 'Murt – is that a serious question?' But the day, or more accurately the two days, belonged to Barry Richards, as Taylor readily agrees.

The pivotal contest of the summer, it was agreed, would be against Worcestershire, their nearest challengers, one that would not necessarily decide the destination of the championship but would go a long way in that direction. The result could not have been more conclusive. Hampshire won at 5.30pm on the second day, by an innings and 44 runs, their sixth win by an innings and their fifth within two days. It was at Portsmouth, not Barry's favourite ground but hey, who cares when you're winning! Worcestershire were dismissed for 94, their lowest total of the season, Roberts leading the charge with 3-17. Thanks mainly to a typically robust and selfless 62 from the captain, Hampshire took to the field with a lead of 142. Significant, it was felt, but not impregnable. Doubters should have thought again. Roberts bowled like the wind. He took 4-29 and Worcestershire were skittled again – for 98. It was a crushing victory for the leaders and by now, with a lead of 31 points over Worcestershire and five games left to play, nobody could envisage, even in his darkest nightmare, anything other than a second successive coronation.

'Eeh, but it's a foony old game,' as Geoff Boycott was fond of saying. At Cardiff, in one of the most bizarre and unlikely sets of circumstances, Hampshire had their one bad day of the summer and as events unfolded over the course of the next few weeks, it could be seen that it most probably cost them the championship. Hampshire, once again in debt to their captain, managed a total of 234, much more than looked likely at one stage. But not to worry. At close of play, Glamorgan had all but thrown in the towel in the face of Roberts's onslaught. They were 43-7, all the wickets going to the Antiguan. 'He was bowling *seriously* fast,' remembered Barry. 'He was out to prove himself that summer and he put everything into it.'

The next morning, Glamorgan struggled to 90 all out but crucially just avoided the follow-on, and certain defeat. It had rained and now Hampshire were caught on a treacherous, drying pitch. Barry made 60 out of a total of 137 and yet again, his skill and technique in difficult conditions were a marvel to witness. 'He played with such soft hands,' Peter Sainsbury later told me, 'which is surprising really when you consider he was brought up on the hard wickets of South Africa.' He meant that Barry did not go hard at the ball, which you can do when the pitch is true and fast, but that he waited and played it softly, gently, to counteract any deviation, up or down or sideways. It was another of Barry's masterful displays and with an unassailable lead of 282, on that wicket, the win was but a formality. 'We woke up the next morning, the sun and breeze had dried out the pitch and it rolled out flat.'

The emphasis that Barry put on the word 'flat' could not have been more disdainful. On the same stretch of turf that he had battled on the previous day, one that demanded all his courage, patience, concentration and technique, had now lost all its venom and even Roberts was reduced to impotence. He bowled 34 overs that day for one wicket. *Thirty-four overs! In one day! That's a sure way to break a fast bowler's spirit, let alone his back, wouldn't you agree?* 'He was over-bowled, definitely,'

Barry agreed. 'You see, in those days, nobody had a clue about managing players – especially bowlers – and their workload. They're better at it now, with squad rotation and proper periods of rest.' He was talking about Andy Roberts but my tacit understanding was that he was referring just as much to his own plight.

I quizzed Richard Gilliat about this particular day and, more specifically, the charge that Roberts had been over-bowled. 'Yes, probably there were times when I bowled him too much,' he agreed, 'but it was so difficult *not* to! He was brilliant at blowing away the tail-end.' That was undoubtedly true. We had all seen, on numerous occasions, that whenever a stubborn stand started to develop lower down the order, Gilliat would only have to turn towards Roberts and rotate his arms a couple of times for the batsmen to start slogging. As for not resting his spearhead of attack? 'That too was difficult,' Gilliat said. 'There wasn't the custom in those days to give players a few days off. The rest of the team would have been distinctly unimpressed. We've got to play every day, they would say, so why don't they? In any case, we were going for the championship and every game was vital. It wasn't as if we were mid-table and the pressure was off.' I can understand both sides of the debate.

I remember playing 30 days of cricket on the trot, shuttling back and forth between the First and Second XIs – and that was in the middle of the 1976 heatwave! Even I felt a bit tired and war weary, and I wasn't a fast bowler. But that was the nature of the beast. Professional cricket was a seven day a week occupation and you just got on with it. There were periods of mental and physical exhaustion but remarkably, all that seemed to vanish if you took some wickets or scored a few runs. Besides, you were young, fit and in your salad days. Professional cricket did exactly what it said on the tin, and it was a tin we were only too happy to buy. But I was a journeyman. Barry and Andy and Gordon were superstars. The pressure to perform was higher and they had bigger fish to fry, in other, different, higher forms of the game. Looking back, it is now as clear as day that full-time cricketers need careful handling. But this is now and that was then. How extraordinary to reflect that current players are escorted to an ice bath when they come off the field. You can imagine, and I can corroborate this, what Barry or Butch White or Peter Sainsbury or any of the others would have said had they discovered that the 12th man had filled the bath with water that was not steaming hot.

To finish the chronicle of Cardiff, with all the time in the world, Glamorgan ground out the required runs and Hampshire had lost a game they seemed destined to win. Had they done so, the rain at Bournemouth would have been a watery irrelevance. 'Aaaagh!' cried Barry. 'Len Hill, the one-shot wonder! I'll never forget him.' And not kindly either. Hill took five hours to amass his 90 runs. But it is only fair to give him the credit he deserves – his team won. 'And that's where we lost it really,' Gilliat acknowledged. 'Were we a bit complacent? Probably. We had such a good side we didn't think we could get beaten.'

All could have been put right, four days later, against the same opponents. Yet another enthralling game evolved and yet again Hampshire were frustrated. The sun was shining on the old Northlands Road ground, Hampshire won the toss and Barry hit the first two balls of the match for four. 'Hello,' remarked Richard, 'Barry's in the mood.' On this occasion, he was no lone ranger. He was joined by the pocket Hercules, David Turner, and the strokeplay was electrifying, both scoring centuries, allowing Gilliat to declare at 393/8 with enough time to snaffle two Glamorgan wickets that evening. The second day was almost entirely lost to rain. Nothing daunted, Hampshire took to the field on day three, confident, with the firepower at their disposal, that they could take the necessary 17 wickets in the time available.

And they nearly did. Glamorgan were 81/8 in their second innings, grimly hanging on for dear life, amidst scenes of the greatest excitement, when the umpires removed the bails and Hampshire were denied their victory and the points haul that would have all but guaranteed the title.

And so to the soggy denouement. Bournemouth is a delightful seaside town but even St Tropez can be a miserable place when it teems with rain. There is nowhere in the world more dismal than a cricket dressing room – and the one at Dean Park was what could politely be called snug – when 12 young men are cooped up for hours on end with nothing to do to fill their time. Boredom is the greatest enemy. Some engage in noisy and disputatious games of cards. Some play indoor cricket and that, with a hard ball, is a threat to frames, both window and human. Others read *The Sun* or attempt *The Telegraph*'s crossword, depending on the intellectual bent of the individual. And there in the corner would sit the captain, chain-smoking, moodily looking through rain-spattered windows out on a bleak scene of a few huddled diehards and a square rapidly filling with puddles. 'It was awful,' Gilliat admitted, 'sitting there watching our championship hopes disappear under water.' Barry said, tellingly, 'It was one of the few occasions in England that I wanted it to *stop* raining!' Mike Taylor had this to say, 'It was ironic that a bloke named Hampshire clearly had it in for Hampshire!'

To explain...the Yorkshire captain was Jackie Hampshire, an England Test player. 'Obviously, the Tykes had no interest in playing. We wanted to get out there, even for an hour or two. So, as the two captains disagreed, it was left to the umpires. And...' His implication was obvious. I sought the opinion of Gilliat. *Was it ever possible to play?* He wrinkled his nose. 'No, not really. I don't think so. Very frustrating but there it was. What could you do?'

Nothing. In the meantime, the skies had cleared enough over Chelmsford for Worcestershire to put Essex in on a drying wicket, just what Norman Gifford, a left-arm spinner *par excellence,* would have ordered for breakfast. Essex were skittled out for 87 in 35 overs, Gifford 7-15, with four bonus points going to the visitors, putting them two points above Hampshire. And so it stayed as the rains came and both matches were washed out. Worcestershire were champions and it was a bitter pill to swallow for the disconsolate Hampshire team. 'Ah well, such is life,' added Gilliat with more equanimity than he probably felt at the time. In an interview at the time, he sportingly congratulated Worcestershire on their success and forbore from mentioning that innings victory a month earlier.

Ah, the politeness of Charterhouse boys. Mike Taylor, late of Amersham College, was not so sanguine. 'Lucky Worcester! They couldn't manage even 100 against us – in either innings!' And Barry, an old boy of Durban High School? 'Pretty miserable sitting there, day after day, hoping it would clear but knowing in our hearts that it probably wouldn't.' *Did you think at any time you could have got out there?* 'It was typical English weather. It would rain and rain and then stop. Thr groundstaff would get out there and try to get the water off. And then it would rain again. Hopeless really. Normally, you'd want the umpires to call it off so you could go home, but...'

Interestingly enough, Barry is of the opinion that had they won the championship in 1974, they could well have won it again in 1975. 'That would have made it a hat-trick of titles and I think everyone would have gone for that.' The team was certainly good enough. It had destructive batting at the top end, a solid middle order and a tail that could wag. It had the fastest bowler in the world to lead the attack, supported by excellent swing and seam bowling. Perhaps it lacked a match-winning spinner (a David O'Sullivan, ironically enough), though the ever-reliable Sainsbury would seal up an end. And the catching and fielding were second to none. It was a team that all counties feared. And the bookies agreed. From 66/1 they won the championship in 1973. In 1975, again they were favourites.

In point of fact, the team did shift one place in the final table but it was in the wrong direction, down to third rather than back up to first. It says something about the confidence and expectations of all at the club that third place was considered to be a disappointment; the players took little consolation in the fact that for a couple of games, when they were unable to bowl out sides of mediocre batting resources, they might well have ended up on top. In the final analysis, we – and I use the first person here because, unlike in 1974, I did take part in several of the matches – felt that we had underperformed and that we did not really deserve the pennant after finishing one point behind Yorkshire in second place and only 16 points behind the eventual champions, Leicestershire, looked like a near miss. Truthfully, however, it never felt like that in the dressing room. Defeats to Middlesex and Glamorgan and failure to bowl Sussex and Derbyshire out twice, having made them follow on, dented our confidence and sense of invulnerability and finally put paid to our chances. There were some glorious performances, both individually and collectively, as you would expect of such a talented side, but the ruthlessness and the tenacity of serial winners were starting to ebb away. And frankly, the team was never the same again.

So, what happened? 'Gordon and Andy started to mess everybody around,' was Barry's uncompromising verdict. 'They were concentrating on their Test careers and were losing interest in the county game.' And here, for the first time at Hampshire, the club versus country conflict, that had bedevilled other counties but not ours, reared its troublesome head. In 1973 and 1974, Greenidge and Roberts were not yet Test regulars, they still had it all to prove and left no stone unturned in order to do so. Furthermore, the team had stayed remarkably free of injury; only 13 players had been used in both campaigns. In 1975, injuries struck hard and no fewer than 18 players were called upon. 'Ah, but were they all genuine injuries,' Barry asked, 'or were a few of them "furfies"?' That is difficult to assess. If a player says he is injured, who can say that he is not? There was no trained, qualified doctor or physiotherapist on the staff to assess each case dispassionately. I have to say that there were dark mutterings on occasions and no side is going to pull together when little factions develop in different corners of the dressing room. 'The truth is,' Barry admitted, 'when your three main players are down, what…ten per cent in their performance, the team isn't going to succeed, is it?'

Andy Roberts missed seven matches and took only 57 wickets, as opposed to 119 the previous year, though to be fair to him, they were taken at the extraordinarily cheap rate of 15.80. He could still turn it on and terrify the wits out of opposing batsmen when he wanted. But he was a canny operator. He had clearly worked out for himself that to bowl at express pace every day throughout the season would be career suicide. And he wanted to make his mark in Test cricket. That he certainly did and who can say that he was wrong to take his foot off the gas at times? 'There you are,' cried Barry, 'It was all down to man management and Hampshire were not good at that.'

Neither were any other counties, as it happened. I am reminded that John Snow at Sussex and Bob Willis at Warwickshire were fast bowlers who were deemed by their cricket committees to be 'difficult to handle' because they would not and could not bowl flat out all the time. And why was it that Bernard Julian of Kent seemed to gain a yard of pace when he played for West Indies? Chris Old at Yorkshire was another England fast bowler who seemed to miss a lot of matches, spending as much time on the treatment table as out in the middle. It was a real problem and it was never satisfactorily resolved, certainly not in our neck of the woods.

As batsmen, Barry Richards and Gordon Greenidge were less likely to get injured or to get away with a 'furfie'. But both had their minds on other things, though for different reasons. Greenidge had already made his debut for the West Indies and scored a maiden Test hundred. He saw himself now as an established international with a big future ahead of him, which was true, and he felt he should be treated accordingly, with due regard and special privilege, which did not always happen. No longer was he the junior dogsbody painting the pavilion seats while everybody else played cricket. It is difficult not to have a certain amount of sympathy with his perspective but his aloofness and occasional carelessness with his batting gave rise to charges of arrogance. But great players are often not the most easily assimilated within a group. The good teams, the successful teams, manage it somehow. I don't think, on reflection, any of us did a very good job in this regard. Whatever was going on in Gordon's head in the summer of 1975, runs for Hampshire – except on a couple of spectacular occasions – was not at the forefront of his mind. His aggregate of 1,120 at 41.48 could hardly be considered a personal collapse in form but 259 of those runs were scored in a single innings against Sussex (and that was a great innings, make no mistake) late on in the season and he only reached the 1,000 mark in the final game, with 168 against Worcestershire. Harsh? Barry thinks not. 'He was away with the fairies much of the time. I don't know what was going on inside there.' But Barry bends the knee to no one in his admiration of the Barbadian's immense talent.

Barry's problem was different. The fact of the matter was that he was getting bored. 'It was different for Andy and Gordon. They were playing for the West Indies and had their eyes on bigger prizes. I had no such motivation. I'd been playing now for 14 years non-stop and was tired of the treadmill.' But he still had his pride. He missed only one match, he scored 1,621 runs and his average was a mightily impressive 60.03. You could say that he had conquered county cricket. What was left for him to prove? How he yearned for the thrill and the challenge of Test cricket. *Were you jealous of the two, younger West Indians?* He paused. 'No, not jealous, envious perhaps. I was as good as them, possibly better, yet they…' He tailed off. His plight was very sad. And it is unfair to criticise Barry Richards for letting the side down in any way up to this point. He may have felt disillusion creeping up on him and entering his heart but he still did the business on the field. It was only later, from 1976 onwards, that moroseness set in and he made less and less effort to conceal it.

To my eyes, he was batting as well as ever. There were times when he seemed to throw his wicket away when well set but he denies that. 'I never threw my wicket away. I may have given it away too easily with a stupid shot but I always tried to bat as well as I could.' That, you see, is the cost of fame; every action, every shot, is closely examined and whenever fault is found, grist to the rumour mill is added – the great man is in decline or his appetite is waning or the 2.30 at Ascot is about to start on the box. No, I disagree. He just played a bad, or I should say, inappropriate, shot. Maybe it was not long after lunch but he had smashed all the bowlers around the park during the morning session and can you blame him for essaying a few extravagant swishes? I know we could all have done with him grinding out another double but come on, Barry didn't do 'grind', we all knew that. Be grateful for what he has given for we shall not see his like again. That's what should have been in our minds. That, on occasions, it was not is to our shame. Sometimes we don't know what we shall miss until it has gone.

But it was not all gloom and doom. Let us remember Barry's dazzling century before lunch against Sussex, narrowly missing another – bowled for 90 well before his ham salad – against Gloucestershire, his towering 103 against nearest challengers Lancashire, which outshone even Clive Lloyd's 112 – and that was not just my opinion – plus other glorious vignettes. But I want to focus on two innings of his that summer, not only for their technical brilliance but because I was fortunate enough to observe and admire from the other end. Or, to borrow that famous saying of Dickie Bird's, 'Where better to watch the great players than from 22 yards? I 'ad t'best seat in the 'ouse.' Except of course, I was wearing pads, not an umpire's coat.

The first was at Southampton against Middlesex. Not for the first time, our groundsman, Ernie Knights, had produced an eccentric wicket that appeared to play directly into the hands of our opponents. Normally the Northlands Road surface was what was popularly known as a 'belter' but on this occasion it was a 'bunsen', a raging turner. Two of England's finest twirlers, Titmus and Edmonds, licked their lips. After a mere ten overs of seam in Hampshire's second innings, on came the spinners and we were doomed. I was not alone in barely being able to lay bat on ball as we were dismissed for 179 but the man at the other end was playing a completely different game. He carried his bat for 71. In one sense it was uplifting to see Barry's footwork and unerring judgement of length, allied to his defensive technique and ability to manipulate the ball into the gaps. In another sense it was unutterably depressing. You wondered what right you had to be on the same field.

Much the same sense of unreality enveloped me as I walked out to bat with Barry to open the innings against Leicestershire a couple of weeks later. We put on 56, by the way. Two things I recollect. One was only having five fingers to help me count to six. And the other was a mid-pitch conference I held with the great man in the midst of this record-breaking stand. I had been peppered with a few bouncers from their opening bowlers, Ken Higgs and Graham McKenzie (the same McKenzie who had been so roughly treated by Barry in that Test series against Australia in 1969/70 and during his famous 356 at Perth the following year). *Why don't they bowl bouncers to you?* 'Probably because I hit them for six.' Very helpful. But he wasn't trying to be funny. He was only stating a fact. And he did give me a piece of beneficial advice. 'Watch the head. It usually goes down at the moment of delivery with the greater effort expended.' I'd like to say it transformed my career but it was typical of his willingness to help, if asked, and his keen eye for the nuances of the game. By the way, he scored 135 not out, despite hurting his leg, which necessitated the services of a runner. A runner? I thought he always batted with one.

That summer, the touring Australians were in town and that was one game Barry was anxious not to miss. So much so, that, in the absence of Gilliat, he took hold of the reins of captaincy. He played the role to perfection, not least winning the toss and leading the charge with the bat from the outset. Everybody was intrigued to see how fast the new sensation, Jeff Thomson, really was. Together with Dennis Lillee, he had terrorised England that winter out in Australia and all reports seemed to suggest that he was the quickest thing since the introduction of overarm bowling. What – quicker than our own Andy Roberts? You're having us on. A few overs on the players' balcony soon changed our minds. Was he quicker than Roberts? 'Not quicker,' was Gordon's assessment on his premature return to the dressing room, 'but quick as.'

Barry seemed not at all rushed when he was facing. That is always the hallmark of a great player, whatever the game. He seems to have *time*. Everything appears to slow down as he unhurriedly gets himself into the right position to deal with whatever is flung at him. And in Thommo's case, I use the word 'flung' advisedly.

He had this unusual, unorthodox, slinging action, with the arm coming over from behind his back, much like a javelin thrower. It was interesting to hear Barry's analysis of his bowling style. 'At the time, everybody thought that Lillee had the purer action, classically side-on at the moment of delivery. But actually, that was not so. You watch – he twisted his back at that moment and as a result had injuries that forced him to adapt and reduce his pace. But Thommo actually had the more easy, fluid action and therefore, I believe, suffered fewer injuries.' Neither of us could understand why Thomson's unique but effective bowling style has never been emulated, with the possible exception of Malinga the Slinga, the successful Sri Lankan one-day bowler.

Whatever speed or mode of delivery the Australians fired at Barry made little difference. He was in majestic form and a memorable century was there for his taking. 'Aaaagh,' he cried in a rare moment of exasperation. 'I was caught on the boundary for 96! Top-edged a sweep. Off the leggie Higgs, I think.' For once, Barry's memory was crystal clear. *It was a great three days. Lovely weather, packed house, batting well against your old mates. You must have enjoyed it.* He agreed. 'Ian Chappell had been my captain for South Australia. And his brother, Greg, was a true friend. And most of the others I had either played with or against.' *We had a good time with them in the evenings too, didn't we?* 'I don't remember,' he said virtuously.

In the second innings, he was batting just as fluently before disaster, on both a professional and personal level, struck. He was poleaxed on 69. I shall put that another way. When his score was on 69, he was hit a sickening blow amidships by Thomson. 'Everybody was on the floor,' remembered Barry, 'including me. They were doubled up with laughter; I was writhing in pain.' I have never fully understood why this should be so in cricket. If you are hit anywhere by a cricket ball and down you go, everybody rushes up to you, concerned and sympathetic. Except when you get hit in the box. And that, for some reason, is cause only for mirth.

'Tell you what, Barry,' remarked an unsympathetic Greg Chappell as Barry was carted off the field, 'ask your physio to give you something to take away the pain without reducing the swelling!' We saw the damage to Barry's manhood when he was back in the dressing room and I can assure you that it was not a pretty sight. In fact it was horrific and any lingering smirks were immediately wiped from our faces. Particularly mine. I was next in.

How quick was Thommo is the question asked of me to this day. One ball I did not see. Literally. But somehow I survived, with my life, my manhood and my wicket intact, 29 not out, to help secure the draw. The Aussies I found an odd mixture, rude and aggressive on the field but charming and companionable off it. 'Have you ever been spoken to like that?' asked Peter Sainsbury of me during a mid-wicket chat. I had to admit I had not. That is, not since I had spat on my brother when we were kids. 'No worse than you got in the Currie Cup,' Barry reminded me.

This wonderful game aside, it was not a fulfilling season. Consolation of some kind was to be found in winning the John Player League that season, the 40-over competition on Sunday afternoons. It seems strange to refer to Hampshire's first one-day trophy as a consolation but that is what it seemed, a measure perhaps of how highly regarded this team was in the mid-1970s. Many years later, I remember talking to Peter Walker, the former Glamorgan player and broadcaster, who hosted the BBC2 television coverage of the league. He said that at the regular meetings with the producer and production staff in order to plan for each Sunday broadcast, the first question asked was, 'Where are Hampshire playing?' That was how attractive the team was to a viewing audience.

Of course, even-handedness had to be applied but it became difficult not to follow the leading team as the season built up to its exciting climax. As a result, we were on the box for the last three games. He also told me that the venue for the final game, at Darley Dale, in a valley deep in the Derbyshire Dales, provided untold problems for their technical crew because of its inaccessibility to the nearest booster mast to put out a strong enough electronic signal. Never mind the inaccessibility of the booster mast and the problems with the signal, it was just as inaccessible for cars. It is the only cricket ground in the country where the players had to queue up to get in. And the least said about getting out of the place the better.

There is nothing wrong with Darley Dale Cricket Club. In fact it is a very pleasant, picturesque, village ground in one of the most beautiful areas of England, but as a venue for the most important match of the competition that season, it was particularly unsuited. Notwithstanding, 6,000 people crammed into the tiny ground while we sceptically examined before play what was no more than a club wicket. It was felt that an extra spinner was required so, in his usual kindly, regretful manner, the captain informed me that I would be 12th man. At least I could observe without nerves how brilliantly our openers, Richards and Greenidge, batted on an uneven surface against an attack that comprised three Test bowlers, Hendrick, Ward and Venkataraghavan. They both scored rapid fifties and pretty well won the game for us, comfortably, by 70 runs.

It was all very satisfying and we enjoyed a glass or two of Champagne inside the dressing room and outside with our jubilant supporters. However, celebration did not go on into the early hours, as it might have done had circumstances been different. We had to get home and Southampton is a long drive from the Peak District. Especially when it takes you one and a half hours to get out of the car park. Most of our jubilation had dissipated by the time we started to head south. 'Never mind trying to get out of the ground,' snorted Barry. 'Remember, we had to queue to get in! At some of these little country grounds, there was nowhere set aside for the players to park! We had to take our chances along with the punters trying to find a space. Which made carrying those heavy coffins from car to dressing room an exhausting business.' Ah, but Barry was a master at enlisting the help of willing schoolboys to carry his.

A glance at the Hampshire batting averages for the Sunday League might have improved my mood, if only they had been immediately available. In fact, they would have made me laugh out loud. They read: First AJ Murtagh 47.00; Second BA Richards 45.93. My subject was incredulous when I read them out to him. *But I have to admit, Barry, my figures read: five innings, four not-outs, 47 runs aggregate.* 'You know I'm not a fact and figures man, Murt.' *Jealousy, Barry, sheer jealousy. Besides, it was Peter Sainsbury who always said that they can't get you out if you're at the other end.* 'I wouldn't know. Not my natural habitat.'

Jubilation may have dissipated on that long, slow journey home but for Barry that was not the only thing dissolving, and rapidly too. He now readily admits that by the time he returned for the 1976 season, he was fed up to the back teeth with county cricket. All of us could sense it. He seemed to take no real genuine enjoyment in what he was doing anymore. It was a job, nothing more, nothing less, one that no longer held any pleasure for him. You only had to look at him as he reluctantly dragged his body up the steps to the dressing room at Northlands Road, his face a picture of gloomy resignation. He reminded me of the schoolboy in Shakespeare's *Seven Ages of Man*:

'Then the whining school-boy with his satchel
And shining morning face, creeping like a snail
Unwillingly to school.'

Barry's satchel was his cricket bag and no one crept more unwillingly into county cricket grounds in 1976 and 1977 than he. He wrote in his autobiography, *The Barry Richards Story*, published in 1978, 'It saddens me when I think of my breathless excitement at walking out to play for Hampshire for the first time…And I know that when I walk off a county ground for the last time – whenever that may be – it will be with an enormous sense of relief.'

Within six months of writing this, he was granted his wish. There was undoubtedly controversy and no little bitterness that surrounded his decision to quit the club mid-season but in truth his total disillusionment with the county game probably meant that it was for the best, for him and for his team-mates. I'm sure some sort of brainstorm would have occurred had he not packed his bag and gone. Whose brain would have exploded first was a moot point. It had got that bad.

The rot might have set in by 1976 but you would never have known judging by the way Barry played that season. He may not have relished the humdrum routine of a professional cricketer but he remained a professional to his fingertips. He talks about being ten per cent down in commitment and performance but his 90 per cent far exceeded what most could ever hope to achieve. Barry may not have clattered down the steps of the pavilion every day when the bell went with a spring in his step and a song in his heart but he had his pride and he still played some magnificent innings. In all, he scored 1,572 runs at a fraction under 50. Next highest in the averages was David Turner with 36.25. Furthermore, Barry scored seven centuries, more than he had ever done in the course of an English season, including one in each innings against Kent, which had particular relevance and poignancy for him, as we shall see. From a playing point of view, in a difficult, injury-ravaged season for Hampshire, most were willing to grab his 90 per cent with both hands.

A perception took hold at this stage in Barry's career that it seemed he couldn't really be bothered to concentrate for long periods of time in order to make the big scores that were expected of him. His public would have to be content with vignettes, attractive embellishments to the innings rather than the framework around which a competitive total is built. This is nonsense. Yes, of course there were occasions when he played a loose shot and paid the penalty but that is the price you pay if you are an attacking batsman. And yes, there were times when his carelessness at the crease would cause howls of exasperation back in the dressing room because everybody sensed, in that moment of recklessness, that our job had just got a whole lot harder. What team's morale is not given a shot in the arm when the opposition's best player has just been dismissed? It was an understandable, human response by his team-mates but not one entirely praiseworthy. It smacked of self-interest. 'Come on, guys,' was Barry's unspoken – for the most part – riposte, 'I can't do it all on my own.' Genius needs latitude, freedom, room to breathe. The trouble was that Barry, almost by the day, was feeling more and more fenced in.

This was no fault of his, though it could be argued that maybe he could have handled the situation with more tact. But put yourself in his shoes. May I suggest that a week in mid-July during the season of 1976 might be as good a time as any for you to lace up his cricket boots. Hampshire were playing Glamorgan at Bournemouth. It was a Saturday and the holiday crowd was a decent one. The weather, let us remind ourselves, was glorious; it was in the middle of the great heatwave of that year.

Barry scored a hundred before lunch. His batting matched the weather – need I say more? Meanwhile, 200 miles north, at a packed Old Trafford, West Indies were playing against England. This was the series made famous by Tony Greig's injudicious comment that he was going to make the West Indies 'grovel'. Greig was the England captain, the same Greig who had left his native South Africa to seek fame and fortune in England where he felt he had a better chance of playing in the top flight.

He was right. Tony Greig could not get in the Eastern Province side but he had worked his way up, via Sussex, to play for, and captain, England. The irony would not have been lost on Barry. Furthermore, to pile injustice upon bitterness, two of his team-mates were playing in that Test match. Andy Roberts, together with Michael Holding and Wayne Daniel, were peppering John Edrich and Brian Close with a continuous barrage of short-pitched bowling that has gone down in infamy as one of the most disgraceful and brutal passages of play in the history of the game. With the bat, West Indies were just as merciless. Barry's opening partner and erstwhile apprentice to his sorcerer, Gordon Greenidge, was launching himself into the international stratosphere with innings of 134 and 101. Barry must have felt as if he had been forced to attend the disco at the local village hall while his mates were living it up in town at Annabel's in Berkeley Square.

Of all the grounds in England, Barry liked Hove as much as any. *What about the slope? And the sea fret? And John Snow bowling downhill with the wind in his sails?* 'I'm not talking about Hove! I mean Brighton. At least there was more going on there in the evenings.' Undoubtedly true and a couple of weeks later, at Hove, he scored another century before lunch against Sussex. The weather remained hot, the beaches were packed, the deckchairs around the boundary were full and it was a moot point whether the crowd were more dazzled by the sun's merciless rays or Barry's blazing shot-making. Perfect, you might think. What more could a man possibly want? At the same time, however, oop north in Leeds, Greenidge was thrashing the England attack all around Headingley for his third successive Test hundred.

There was another poignant moment during that stiflingly hot summer. Over a Bank Holiday weekend, in front of a full house at Southampton, Barry scored a century in each innings against Kent. His parents were watching, proof positive to his multitudinous admirers, and one or two of his detractors, that Barry Richards could score runs at will. He scoffs at the very idea. 'Come on, Murt, you and I know that there is more to batting than that. I could have got an unplayable delivery first ball.' Of course he is right.

Nobody, even Bradman, has been able to deliver innings on demand. It's just that is the way it seems when great players stride out into the spotlight and seize the moment. I watched both innings and now I come to describe them, words fail me. On the first morning, he was one run shy of yet another century before lunch. While he was at the crease before he was dismissed for 159, his partners, Lewis, Turner and Jesty, all considerable shot-makers in their own right, were reduced to the roles of bit part players in comparison – a comparison with which they would have heartily concurred.

His second innings of 108 was compiled – no, compiled is a wholly inadequate verb, more like plundered – in only 83 minutes. Do not forget that this was a three-day county match against a bowling attack comprising Jarvis, Shepherd, Underwood, Hills and Woolmer (three Test bowlers) in the days before heavy bats, short boundaries, helmets and the different mindset of a generation not brought up on T20 slogging. I may labour the point but it is important to put into perspective the unusually rapid rate of scoring that Barry was spearheading.

You __must__ have been inspired by the presence of your mum and dad? 'No, they just happened to be on their travels and wanted to come and see me play.' *How were you getting on with your father at the time?* 'Look, it was not so bad. I was concentrating on my career and he was looking after the money at home. It was only later, when I was in Perth, that things broke down completely.' *So you didn't try to put on a show for them specially?* 'Nah. I was just hitting a good patch, that was all.' And then he grinned. 'But it was narse, hey!' Barry does not have a thick, grating South African accent that one frequently hears from, largely, Afrikaans speakers. The Natal inflexions are gentler on the ear but the intonation of that word 'nice' imbued it with far more expressiveness than any of its usual anodyne meanings.

There was another special innings of Barry's that summer, remembered with fondness and sadness in equal measure. It was in the John Player League against Essex on anther sun-drenched day at Southampton. Essex made an unremarkable 168 off their 40 overs, thanks in large part to Gooch's 65. Hampshire gobbled up that total in only 33 overs, led by an imperious 101 from Barry. His hundred contained 15 fours and two sixes. He was the first out when his side's score was 127. Do the maths. I didn't even need him to tell me. So far, so Barry. But the mere mention of the name of his opening partner, Peter Barrett, unfailingly brings a tear to the eye of anyone who knew him, and whether that is a tear of laughter or of grief is always difficult to tell. Peter – his nickname is unrepeatable – had a short and undistinguished career for Hampshire. A local lad, a bit of a rough diamond, he made only six first-class appearances and this single one-day match for his county: at the end of the season, he was released and he dropped out of the game. Yet he had more talent in his little finger than others of us on the staff had in the whole of our being. So why did he not make it? Why did he not fulfil his incontestable talent?

You see, cricket, probably more so than any other game, with the exception of golf perhaps, is played in the mind as much as on the pitch. And dear old Pete, it has to be said, did not have a mind that often stirred itself. He just could not work things out, he did not learn what it took to make a professional cricketer, he lacked insight, perception, common sense. In one way, that is what made him so likeable, he did not possess a nasty bone in his body, he was utterly guileless and gullible. We all remember tipping him out of the car just before the Severn Bridge. We were on our way to play Glamorgan and as Wales was a foreign country, he would have needed a passport, which of course he did not possess. He was distraught. He thought, by this careless oversight of his, he had let the side down and we would have to play with ten men. All right, the joke is an old one and, don't worry, we went back to fetch him – his language was as predictable as it was colourful – but it seemed incredible to us that he had fallen for it. Barry will forgive me for this digression about Pete, for he was as amused and baffled by Pete as anyone, yet the story does emphasise the incontrovertible fact that talent alone will not a success make. Remember those countless hours that Barry spent as a young boy in the nets and consider how he soaked up advice, knowledge and experience like a piece of blotting paper?

One story will suffice as illustration. Barry would have been keen to play against the tourists in 1975 because his opponents were old mates in the Australian team. He had no such personal ties in the West Indian team that was touring in 1976, so he decided to take a rest. Shrewd move. In the same way that Jeff Thomson had only just burst on the scene the year before, everybody was keen (except the Hampshire team) to witness at first hand the pace of the new fast bowling sensation, Michael Holding. The sight of him, pushing off from the sightscreen at Northlands Road, as he accelerated into that long, fluid, lissom run-up and gathered himself for the beautifully balanced and graceful delivery, was awe-inspiring. The memory of the experience of facing him from 22 yards has been erased from my mind. I am still here so I guess I must have survived. 'Whispering Death', Dickie Bird so memorably named him. In the absence of Barry, Peter Barrett opened the batting. He was left-handed. But he only possessed a pair of right-handed pads. There is a difference. Batting is a sideways activity; it stands to reason therefore that extra padding is provided on the side of the knee more vulnerable.

This fact seemed to perpetually escape Pete. Stubbornly, he persisted with his favoured right-handed pads. Against the pace of Holding, the inevitable happened. He was hit a sickening blow on the inside of his right knee as he thrust his front leg forward and down he went like a sack of potatoes. The following scene was recounted to me many years later by Clive Lloyd, the West Indies captain, when his son was a pupil of mine at Malvern. Pete Barrett was lying there groaning in pain. Eventually, he opened his eyes and all he could see was a circle of black faces, none of whom he knew, peering down anxiously at him. Then he recognised Lloyd, probably because he was the only one wearing glasses. "Ere Cloive,' he said in his Hampshire accent, 'tell your fahst bowlers not to bowl so f*****' fahst!' Everybody laughed. The West Indians were never unpleasant on the field. They never sledged. They had no need.

The sad postscript to this story is that a mere eight years later, Peter Barrett was killed in a motorbike accident. It was a shock to us all but scarcely a surprise. Poor Pete. He just did not have the wherewithal to survive in the harsh world of professional sport. But what a talent. If only someone could have hit on the formula to polish that rough diamond. Even Barry, who didn't know him as well as some of the rest of us, smiles at his memory. As for Barry's memory of that partnership with Pete, he has this interesting anecdote to recount. He had played brilliantly; he needed no affirmation of that. As it had been televised, he approached Richie Benaud, one of the commentators, with a casual enquiry. Did the BBC have a copy of the tape of his innings? Benaud promised to make enquiries. He came back with the answer that yes indeed, there was a tape, but that it would cost him £800! 'Tape was very expensive,' Barry explained. 'So they used the same tape again and again.' I would imagine that the tape of Barry's scintillating innings is now gathering dust in the BBC archives somewhere, overlain with countless episodes of *EastEnders*. I would give anything to see that cherished Victorian pavilion once more.

Barry returned to England for the 1977 season, in early April. No, he had not been so fooled by the Saharan weather the previous summer that he now believed in global warming, that England had a Mediterranean climate and that Southampton in spring would be as balmy and pleasant as Marbella. Money drove him to don his longjohns and extra sweaters, specifically his benefit. The practice of counties awarding a benefit to deserving professionals was a relic of 19th-century practice and as such reflected the social and financial conventions of the time. It served its purpose and was a useful and mutually beneficial means by which a club could reward a loyal and stalwart servant at a time when the average wage of a professional cricketer was nothing to write home about. But by the time of a more egalitarian and prosperous era of the late 20th century, the system was surely outdated, anachronistic even. It seems doubly preposterous that the tradition holds as much sway today in the 21st century as it ever did. By and large, it worked like this. During the course of the year, the beneficiary would hold a series of fund-raising dinners, auctions of sporting memorabilia, golf days, celebrity cricket matches, pontoon boxes and of course the entire gate money of one day of a match of the player's choosing. Yet another one of the few occasions in Barry's county career when he did not pray for rain, I imagine.

Hampshire had awarded a benefit to their South African overseas player for the 1977 season. No one could possibly deny that he deserved it. He had given eight uninterrupted years of service and pleasure to the club and its supporters and had consistently been their top scorer and major match-winner. Besides, Barry did not invent the benefit system; that had been in place for well over one hundred years. 'In any case,' he said, 'I needed the money.' Barry had no choice but to maximise the revenue that a benefit could bring. Hence his early arrival on these shores in 1977. He usually left it as late as he could possibly get away with.

I cannot imagine anything on earth that you would relish less than going around the county asking for money. He screwed up his face. 'Legalised begging! I hated it,' he practically spat. 'Such a humiliating way to be rewarded, having to go into pubs and bars to drum up trade.' For some that might have been no hardship. To one or two, the alcoholic temptations proved ruinous. Barry, however, was no pub animal. Essentially shy, he shunned the limelight and preferred the company of his tight circle of loyal friends. The only time he ever came alive in public was when he had a bat in his hand. 'Some people, like Botham, Flintoff, Pietersen, love the fame and the bright lights,' he said, 'and lap up all the celebrity circus stuff. I never enjoyed it – made me more insular and withdrawn, probably.' Remember the story his Natal team-mate, Denis Gamsy, recounted about the way Barry would shrink back into his chair whenever he was publicly recognised on visits to the hotel bars of Durban's beach front?

At that time, Barry was going out with a delightful girl called Shelley Sullivan (now Morris), an Australian, who was very popular with the Hampshire players and wives. She and my wife struck up a firm friendship that continues to this day and the four of us spent many a convivial evening together. Naturally, Shelley was conspicuous in helping Barry with his benefit and she can confirm what an excruciating experience it was for him. 'People thought that because Barry was out there in the middle swiping those bowlers all around the place and entertaining thousands of people then he must have enjoyed the limelight,' she told me, 'but he didn't. He loved the batting and the challenge and he preferred it if there was a large crowd because that made it more of an occasion. But once he was off the field, he hated being the centre of attraction wherever he went. I think he was quite shy, actually. He certainly didn't think he was public property and he tried to protect his privacy as much as he could.'

So going around all those pubs, cap in hand, must have been purgatory? She shuddered. 'I can't imagine anything worse for him. He wasn't a "pub" man. He enjoyed a drink with friends but it was not his first choice of venue.' I can corroborate that. As a non-smoker, Barry hated the fug of tobacco smoke that permeated through pubs in the days before the ban. We all did. But where else was there to meet?

As an Australian, and therefore unused to this concept of entitlement that professional cricketers had of their 'golden handshake', Shelley had an outsider's perspective that probably mirrored her South African boyfriend's ambivalent attitude to the whole business. 'Barry believed that his benefit was deserved; he should have it. But it was the "show me how much I am worth" that laid him bare.' What a very perceptive phrase – 'laid him bare'. 'Constant conversation and praise about his talent flummoxed him,' said Shelley. 'He didn't have the banter that comes readily to others. And I say this with affection.' Vintcent van der Bijl had made the same point to me earlier. 'A friend of mine told me that Barry had once admitted to him that he wished he had the same easy and conversational gifts with people that I had. I was astonished, quite frankly.'

Clearly, some people sensed Barry's unease at successive benefit functions and felt that he should have put on a more jolly face, especially as he was relying on their generosity. But I have never known Barry to put on a face. He is arguably the worst actor I have ever met. His face is a window into his soul. That is why his smile is so gratifying. It doesn't come easily. Barry is different. And *'vive la différence'*, as Spencer Tracy once memorably said, though I'm sure the French had long been using the phrase before him. It is the same with actors, seeing as I have just mentioned one. They come off stage, take off their costume, remove their make-up and revert to whom they really are – and people are surprised that it's not the same person. I've not met many actors but I have heard that a number of them shun the spotlight off stage as Barry did. No wonder he hated signing autographs. The curtain had come down on his performance, he had taken his bows and now he was trying to slip quietly away through the theatre's side door. During this year however, he was forced to stride cheerfully through the front door. How often he must have sat in his car in the car park outside summoning up the mental resolve to get out and make his entrance.

So, how much did your benefit realise? His answer was immediate and unequivocal. 'Thirty-five grand.' And then, as a grim rider, 'Which was about half the amount that was generated.' I did not pursue the financial details. It was not uncommon then for sums of money raised for the beneficiary to go 'missing'. Unsurprising really. Benefits were starting to become big business and few cricketers are expert businessmen. How they were expected to keep their eye on two balls at once – one out there in the middle and the other on a spreadsheet of accounts in someone else's briefcase – was always beyond me. 'Look,' said Barry, by way of explanation, 'those pontoon boxes – they were really no more than cardboard fruit machines. You'd put your money in and have a gamble. Some of the proceeds were meant to go to the landlord and the rest to the beneficiary. But, as you can imagine, with money swilling around in a pub... well, let's just say there was a fair bit of spillage!' He rather liked the pun.

Nonetheless, £35,000 is a not inconsiderable amount. Up until that year, the largest figure for a Hampshire player had been £7,000. He was not ungrateful to the Hampshire supporters for their generosity and even now he looks back on the whole venture with some shame mixed with the embarrassment. 'I could have been more openly appreciative. It's just that sometimes I found it difficult to pitch it right, to find the appropriate words, without sounding too grovelling.' *Did the amount cause friction in the dressing room?* I knew the answer of course but the question had to be asked. 'Probably,' he replied, a little mournfully. I guess it was about now that the tag, the Happy Hants, had started to wear thin.

One of the problems facing Barry was that the system, as well as being anachronistic, was also inequitable. There were rich counties, who did their beneficiaries proud, and there were poor counties, who struggled to make ends meet, never mind lining the pockets of their favourite players. In the top bracket were, obviously, the larger, city-based counties, such as Surrey, Middlesex, Warwickshire and Lancashire. Kent also did well with their wide base of fanatical supporters. Hampshire, together with Derbyshire, Gloucestershire and Somerset, were the poor relations. Accordingly, an average, though loyal, employee of a rich county could expect to double, or treble, what a superstar from another county would expect. Cricket followers (to say nothing of the tax man) were staggered at the £14,000 raised for Cyril Washbrook of Lancashire in 1948. Another man of the Red Rose county, Jack Simmons, broke through the six-figure barrier in 1980 with £128,000. Graham Hick, of Worcestershire, raised £300,000 in 1980. Andrew Flintoff, sometimes of Lancashire, but more popularly of England and the World, was reputed to have made several million in 1999. You can see the exponential increase in the figures and it is no wonder the system is coming under increasing public scrutiny.

Barry had another, more altruistic, objection to benefits, which is all of a piece with his opinion of county cricket. 'People hang on too long in the game, long past the time when they are at their peak, just to get a benefit. It clogs up the system and prevents the younger players from coming through.' There was definitely some truth in what he said. We could all point to examples of players well into their 30s, even older, who were wily and experienced enough to do enough to guarantee another contract, their best days a distant memory. Some may not have wanted to quit, it is true, and some may not have wanted to think about what they were going to do after a life in cricket. But the financial carrot of a benefit usually proved irresistible and rather like the crusty old bachelor in his favourite armchair in the school common room, he was unbudgeable.

'It never happened in provincial cricket,' Barry added, 'for all the inadequacies of the financial organisation of the Currie Cup. We were all amateurs.' *Except you.* 'Except me. But I was the only one. And that was another reason why I never wanted to captain a side of professionals. I was okay on the field but captaining an English county side was so much more than that.'

Who would explain it better than Richard Gilliat, our captain at Hampshire? 'You want to know what it was like being a captain? Most of my time, I seem to recall, Murt, was spent trying to get people like you into bed at a reasonable time.' Putting aside a burning desire to sue for slander, I persisted. 'Well, all the teams I played for, I captained, all the way up the ladder, from school onwards. Then I had a few years under Roy Marshall and I always had an inkling that I wanted to do the job.' *Did you enjoy the responsibility?* 'Yes, I did, though I think I could have been a much better batsman if I'd had a few more years concentrating and working on improving my batting rather than worrying about everyone else!' *And what was your philosophy?* 'Two-fold really. To enjoy it. And to play attacking cricket. That last year – 1978 – after Desmond Eagar, the club secretary, died, I felt I was no longer enjoying it and that it was time to finish.' *What was it like captaining the three superstars?* He gave a rueful smile. 'Not always a bed of roses. But my view was to try to get them on board. Perhaps one or two felt that I gave in to them too much but I don't think so. We wanted them out there on the pitch performing. It was no good if they got the sulks and downed tools.'

Specifically, how was Barry with you? 'Very helpful. He was no real trouble. A few of the older players resented him a bit. The younger ones didn't.' *And what about the charge that he was a bit mercenary, only after the money?* 'Hmm, a tricky one. When I first took over, there was friction over bonus money, a throwback to another era, really. People were saying it's all right for him to walk off with the bonus but someone's got to stand at the other end while he's batting. Similarly, with the bowlers. They get the money for taking the wickets but you need fielders to fetch the ball and catch it from time to time. The system seemed outdated to me so I got it changed. Everyone got the same bonus, depending on how well we did. All right, some players got paid more than others but that seemed perfectly fair, as they were better. But we were all on the same bonus after that and the mood, team morale, definitely improved thereafter.'

He seemed more proud of that initiative of his than any other. But he was ever a fair man, our captain. I wondered what Barry thought of the new deal. 'As I recall,' he said, 'there were two or three changes to the bonus system when I was there. Certainly it was better that we shared out the bonuses. But where I took issue with the cricket authorities – and I was not alone in this – was that the better players should have been better rewarded. This was pre-Packer but a stage on from the old amateur and professional ethos – a sort of halfway house, if you like. It helped but it was never going to cure the problem.' *And it was reasonably amicable between you and the captain over all this?* He nodded. I wondered if Richard Gilliat felt the same. 'Well, our paths have not crossed that often,' he answered, 'but it's always good to see him, at players' reunions and the like, and we get on well. We always did, really.'

Gilliat saw 1978 as the season when the wheels started to fall off what had been a very fine team. My impression was that the wheels developed a distinct wobble the year before, 1977. Certainly, Barry's chariot was getting rusty, with bits falling off all over the place. For the first time in his Hampshire career, he failed to complete 1,000 runs for the season; he made only 927. Injuries had restricted him to 16 out of the 22 matches, he scored only two centuries that summer and the distractions of running his benefit had obviously had a deleterious effect on his commitment and concentration. For all that, his average remained respectable, 42.13. However, there is no getting away from the fact that, by his levels of excellence, it was a poor season. Were his standards slipping? Were his reactions not what they were? Had his eyes started to go?

'Look,' he tried to explain, 'no one is as good at 33 as they were at 23. But that wasn't the reason. I'd now been playing cricket for 16 seasons on the trot, without a break. And I'd run out of challenges.' As we know, and as he has emphasised, weight of runs in themselves, number of centuries scored, with the magic figure of 100 of them on everybody's lips, where he stood in the national averages – he had long given up reading them in *The Daily Telegraph* in the morning – none of these motivated him. With the acceptance of South Africa back into the international fold no more than a pipe dream, nothing was left for him to achieve. He'd done it all. Now he was only marking time. As he wrote in his autobiography, 'In 1967, no young man could have loved cricket more than B.A. Richards; ten years later, there could be no more disenchanted player in the first-class game.'

In an attempt to unearth Barry's true state of mind when he wrote that, or at least to discover whether he was as desperate as it sounds, I contacted Martin Tyler. Now an eminent football commentator on Sky Sports, he loves his cricket and was no mean player in his youth. He was a great friend of Bob Willis, the former England captain and fast bowler. I believe they were once flat-mates, together with Geoff Howarth, the New Zealand and Surrey batsman. Barry knew Geoff well and through him, he was introduced to Martin. The two of them came to an agreement for Martin to ghost-write Barry's autobiography. In fact, one or two sessions of their collaboration took place in my brother's flat in south London when Barry was playing in the capital. It occurred to me that I was in the same position as Martin Tyler all those years ago, having the privileged, not to say unique, window into Barry's soul. Martin would surely be a useful source of thoughts and opinions on the state of mind of our mutual subject at this difficult stage of his career.

'The crux to understanding Barry,' Tyler said, 'was the relationship he had with his father. It was, by all accounts, not an easy one. For one reason or another, Barry never felt really loved or appreciated by his father and that, as we all know, can have an unhappy effect on one's childhood.' I agreed. 'The other thing to remember,' continued Tyler, 'is that South Africa's isolation from Test cricket hit him hard. So two significant influences on him that would have defined him as a person, his father's love and support and a successful career in the international arena, were denied him. It wasn't that he was *bitter* about his misfortune but it hurt and saddened him.

I think it definitely had an effect on him for many years, despite what he may say to the contrary. He felt unfulfilled.'

How did you get on with him? Was he an easy subject to work with? 'No problems at all. We respected each other. We were pretty close for five or six years and though our contact has inevitably dropped off since his playing days ended, we still keep in touch. And what's this utter nonsense about him being mean and not paying his way?' *Well, that wasn't on my list of questions, Martin, but since you brought it up...* 'That's what it was – nonsense! He bought drinks and meals while we bickered about the terms of the contract. That's a joke, by the way, there was no bickering. Well, there was but it was all in jest.' I told him that the experiences that he had outlined in his journalistic dealings with Barry exactly mirrored my own.

Most of the interviewing and researching for the book took place during this 1977 season. In some ways, that was a pity, for Barry was not playing at his best. But in a perverse way, the fact that Barry was not spending long hours at the crease meant that Tyler had more time with him in front of the tape recorder. 'I remember one match at Guildford against Surrey,' Tyler said. 'He was out in the first over of the day, caught Skinner, bowled Jackman [for] none. He joined me after a while for a session and he was a bit grumpy.' *Not surprising – he'd just got out.* 'I know. But he soon warmed up and we had a very productive few hours. He was always easy to talk to, very welcoming, very friendly. Not at all like his reputation.' Not for the first time, then and now, I reflected on this 'reputation' of Barry's for being difficult, uncommunicative, even rude at times and, as always, I remain baffled. It is true that he could be blunt, even brusque at times, but I am convinced that people, some people, just took him the wrong way. 'He should have had me as his PR agent,' was the cry of Barry's schoolboy friend, Dave Anderson. 'I could have saved him so much trouble.'

'There was another memory I have of our association, something I shall never forget,' Tyler said in conclusion. 'It was on 12 July at Northlands Road in Southampton. Hampshire were playing Sussex and later that evening, when Barry and I met up – Steve Coppell was also with us, as I recall – Barry was not out overnight.' It started to come back to me. Barry was out of sorts and out of form and had struggled to survive the few overs before stumps. 'When we were chatting that evening,' continued Tyler, 'I mentioned to Barry that I had never seen him score a hundred.'

Challenge! 'I beg your pardon?' *A challenge! Barry thrived on challenges. I know what's coming next.* 'The following morning, he thrashed the Sussex attack all round the ground. His first fifty came in 74 minutes. His hundred came up 23 minutes later!' And having got his hundred, he promptly had a slog at the gentle off-spin of Barclay and was caught on the boundary for 100 exactly. Typical. But unforgettable for those who were there. 'I like to think he did it for me,' said Tyler. 'I'm sure that probably wasn't the case but I was bloody grateful nonetheless.' I wouldn't have put it past Barry, myself. He could do that sort of thing. The rest of us mere mortals would never dream of it.

There was another reason for his brown study that season, a source of confusion, controversy and discord among us all, players, administrators, media and fans alike. Six months previously, Tony Greig – the England captain! – had been secretly signing up players from around the world for what was to become known as the Packer Circus. The news broke early in 1977 and at a stroke, the cricketing world was split asunder. In any civil war, brother is set against brother and the same was true in the county game during that fractious English county season. Barry of course had been one of the first to sign – '*the* first' he assured me. And why ever not? 'It gave me the chance, late on in my career, of what I had craved all these years – competitive cricket on the world stage.'

That was not what was causing the problems in the team. Nobody would want to deny him that late stab at glory. But should the pirates, as they were called, be allowed to play in the English domestic game when they had signed up to play for an organisation that was totally outside the jurisdiction of the game's governing body? Or bodies, as the mutiny had spread worldwide. These were sporting, ethical, patriotic, financial and loyalty issues, exposed by the upheaval, which will be examined in detail in a later chapter. But it did make for a strange, uneasy season, no better illustrated than by a rather bizarre little ritual enacted on the pitch at Bristol before the start of play against Gloucestershire on the final day of the season. It had been planned but the targets were quite in the dark. Both Barry and Gordon Greenidge, two obvious recruits for Packer, both of whom everybody expected to be banned and therefore playing in their last match for their county, were surrounded by the rest of the team and subjected to a loud but tuneless rendition of *Auld Lang Syne*. Barry describes the moment in his autobiography, 'I would like to think that the feelings that inspired the gesture were sincere; at the time I was sure that they were enjoying a huge joke.'

I was not there so I cannot comment. My guess is that it was a little of both. Cricketers are not known for their sense of seriousness and earnest solemnity. Everything is reduced to levity and mirth. I have not spoken to any one of the Hampshire all-male choir who does not double up with laughter at the memory of the moment. Yet underneath there was a genuine sense of respect and regret. Both Gordon and Barry were great players and even the most intractable of their team-mates readily accepted that. And what tremendous innings over the years both had played, innings which left even hard-nosed pros, who reckoned they had seen it all, open-mouthed in awe and wonder. So, on balance, it had been a privilege to play with them. At any rate, *Auld Lang Syne* beat giving them a carriage clock.

8

Natal Success 1973–76

*'Congratulations! You out-bowled, out-batted, out-fielded and **out-captained** us throughout.'*

**Ali Bacher, Transvaal captain, to Barry after he had led
Natal to Currie Cup triumph in 1974**

O N a hot, still, cloudless morning in early March 1974 in Port Elizabeth in South Africa's Eastern Cape, the packed main stand of St George's Park erupted into a tumult of whistling, cheering and shouting. Little had disturbed the torpor of the morning's play; Natal's opening partnership had progressed without alarm in the first crucial session of their Currie Cup match against Eastern Province. It was towards the business end of the season and Natal, following a depressingly fallow period, were within touching distance of upsetting the odds and making off with the cup. Clearly intent on taking full advantage of a sluggish pitch by posting a commanding first innings score, all was going well for the visitors. The crowd were restless. A wicket would do.

So what had occasioned this sudden outburst of enthusiasm? Was it the wicket Eastern Province so desperately craved? Had it been an astonishing catch? Or an athletic piece of fielding? Or possibly a soaring six? In fact it was none of these things. Blithely unaware, a young English girl, dressed in a fetching top and short skirt, was making her way past Castle Corner and in front of the stand. Now, it is important to understand that in South Africa, Castle Corner rivals, if not surpasses, all the great ungovernable spectator areas in cricket grounds the world over for its alcohol-fuelled raucousness and uninhibited appreciation of the female form. Still blissfully unaware of the cause of the commotion, the girl strode towards her designated seat in the grandstand. As she eventually took her place, the reception she received from the St George's faithful bore comparison with any acclamation accorded Eastern Province's favoured son, Graeme Pollock, after another of his magisterial innings.

The eyes of all participants out in the middle, including those of the two umpires, swivelled in the direction and cause of the clamour. The said Graeme Pollock, captain of the EP side, turned to me and enquired loudly, 'Jeez, Pommie, is that your missus?' Linda Burrows was not yet Mrs Murtagh (and when she belatedly realised what was going on, it is a surprise that she did not resolve, there and then, never to agree to the name change), so, strictly speaking, I could have denied that fact and retired mortified to my station in the covers. But the rest of the fielding side, now hugely amused, were in no mood to spare me any blushes.

At length, things settled down and business was resumed. 'Seeing as your missus has turned up,' announced Pollock, 'I suppose you'd better come and have a bowl.' He didn't sound very encouraging. Perhaps that was just his laconic manner; in fact, when you got to know him, he was as affable and as well disposed as they come. More likely, it was the unpromising situation he had found himself in, fighting heavy artillery with pea shooters. I was one of several injury replacements for his usual bowling attack. And Natal had pretty well broken through our lines. I measured out my 12-pace run-up, turned, checked my field, eyed my opponent and blew out my cheeks. The batsman facing stared back at me, gimlet-eyed and ready to pounce. I knew it. I just knew it. It had to be, didn't it? Barry Richards was set, determined, in fine form and 70-odd not out. I didn't remember ever getting him out in the nets. I didn't ever remember getting one past his bat. Was I to be the second sacrificial Pommie that day?

Unexpectedly, the maestro did not tear me apart in my two, short, unsuccessful spells. He *filleted* me. A century was what he wanted and a century was what he got. I get cross when his critics maintain that he was a dilettante with a bat in his hand, quickly bored and prone to tricksy shots and flamboyant showmanship. He saved the extravagance for exhibition time, when games were unimportant or dead. He was captain of this Natal side, he led from the front – he always did – and he had a Currie Cup to win. He needed runs on the board and to take 20 Eastern Province wickets. That he was denied the victory was no fault of his, nor of his opening partner, Dave Dyer – they put on 176 for the first wicket – but an apocalyptic thunderstorm, as well as a stubborn 62 not out in the second innings from Pollock, which put paid to that. No matter. The bonus points accrued from this truncated game put Natal on top of the table and in pole position to win the Currie Cup outright in the next round of provincial matches.

How come you were now captain, a role that you had always eschewed at Hampshire? 'Captaining a side of professionals never really interested me,' Barry replied. 'For two reasons, I think. Being captain of a county team means much more than getting the best out of 11 individuals on the field, developing a strategy of how to play, putting those plans into action on the field and reacting as situations develop. That bit I enjoyed, being in control and influencing matches. As a captain of a county, you are responsible for so much more, all that stuff that goes on off the field. And secondly, I couldn't be bothered with the petty squabbling that sometimes went on, each individual more concerned about his own performances than he was about his contributions to the team.' I took his point, though I had a little more sympathy than he did for the run of the mill county player, probably because I was one once. But I guess this self-centredness – I would not put it as strongly as selfishness – is inevitable when each run scored, each wicket taken and each catch taken, or dropped, is vital to a player because it had a bearing on whether he would get another contract next season. And none of this applied at Natal. They were all amateurs.

I was reminded, during this assessment of Barry's lack of ambition to captain Hampshire, of the words of Richard Gilliat at Hampshire when he described his own experiences as a captain. Surprising as it might appear to the outsider, there were more than a few passing similarities between him and Barry in their approach to the game. 'In some ways,' Gilliat said, 'I regret being made captain so early. It stopped me from concentrating on becoming a better batsman.' Barry would agree with that. He could have been a more than useful off-spinner had he worked at it but the time and the mental effort would have deflected him from what he was good at, and what he was born to do, namely batting.

Furthermore, there was much else to concern a county captain, Gilliat went on to explain, 'In my day, the captain was in charge of the team on away trips at all times and had to handle everything that went on off the pitch as well as on it. And that included all the media stuff. There was no manager or backroom staff to take any of the pressure off you.' Can you imagine Barry organising travel, hotel rooms, logistics, being responsible for discipline and curfews, sweet talking local radio and pressmen, exchanging polite and pointless pleasantries with club officials and bores, all the while when he had a match to win? No, neither can I. At least, not when he was playing. Later on, in his career in administration, of course, he did it willingly, and well. Gilliat took to it like a duck to water even when playing, and successfully too, but then he felt the enjoyment begin to drain from him and he resigned, turning his back on the game. Now, who does that remind you of? Except that Barry could not resign. He had no other interest to pursue, no other career to fulfil; he was set on the treadmill.

And the parallels between the public school and Oxford educated Gilliat and the largely self-taught genius from the colonies do not end there. Listen to this from Gilliat and reflect on the echoes you hear of Barry speaking, 'I don't think I could have played for more than a few years really because not being a bowler, as a batsman who is only in the game for a short while, I would have got thoroughly bored just fielding.' That is why he enjoyed the challenge of captaincy.

And that search to stave off boredom and staleness is why Barry took on the captaincy of Natal. However, before we examine Barry's leadership of his province, we have to ask ourselves what he was doing back in South Africa at all. Why had he not returned to Adelaide for another season after 1971 and further seasons after that? 'It was all to do with the Kingsmead Mynahs,' he told me. And thereafter, whenever the subject of the Mynahs cropped up, he spoke of them with the sort of reverence that is usually reserved for an admired religion, or beloved mother, or respected housemaster, or influential coach. In this case, it was a former coach who altered the course of Barry's life at this juncture, none other than his old mentor from Durban High School, Les Theobald.

The Kingsmead Mynahs Club was set up for the very simple purpose of luring Barry back to his home town, Durban, from Australia, where he had been making such a spectacular impact. Hang on, Theobald and other influential figures in Natal cricket might well have said, Barry is one of ours, why is he not playing for us? The reason, as ever, was money. In short, Natal could not afford him. Not that they would have dug deep into their pockets had they been able; provincial cricket was run by amateurs. In a deeply conservative country, the administrators of South African cricket had their heads buried in the sand even more than other cricket boards around the world. Instead of the springbok, the national emblem should have been the ostrich.

'When I first played for Natal back in 1969,' Vintcent van der Bijl told me, 'they had had a lot of success over the years under Jackie McGlew. Then there had been a succession of captains with poor results, despite having many Springboks and some good players. I, together with Dave Dyer, the opening bat and a good strategic thinker, and one or two others met in a pub during the winter to discuss what to do about the situation. We decided to set up a think tank and invited all interested parties, the Natal team and captains of the league teams, which included Norman Crookes and Grayson Heath, with Denis Dyer – Dave's father – to suggest a raft of far-reaching ideas.

The proposal was presented to Denis, president of the Natal Cricket Association. It was pretty radical, ranging from calling for a vote of no confidence in the selectors to demanding Lifebuoy soap in the showers! It was more or less accepted and the selectors were changed. A manager was appointed and Barry sounded out to be our captain. Amazing really. Usually, players' opinions were neither sought nor listened to. Once Barry was approached, he became more and more enthusiastic and it all took off from there.' Without a hint of irony, he added, 'It was like one big, cheerful family, really.'

There was still one big problem to overcome first. Barry was a professional; he needed to be paid. However, Natal would not countenance any sort of professionalism in an amateur game (though much like rugby union before professionalism, the lines were often deliberately blurred). So, Les Theobald gathered together a group of like-minded individuals who each guaranteed differing sums of money in order to finance Barry's season. Of course, it all had to be done privately; Natal could not be seen to be paying their star performer. Thus, the Kingsmead Mynahs Club was formed and Barry signed on the dotted line with alacrity. *Was it a proper contract?* 'Yes it was. For three years. I was employed as their professional – others came after me – and I had to do lots of coaching, as well as playing for Natal.' *Would you have been expected to play for Durban High School Old Boys as well, by any chance?* He laughed. 'Les Theobald wasn't **that** philanthropic! He wanted his pound of flesh.'

The prodigal son returned and the fatted calf wheeled out for the braai but the captaincy as well? How come? 'Well, as I told you, when I captained the SA Schools, it's usually the best player who was given the role.' *No, I mean, did you seek it?* 'I suppose in a way it was what I wanted. It certainly was what was needed. We were the Currie Cup whipping boys and we needed to take ownership of our performances. That's why I was determined to pick the guys I wanted, the ones who would follow me.' *And did they?* 'I was the big name, so they all looked up to me, I guess. Look, it was fine, no problems at all. They were all amateurs, they wanted to play, they wanted to improve and as I was the experienced pro, they listened.'

How would you describe your style of captaincy? He gave this some consideration. 'Thoughtful. I was quite authoritarian. It was my team. I made the decisions. And I got away with being demanding because they respected me as a player, I suppose.' *Were there any difficult characters to handle?* 'Like me, you mean?' he laughed. 'They were all very different personalities but easy to captain.' *Who were the big egos in the dressing room?* 'No one really. Vince van der Bijl was a great help as well as being a great bowler. But he was very genial and easy-going. Sometimes I'd have to kick him to bowl a bouncer. "I can't do that," he would say. "I'll kill him!" But he was a crucial performer for us.'

Further probing about Barry's three-year stint as Natal captain threw up some interesting details. Tich Smith, the wicketkeeper, was a case in point. Apart from being an excellent gloveman, he was vital as a sounding board, as you would expect of one in the best position on the field to see what was going on. But off the field and away from his cricket, he was the original hell-raiser. I use that term advisedly because of what happened to him later; he turned his back on hell and raised his eyes to heaven. 'He found Jesus,' Barry put it simply. In Smith's own words, 'I ended up in a home for alcoholics at the age of 35. It was then that I decided to devote my life to Jesus and chose to walk His way, never looking back.'

And neither did he. Everybody to whom I spoke about Tich Smith shakes his head with a mixture of bewilderment and grudging respect, as if the transformation from profligate rogue to born-again Christian was a miracle. Which, I suppose you could say, it was. And Smith certainly puts his money where his mouth is. He has raised millions of rand to found a village for orphans in his home province and has ploughed all the proceeds of the various companies he has set up into the project. It is indeed an inspiring story.

Perhaps we could do something similar, Barry, for the abandoned and neglected children of ex-cricketers? 'You mean with my money and your kids?' he responded drily. 'But it's extraordinary what has happened to him when you remember just what he was like in our playing days,' he went on. 'I remember one occasion…We had won the Nissan Shield, the premier one-day competition in South Africa. As a reward, the NCA flew us to Lesotho for the weekend. Gambling wasn't allowed in South Africa but Lesotho had a casino, which Tich made the fullest use of. At one stage during the night, he had won a packet. Sensibly he gave some of it to the manager for safe keeping, on the strict understanding that he should not give it back to him. Under any circumstances. The manager duly handed it to Tich's wife. Tich came home and turned his bedroom upside down – literally – in his search for more of the money he thought his wife had hidden from him.'

Switching the subject back to his captaincy, Barry made an admission that at first surprised me but on further reflection, perhaps not, because it was all of a piece of his attitude towards the game. 'Sometimes, during a passage of play where nothing seemed to be happening or the intensity of the contest had gone off a bit, I would switch off. I found it difficult to stay focussed if the game was meandering towards a draw.' That cannot have happened very often. There were only six matches a season and in the three years Barry was in charge, Natal were always battling for top spot. 'My approach was to plan well. We had tactics for each batsman and we stuck to them. Everybody knew what they had to do. It seemed to work.' Van der Bijl agreed wholeheartedly, 'We were a damn good side. We beat all-comers – even the great Transvaal – at a time when provincial cricket was very strong. And a lot of it was down to Barry. He didn't seek the captaincy but when it fell into his lap, he relished it. In fact, I would go so far as to say that he was the second best captain I have ever played under.'

The second! Which begs the obvious question, Vince – who was the best then? 'Mike Brearley.' Fair enough. In the same way that Barry cedes first place to Don Bradman in the Test batting averages, so is it unarguable that he should be pipped at the post in the captaincy stakes by the Cambridge psychoanalyst. Rodney Hogg used to say that Brearley had a degree in people. Van der Bijl fell under his spell during his season playing for Middlesex when they won the County Championship in 1980. It has to be said that the admiration was mutual. Brearley commented, 'Vince was a breath of fresh air…and an excellent influence in the dressing room,' and compared his bowling to Joel Garner's.

Barry too rated his opening bowler highly. 'Vince was brilliant for us, a match-winner. And a great help to me on the field as well.' Although no harsh disciplinarian off the field – that would have been against his nature – Barry was a demanding taskmaster out in the middle. 'I'd get cross if anyone was falling short in his job. If I demanded high standards of myself then I would expect everyone else to do the same.' He took his lead here from Ian Chappell, his captain at South Australia, who would never ask one of his team to do anything that he himself would not do. 'Barry would get cross if the guys weren't focussed,' said van der Bijl. 'He expected the same level of application and concentration that he gave and he could be sharp if he thought you weren't pulling your weight.'

I then remembered an exchange between him and Barry on the field during the very short time that I was at the crease in the game I have already described. It seemed to me that the burly, indefatigable Natal fast bowler was being given a few choice words by his captain, notwithstanding his previous sterling efforts during 20 overs on a hot day. 'That used to bug me,' nodded van der Bijl. 'He'd have a go at me no matter how well I was bowling when it was at nine, ten, jack. After a while, my patience snapped and I had a go back, "Hey, what's eating you, man?" He later admitted that he would get a bit tense at those times because he was mentally preparing himself to open the batting and he didn't want to be fussing around prising out tail-enders. It would drain him emotionally.' No opening bat does, I guess, so Barry could be forgiven for the odd bout of tetchiness if a stubborn last-wicket stand threatened to develop.

Van der Bijl was of the firm opinion that Barry grew into the job. 'He found that he enjoyed it, making him feel part of the family.' There we are again. Having been starved of love as a child from his father, Barry needed to feel appreciated, especially by his peers. It didn't require a psychiatrist, van der Bijl and I agreed, to deduce that Barry craved affection and reassurance. From the Natal team, he got both, unconditionally. 'It brought him out as a person,' continued van der Bijl. 'He had to think of other people in the team, not just himself. We were all young, you see, and we looked up to him.' Dave Anderson confirmed this assessment of his old club-mate's emotional insecurities. 'He's like me,' he said. 'We're both Cancerians.' The motif of the star is a crab. And crabs tend to retreat beneath their shell when threatened. 'That's right,' Dave confirmed. 'We both have a protective carapace which is difficult to penetrate.' *Moody, crabby, tenacious, strong-willed and like their own way. Shall I go on?* He laughed. 'But we're kind underneath.' And as if to underline the point, he called for another two beers.

Van der Bijl cited as an example of Barry's newfound maturity and developing skills at handling his team the way in which Pelham Henwood thrived under his captaincy. Hitherto, Henwood had been a relatively successful left-arm spinner, capable of doing an effective job for the team as a defensive bowler but not one that you would expect to bowl sides out. In point of fact, few in the game would have begrudged him even this small measure of success; every ball he bowled, fired in to a regular, packed, off-side field, was a bonus for him. Lucky to be alive following a horrific car crash, he probably counted his blessings that he could bowl at all. But Barry persuaded him to alter his whole mental strategy by switching his line of attack from off to leg stump.

At the time, this was considered an unusual tactic. Barry had seen it used sporadically in one-day cricket in England and believed it could be adopted with success for Henwood in the longer version of the game. 'Barry gave him the confidence to do it,' said van der Bijl, 'and it worked. Look – he bowled out Transvaal to win the Currie Cup. That wouldn't have happened without Barry's influence.' *How was Barry tactically?* 'Very positive. "Look, guys," he'd say, "if the first ball of the day or the last ball of the day is a half-volley, hit it for four!" And he was very thoughtful about the fields he would set. I remember him taking an age – five minutes, at least – to set a field for someone, putting the fielder in a very odd position. And then the batsman, Dopey de Waal, slogged it straight down his throat!' It is difficult to exaggerate what a boost to a bowler's confidence it is to have such a staunch supporter of your cause as your captain. Henwood clearly relished the faith shown in him; he was anointed as one of the five South African Cricketers of the Year at the conclusion of the season.

However, had anybody hinted to the Natal faithful after the first match of Barry's reign that their cricket team was being led by a fledgling Napoleon, he would have been greeted with hoots of derision and suggestions of having imbibed one too many Castle lagers. Western Province had won by nine wickets, despite Natal declaring their first innings on 278/4, with their captain on 186 not out. *How come, Barry?* 'It was the first year of a new system of bonus points that they had introduced to try and spice up the games. Nobody was quite sure how it was all going to pan out. We couldn't get any more points batting so I immediately declared.' His action, as ever, had a positive intent.

It is never easy to take 20 wickets in three days, especially in the southern hemisphere where wickets tend to be truer than in England and where the light can deteriorate more quickly, curtailing play early. In the English County Championship, there had always been a tradition of trying to manufacture results by some judicious declaring. Strictly speaking, you could call it collusion. Often you would see the two captains in deep and private discussion before play on the third day trying to agree how and when a realistic fourth innings chase could be manufactured. As long as it was done with a genuine attempt to win the match, a blind eye was turned to all the machinations that would go on to reach that stage and there was never any hint of bribery or foul play. Ah, happy days, untainted with greed and corruption. In the present climate, the four-day game should militate against any need for dodgy declarations.

*But your declaration **was** dodgy, in the sense that it backfired, not that it had nefarious intent.* 'Yah, I got serious grief from the press, that was for sure. But I was trying to win the game. Unfortunately, we were skittled out for a low score (130) in the second innings and lost by nine wickets.'

It was a body blow but not a grievous one. Natal had been outmanoeuvred, not outplayed. Usually a good side responds to a setback like this. They do not shrug their shoulders and pass it off as a bad day at the office. They are furious with themselves and vow never to let it happen again. Pride has been hurt. 'We are better than that,' Barry told them. 'And we were,' agreed van der Bijl. 'He instilled in us a great belief in ourselves.' That belief in their abilities coursed through the team. Under Barry's three-year tenure as their leader, they were to lose only two more matches, a record of which he is quietly proud.

They so nearly banished any residual demons in their next match, failing by just one frustrating wicket to beat Rhodesia, and then drew comfortably with Transvaal. Sufficient bonus points had been gleaned to keep them in the hunt but they desperately needed a win to establish themselves as genuine title contenders. This came in a thumping demolition of Eastern Province, by an innings and 65 runs. Barry led the charge with a characteristically dominant innings of 152 but he was more pleased by the contributions everyone made with the bat (lowest score was Woolmer's with 24) than with his own crucial century. Revenge for the calamitous misjudgements against Western Province was duly taken in the return fixture. This time Barry got his declarations spot on and largely thanks to a herculean bowling performance from van der Bijl (match figures of 12-85), Natal edged to the top of the table with a 221-run victory.

I should like to say that a valiant rearguard action by Murtagh prevented Natal from polishing off Eastern Province but in fact it was Graeme Pollock's undefeated 62 which held them up until the final match of the season, a winner-takes-all encounter with Transvaal. First blood, you might say, was drawn by Transvaal, who beat Natal by ten runs in the final of the Gillette Cup a week before but any disappointment at this second successive stumble at the final hurdle in the one-day game was banished by a comprehensive victory by an innings and 48 runs. The Currie Cup was theirs. I love the photo taken in the dressing room following their triumph. A beaming Barry is not holding the trophy aloft. However, the lid of the cup is being placed jubilantly upon his head, much as the Archbishop of Canterbury crowns a new monarch, by a worshipful and supplicant Pelham Henwood.

As well he might. He had repaid his captain's confidence in him by bowling out Transvaal for 130 on the final afternoon with the remarkable figures of 32-17-34-7. Barry does look pleased, it has to be said. 'Congratulations,' the Transvaal captain, none other than Ali Bacher, said to him. 'You out-batted us, out-bowled us, out-fielded us and out-captained us.' Praise indeed from the South African Test captain. *Was it some comfort for being banned from Test cricket?* 'Not sure about that, buddy. Nothing can replace playing for your country. But certainly it gave me a lot of satisfaction.' *So now you had the full set?* 'Eh?' *You'd won the County Championship with Hampshire, the Sheffield Shield with South Australia and now the Currie Cup with Natal. I bet there is no one else who has ever managed that.* 'I guess not.'

His undemonstrative response set me thinking. He is not oblivious to his achievements, both individual and as part of a team. He takes satisfaction in winning, otherwise, what is the point of competing? And he **hates** to lose. But like all great players, success does not surprise him; he almost expects it. That is what the best players do – they win. Yet individual records, personal performances, statistics, career analyses hold little appeal to him. It is enough that he has competed and won the individual duel…and played a few decent shots along the way.

The contrast between him and the subject of my previous book, Tom Graveney, could not be starker. Graveney remembered with total clarity every blade of grass that he played on. Invariably, my later research would reveal that he had recalled innings and scores and incidents with complete accuracy, down to the smallest detail. His memory was phenomenal. Barry is cut from different cloth. 'Not sure, Murt,' he would say. 'You'd better look that up.' It became quite endearing as time went by.

He is not consumed by his ego. He is not a jealous guardian of his legacy. All he wanted was respect, recognition. He is still not sure that he has got it, having been denied any sort of proper Test career but I, along with a host of others, am convinced that he has. 'Look,' said his friend, Vince van der Bijl, 'Barry is recognised wherever in the cricket world he goes. And it's not for his good looks either!'

Barry's batting throughout the season had been consistently brilliant. Or should I say, brilliant and consistent. Look at his scores: 186 not out, 0, 48, 60, 78, 66, 152, 9, 61, 80, 106, 52. To save you the mental arithmetic, that adds up to an aggregate of 868 runs at an average of 81.63. Top of the Currie Cup batting averages, needless to say. All that is missing to draw a comparison with his *annus mirabilis* in Australia, I suppose, is a triple century.

Three quick points need to be made here before we move on. Barry batted just 12 times. In an English season, he would have had three times more innings than that. As he always maintained, in his case less meant more. Secondly, note that I have made mention of his batting exploits almost as an afterthought, as if the remarkable was becoming the commonplace. And thirdly, as I studied these figures at the time in the *Eastern Province Herald*, I was struck by a sadness that such a genius was still denied the world stage that his talent and temperament craved. And what's more, even to my politically untrained eyes, the padlock of international isolation looked as if it was beginning to rust on the gate's bolts.

Any big celebrations? Open-top bus parades? Freedom of the city of Durban? Commemorative banquet hosted by the city mayor? It was a fatuous line of enquiry. I already knew the answer. And he knew I knew so he contented himself with a snort of derision. That made his determination to repeat the success the following season not a jot less intense. But it was not to be. Natal were to be denied back-to-back triumphs in the most frustrating of circumstances, much like Hampshire had been six months earlier. In September 1974, Hampshire lost the championship to Worcestershire by two points. In March 1975, Natal lost the Currie Cup to Transvaal by one point! 'Frustrating!' was Barry's terse summation. 'And we went through the season unbeaten.'

The pipe opener was against Rhodesia, batting against two bowlers who ran in at him more than most in his career – Mike Procter and Robin Jackman. In the first innings he was bowled by Jackman for a masterful 162, out of a total of 284. In the second innings, he was caught by Duncan Fletcher (a future England coach) for four, once again off Jackman. Nothing much out of the ordinary there. Barry would usually be expected to make runs in the first innings, when it counted, and to fall cheaply in the second innings when a game was meandering towards a stalemate, when it certainly didn't matter. And Jackman, as we know, dismissed him in his career more than any other bowler. It was about time, I resolved, to investigate this head-to-head rivalry between the two.

Did Barry have a 'thing' about the Shoreditch Sparrow, as Jackman was known, like Atherton had a 'thing' about Glenn McGrath? After all, most batsmen have their bogeyman, as bowlers have their 'bunnies'. Robin Jackman was good enough to give me a generous portion of his time to consider this marvel of a statistic. 'Did I have the Indian sign on Barry?' he laughed. 'You've got to be joking! I only got him out more times than anybody else because I had the misfortune to bowl to him more times than anybody else, for Surrey, Rhodesia and various other representative sides.' Nonetheless, it is a fact. He dismissed Barry 16 times. The next highest on the list was Eddie Barlow, 11 times. 'For the record,' Jackman insisted, 'I played against Barry in 25 matches. He had 41 innings, three not outs, 2,279 runs, highest score 197, at an average of 59.79. Indian sign? More like Indian takeaway!'

The second match of the campaign, against Eastern Province at Port Elizabeth, made the news because of an extraordinary incident, with Barry at its very heart. At the time, the *Eastern Province Herald* headline screamed 'Richards On Sit-down Strike'. The bare fact of the scorecard states that Barry was run out for 17. 'I hit Dave Brickett through mid-off and set off for three runs. That would mean I was going to be running towards the danger end, the bowler's end, for the third. There was a bit of a mix-up with Dave Dyer, my partner, over the calling and at first he didn't realise I was going for three. But belatedly he set off for the wicketkeeper's end. The ball came in to the bowler, who instinctively took off the bails. But I was safely home. Not out. However, seeing Dave struggling to make his ground, Brickett threw the ball to the keeper's end and hit the stumps direct. Dave was out.'

So far, so straightforward. But the Eastern Province players had noticed that the umpire at Barry's end had raised his finger for Brickett's original appeal and then swiftly put it down again, presumably realising he had made a mistake. Now, whose wicket did Eastern Province crave more – Dyer's or Richards's? Unsurprisingly, they appealed again to the bowler's umpire. Under some considerable pressure, the callow official – this was his first provincial match – admitted that he had given Barry out. So the original decision stood. The umpire refused to change his mind, which he was fully entitled to do under the laws of the game. Barry was incensed, believing he had been the victim of sharp practice. 'I was in – by a yard. And Dave had already walked off the field. So I sat down!'

You what? 'I sat down.' *You refused to go?* Sheepishly he nodded. Finally the other umpire, Sandy Matthews, was called over to consult and it was agreed by the two of them that Barry was indeed out and that Dyer should be called back to resume his innings. Slowly Barry hauled himself back to his feet and departed, much aggrieved. He knew that it hadn't looked good and later regretted his public show of dissent. Two factors occur to me at this point. Doesn't the game provide a bottomless pit of controversial incidents and strange altercations? You think you've seen it all, heard it all, and then something else crops up that you have never before even considered. And I would have given anything to be a fly on the wall when Barry finally made it back to the dressing room.

He was in trouble again in a later match against Western Province. The game in South Africa was still very much run by amateurs, in the resolutely determined amateur fashion. The same applied to the umpiring. Although there were some experienced umpires standing in provincial matches, I think it would be fair to say that they were thin on the ground. The panel of officials in the first-class game was not professional, in any sense of the word, as it was in England. This would have annoyed Barry. On occasions, his frustrations would erupt, like a festering boil. It happened at Newlands. At a crucial stage of the match, Jack Nel, the Western Province opening batsman, was caught at cover…and given not out!

Not out? How on earth was that decision arrived at? 'It hit his pad, then his bat and lobbed up to cover.' How a ball could reach cover on the full without the intervention of some wood is a moot point but there we are. The umpire had given his decision and according to the spirit of the game, which tacitly makes clear that the umpire is always right, even when he is wrong, Barry should sensibly have left it there. But he didn't; he questioned the decision. The umpire unwisely then admitted that his view had been blocked by the considerable bulk of Vintcent van der Bijl as he followed through. The next step was obvious – consult the square leg umpire. The bowler's umpire declined to do so. The decision stood. Barry seethed.

Uncannily – the game has a habit of throwing up such dramatic moments – two balls later, after Nel had taken a single, Eddie Barlow was caught behind. South Africans do not walk, it has to be stated, and Barlow usually needed a crane to remove him from the crease. Yet again, the verdict was unfavourable to the Natal side. Barry was now apoplectic. In the space of three balls, both openers should have been back in the pavilion. The next delivery hit Barlow plumb in front and on this occasion, the umpire gave him out. Barry fell backwards on to the turf in mock astonishment and even had the temerity to wave his cap ironically to the umpire. *That's just not cricket, old boy.* 'I know. I got rapped over the knuckles and had to apologise.' Again.

The final match provided another thrilling, if ultimately fruitless, climax to the season, yet again against Transvaal. Victory for Natal would vouchsafe them the Currie Cup for the second year running – provided they secured the requisite bonus points as well. Barry and his team were not going to die wondering. This time, Barry's bold gamble to declare, when behind on the first innings, was vindicated, because his opposite number and old friend from school, Lee Irvine, took up the gauntlet and declared himself, setting Natal a stiff, but achievable, target of 217. I guess, like everybody else at Kingsmead that day, Irvine thought that the outcome of his challenge would depend on Barry. He was not wrong.

Barry raced to the fastest hundred of the season and secured victory for his side by six wickets. Once again, the old measure of determining the length of an innings, minutes spent at the crease rather than balls received, frustrates us here. His hundred came up in 103 minutes. Obviously rapid and obviously wonderful to behold but how many balls did he face? We shall never know. If this is frustrating, looking back over 40 years, it pales into insignificance compared to the frustration felt by Barry and his team-mates at failing by a single bonus point to overhaul Western Province. The tension felt back in Cape Town, their programme having already been completed, must have been excruciating as the Western Province team listened to events in Durban unfold on the radio (there being no television in South Africa, don't forget) before the news came through that they were indeed crowned as champions. *Where was the bonus point lost? Where was it to be gained? What **was** a bonus point?* Barry did not know; he couldn't remember. If batting statistics do not greatly interest him, humble bonus points would pass well below his radar.

Consolation prizes do not enthuse him much either, though there was one to be had in winning the Gillette Cup that year. 'Vince won it for us,' he recalled, 'not least for an astonishing catch at long leg. He smashed a few runs too.' This sounded interesting, so I quizzed the aforesaid match-winner. As is the way with all bowlers, he was more than happy to discuss his batting exploits. 'I slogged a few,' he said modestly, for in truth, he was not a bad batter, 'which got our score up to a reputable 179. I scored a quick 28, which included the biggest six you've ever seen. Then I took a few wickets.' That it was Western Province, Eddie Barlow, Jack Nel *et al,* made the victory all the sweeter.

To reclaim the Currie Cup in Barry's third year as captain in 1975/76 ought to have been a most satisfying and joyful triumph. It was a triumph all right, both personal and collective, but some of the gloss was rubbed off by controversy, this time off the field rather than on it. Controversy seems to have stalked Barry throughout his career, some of it bad luck, certainly, but more often than not because he had been standing slap bang in the path of the juggernaut and refused, for good reason or bad, to get out of the way. Politics or money usually lay at the heart of the storm; on this occasion, you might say that both conspired to injure his reputation with the South African press and public.

First, however, let us deal with the cricket. In Barry's estimation – and the figures bear him out – he was still at the very peak of his powers. Top again of the batting averages, he played in all eight provincial matches, batting 15 times, with four not-outs and a total of 868 runs at an average of 78.90, with three hundreds to his name. Hereafter, he believed, saw a slow, almost imperceptible, decline, arrested only by his superhuman efforts of will as much as by sheer brilliance in his late flurry with World Series Cricket.

Now, was this decline on account of waning powers or waning appetite? He agreed that was a moot question. His enthusiasm for county cricket was now on a steep and slippery slide. He had proved himself in Australia and he had swept all before him in his own country. Barely a single batting record in domestic cricket had not fallen to him. What was left for him to achieve? That is perhaps the reason that the reclaiming of the Currie Cup, though eminently pleasing, did not hold quite the same euphoria for him as the first. He was, as he later admitted, already casting around for a change of scenery. Even provincial cricket had now become stale and unprofitable.

Despite losing twice, to Eastern Province (he got out to the worst shot of his career, off a slow full toss from the occasional bowling of John Stephenson) and to Western Province (Denys Hobson bowled them out twice, to record match figures of 14-113), Natal had already secured the cup by virtue of two thumping wins against Rhodesia and Eastern Province and plenty of bonus points this time, by the time they took their traditional curtain call against Transvaal. This was to be the last match before retirement of Pat Trimborn, a tireless and selfless servant of Natal cricket. His treatment by the authorities came as no great surprise to Barry but it shook him to the core nonetheless and convinced him that his desire to leave was the correct one. 'After 17 years, bowling, I don't know, all those overs, latterly on a gammy knee, do you know what the Natal Board gave him in appreciation? A mounted cricket ball! Can you believe that?' No, I could not, in all honesty. It did seem a piddling memento for such a fine cricketer. I was given a mounted ball once. I still have it. It was for taking a few wickets in a school Under-11 match.

Now, what was the strike all about? 'It was no strike. I just refused to play in a match against the International Wanderers.' Who were the International Wanderers, you might ask. Derrick Robins is already a name familiar to the reader. A millionaire businessman and former chairman of Coventry City FC, he was a great friend and benefactor of South African cricket. Sensing a need, nay, a longing for international competition in the cricket grounds of the country following sporting isolation, he organised and bankrolled several unofficial tours in the early 1970s. His teams comprised mainly Englishmen but with an increasing number from other countries. Two were of particular interest to the South African public because they were 'non-white', to put it in the official jargon of apartheid, Younis Ahmed of Pakistan and John Shepherd of Barbados. Officially, they were given the status of 'honorary whites' – you can see how ridiculous the system was.

Both conducted themselves with dignity, not to say aplomb, and proved to be huge hits wherever they went. John Shepherd in particular endeared himself to the crowds, black and white, who flocked to see the games. Those who have ever played with or against Shep will be unsurprised at this; he really is the most genial of men, with a smile that splits his face, and was a very fine cricketer. Barry laughs at one memory he had of Shep during one of these matches. 'While we were all milling around the foyer of the hotel where we were staying, one of the female guests mistook Shep for a bellboy and instructed him to bring her bags up to her room. Instead of putting her right, he decided to play along and with a beam and a funny accent, he politely did as he was told, picked up her bags, took them to the lift and disappeared with her upstairs.' *Did he return? Knowing Shep, it could have been some time.* 'Not sure about that, pal, but I do know all the guys were creased up with laughter at his antics!'

This led Barry on to an important point he wanted to make. A lot of the overseas players who turned out for Robins and on later rebel tours made huge sacrifices to come to South Africa. 'All right, they were paid, possibly a lot, but the stick they got when they returned home, especially the West Indians, was cruel and merciless. I take my hat off to them. They were acting out of noble sentiments, trying to do good for cricket in South Africa of all races. They were heroes, in my eyes.' He then went on to list a large number of West Indians who became pariahs in their own countries because they had challenged the sanctity of isolation and braved official opprobrium in the name of multi-racial cricket. 'Lawrence Rowe was the most significant casualty. After he led a rebel tour, he was ostracised by his countrymen back home and eventually hounded out of Jamaica to settle in Miami. That was sad.' Collis King, Hartley Alleyne, Franklin Stephenson, Sylvester Clarke, Richard Austin, David Murray, Ezra Moseley, Albert Padmore, Bernard Julian, Colin Croft – all were heroes in one country and outcasts in another.

Even today, the wounds have not fully healed. Collectively, they were known as 'The Unforgiven'. 'Yet they did more for integration than any politician,' said Barry. 'They were good guys and they got no credit for what they did, how they behaved and how they related to the blacks in our country. Albert Padmore!' he practically spat, 'He's now living under a railway bridge.' Aye, and Richard Austin was reduced to begging on the streets of Kingston. As Barry said, it is all very sad.

Of course it were better that these unofficial tours had no need to take place, against the backdrop, as they were, of apartheid and world denunciation. But

South Africa was where it was and its public was starved of international cricket. No wonder the arrival of the International Wanderers in March of 1976, another team got together by Derrick Robins and this time truly international, was so keenly anticipated. The team was managed by Richie Benaud, captained by Greg Chappell and included his brother Ian, Dennis Lillee, Phil Edmonds, Ashley Mallett, Glenn Turner, Derek Underwood, Max Walker and others. Intriguingly, the South African side would include a number of coloured players, a condition of the tour in the first place. Why on earth would Barry not want to play? Surely, this was the sort of stiff examination of his mettle that he had been craving. He wanted to play all right, but he wanted to be paid to play, or at least to receive an amount commensurate with what the Wanderers were going to get. It takes two teams to make a contest, was his reasoning, so why should one team be paid more – much more – than the other?

And now we arrive at the very nub of the question that has dogged Barry throughout his life. You have probably heard whispers of it from time to time in this story only for me to delay the inquest for the appropriate moment. Well, now is the moment. How does he answer to the charge of becoming a mercenary, a hired gun who sold his expertise to the highest bidder? Even today, his face clouds over whenever the thorny subject pricks. The barbs evidently hurt and hurt still. 'Some people never forget and yet I firmly believe, and still do, that my actions paved the way for professional cricket in this country.' For which he gets scant praise. Nonetheless, there are those, some of whom remain close to him, who judge that he may well have been genuinely motivated but mishandled the whole tricky question. 'You mean tactlessly?' he said with a wan smile.

First, let us deal with the issue of the moment. Barry, as you would expect, was invited to represent the South African team to play against the International Wanderers at the tail end of the 1975/76 season. The words I choose are telling; 'invite' and 'represent' hint at a patriarchal and amateur administration, which is precisely how it was. An appearance fee of R900 was promised to the home players. To most of the South African players selected, white or coloured, the amount would have been irrelevant, though no doubt welcome to one or two; what would have counted was the thrill and honour of having the opportunity to represent their country. Three of their number begged to differ.

Graeme Pollock, Lee Irvine and Barry Richards asked to be paid the same amount as the opposition, roughly three times as much. 'I didn't mind Dennis Lillee trying to knock my head off – well, I did but that's part of the game, isn't it – but I felt I deserved to be paid the same.' The contest between bat and ball among some of the world's premier players, to say nothing of the groundbreaking agreement to field coloured players in the same national team, had caught hold of the public's imagination and meant that the games were bound to be sell-outs. As part of the spectacle – indeed, some might say, topping the bill – Barry believed that he should be paid commensurate to the occasion. Or, at the very least, the equivalent. So why should Max Walker, who had a job, by the way, be paid thrice the amount as Barry, who was, after all, a professional? He had no other job. 'You need a plumber?' Barry said, 'You call him out and you pay him for his services. You need an opening batsman to take on Lillee? You pay him the going rate. What's the difference?' The difference was that cricket in his home country was not yet ready – not by a long chalk – for the advent of professionalism.

'Verily I say unto you, no prophet is accepted in his home town.' It might be stretching the judgement of avid readers of the King James Bible to compare Barry to a prophet (though he did have an uncanny ability to foretell where he was going to hit the ball) but it can be argued that he was something of a soothsayer. Nowadays, nobody would turn a hair at cricketers demanding a decent return for their labours, in South Africa or anywhere else. Hairs would be turned if they did *not* seek remuneration, or if they were refused adequate payment. And, to add insult to injury, Barry was not accepted in his home town. In fact he was made to feel like a pariah. 'I tell you, I was not popular. The press had a field day.'

I asked another of the 'refuseniks' why he had declined the invitation from the South African Cricket Board. Lee Irvine agreed that the 'bottom line', as he called it, was money. 'We found out pretty early on that the tourists were going to be paid considerably more than we were,' he said, 'so four or five of us went to the board and told them that this didn't seem very fair.' *Four or five of you? I thought there were only three.* He gave an arch smile. 'Eddie Barlow was one of them – that was not generally known at the time. We went to the board and aired our grievance. We were given short shrift. Take it or leave it, we were basically told. So we said that we would leave it.' *But Barlow played, didn't he?* 'They turned Eddie at the last minute, making him captain and asking him not to rock the boat.' *So the three of you were left out on a limb?* 'That's exactly right. We were made out to be the bad guys, who wouldn't play for their country because of some trifling dispute over money.'

Then what happened? 'The home team was *whupped*. So the board came back to us and wanted us in the team for the second game.' *More money?* 'Well, at first, they tried to hoodwink us, saying that the pay was the same as the tourists. We explained to them in words of one syllable that we knew *exactly* what the other guys were getting. Come on, they're friends of ours, some of who we know well from our county days. So don't lie to us.' In the end, terms were renegotiated and the three then came on board. In this respect, his memory diverges from Barry's, who thought that no more money had been forthcoming but in their disdain for the self-serving machinations of the game's governing body, they were united in their opinion.

It was all to do with perception, what cricket meant to a generation who had been brought up in another era, before money had reared its ugly head. Of course money has reared its ugly head in the game of cricket since it was invented – and continues to do so – but some people still clung vehemently to the old amateur principles and orthodoxies.

Dave Anderson rushes to the defence of his old friend even now. 'Look, Barry was a trailblazer, if you like. He was the first of the professionals in this country. He was only doing what he felt was right. The game was going to go professional at some stage or other, whatever the administrators thought or did. So he was standing up for those who came after him. Nobody gives a second thought about players making money from the game now. Some do very well for themselves, and why not? Jeez, Jacques Kallis is a *multi-millionaire!* And fair enough – he deserves it.'

Dave was getting quite animated here, as he warmed to his theme, but he did check himself to admit that he did not have the ear of Jacques Kallis's bank manager and could not therefore be absolutely specific about the recently retired all-rounder's financial affairs. But we both agreed that Kallis was more than likely a wealthy man. 'Without Barry, the word "professional" would not have existed,' Anderson continued, 'and because of that, he was labelled a mercenary. And to some extent, his name is still tarnished by that image.' With which, Dave sunk his beer. South Africans have a habit of doing this, sinking their beer, to emphasise a point, as if the last word has been spoken.

But it hadn't. In the interest of balance, it has to be said that not everyone was wholly in accord with Barry's stand. Vince van der Bijl, for one, had a completely different perspective on the affair. 'It was very sad those three didn't play,' he told me. 'I remember Graeme Pollock phoning and asking me not to play. Look, I said, I've waited all my life to play against these guys and now you want me to say no! I don't think he was very impressed. I suppose we had different lenses. He had played Test cricket. I hadn't. Most of the guys would have played for nothing. The three dissenters didn't seem to appreciate that it was a great honour for us to mix with the greats.' He also went on to point out that it was potentially a seminal moment in inter-racial cricket in South Africa. Perhaps the bonds of apartheid were being loosened a little? Van der Bijl was not to know that just three months later, the Soweto Uprising would leave close to 600 dead, precipitating worldwide condemnation and a crisis in the South African government.

Far from being loosened, the bonds were tightened, overseas tours were banned and no international cricket was seen in the country until the first of the rebel tours in 1982. And we all know how controversial and bitterly divisive they were. As for inter-racial cricket, that remained a distant pipe dream. Van der Bijl accepts this but still insists that the great fight had to be fought. 'Maybe those guys who played for us, who wouldn't normally have been allowed, might not have been good enough to play for the full Springbok side. But a start had to be made, hey?' His argument was lucid and persuasive. It is impossible to take a player out of sub-standard cricket and shove him straight into the international arena and expect him to cope. But with the proper framework, encouragement and coaching, the sky is the limit as far as potential among the non-whites is concerned.

'Look at Philander. Look how well he's done. It just goes to show. There must have been so many D'Oliveiras or Philanders we've missed along the way and we shall never know their names. How sad.' Van der Bijl is nothing if not messianic about South Africa's future. 'Transformation' is the word he uses.

I ask Barry if he is equally sanguine about his country. He sighed. 'What did I say about politics dominating my life? It did then and it does now.' He swayed out of the way of the bouncer I had just delivered (as if I have ever bowled a bouncer in my life!) and instead tried to steer the conversation back to the original point at issue – the principle of fair pay. *Did you get what you were asking for?* 'Nah. All we got was a lot of flak. We were told that it should be an honour to play for your country. Well, I knew that as well as the next guy. But that wasn't the point. The Aussies – Lillee, Marsh, the Chappells – they had all come to the same conclusion about the cricket authorities and they too thought they were all dinosaurs. And no one could accuse those players of not having pride in playing for the Baggy Green.' Sadly, he told me that, when he declined to play, he was refused accreditation to report on the match at Newlands for one of the national newspapers; he wasn't even allowed into the ground.

The three rebels all made themselves available for the rest of the series. Pollock made an imperious 124 in the second match. Van der Bijl remembers the hysterical reaction of the South African press to the innings and laughed ruefully at its repercussions. 'GP tames Lillee', screamed the headlines. Well, that was like a red rag to a bull. In the second innings, Dennis ripped through us and took seven wickets.' The memory Barry has of the exchanges is necessarily more vague. He was hit a nasty blow on the head by Alan Hurst and spent the night in hospital under observation. How he must have loved that. Three weeks later, he was back in England, playing against Somerset at a windswept Taunton, and he would have loved that even more.

Mention of Graeme Pollock, who has interposed himself from time to time in these pages, brings to mind an argument that ran on throughout my time in South Africa. At many a dinner party – except that in that country, it was never a dinner party but a *braai*, and very nice they were too – the question invariably posed was who was the better player, Graeme Pollock or Barry Richards? Hmm, now that was a tricky one, and still is. Who was the greater composer – Mozart or Beethoven? Who was the better poet – Chaucer or Milton? Who was the more successful general – Caesar or Napoleon? If we narrowly define the parameters of what we mean by 'greatness', thus reducing the number of candidates, the choice invariably becomes one of personal opinion. What are the criteria? Runs accumulated? Number of centuries? Batting average? Orthodoxy, or otherwise, of technique? Elegance of strokeplay? Strength of opposition? Quality of pitches? Already the debate loses its rigour and emotions start to brim over. In the end, of course, it can be seen as a futile and unachievable exercise...but, my God, what fun can be had and what passions stirred. Especially when fuelled with a few 'toots'.

To have two indisputably great players in the same team slugging it out toe to toe, so to speak, for the ultimate honour of being top notch in people's minds would be uncommon, though it has to be stressed that the prism through which South Africans were peering was a narrow one. Pollock and Richards were not the only contenders on the world stage at the time. In fact, Pollock and Richards were not on the world stage at all. Viv Richards, Greg Chappell, Clive Lloyd, Sunil Gavaskar, Majid Khan and Zaheer Abbas were all strutting their stuff in Test match arenas around the world at the same time. But my friends, dimly made out through the smoke of sizzling steaks, to a man (and in South Africa, a male dominated society, it was always the men) were wearing blinkers. It was either Richards or Pollock. Nobody else was in the frame. South Africa was isolated from international competition. Cricket fans had heard about these shadowy, exotic figures but they had never seen them in the flesh. And, let us not forget, there was no television to bring them into their sitting rooms.

So come on, Pommie, you tell us who is it to be – Richards or Pollock? For the time being, I shall sidestep that one and enlist the opinions of others, contemporaries of both, all of whom had their firm ideas. As ever, Vince van der Bijl made some interesting and thoughtful points. 'Barry was the rapier, GP was the bludgeon. Barry would not look to see where the fielders were placed; he would look instead for gaps, holes, where he could hit it. Graeme would simply wait for the right ball and smash it with such power. He was sublime! Barry sometimes fell foul of rashness or loss of concentration. GP *never* gave it away, even in club games. Who would I have batting for my life? Barry, to get the first 50. GP, having got to 50, to go on and make a big score.' Their respective statistics would seem to bear this out. In their first-class careers, Barry made 152 fifties and went on to convert 80 of them into hundreds, whereas Pollock made 99 fifties and converted 64 of them into hundreds. While we are bogged down in figures, let me just remind you that both of them had significantly higher Test than first-class averages – Pollock 60.93 as opposed to 54.67 and Richards 72.57 against 54.74. Both clearly relished the grand stage and rose to the occasion.

'Comparisons are odious,' said Lee Irvine in response to my query but then went on to give this informed respective assessment, 'Barry's technique was perfect, well nigh impregnable. He thrived on challenges and surely would, had he had a proper Test career, have been considered one of the greatest. But GP was run-hungrier. He may have had one or two little flaws in his technique but once he got going, he was unstoppable.' So was Lee, in this mood. Unbidden, he started to give me his opinion of a range of players of his generation. 'Best all-rounder? Without a shadow of a doubt, Garry Sobers. Best wicketkeeper? Alan Knott? Worst pitches? In Essex! Gordon Barker knew all the groundsmen in the county. He'd chat to them and come back into the dressing room and say that 20 would be a good score on that cabbage patch. And he'd be right!'

By now, he was laughing uncontrollably. 'One game, we played Warwickshire on a ploughed field at Leyton. Rohan Kanhai came in and the first ball beat him all ends up and went straight to first slip. He turned to me and asked how was he expected to bat on that. I shrugged and replied that I hadn't a clue. Well, stuff this, he said, I'm not going to get out of form playing on this pile of ****, I'm going to get out. So he slogged the next ball up in the air and strode off. He got a duck in the second innings too, I seem to remember.'

Regretfully, I hauled Lee back from his hilarious anecdotes of the Essex dressing room to the issue at hand and he came up with a surprising observation. 'McLean, Pollock and the others – they all pinched the strike. Barry didn't, unless it was in the team's interest to do so. He wasn't a selfish player.' I had to agree. At no stage in Barry's Hampshire career was any plan hatched in the team dressing room to send out a sacrificial scout to try and run him out, as Ian Botham was instructed to do to Geoff Boycott in a Test match in New Zealand. We were concerned that he batted *more* selfishly. You see, selfishly we wanted him to score all our runs, which he could, and sometimes did.

At a recent golf day in Cape Town in 2014, I had the opportunity to ask Pat Trimborn, the former Natal fast bowler and erstwhile team-mate of Barry's, what he thought of Barry as a batsman. 'Barry Richards!' he exclaimed loudly, not at all abashed by the number of people who paused mid-drink to listen, 'The best batsman I've ever seen, bar none! And that includes Graeme Pollock.' I had been told that Trimborn took no prisoners as a bowler. Needless to say, his opinions equally bore little self-doubt and he had those near about nodding their heads in agreement. Garth le Roux, another South African fast bowler, who was to join Barry playing World Series Cricket, was just as fulsome in his praise. 'I first bowled against him at Newlands in 1974, or was it 75? He took two steps outside leg and hit me over cover for four. My eyes bulged in astonishment. Nobody had ever done that to me before. Nobody ever did that to anyone!' Le Roux, it should be remembered, was one of the fastest bowlers around at the time.

'Do you remember that 356 he made at Perth?' *Well, I wasn't actually there but I have heard plenty of descriptions of it from a number of people who were.* 'He wasn't wearing a thigh pad!' *What?* 'He wasn't wearing a thigh pad. All he had was a sock in his pocket. I asked him why he had been so foolish. 'Why on earth would I want to wear a thigh pad?' he answered, 'That would mean I missed it, wouldn't it?' What a player! What talent! He had all the shots in the coaching manual and a few that weren't too.' *What about Pollock?* 'GP was never a hooker, more of a puller. Barry was more classical in his technique. He would adapt his strokeplay as the situation demanded. GP would simply bide his time and hit it. And he never missed it or hit it to a fielder. If it was a bad ball, it *always* ended up hitting the fence.'

Who can I turn to, therefore, who is unlikely to be biased, for a definitive judgement? As it happened, Robin Jackman was standing right beside Pat Trimborn when he, Trimborn, made his ardent declaration of admiration and Jackman was only too happy to give a more forensic analysis. 'Barry was the most complete right-handed batsman I have ever bowled to in my career,' he started off adamantly. Interestingly, he drew on two other players for comparison but not Pollock. The reason was simple. 'GP was left-handed. Let me compare Barry with two right-handed batsmen I played a lot against. Boycott was difficult to get out because he had a sound technique and he put a huge value on his wicket. Because of this, he would rarely, if ever, hurt you. Bowling at him therefore became risk-free. No real winner in that contest.' By contrast, he maintained, Viv Richards was an entertainer, which meant that he would take calculated risks in order to dominate. 'So, as a bowler, you always had a chance.'

Jackman then admitted ruefully that those chances came along all too rarely. 'I will never forget my Test debut in Barbados on the 1981 tour of the West Indies. Having made a duck in the first innings, Viv smashed us to all parts for 182 not out in 256 balls, with 23 fours and two sixes. There was a winner in that contest!' *How did Barry compare with those two diametrically opposed approaches to batting?* 'He fitted both profiles in as much as he had a very sound technique but could really hurt you when he put his mind to it.' Jackman then mused aloud what it was that made Barry so good. By way of illustration, he described watching Barry have a net before Western Transvaal took on Natal before a Currie Cup match. He enlisted the help of a bystander and asked him to shout out 'now' the moment van der Bijl, who was getting up a fair head of steam bowling to Barry, let go of the ball.

Meanwhile, Jackman had his eye firmly fixed on Barry as he faced up to each delivery. 'Barry had a very relaxed stance, eyes level, with the bat just tapping the crease a few times as the bowler was running in. When I heard the shout "now", Barry had not moved other than to complete his backlift. There was no trigger movement, like you see so many of the modern players incorporate into their pre-shot routine. He had remained stock still and only moved when he judged whether he was going to play forward or back.' I could scarcely contain my excitement. *We used to play the same trick on him in the nets at Hampshire! It's true – he remained motionless. That proves he must have had quicker reactions than the rest of us mere mortals.* Jackman agreed. 'It was a revelation to me and I have never forgotten it.'

Poignantly, Jackman told me of an interview that he had with Barry on South African television after he had retired. In the interview, Barry admitted that he regretted not scoring 100 hundreds. 'He said that with a hungrier attitude he could easily have attained that historic milestone,' said Jackman. 'He would get bored, you see, and give his wicket away. All I can say is thank goodness he did!' *Sixteen times when you played against him, Jackers.* He laughed. His comment put me in mind of an observation by Wilfrid Weld, chairman, president and patron of Hampshire CCC, who knew Barry well. 'Barry told me once that he wished he had scored fewer runs and made more friends during his time at Hampshire.' That is a sad epitaph to Barry's county cricket career and one that he would not now honestly discount. As we shall see, his association with his home province, Natal, has not been wholly amicable since his retirement either but for this he is surely less blameworthy. 'Politics, Murt, politics.' As he was forever reminding me.

It is time, is it not, for me to climb down from the fence and declare for one or the other, Pollock or Richards? I had the privilege of playing with both and the tribulation of playing against both. My qualifications for any sort of pronouncement are hardly in the same league as those I have quoted but here it is anyway – a personal opinion. Barry was the best right-handed batsman I have ever seen and Graeme the best left-handed batsman. That was a shirking hard decision to make, I know, but what I will say, without equivocation, is that I, in common with just about anyone else who has ever been on the same pitch as them, immediately sensed I was in the presence of greatness.

Satisfied? Probably not. But what is certainly true is that Barry, at this stage of his life and career, was far from satisfied himself. One wondered, given the circumstances that he found himself in, what would have satisfied him? Test match fulfilment? Sadly, out of the question. Contentment on the provincial and county circuit? Monotonous and tedious. Stockpiling runs and records? Uninspiring and wearisome. Trophy hunting? He had them all in his locker. Retirement? He was still in his early 30s. Change of career? What else could he do? Cricket was his life. Go home and count all his money? A hollow laugh for that one. He wasn't penniless but his financial wellbeing was far from secure. There was nothing for it, he reluctantly came to the conclusion, but to return to the treadmill of county cricket – for that was his job – and take what enjoyment there was to be had playing club cricket in Perth, Western Australia, where he had been offered a post, during the English off-season.

And then a single phone call changed everything.

9

The Packer Revolution 1977–79

*'Some called it a circus. Oh no it wasn't. That was by far
the most competitive cricket that I played in.'*
Barry Richards on his experiences in World Series Cricket

I HAVE often wondered, as I watch favoured guests bobbing and bowing before the Queen, whether there are circumstances where anybody would *not* wish to meet Her Majesty. Maybe there are a few hard-line republicans or Amazonian pygmies or Colombian drug barons or Islamist jihadists who would prefer to take a rain check but judging by the nervous look of expectancy on the faces of those in the queue, the overwhelming majority would not have missed it for the world. Heads of state, minor royalty, politicians of all hues, church leaders, captains of industry, film stars, celebrities, the great and the good of all countries, even American presidents, fall over themselves to take the hand of this tiny, elderly, unremarkable woman.

However, on 17 March 1977, 22 cricketers, locked in fierce combat on the last day of one of the greatest Test matches ever played, might have been forgiven a moment of exasperation as they were instructed to forgo their tea interval, don their blazers and line up to meet the Queen on the outfield of the Melbourne Cricket Ground. She was there as part of a tour of the country to celebrate her Silver Jubilee. They were there to play the Centenary Test, marking the 100th anniversary of the first ever Test match. She does not much like cricket and would probably have preferred a visit to the nearby racecourse, where the Melbourne Cup is run. They would rather have had the opportunity of putting their feet up for a few more minutes – especially Dennis Lillee, who had practically bowled himself into the ground – but there it was. The Queen is nothing if not forever dutiful and the players recognised the momentousness of the occasion so everybody put on a good show. Duty called, even though the participants had now been slugging it out, toe to toe, for all five days and the match was still in the balance. The Queen, they might have reminded themselves, had been responding to duty all her life.

For sheer extravagance, panoply and historic significance, few cricket matches have rivalled the Centenary Test of 1977. Notable absentees for the inaugural match one hundred years before, on the same Melbourne ground, were W.G. Grace for England, who had decided not to tour, and the 'Demon' Fred Spofforth, who had had a tiff with the Australian selectors. The result was a win for Australia by 45 runs, unexpected at the time, though it was said that the Englishmen were handicapped by seasickness following their voyage from New Zealand, the loss of their wicketkeeper, arrested on a charge of assault, and the consumption of large quantities of the amber liquid during the lunch breaks.

There were no absentees from the guest list of this jamboree; notable ex-players were in evidence as far as the eye could see. The likes of Percy Fender and Jack Ryder – the oldest from both countries – O'Reilly and Grimmett, Compton and Edrich, Tyson and Statham, the Bedser twins *et al*, were hugely enjoying the party. And no doubt imbibing large quantities of the amber liquid too. Some things never change. The players presumably were not – though one could never be sure with Rodney Marsh in the team – however much the low first innings scores might have suggested otherwise. The probable explanation for the double collapse was nerves; even the best players can sometimes be affected by the occasion.

Normal service was resumed by a better showing from the Australian batsmen in their second dig, setting England 463 runs to win. An unlikely target, but evidently no one informed Derek Randall of this. He played the innings of his life, an impudent, defiant, courageous 174, full of audacious shots and cheeky pugnacity. Everyone has the image ingrained in his mind of Lillee putting him on his backside with a well directed bouncer and Randall springing to his feet to doff his cap at his tormentor, a grin splitting his features. On another occasion, when Lillee hit him a painful blow on the back of his head, he cheerfully informed the concerned huddle of fielders gathered around, 'There's no point in hitting me there, mate – there's nothing in it.' It was enthralling, riveting stuff and the crowd lapped it up.

It almost took England to a famous victory. In the end, Lillee gathered himself for one last effort – he was in agony from a back injury – to have Knott LBW, whereupon he sank to the floor exhausted as his team-mates rushed to chair him off the field in triumph. He had taken 5-139, and 11 wickets in the match, to see Australia home. It took the scorers a minute or two to realise that they had won by 45 runs, the exact same winning margin as the very game that they were celebrating 100 years before.

The whole occasion had been a resounding triumph. No one was in the slightest doubt about that. A fiercely contested match from first to last had gripped large crowds – and enormous television audiences – with absorbing, sometimes exhilarating, cricket, fluctuating session by session. The marketing men were in raptures. The executives of the Australian Broadcasting Corporation, who had the sole television rights for the game, were jubilant. The players were shattered but satisfied. They knew they had been part of something special and they had not let themselves down. Sir Don Bradman was exultant. In a speech at a banquet after the match, he said, 'This will go down in history as one of the greatest sporting events of all time.' Hear, hear, agreed the gentlemen in the committee rooms of the Australian Cricket Board, convinced that all was well in their world. Here's to the next hundred years, they toasted each other.

But all was not well and those self-satisfied committee men would have spluttered in their gins and tonic had they had any inkling of what was about to hit them. For one man must have looked at the television ratings with a deep sense of frustration, not to say seething anger. Kerry Packer, the Australian media magnate, owner of Channel 9 among other business outlets, had long been trying to crack the monopoly of the broadcasting rights for cricket in Australia, owned solely by the Australian Broadcasting Corporation. But the ruling body of Australian cricket, the Australian Cricket Board, were more than happy with their cosy relationship with the national broadcasting corporation and were not prepared to do business. 'It would be easier to get an audience with the Pope,' Packer famously quipped, 'and I'm not Catholic.' He was not alone in believing that the initials for both organisations, ABC and

ACB, were practically interchangeable. Nonetheless, Packer, shrewd businessman that he was, recognised that the administration of both bodies had become lazy and complacent and were easy meat for a predator. Packer sharpened his claws.

In order to gain exclusive rights to broadcast cricket on Channel 9, he set about planning nothing less than a complete takeover of the game's establishment. He never made any bones about the fact – either at the time or subsequently – that this was his sole objective. He didn't want to run the country's national sport. He was a TV man. And he wanted his own way. It is often forgotten, however, that he loved his cricket. 'I wouldn't entirely agree with that,' demurred Barry. 'He liked his cricket but he *loved* TV.' Nonetheless, Packer was only too happy that his planned coup would also benefit the players – provided he got what he wanted. He joked that he had once been asked whether his actions were half philanthropic. 'Half philanthropic? That makes me sound more generous than I am.'

Whatever the causes of the perfect storm that was about to be whipped up, he was determined to step in and take advantage. Anyone who has studied political philosophy will know that revolution throughout history has usually been the result of an uprising by the people of a nation to overthrow a government that is seen to be acting against their interests. 'It was the easiest sport in the world to take over,' Packer maintained. 'Nobody bothered to pay the players what they were worth.' Such reasoning would have come as no surprise to Barry. He had been arguing that players had been underpaid for years. As an illustration, he has a memory of one quarrel he had with his own provincial administration in Natal. 'The guys in the team were not paid,' he told me. 'All of them had jobs and had to get leave of absence from their employers to play, sometimes to their financial disadvantage. I went in to argue that, at the very least, they should be paid a meal allowance. The request was refused. For just three rand! Jeez!' Actually, his expletive was a little more colourful than that but his anger was palpable. And for this niggardly action, and countless others, great and small, by cricket authorities the world over, the price they would have to pay was huge.

Packer's first move was to get the players – the third estate, if you like, of the revolution – on board. Here, he knew that he was pushing at a door that was already ajar. Test cricketers in all countries were slowly waking up to the fact that they were an integral part of the entertainment business that was filling stadiums yet precious little of the revenue generated was finding its way into their pockets. Barry was fond of pointing out the huge difference in earnings between him and a contemporary, another great South African sportsman, Gary Player. 'And while we are on the subject of golf,' he said, 'what about Rodney Marsh? His brother, Graham Marsh, was a successful pro golfer who earned lots more than Rod, who was just as well known to the Australian public.' *Yes, but golf is different. For a start, it is an individual game and you don't share your winnings with ten other team-mates.* 'That's true. But there was much more money sloshing around in golf. Why? Because the game was fully professional. It knew its market value and maximised its earning potential. Cricket was in the dark ages.'

Another classic example of this inequitable state of affairs, we both agreed, was Dennis Lillee, he who had just broken his back – almost literally – taking 11 wickets in the Centenary Test, all in the cause of Australian cricket. There was probably no more prominent and charismatic cricketer on the planet than Lillee, with his flowing mane, his bristling moustache and the raw aggression of his bowling. He was truly a household name, helping to fill the Melbourne Cricket Ground (250,000 over the five days) and was the star of the team who were, at that time, the undisputed world champions. Yet he was being paid peanuts. It was said that Packer was appalled when he discovered the terms and conditions of his contract with the ACB.

Greg Chappell made an interesting comparison to underline how far behind Test cricketers had fallen in terms of their remuneration. 'My grandfather, Vic Richardson, who captained Australia in the 1930s, was paid £1,000 when he toured England,' he told me. 'With that money, he was able to buy a large house and some land – and still had some left over. When I toured England in the mid-70s, I was paid $2,000 – on which I had to pay tax!' I am no mathematician but even I can see at a glance that, over the years, pay had regressed startlingly. 'Here's another fact,' he continued, 'After the very successful series against England in 1974/75...' *Er, very successful for you, Greg, not for us.* 'As I was saying, after the hugely successful series against the Poms in 74/75, we were told that the ACB had grossed over $1m. Yet it had only cost them $2,400 to hire the performers who filled the stadiums. That worked out at $200 per player.' The inequity and the iniquity of this state of affairs was beginning to rile the Australians, in particular.

Barry had enormous sympathy for their plight. He had been banging on about the same unjust system for years. As he and I pondered what was happening back then to the game we loved, a sudden thought came to me, an unworthy one perhaps but something that had not occurred to me over all these years. *I wasn't paid a penny to turn out for Eastern Province in that match against your lot in 1974. Yet the ground was packed, as I remember. Where did all the gate money go?* Barry gave one of his sardonic laughs. 'Straight into the coffers of the Eastern Province Cricket Association. Same with all the provinces. That is why the blazers turned left at the top of the steps leading up to the door of the plane and we players turned right.' The thought was unworthy because I did not expect to be paid; it was truly an honour to step on to the same field as the great GP. And yet, and yet...I was a professional cricketer, just like Barry – well, truth to tell, *nothing* like Barry – and the public had to pay at the gate to watch us play. Yes, on reflection, Barry is right. The game needed a really good kick up the backside and, by golly, it certainly got it.

So Packer made his move. Having been turned down flat by the ACB in his offer to negotiate, his response was immediate and unequivocal. If anyone was going to take aim with his boot, Packer was that man. Intrigued by his reputation as a hard man, I asked Barry whether it was justified. 'Look, all that stuff was media hype. He was portrayed as a bully. But that was not fair. He was a tough, shrewd, astute businessman, who didn't suffer fools gladly. Typical forthright Aussie, if you like, not at all worried whose toes he trod on. But his word was his bond. If he shook hands on a deal or a contract, he would honour it to the last letter.' Barry came to trust him, as did all the players who signed up for his organisation. And no one could accuse the likes of Greig and the Chappell brothers, any more than Barry, of being innocents abroad. 'I'd never met Kerry Packer,' Greg Chappell stated, 'but of course we all knew who he was. Apparently, he had struggled at school, as an undiagnosed dyslexic. He hadn't been the choice of his father, who owned Channel 9, to inherit the business. But when his elder brother, the favoured one, had shown a disinclination to run the family business, Kerry took over and grew it from a multi-million concern to a multi-billion one. People underestimated him at their peril.' *How did you get on with him?* 'Look, we were not friends. But we had a good working relationship.' *Was he as straight as a die, as Barry claims?* 'Kerry honoured every contract to the last letter.'

The tiger, having had his tail tweaked, started to stalk the corridors of power, smelling blood. His prey shut themselves away, terrified that the predator was now on the loose and they were powerless to do anything about it. But instead of clawing at the doors of the ACB, the tiger went away to form his own circus. For circus was the word that the unsympathetic press latched on to to describe Packer's troupe of itinerant cricketers. Barry laughed at the suggestion. 'Some called it a circus. Oh no it wasn't. That was by far the hardest cricket I ever played.' And I have yet to hear of a single player who was involved in World Series Cricket who would not agree with this assessment. Greg Chappell certainly does. 'The toughest. I've never had to work so hard for runs in my life.' As we come to look at some of the matches and the quality of the combatants – 'It was war out there at times,' said Barry – I think you will agree too.

Central to Packer's plans was the recruitment of two major players, respectively the captains of Australia and England, Greg Chappell and Tony Greig. Chappell was arguably the finest batsman in the world at the time and as the affair was largely an Australian one, the whole project would have been dead in the water without him. Chappell's signature was non-negotiable, Packer told his associates. *Tell me, Greg, was it a done deal from the outset for you?* He shook his head. 'Aw look, I was the Australian captain at the time. I was fully aware of my responsibilities to the post and to the team. That's why I wanted to see what players he was recruiting before I signed. Once I realised he was serious, it was a no-brainer. I knew it was something I had to do, for me personally and for Australian cricket in general.'

In many ways, the recruitment of Tony Greig was equally important. He had just led an MCC tour to India, which had been a great success, England winning the series 3-1. From the very moment his team landed on the subcontinent, he charmed the Indian public. 'What do you think of Indian umpires?' he was asked at his first press conference. Here was a potential banana skin and he knew it. This was in the days before neutral umpires and Indian umpires were notoriously partial. Greig's fingers had been burnt once before with his infamous promise to make the West Indies 'grovel'. A recent but wholly enthusiastic convert to the value of good PR, he turned to his inquisitor and with a beaming smile announced, 'Indian umpires are the best in the world.' Thereafter, he had the whole country in the palm of his hand, including the umpires who gave his side more LBW decisions on that tour than in every other tour put together. Oh yes, Packer knew well enough that Greig was crucial to the cause.

Were you close to Tiny Greig, Barry? 'Tiny Greig? Is that your idea of a joke or are you making fun of my South African accent? As it happened, we did both come from the same background and had the same sort of upbringing. So, yes, we always got on well and continued to do so throughout our careers and beyond, when we both were on media watch. He was a loyal friend but, hell, you wouldn't want to cross him! Sad he's gone. He was a larger than life character.' I should say so. I remember when I first met him. He strode into the Sussex pavilion at Hove, greeting everybody cheerfully, from the doorman to the catering lady to familiar faces in the Hampshire team. It was as if a god had entered our presence, a 6ft 7in, blond, beanpole of a man, exuding power, influence, charisma, sex-appeal. 'You just couldn't ignore him,' said Barry, 'whatever he was doing.' And this was from one who was very much in the public eye himself. 'Packer needed him for two reasons,' went on Barry. 'As the England captain, he was in the best place to recruit. And, if you needed someone to mould a team of superstars from scratch, he was your man.' *No problems about playing under him as your captain?* 'None whatsoever.'

I was intrigued, at this point, what were Greg Chappell's feelings when he discovered that he was expected to play under another's captaincy, namely his brother. The story goes that Packer approached Ian, who had by now retired and been succeeded as Australia's captain by Greg, and asked him to lead the side. Ian replied that he would have to consult his brother first, before giving an answer. 'What do you think this is, son?' retorted Packer, 'This isn't a f****** democracy. You're the f****** captain!' *That seemed pretty conclusive. But were you happy with that?* Greg replied, 'Perfectly happy. I'd done the job for a while. And I was to do it again. And I'd played under Ian before. I was happy to try and concentrate on my batting.'

What thoughts I wonder assailed the official captains of England and Australia as they signed on the dotted line. Both were the supreme commanders of their country's forces, if you like, entrusted with command by their political masters and given custody of their supporters' goodwill. The notion of betrayal must have crossed their minds at some point. It mattered not, in the court of public opinion, that they themselves felt betrayed; how could they turn their backs on the legacy betrothed them by Darling and Armstrong, Woodfull and Richardson, Bradman and Hassett as well as Grace and MacLaren, Chapman and Jardine, Hutton and May? Not the least irony of the affair was that Vic Richardson was Greg Chappell's grandfather.

The decision cannot have been an easy one, no matter how disillusioned both Chappell and Greig had become with their lot. There was no guarantee that the project would even have got off the ground, let alone become a viable commercial prospect. Sadly, Tony Greig is no longer with us but Greg Chappell most certainly is. 'Yes, we all had fleeting doubts from time to time. But we never discussed failure. It was inconceivable. What united us all in our determination to make it work was a firm belief that if we provided exciting, competitive cricket then people would come to watch. And after the initial scepticism, people did, in droves.'

I guess, as with the success of any new adventure, much depended on the single-minded tenacity, self-assurance and strength of character of the main driving force, Kerry Packer. He was a multi-millionaire with enormous resources at his disposal. He was in it to win it. 'What Packer wanted, he got,' was Barry's appraisal. Still, Greig and Chappell had much to lose. Chappell was the captain of his country's team. It is difficult to think of a higher profile job in that country, saving the prime minister's perhaps, and Greg was fully aware of what he was sacrificing. 'We knew that we would never play Test cricket again,' he surprised me by saying, 'I'd been playing at the top level for seven or eight years. I now had a family and a mortgage to pay and I simply couldn't afford to go on playing, away from home such a lot, without a decent salary.' In fact, he was to play Test cricket again, for a further six years, and we can all breathe a hearty sigh of relief for that. I would have hated to have to write another book about a lost genius to the game.

At the time of the Centenary Test, Tony Greig's stock could not have been higher. He was the golden boy of English cricket, the favoured adopted son of his lords and masters at Lord's, a successful captain, an irresistible leader, a popular figure and a powerful magnet for sponsors and advertising contracts. And not a bad Test cricketer either, it should be remembered. He found himself mercilessly pilloried as a traitor and a foreign mercenary by the English media when the news broke.

'Test Pirates!' railed the popular press. Barry utterly disagreed with this caricature. 'What Greigy did,' Barry said, 'immeasurably improved the lot of the professional cricketer in England, much as I was trying to do in South Africa.' The passing years have vindicated Barry's assertion and largely restored Greig's reputation in the eyes of cricket's establishment. But it was very different in 1977. Well, what do you expect if you put a South African in charge of the England team? That was a view I heard expressed many times on the county circuit, and from people that you would normally have expected to be more supportive.

In 2012, Tony Greig gave the keynote speech at the MCC Spirit of Cricket/ Cowdrey Lecture at Lord's and took the opportunity to right a wrong. He read out a letter he had written to Packer all those years ago, which set out his reasons – and the justification for them – for signing for WSC. In it, he claimed that money was not the bait. He was not poor, not by a long chalk. But job insecurity stalked him. The captaincy of England was a precarious position. All recent incumbents – Close, Illingworth, Cowdrey, Denness – had been sacked.

'I am 31,' he wrote, 'and probably two or three Test failures away from being dropped by England. Ian Botham is going to be a great player and there won't be room in the side for both of us.' Prescient words. He continued, 'I don't want to finish up in a mundane job when they drop me. I'm not trained to do anything. I went straight from school to playing for Sussex. My family's future is more important than anything else. If you guarantee me a job for life working for your organisation, I will sign.'

Packer did. And Greig signed. And, as Barry said, Packer always kept his word. Greig was still working for Channel 9 when he died, at the end of that year, 2012.

And there you have it; an age-old grievance had stirred. Barry was not the only professional cricketer racked by insecurity. If the acclaimed Tony Greig, literally head and shoulders above his contemporaries, a totem pole of affluence and success, was fearful of the future, what misgivings assailed the minds of the ordinary county player? 'And people moaned at me because I was trying to protect my future,' complained Barry. Mark Nicholas, former captain of Hampshire and in many ways Greig's natural successor as an international broadcaster, put it better than most, 'At that time, England were paying £210 per Test match, less than the cost of the tickets that Greig had to buy for his family to attend the Centenary Test.' That says it all. 'Look Murt,' Barry insisted, by way of the final word on the matter, 'If Packer hadn't done it, someone else would.' The governing bodies of the game were obsolete structures, built on rickety foundations, and the tremor that was World Series Cricket brought them crashing to the ground. And Barry Richards, for one, had no problems with that.

Greg Chappell went to great lengths to emphasise to me that the rebellion was not solely about money. 'Yes, money came into it. But we weren't asking for much. It was *respect* we wanted. The players never had a voice in the running of the game. For years, Ian had been trying to negotiate with the board over salaries and conditions of service. There was no thought of the players' welfare or their future security. You were paid match-by-match and very little, considering the vast sums of money pouring into the board's coffers. For example, Ian tried to get them to set up some sort of pension scheme for guys who had played 20 or more Tests.' *And how was that received?* 'Basically he was told to get lost. We were only asking for a few thousand dollars more. Someone on the board went public with a statement to the effect that if these blokes don't want to play for Australia, there are 50,000 others out there who would – for nothing!' Even from a distance of nearly 40 years, that still sounds like intemperate, if not to say inflammatory, language. 'We wanted to form a cricketers' trade union,' Greg continued. 'Bob Hawke, later our prime minister, advised us to call it an association, because of the obvious connotations of the word "union". But we got nowhere. Trust, that had been eroding for years, had now broken down completely.' *So, not many Australians were going to reject the offer then?* He laughed hollowly.

The irony of all ironies of the whole affair was that the recruitment for World Series Cricket started in earnest during the Centenary Test, just when the respective boards of Australian and English cricket were congratulating each other on their great success. History is littered with examples of the unwary being caught out when they least expect it, frequently with disastrous consequences. The ignominious fall of Singapore to the Japanese during the Second World War is routinely blamed on the fact that the large defensive guns of the military garrison were facing the wrong way, out to sea. The British expected a seaborne invasion and never believed that the Japanese could invade by land, through what they thought was impenetrable jungle. They underestimated their foe calamitously.

The administrators of the ACB and the TCCB (their English equivalent), basking in the success of the one-off celebratory Test match, had taken their eyes off the ball and were astonished to turn round and see the enemy climbing the barricades behind them. In point of fact, the game was a perfect opportunity for Chappell and Greig to go round their respective dressing rooms, pen and contract in hand; the majority of potential recruits were conveniently situated at the same time under one roof.

Where were you when all this was going on, Barry? 'I was in Perth at the time playing club cricket.' *Did you watch the Centenary Test on the box?* 'I was *there*, man!' That I had not realised. *So you knew what was afoot?* 'I'd already signed and I knew people were being recruited. But I didn't go anywhere near the players. That would not have been right.' Of course not. We both understood the sanctity of the dressing room.

Secrecy was paramount. There had to be a critical mass of top players willing to throw in their lot with Packer for the embryonic venture to stand any chance of getting off the ground. And not all of the potential targets were in Melbourne during those five days. There were West Indians, South Africans, Indians, Pakistanis to be sounded out and they were scattered about the globe. If word got out what was afoot, the coup would have been nipped in the bud. There were also compelling commercial reasons to keep everything under wraps. The last thing Packer would have wanted was for his competitors in the media world to get whisper of what was in the offing. And reporters are not called newshounds for nothing.

With one exception, it would appear, the identity of whom will emerge shortly. *I guess, then, Barry, that you must have been one of the first to be asked?* '**The** first,' he put me right. And that would seem to be entirely logical. He was an obvious choice. His pedigree was unquestioned. He was living in Australia at the time. He had no Test commitments, no national board to which he was beholden. And he had always made it clear that he would follow the money. If it was a travelling circus that you were setting up, the authentic cricketing troubadour was your obvious man. 'Have bat, will travel' could have been emblazoned on Barry's cricket bag.

What did he say when he contacted you? 'Who – Packer? No, it wasn't him. He employed others as his negotiators. It was a man called Austin Robertson who rang me, quite out of the blue.' Austin Robertson was a former Aussie Rules footballer and together with John Cornell, a partner of Paul Hogan (yes, he of *Crocodile Dundee* fame) in a successful Channel 9 chat show, they acted as Packer's chief spear-carriers in the recruitment process. 'I was struck by the magnitude of the whole thing,' said Barry, 'the sheer breathtaking ambition of the project. Once I heard who was already involved – the Chappells, Lillee, Marsh, Greig – I knew it was serious. I didn't take much persuading to sign up.'

In many ways, the offer had come as a godsend to Barry. He was at a crossroads in his career; he feared that it might be a cul-de-sac. He had finally come to the conclusion that there would be no more Test cricket for him. He had severed his ties with Natal. He was playing club cricket in Perth but that wasn't going to pay many bills. He still had his contract with Hampshire but we know how disillusioned he had become with county cricket. And here, totally unexpected, had come knocking on his door the opportunity, a late one, it was true, but welcome nonetheless, to pit his skills against the very best. He could scarcely contain his excitement.

How much was the contract worth, if you don't mind my asking? 'Twenty-five thousand dollars a year,' he replied without hesitation. 'Bit more than we were getting at Hampshire, eh, Murt?' For a cricketer in the late 1970s, that was serious cash. You might even say, unheard of riches. *It was for you a no-brainer then?* 'It was a no-brainer for two reasons. One, it was my last chance to play international cricket. And two, the money guaranteed at last some sort of financial security. So yes, you could say I was excited at the prospect.' *Did you, at any stage, have any reservations?* 'Well, obviously it was a gamble. We were stepping off into the unknown. But I knew that Kerry Packer was a serious player on the world stage and, hell – what did I have to lose?'

I imagine you too were sworn to secrecy? 'I said nothing for six months, until the news broke.' *Did you chat about it with any of the other players?* 'No, not really. I mean I'd look at one or two of them and they'd sort of look at me and we would guess what was in each other's mind but it was all hush-hush.' He did however talk to one person about the whole business and that one person happened to be a reporter. He was John Bishop, a personal friend, who worked for the *Natal Witness*. 'I trusted him. Look, pal, I said, if you keep your mouth shut about what I'm about to tell you, I promise I'll give you an exclusive when it all comes out.' Both were as good as their word.

Even more extraordinary than a newspaper reporter keeping the lid on a major scoop was the collective silence of scores of international cricketers as one by one or in groups they were signed up for the biggest revolution in the game's history. That the news did not leak out for six months beggars belief. I asked Greg Chappell about this. 'I talked to my brother and my wife about it. *And no one else*. Not even my parents.' Meanwhile, the cricketing authorities sleepwalked towards cataclysm as Packer planned, plotted and got all his ducks set up in a row.

When you stop to think about it, the secrecy really was nothing short of a miracle. Cricketers are not the most discreet of animals and nothing remains hidden for long in the claustrophobic confines of a dressing room. There were team-mates in the know and others who were oblivious. One member of the England touring party for the Centenary Test was Mike Selvey, later to become a cricket reporter himself. He was not part of Packer's plans and was not approached by Greig. He later admitted that he never heard so much as a whisper of what was going on. A good friend of mine, Roger Tolchard, was also in that team and was not approached either so I asked him whether he too had been kept entirely in the dark. 'Well, I was aware something was going on,' he said. 'You know what it's like, there are huddles in the corner and people looking about conspiratorially. But I thought it was Greigy planning some sort of charity jamboree or a benefit game or a money-spinning private event. And as he didn't talk to me, I assumed that I didn't feature in his plans so I forgot all about it. I was more concerned about being dropped for the Test, which in truth I knew was going to happen. I hadn't got enough runs in India, you see.'

Quite possibly, Roger, but what was happening under your nose might have put paid, quite realistically, to Test cricket, in India or anywhere else. Are you sure you had no inkling? He assured me that he did not. Whether that says more about his noted powers of concentration on the match in hand or the extraordinary guardedness of the pirates, as they were soon to be labelled, is hard to determine. Or perhaps they were so intimidated by Mr Packer and his tough, no-nonsense negotiating team – so unlike the bumbling amateurish governance of their own cricket boards – that they were cowed into silence. The upshot was that several weeks later, pretty well the same band of cricketers assembled in England for the resumption of official hostilities, the 1977 Ashes series.

Meanwhile, the English county season cranked into life in early May as it had been doing so for generations and still there was barely more than a gentle breeze rippling the calm seas. And all the while, the big names of Test cricket were eagerly seizing the proffered pen and signing up with alacrity: Viv Richards, Lloyd, Holding, Roberts, Daniel, Croft, Fredericks, Garner, Rowe, Imran, Barlow, Majid, Asif, Javed, Procter, Rice, Zaheer and many others. Rebellion was afoot and the man on the Clapham omnibus on the way to the Oval or the Kent supporter unwrapping his sandwiches in the rhododendron-lined ground in Tunbridge Wells was blissfully unaware of the tidal wave that was about to engulf the game he knew and loved.

Why no Indians, Barry? I should have thought that Gavaskar, Kapil Dev, Bedi, Vishy, would all have been useful additions? 'I think they were more closely tied in by contract with the Indian board. And there was a series scheduled in Australia at the same time.' That was true. The Indians lost an enthralling series 3-2 and proved to be popular and well supported tourists. 'In their own country, the Indians were regarded as demigods,' Barry continued, 'so it would have taken a huge leap of faith for them to turn their backs on their board and their countrymen.'

But were any of them approached? 'Gavaskar was, obviously, but he was the captain and was probably put under huge pressure by his board. Anyway, he hummed and hah'd and in the end, Kerry lost patience. Besides, I don't think the fast wickets in Australia would have been to the Indians' liking. Their strength was in their spinners and spinners did not feature much in Australia.' It was well documented that the subtle tussle between slow bowler and batsman did not greatly enthuse Mr Packer. He preferred the violent clash between the fast men and their hunted prey, red in tooth and claw. 'The Indian tour also meant that all the Test venues were booked for that year,' Barry reminded me. This was a huge problem for Packer and one that he was not able to sort out until the second year of WSC.

And what about Pollock? He was originally signed, I see, but never played. How come? This elicited one of Barry's derisory snorts. They usually presented themselves whenever the thorny problem of politics intruded into the story, with all the cant and hypocrisy that went with it. 'Those of us South Africans who were playing county cricket were considered "cleansed". Those who were not – GP, Irvine, van der Bijl, Denys Hobson, the leg-spinner – were considered to be pariahs.' Doubly damned then – prevented from playing Test matches and now not even allowed to join the pirates.

Barry's use of the word 'cleansed', with its nuance of sanctimonious preachiness, set me thinking. In my time in South Africa, during the apartheid years, closer contact with the morally repugnant system did not breed in me complacency and acquiescence. I found apartheid just as appalling at the end of my stay as at the beginning. But I recognised too that there were plenty of anomalies and double standards operating on the margins of the divide. Was I alone, I mused, as I looked around the Boeing 707, flying out of Heathrow, bound for Johannesburg, and crammed with prosperous businessmen…was I alone in wondering why it was iniquitous to have sporting contacts with South Africa yet perfectly defensible to maintain close trading links? South African cricketers who played county cricket were tainted but had been 'cleansed'. So that was all right then, they could join. The rest, even the great Graeme Pollock, were stigmatised and no one wanted to play with them.

Still curious, I contacted Lee Irvine and asked him if it had ever been explained why he had not been approached. 'But I was!' he exclaimed. 'They were looking for a wicketkeeper batsman. They had Knotty but they needed cover so I was asked to sign. I was absolutely delighted, I can tell you. I thought my playing days were over.' He had retired from the captaincy of Transvaal after two unhappy seasons in charge, finding the job of captaining the side, keeping wicket and opening the batting too burdensome. So, at the age of 33, he chucked it all in. 'But I got a hundred in my last game!' he announced proudly. 'Against EP. And then Packer came calling.' *So, what happened?* 'I had to get leave from my job. In the time that my employers took to decide, the offer from Packer was withdrawn. Apparently, the West Indians didn't want to play with or against South Africans. But if you were playing with or against them in county cricket, that was considered all right.' And he laughed. Like Barry, he was bemused by the constant trimming of principles. 'So I never signed. But Pollock did, straight away. The offer was withdrawn, yes, but as he had already signed, they had to pay up. $25,000. And he never went. Had I been quicker off the mark, I too would have got the money.'

A shame, I agree. But did you regret not being able to play? 'I would have loved it. Like Barry, I wanted to test myself against the best. Test cricket was out but Packer would have given me the opportunity of top-class competition. I always fancied myself against the quicks. And there wasn't much else out there other than fast bowling, was there? I'd have gone for nothing. It was massively disappointing.'

Let us return to the story, which was now being played out during the English summer of 1977. It must have been strange for Barry and the other signatories to travel the country playing against each other and exchanging knowing looks and occasional half-smiles, wondering when the storm was going to break. It came in mid-May, while Sussex were entertaining the touring Australians. Ironically, Tony Greig was hosting the tourists to a party at his home, when it is alleged a couple of Australian journalists unearthed the secret – from whom it has never been discovered – and published the story in the following day's newspaper back in Australia. The report took a day or two to come back to England but when it did, all hell broke loose. I remember the furore very well. For the rest of that summer, it dominated discussion in dressing rooms, committee rooms, pavilions, bars and stands up and down the country. Television, radio and newspapers talked of little else. Nobody seemed sure what to make of it. Of three things, however, everybody was agreed. Greig was a traitor and should be sacked. Packer had committed the biggest larceny since the Great Train Robbery. And cricket would never be the same again.

It seemed certain that the Packer 'pirates' would be banned from Test and first-class cricket. And Greig had to go. His position as England captain had become untenable. Sure enough, within the week, he had been stripped of the captaincy and Mike Brearley appointed in his place. This can't have come as a surprise to Greig; he must have expected that something like this would happen. What he did not expect was the amount of vitriol poured over his blond locks. The establishment turned their backs on him and so did the British public. He retained his place in the England side, thanks solely to Brearley's insistence, but he was booed whenever he made his way to the wicket. He had a quiet series and in the last Test that summer at the Oval, he made his final appearance for his adopted country. Thereafter, his life was bound up with Packer's organisation and he moved, lock, stock, barrel and family, to live in Australia.

England thrashed the Australians that summer, incidentally, to regain the Ashes. Their opponents put up a lacklustre show, hardly surprising really. They were a divided and dispirited team. Thirteen had their minds on other things; the remaining four were left wondering why they had not been invited to the party. The management were furious with the rebels and kept on issuing veiled threats about their future careers and the legitimacy of what they were about to embark on. 'They were not a bunch of happy campers,' was Barry's wry comment.

Meanwhile, Packer decided that his signees needed having their resolve stiffened, so he flew into London to take on the grandees at Lord's and the TCCB, not to mention public opinion, in the war of words that was to follow. Packer was an articulate and skilled PR operator so there was only going to be one winner. He did not deal in defeat. Chappell laughs at the memory. 'There we had in opposition an uneducated roughneck from the colonies taking on the face of the establishment, Robin Marlar, Harrow and Cambridge, experienced and outspoken cricket correspondent for *The Sunday Times*. It was an unfair contest. Packer wiped the floor with him!' *When did you first meet him?* Not until he came to London during the summer of 1977. Some of the boys were being put under intolerable pressure by the management and were beginning to waver so Kerry flew in to reassure them and gee them up. And then there was the famous court case and after that there was only going to be one winner.'

When did you first encounter Packer, Barry? 'He called me on the phone at the ground at Southampton. I though it was a joke at first. He asked me what I thought of this chap Greenidge. Needless to say, the next day, I was driving Gordy up to London for Packer to sign him on. We walked into the Dorchester and there was John Snow. Packer came in and told Snowy that he was over the hill but he'd sign him anyway. Snowy went puce – he had steam coming out of his ears. But Kerry was like that, brash and forthright.'

More and more players were signed up and the cricket authorities were well and truly caught on the hop. By now, Packer had over 40 under his wing, with the promise of more to follow. The scale of the rebellion was staggering. It was a standing joke in the dressing room at Hampshire that every morning we would greet each other with an enquiry as to whether any of us had had a phone call from Packer the previous evening. Barry, as I remember, together with the two others, Roberts and Greenidge – whenever they passed themselves fit to play – maintained a sensible and dignified silence. As in most dressing rooms on the county circuit that summer, it was an awkward place.

Looking back on it now, I wish I had adopted a more mature and inquisitive attitude to unfolding events. Daily it seemed there were rumours, counter rumours, leaked reports and official pronouncements. We knew nothing and as ever when the difficult, the problematic, even the unpalatable, reared its head, we treated it as a joke. And all along, the man who could best explain was changing next to us. If only we had bothered to ask. After all, he had been banging on about pay and working conditions ever since he had come to the club. And now, at last, he was about to be vindicated. The distinction between amateurs and professionals had been abolished ages before, in 1962, but the old ways still lingered. Now, they were about to be swept away forever. And not before time, was the prevailing opinion, in spite of the disappointment over Greig's perceived betrayal and the worrisome threat to Test cricket. Packer did not cause this revolution; he was the catalyst. We could all see that. The players, particularly the Test players, had been dissatisfied and disillusioned for some time. You need a match to light a bonfire. But it will not ignite if the wood is not tinder dry and ready to burn.

Barry's despondency with the daily grind of county cricket and its meagre wages has been well documented. The wages may have been low in the 1970s but at least the game was professional; you could make a living out of it, albeit an insecure one whose lifespan was limited. In the non-professional countries, you played for love. Fine when you are young and you have few responsibilities. But at some stage, you have to think of the future, especially when you have a family. In the past, the best players, Bradman foremost among them, had been provided with nominal jobs by sympathetic employers but, by now, the world was becoming a more competitive place and fewer sinecures were to be found. Players were retiring earlier. The game just wasn't worth the candle. 'Everybody was becoming fed up with their boards,' said Barry, 'especially the Australians and West Indians. In the Caribbean there may not have been much money sloshing around. But that certainly wasn't the case in Australia. The Chappells, Lillee, Marsh, were all at loggerheads with their boards, all the time, it seemed to me. Ian Chappell, in particular, had constant battles with officialdom.'

So much so, according to his brother Greg, that he retired. In his early 30s, he'd had enough, rebuffed at every turn in his quest to legitimise and raise the status of the professional cricketer in his country. 'People called us rebels,' said Greg, 'and said that we were trying to do away with the traditions of the game. But they didn't, or wouldn't, understand. We were traditional cricketers too and had as big a stake in conserving the game as anybody. We didn't want to run the game ourselves. But it was pretty clear to us that the game was going backwards and we had to do something about it before it died on its feet.' His frustration was shared by Barry, who would probably have retired by this time as well, if only he could have afforded it. Everywhere, there was this feeling that cricket in each country was being run by a monopoly, an inner circle of reactionary diehards who were totally out of touch with reality.

During the summer of 1977, while Barry was wrestling with the parochial complications of running his benefit, World Series Cricket seemed to be generating more heat than light. Rather like the phoney war that prevailed in Europe from September 1939 until hostilities commenced in earnest in April 1940, not a lot seemed to be happening as both sides, Packer and the International Cricket Conference, the game's governing body, faced off uneasily. At length, they met at Lord's in June to seek a compromise. I say 'at length', but the meeting lasted barely 90 minutes before Packer, exasperated by the refusal to grant Channel 9 exclusive broadcasting rights – the ICC claimed they had not the power to make such a decision – stormed out and delivered his own declaration of war, 'I will take no steps now to help anyone. It's every man for himself and the devil take the hindmost.'

The ICC responded by outlawing WSC, stating that none of the games would be allowed first-class status and that the players involved would be banned from Test and first-class cricket. It is never a good idea to tweak the tiger's tail. Packer's reaction was uncompromising. Getting wind of the fact that some of his players were beginning to waver in the face of this prospective ban, he took the ICC and the various boards to the High Court. Tony Greig, Mike Procter and John Snow, backed by the best lawyers Packer could hire, sued for restraint of trade.

I'm guessing you were not one of them, Barry. After all, restraint of trade might have been very welcome to you. 'Correct. Prockie had much more to do with it than me. Look, banning me from Test cricket was meaningless because I was already banned. And stopping me from playing for Hampshire was no big deal. In fact, it was a welcome release. So, no, I wasn't bothered. But I could see that some of the others, especially the English players, felt they were caught between a rock and a hard place.' He was correct. Many in England, supporters and players alike, were very worried about the future of Test cricket.

And not just Test cricket. The English counties wrestled with what strategy to adopt with regard to their 'pirates' and by no means could it be said that they came to a unanimous conclusion. The reaction from committee rooms up and down the country differed wildly. Some were strident in their condemnation; others preferred to put their head in the sand and wait to see what happened. Derek Underwood recounts an extraordinary story about what occurred in the Garden of England, one that left me in two minds whether to laugh or cry. 'All of us Packer signatories, the Kent boys, me, Knotty, Woolmer, Denness, Asif, were told to report to the County Ground at Canterbury. We were informed that our contracts at the county were not going to be renewed at the end of the season. And, to add insult to injury, we were told that if we wanted to leave immediately, no one would stand in our way! We were all in shock. Poor little Knotty was practically in tears.' I'm not surprised. Alan Knott was a man of Kent through and through, a integral a feature of the county as its orchards and hop gardens. 'It was farcical, really,' Underwood continued. 'Within days, we were being rung up by other counties asking us to go and play for them!'

So much for a concerted response by the TCCB. 'Exactly. The last straw was when Eddie Barlow, captain at the time at Derbyshire, got in touch and asked me to go and play for them.' *What was your reply?* 'Bugger off, Eddie. Play at Derby? You must be having a laugh.' Underwood's jocular tone belied a real concern for his county future. *But the court case put paid to all that nonsense, didn't it?* He nodded. He said that he and Asif went up every day to London to listen to the proceedings in the High Court. *Packer wiped the floor with the cricket establishment there, didn't he?* 'Absolutely demolished them,' he replied, with a little smack of the lips that he must have given – many times – whenever he scrutinised a wet wicket. 'Probably at Westcliff,' Barry observed tartly.

To put it bluntly, Packer was seen as a clear and present threat to the very fabric of the traditional form of the game. 'England is a deeply conservative country,' Barry offered, 'especially when it comes to their love of the time-honoured customs of the game. That is why the outcry was so vehement in your country. Other countries were less hidebound by tradition and perhaps more open to change.' Well, yes and no. My opinion, then as now, has always been ambivalent over the Packer affair. Yes, I could see that the administration of the game was moribund and needed shaking up. In all other walks of life, employees were no longer satisfied or willing to remain mere lackeys of their masters. And in this social revolution, cricket was lagging far behind.

On the other hand, I really did believe that Test cricket was the highest and sternest test of ability and temperament (after all, why are they called Tests?) and in my mind, the future, to say nothing of the history, of this form of the game, was sacrosanct. In many ways, the same conflicting forces are at work today with the advent of the Indian Premier League. Test cricket in this country is popular and well supported. Sadly, this is no longer the case in other countries where the razzmatazz and the gaudiness, as well as the naked commercialism, of the 20-over slog has superseded the pre-eminence of the longer game. Whither Test cricket? The misgivings are as real now as they were back in 1977.

Did the fact that you were one of the 'pirates' affect in any way the support for your benefit that year? Barry gave this some thought but reckoned, on balance, that it had not. 'It might have been different had I been one of the English players. But I think it was generally regarded as reward for my ten years' service to Hampshire in county cricket and Packer had nothing to do with it. In fact, a lot of people could fully understand why I had signed up, as I couldn't play Test cricket.' *Still, I have heard it whispered that there was a bit of ill feeling towards you three for abandoning Hampshire.*

Was that true? He rubbed the side of his nose, a sure sign that he was considering his response very carefully. 'I don't think that was true of Gordon. He still wanted to play county cricket so the ban would have hurt him. Fruity had worked out that the daily grind on the circuit was no way to prolong a fast bowler's life. As for me… Look, I'd been playing non-stop for ten years. In other words, 20 seasons without a break. So it was hardly hello today, see you tomorrow.'

That is true. He had become stale and bored and God knows what ructions would have ensued had he been forced back on to the treadmill. But if I have one quarrel with Barry – hardly a quarrel, more a difference of opinion – it is that he was, in my opinion, a little too obvious in his delight at the banning order. I remember him coming into the dressing room and announcing the news with a beaming smile, as if he had just won the lottery. No doubt that was how he felt. But it might have been more politic had he shown some restraint. After all, his team-mates were in no such enviable position. They still had to take to the field day after day, to grind out the results and to eke out a living. Some of them were less than impressed by his attitude. 'That's probably right,' he sighed. 'No marks as usual for tact. I was young and brash. I wish…' His words petered out. Barry wishes many things in his life had been handled better or turned out differently

The clash between Packer and the establishment, heard in London's High Court in September, held the country in its thrall. Nothing in the cricketing arena since the D'Oliveira Affair, nearly a decade earlier, had stirred up so much public interest. Who can possibly forget that famous photo emblazoned across the front pages of all the newspapers of Kerry Packer and Tony Greig as they emerged together from court – the sorcerer and his apprentice, Packer an avuncular guardian and Greig, done up to the nines in his suit, with bulging briefcase in one hand and bundle of files under the other arm, looking like no cricketer ought in the 1970s? A report on the trial gives just this bald conclusion – judgement was given for the plaintiffs in both actions with costs. The actual length of time that it took Lord Justice Slade to read out his judgement took five and a half hours but the verdict was as electrifying as if he had merely confined himself to these short words, taken from his speech, 'A professional cricketer needs to make his living as much as any other professional man.'

The ICC were therefore wrong to prevent cricketers from doing this, even if they believed their own interests were being harmed. The costs were estimated to be in the region of £250,000. 'They talk about not being able to pay the players enough,' announced a scornful Packer afterwards. 'They could have had that money to do it.' Meanwhile, Barry was doing the rounds of clubs and pubs, collecting the sparse takings from the collection jars and pontoon boxes for his benefit. Born in the wrong era, as he continually points out, at least he could content himself with the thought that those who came after him would more than likely not have to prostitute themselves 'begging' for money as he was doing, once that epochal judgement had been handed down from on high.

The result of the court case may well have left him in two minds about the rescinding of the banning order but what was not in doubt was his impatience to leave the dreary England autumn behind him and get stuck into his new career with WSC. 'I was determined to do well. First and foremost, I had to get myself fit, which I did.' Beneficiaries in the English game often find their duties a strain on the liver as much as their stamina. Barry was no boozer and he would have had little difficulty in resisting the blandishments of even the most persuasive landlord but he was no longer young and though possessed of an inner core of natural fitness, he knew that he would have to be at his sharpest, both mentally and physically, for the challenges ahead. One upshot of the new fitness regime was to shave off the ill-advised beard that had been decorating his face. W.G. Grace grew his according to the fashion and credence of the time. Victorian doctors believed that a long beard would catch impurities in the air and the good doctor was never afraid to put his mouth where his heart was. The occasion for Barry's beard was equally dubious. And off it came.

What were your feelings once you arrived in Australia? 'Very excited. I was 34 and this was my last shot at proving myself in international cricket.' *Did you practise?* 'Did we practise?' he repeated incredulously. 'I was going to point out that he was never the greatest netter at Hampshire but I knew that he felt quite differently about WSC as he did for county cricket, at least in his latter years. 'We wandered across to where the Aussies were practising. We all knew each other and I was quite prepared for some of them to bowl to me, if they wanted. But it was Bunter who stopped us. He said they were the opposition – the enemy – and it wouldn't be right.' This was of course the same Eddie Barlow who had cautioned against complacency when the South Africans went one up against the Australians in the 1970 series. 'And he was absolutely right,' Barry assured me. 'We were there to do battle. This was no showbiz carnival.'

As if to emphasise the point, he recounted the pep talk that Packer gave them all before hostilities commenced. 'He told us in words of one syllable that if he unearthed any evidence of collusion between the teams, we would be on our bikes. And that included any talk of sharing out the winnings between both teams. You see, the money was for the winners of the series, not for each match. He wanted it to be competitive. And it was, believe me.'

Packer underlined this very point in his comments to the press, 'I make no apologies for the fact that the contract is tough. I told every player, "This is a tough contract and you'll do as you're damn well told!"'

He also said, to some amusement that there was only one way a player could get out of the contract and that was to get pregnant. Barry had no intention of reneging on his contract. Nor did he want to get pregnant.

What were the practice facilities like? 'Variable. The Indian touring side had booked all the big grounds so we had to make do with what was on offer.' The Packer organisation pulled out all the stops to ensure that everything was of the highest standard but inevitably there were teething problems. When an official tour is in the offing, you presumably get hold of the file from the previous visit and follow the blueprint, improving and changing where necessary. But in any new venture, with inexperienced staff in the firing line, there are bound to be hiccups. 'No expense was spared,' said Barry, 'and when there was a problem, Kerry would step in and sort it out. Some of the changing rooms weren't great and the kit was sometimes sub-standard but, hey, we just got on with it.' I'm pretty sure they didn't have to change in shifts, as we had to do at Basingstoke, and I seem to remember that Barry was not greatly impressed by this. But, hey, the $25,000 pay cheque probably helped.

He then went on to talk about drop-in wickets. Necessity is the mother of invention and this new and novel way of preparing pitches – not the only innovation born out of WSC and now taken for granted – was required because they were reduced to using stadiums that were not cricket grounds. *What were they like, these wickets?* 'Some were okay, some were shocking. After we complained, Packer got in the best groundsman, John Maley, from Perth, to oversee their preparation and then things began to improve.' I tried to summon up a picture in my mind's eye of what it would have been like to face the world's fastest bowlers – and goodness me, there were a few around at the time – on sub-standard pitches but the vision was too terrifying to contemplate. 'There was one wicket we played on at the Gabba in Brisbane that was an absolute shocker.'

But the Gabba is a Test ground, not a football stadium. 'Yes, but because of the previous commitments, the wicket had been under-prepared.' It is well documented that Barry came back into the dressing room after his dismissal and let rip with some choice observations in the most colourful language. *Is it true you threatened never to play again on a wicket like that?* 'Something like it,' he grinned. Garth le Roux was playing in that match and he remembers the incident very well. 'We were bowled out for 90, I think. The wicket was under-prepared, much too green. Especially as the West Indies could call on a pace attack of Roberts, Holding, Garner, Croft, Daniel. Barry stormed into the dressing room and shouted – at no one in particular – 'If you ever make a wicket like that again, you can say goodbye to me!' I think actually he might have added one or two swear words for good measure.' *Was anybody listening? I mean, officials, managers and the like?* 'Oh yes, all the guys were there. But he was only saying what everybody knew. As usual with Barry.' To be fair, Garth continued, the pitches did get better as the technology quickly improved.

He then started to laugh. Something else had obviously stirred in his memory. 'I can't remember which match it was but we had already pretty well won when in strode Joel Garner, last man in. "Give him a bouncer," Greigy said to me. Well, what could I do?' *He was your captain. And like all dutiful and compliant fast bowlers, you did exactly as your captain told you.* 'Exactly. So I gave him one. It hit Joel smack on the hand. The bat went one way and Joel went the other – straight back to the pavilion!' *Would you say that WSC was the toughest cricket you ever played?* 'Without a doubt, man. I never played Test cricket, though I believe that some of those Currie Cup matches must have been as competitive as some Tests. I just loved it, playing and rubbing shoulders with all those great players. It was what had been denied me by our international isolation.'

How did you, as a South African, get on with all the other nationalities? He looked at me in amazement, his great moustache quivering. 'Like a house on fire, man.' I had little doubt. Garth le Roux was a beast with a ball in his hand but one of the most sociable of men off the pitch. 'I roomed with Imran,' he told me, as if anxious to prove his credentials for inter-racial harmony. As if I ever doubted them. 'Hell, I could tell you a few stories about that man and what we got up to.' I bet he could. And he did, none of which shall be repeated in print. If Tich Smith's conversion to godliness was a surprise to his friends, Imran Khan's political and personal makeover is nothing short of miraculous. 'Imran!' confirmed Barry. 'An interesting man!'

From the very outset, all of the Packer recruits quickly realised that this was very different to anything that they had ever experienced before. 'There was a lot of razzamatazz,' said Barry. 'This was an entirely commercial undertaking and Packer had to sell his product. To me, coming from a very conservative background, where cricket was an amateur sport, it was all very strange…and somehow exciting.' The Australians, naturally, because they were the home side, and the West Indians obviously, because they were colourful, exciting and marketable, were used a great deal in the PR offensive that was launched in the face of initial public scepticism. The South Africans, by contrast, were largely kept in the background, rather like the embarrassing aunt whom nobody wants to ask to the wedding but can't really be left off the guest list.

Barry was used to it now; he just shrugged his shoulders in resignation. Besides, the publicity, the media attention and the glare of the limelight were of no significant interest to him. Fame never captivated him. He was more concerned about putting on view to the world what they had missed. He was also anxious to prove to himself that he still had it in him.

Were you confident you would cope? Yet again, there was that ruminative rub of the nose. 'I was pretty confident that I could still hack it, but I had to be at my best.' The impression I got was that he believed those carefree days of his youth when he could march down the wicket to Dennis Lillee and smack the ball back over his head were gone but that increased experience would allow him to mix judicious defence with attack whenever the position demanded it in order to construct decent scores. *No more aiming for the swimming pool, no more hitting round the clock, no more stepping outside leg to hit it on the off, no more playing with the edge of the bat?* He gave me a contemptuous look. 'Hey, this is World Series Cricket we're talking about here.' He was motivated all right.

And then he made an admission that took me quite by surprise. 'To be truthful, I did have my doubts. I was having trouble with my eyes. I no longer had 20/20 vision. I tried contacts for a while but gave them up. The funny thing was that they helped me to see the ball more clearly but I found I couldn't judge distance. You know when I was hit on the head by Hurst?' It was when he was playing for South Africa in the third match of the series against the International Wanderers the previous year, the first one of which he had missed in that protest about equal pay. 'I was dazed, definitely, but I remember scrabbling around on the ground looking for one of my missing contacts.' *And no one knew?* He shook his head. On reflection, that would seem to be perfectly reasonable. No player admits he is carrying an injury or is incapacitated in any way or is suffering from some sort of crisis of confidence. 'I had to adjust,' Barry continued. 'I used to be able to see the seam on the ball rotating, so I knew which way it was spinning. From then on, I had to *fashion* my innings, rather than playing instinctively.'

Two points arise here. First, what extraordinary eyesight he had in the first place, to be able to detect the seam of the ball as it rotated in the air. Most of us were just happy to spot a round, red object as it whirred towards us. And secondly, his use of the word 'fashion' intrigued me. Despite its voguish, stylish overtones of *haute couture* and the clothing industry, it actually comes from an old French word – as does so much of our vocabulary – meaning to suit or to adapt, to mould according to a pattern. Nothing trendy or chic about it; it is a word steeped in the tradition of labour, toil, exertion. In other words Barry's innings had become pieces of careful engineering rather than inspirational works of art. More of a struggle, I guess, and not so joyful. But no less admirable for that.

Packer's original concept was to have a series of matches between the Australian team and the Rest of the World but so many West Indians had signed up, proof of how poorly they were being paid by their board, that it soon became clear that they could have their own team, and an extremely competitive one too. This would explain, during the first season at any rate, why sometimes the West Indies played as a separate unit but at other times some of them were drafted into the Rest of the World side. Therefore, Barry would be playing with and against his Hampshire team-mates, Andy Roberts and Gordon Greenidge.

How did you all get on? Puzzled, he replied, 'We knew each other well. Absolutely fine. We weren't bosom buddies but there, we weren't at Hampshire either, were we? But as for...' *No, I meant with all the others. What was the atmosphere like between the combatants?* 'Most of us knew each other from county cricket, so relations were cordial off the pitch. Of course, you wouldn't be chatting amiably over breakfast if you were in opposition that day.' Often they would all be staying in the same hotel and naturally they would bump into each other in lifts, foyers and restaurants. And sometimes, they had to share transport. Barry remembered one terrifying flight between venues when they hit bad weather. 'The sick bags were much in evidence. Some of the West Indian guys went as white as us!'

Were the West Indians all right with you, as a South African? 'No problems. It wasn't as if I was representing my country, which they would have objected to. We were all cricketers and cricketers tend to get on.' That is true. Cricketers, by and large, are not the most strident engagers in social issues and current affairs; they tend to exist in their own bubble where the state of the pitch is of more concern than the state of the nation. But neither are they stupid. The West Indians would have had their own feelings about apartheid but Barry and the other South Africans were not seen as their country's representatives, or even apologists – they were cricketers who happened to be South African and as such worthy of having a game with. Insofar as anyone facing a barrage of 90mph bouncers can call it a game.

At last the phoney war was over and hostilities started in earnest. After a couple of trial matches which had passed off without any major hiccup, on 2 December the first of what were to be called the Supertests (the ICC had banned Packer from calling his matches Tests) between WSC Australia and WSC West Indies got underway at the VFL Park in Melbourne, a converted Aussie Rules football stadium. The capacity was 79,000. The actual attendance was 2,000. *What had gone wrong, Barry?* 'Nothing we could specifically put our fingers on. First, the Indians were playing Australia – admittedly their Second XI – and they had first choice of all the cricket grounds. Second, this was all new to the Australian public and it took a while for them to cotton on to what was happening. And third, don't forget this was a battle between Packer's media empire and the rest of the media outlets. So all the rival newspapers were going bozo to do it down!'

Greg Chappell explained to me just how vicious this media war was. 'Channel 7 were televising the Australian Open tennis at the time. They took out a full-page ad in all the newspapers – except those owned by Packer of course – with a photo of six lonely people in an empty stand where we were playing at the Waverley AFC ground, with the caption, 'These are some of the people **not** watching the tennis on Channel 7!'

Were you at all discouraged? 'No. We knew it would take time. Packer was not one to give up easily.' You could say that again. Packer's response was to pour money and resources into marketing and advertising, using the players in a PR blitzkrieg. 'This is where he got it so right,' said Barry. 'He got experienced and knowledgeable people around him, many of whom were former players. People like Andrew Caro, Bob Cowper, the Chappells, Johnny Gleeson, even Paul Hogan.' The final piece of the jigsaw, which gave the whole project credibility and legitimacy in the public's perception, was the procurement of Richie Benaud, the doyen of cricket commentators. With Benaud on board, WSC could not fail. Sadly, it drove a wedge between him and Sir Donald Bradman, who was firmly in the establishment camp. Hitherto, the two of them had been close and respectful friends; thereafter their relationship was never quite the same.

Barry's first Supertest was held at the RAS Showground in Sydney, not a cricket ground but a multi-purpose arena that had held as diverse spectacles as agricultural shows, rugby league matches, speedway meetings, stock car racing and rock concerts. At its peak, it could hold 90,000 people. There were not 90,000 to watch the finest cricketers of the day take the field, just a mere 3,000, though perhaps there should have been. Consider the talent on show. For the World XI: Richards B.A., Fredericks,

Greenidge, Richards I.V.A., Lloyd, Greig, Knott, Procter, Roberts, Garner, Underwood. For Australia: McCosker, Laird, Chappell I.M., Langer, Chappell G.S., Kent, Marsh, Gilmour, Bright, Walker, Prior. No Lillee – how come? Barry's hazy memory let him down here. 'Must have been injured,' he surmised. 'People have never really heard of Wayne Prior,' he continued, 'but I tell you he was genuinely fast.'

Prior must have been one of the unluckiest bowlers not to play in a Test match for Australia. His career coincided with Lillee and Thomson, he played for WSC for two seasons and thereafter, his cricket was restricted by his farming commitments. *Still not big crowds?* 'No, that came the following year.' It must have been odd, strutting their stuff in a near empty, cavernous bowl but such was the life of the travelling troubadour in Packer's troupe. Besides, Barry was used to playing in front of one old man and a dog. In both innings, Barry got a start (57 and 48) but failed to capitalise on either occasion. WSC World XI's four-wicket victory was largely based on Viv Richards's hundred in the first innings and Andy Roberts's six wickets in Australia's second innings.

There's something in the air at Perth that you enjoy, is there not? 'It wasn't at the WACA, you know.' Indeed, I did know. The second Supertest was held at Gloucester Park, a harness racing course for trotting horses but in Perth nevertheless, the city where he made his famous 356 for South Australia. Now it became the scene for another one of Barry's indisputably great innings. How the Hampshire members would have purred as two of their own, Richards and Greenidge, strode out to open the innings, had they only been able to see it. Sadly, back in England, there was little coverage, in the papers or on the news, of the match, or indeed of WSC in general. Together, they put on 234, unbeaten, against an Australian attack of Lillee, Gilmour, Walker and Bright. How Dennis Lillee must have loved bowling to Barry in Perth.

'Yet again, Gordy had to retire hurt,' said Barry. 'I can't remember why.' Gordon retiring hurt was not an uncommon occurrence. We all believed he had more muscles to pull than there were days in the year. Opponents used to dread when he started to limp for it always signalled his intention to take no further singles and deal thereafter only in fours and sixes. With Gordon's enforced departure, there was no respite for the toiling Australian XI. Taking his place was the sauntering peacock, with his cap at the normal jaunty angle, the unmistakeable figure of Viv Richards, currently in the form of his life. For the next few hours, arguably the two best batsmen of their generation treated the crowd (well, I say a crowd but only 3,500 were there to witness it) to a joyous celebration of batsmanship of the highest class. Those fortunate to witness it first hand speak of it in the same tones of awe that spectators remembered that golden hour of South African cricket at Durban, back in 1970, when Barry and Graeme Pollock matched each other, stroke for stroke, in that magical hour after lunch.

How did you play? 'I slogged it,' Barry grinned. 'Mind you, it was a good wicket, fast and true.' *Oh, come on, it can't have been that easy*. 'All right, maybe not. I didn't play with the carefree abandon of the 356 knock. I was 34 now, not 24. But I felt in *control* throughout.' Vince van der Bijl compared Pollock as the bludgeon with Richards (Barry) as the rapier. The same might be said of these two: Viv the broadsword and Barry the stiletto. But on this occasion, the older man outscored the younger. Barry scored 93 to Viv's 41. But who's splitting hairs? If Packer's objective was to bring the world's best to his table, he must have been sitting above the salt with a large grin creasing his craggy features. But he wasn't there. He was back in Sydney checking up on one of his WSC coaching clinics. And neither were the world's press and TV. It reminded me of another of Barry's masterclasses, at an empty, windswept Lord's, in 1974. It remains a crying shame that so little footage of his greatest feats remains extant. As someone once memorably put it: Barry Richards, never the groom.

Finally, he holed out at deep mid-off, to Greg Chappell off the bowling of Ray Bright, for 207. Bright later recalled, 'Only someone of Greg's concentration could have taken that catch. Everyone on the boundary was thinking of stopping fours and getting those sixes back.' There had been four of them – sixes – and 28 fours. After only 60 overs, the score was 369/1. Viv went on the next day to score 177 of his own and the WSC World XI finally amassed 625. Unsurprisingly, they won by an innings and 73 runs, Imran and Roberts doing the damage in the first innings and Imran (4-24) in the second. But for an inspired piece of defiance, combined with sublime elegance, a matchless innings of 174 from Greg Chappell, the margin of victory would have been much greater.

Barry had this to say about his friend, team-mate, opponent and fellow coach, Greg Chappell. You might say fellow great batsman too. At this time, he was at the peak of his powers. 'Yup, that was a superb knock, no doubt about it. He was their gun player.' *I beg your pardon?* 'The one you always go to when you're in trouble. Your main man.' *Presumably then, he would be the one that the opposition targeted?* 'Precisely. He had to face the four fastest bowlers in the world, who were constantly at him, with no respite – and no lid!' he added, referring to Chappell's experience against the West Indies. 'So take his Test average – 53.85 – and add another five for difficulty.'

That is a favourite theme of Barry's, that Test averages compiled by today's players include some very easy runs made against moderate bowling attacks, some of which scarcely deserve the status of a Test match. 'In the end, this constant bombardment from the four-pronged pace attack by the West Indies got to Greg. And he was the toughest of the tough. And still he got runs.' Greg agreed that he was probably at his best at this stage of his career. *Was that innings your highlight?* He demurred, citing his 246 not out later on that season as his best. The following year, he did not do so well and admitted he found the relentless diet of hostile fast bowling wearying.

For this was the Age of the Fast Bowler. Of course there had been fast bowlers wrecking batsmen's confidence and technique down the years: Gregory and McDonald, Larwood and Voce, Lindwall and Miller, Trueman, Statham and Tyson, Heine and Adcock, Hall and Griffith. However, Lillee and Thomson had raised fast bowling to a new, more brutal level. In a searing Ashes series in Australia in 1974/75, experienced onlookers believed that the sustained ferocity of the speed attack had rarely been equalled. *Wisden* recorded, 'Never before in the 98 years of Test cricket have batsmen been so grievously bruised and battered by ferocious, hostile, short-pitched balls.'

Some of the Englishmen returned from that tour mentally scarred and were never the same players again. Worse still was to befall the West Indians in the following series in 1975/76. They lost 5-1 and if anything, Thomson bowled quicker and more dangerously than he had done the previous year against England. The humiliation left Clive Lloyd, the West Indies captain, with the conviction that fast bowling, and fast bowling alone, was the way forward. He initiated the tactic of the four-pronged pace attack that may have offended the purists – and broken a few bones – but was to underpin their dominance on the world stage for the next 15 years or so. The legend of the ceaseless production line of fearsomely fast West Indian bowlers was born.

Barry now launched into a monologue about this phenomenon that I was only too happy to listen to. 'To compare batting then to now is to try to compare apples and oranges. They're both fruit but…well, you get my meaning. At that time, fast bowlers reigned supreme and spectators had got used to – in fact they had come to love it – seeing batsmen duck and dive.' This gladiatorial atmosphere had started in Australia. We all remember the catchphrase, 'Ashes to Ashes, dust to dust, if Lillee doesn't get you, Thommo must.' And the increasing crescendo of the crowd's exhortation of 'kill kill kill' as they ran in to bowl was much as I imagine went on in the Roman Colosseum. 'Batsmen were battered into submission,' went on Barry. 'Look, you'd go into lunch, if you were lucky, at 50/1, having faced at the most one or two balls an over that you could possibly have scored off. Before, you could see off the quicks and then attack the medium-pacers or the spinners. But there would be four of them. Two would bowl for an hour and then the other two would come on for the second hour. And so it went on all day, the four fast bowlers being regularly rotated.'

No chance of a century before lunch then? 'Huh. If you scored a hundred by the close, you'd done mighty well. And they slowed the over rate down so much that they were bowling only 13 an hour.' In many ways, it was a negation of everything that he believed in the game – a fair contest between bat and ball – but he had to admit that it was brutally effective. 'If you scored a four early on in the over, you would expect, and get, four bouncers on the trot, which you couldn't reach. It destroyed any momentum that you were trying to build up.' Greg Chappell further spelt out the problems facing the batsman. 'Aw look, if you only get 50 per cent of the strike, which would not be unreasonable, and only 50 per cent of the balls that you faced could you possibly score off, and they were only bowling ten overs an hour, that meant you would only realistically have in total three or four overs an hour to score any runs.' His brother, Ian, put it more succinctly, in his own inimitable way, 'How the f*** could you get back into form when you were playing Roberts, Holding, Garner day after day?' And yet again, Barry reminded me that this was in the days before helmets. 'It's all so different now – helmets, better protective equipment, bigger bats, smaller boundaries, slower wickets.'

And restrictions on the number of bouncers allowed per over. Were there any restrictions in place for WSC? 'Nah. That's the point. Packer loved the atmosphere of fast bowlers trying to pin batsmen and the primeval thrill it gave to the crowds. Spinners weren't really in his calculations. I remember Dennis Lillee in the first over of the day bowling six bouncers to Viv Richards, all of them sailing over his head. Six bouncers! A maiden, therefore.' *One way to keep the Master Blaster quiet, I suppose.* 'They worked you over and wore you down. A half-volley was something you only read about in the coaching manuals. I'd like to see some of the modern players having to cope with that.'

How did you manage? 'That's it, I guess – I managed. But I can't say it was very enjoyable.' Managed? I should say so! The 34-year-old Barry Richards, who had not played international cricket for eight years, had scored 388 runs in five innings, second only to his namesake Viv, who had scored 502. If his intention had been to prove to everybody, including himself, that he could still cut the mustard at this level, he had given his answer in the most emphatic manner possible. Not that any reasonably informed onlookers had ever had any doubts. Those fortunate enough to witness it – all too few, sadly – could only shake their heads in regret and wish that it all had been so different. 'If only I'd had the opportunity when I was at my peak,' he said regretfully. And listen to this pertinent point offered by his friend, Greg Chappell. 'At the time, I had been playing Test cricket so I was, in a sense, ready for it. Barry hadn't played in a Test match for seven years. To make the step up from county and provincial cricket to the toughest ever played, just like that, made his efforts even more remarkable.'

When did helmets come in? Barry replied, 'David Hookes, the pin-up boy of the whole advertising campaign, was hit by Fruity and had his jaw smashed.' Yes, we had both been close witnesses to that sort of thing from Andy Roberts. 'Packer was insistent that Hookes went out again. But that was ridiculous, he couldn't. So Packer said, "Look, if I put you in a crash helmet, will you go out?" So the helmet was born and the game changed forever.'

That is not strictly true, that WSC gave birth to the helmet. In much the same way that Samuel Morse did not invent the telegraph, Alexander Bell did not invent the telephone, and Thomas Edison did not invent the light bulb, credit for the concept of the cricket helmet cannot be laid solely at WSC's door. The misconception is known as the myth of the single inventor. Very often, unsung experimenters had paved the way for others to take all the credit. In 1933, Patsy Hendren wore a sort of rubber helmet under his cap to protect him against the fast bowling of Martindale and Constantine. And in 1977, Mike Brearley had taken to wearing a plastic skullcap under his cap for the same reason, later popularised by Sunil Gavaskar. But of course, the injury to Hookes and the insistence of Packer to protect him, provided the impetus to produce various prototypes, which spawned the helmet familiar to us today.

Did you wear one? 'Of course I did. We abandoned the crash helmet first worn by Dennis Amiss after there were four run outs on the trot! They got better though. But I didn't like the visor they had, so I wore one without anything in front of the face. I reckoned I was still quick enough to get out of the way but I may as well protect my skull.' He believes that the helmet has revolutionised batting today. 'They go after it much more because they know that if they miss it, the worst they will get is a headache. Before helmets, if we missed it, we'd end up in hospital.' It has amazed me that whenever I watch a Test match these days, someone always gets hit on the helmet. In the past, Accident and Emergency departments would have been full to overflowing if batsmen had adopted such a gung-ho attitude to hooking.

Back to the final Supertest of the series. Barry scored a half-century in the first innings and a duck in the second, in a match that the World XI lost by 41 runs. No matter, they had won the series and with it the $100,000 prize money. *How was it shared out?* 'Equally among the squad. So I got about $7,000.' Still not a fortune but you could see that the landscape of the money within the game was beginning to change. *Rather more than the £100 you got for Hampshire as a bonus at the end of the 1968 season, eh?* 'And I had to share that with Bob Cottam,' he reminded me.

At the conclusion of the first season of the head to head contest between WSC and the official Test series between Australia and India, it was time to take stock. By any yardstick, WSC had been well beaten into second place. And second place was unfamiliar territory for Kerry Packer. Despite the talent on show, the intensity of the competition and all the hype, the Australian public had not warmed to the new brand of cricket. *Was there any doubt in your mind at that stage about your decision to join?* Barry was emphatic. 'No. For two reasons. For me, there was no alternative. And Kerry was no quitter. If it's not working, make it better. That was his mantra.' In fact, it was a miracle that the unofficial series had got off the ground at all. They had started with no organisation, no teams, no infrastructure, no tradition, no grounds, no wickets, nothing other than a burning desire to prove the naysayers wrong. And to secure the exclusive broadcasting rights for Channel 9.

'We all knew what was the endgame,' said Barry. 'Once he had won and got what he wanted, he'd call off his attack dogs and that was going to be the end of WSC. We all recognised that it was no more than a short-term contract.' In the meantime, he had secured the services of the world's top 50 or so players, he had some revolutionary and exciting ideas and he was paying good money. It was inconceivable that he would fail.

Greg Chappell tells an amusing story about the early teething problems of the fledgling organisation. Amusing now in hindsight no doubt but he assures me that it was anything but at the time. 'It was a day/night game at the Waverley Park Australian Football League Stadium in Melbourne against the West Indies. There was a local by-law, which stipulated that the lights should be switched off no later than 10.30pm so the local residents could get to sleep. In other words, the game had to finish at 10.15pm at the latest to allow the crowd to disperse in safety. Anyway, in the second innings, when the West Indies had been batting, there was a rain delay.' In circumstances such as this, the runs target would be reduced commensurate with the number of overs lost. It was not a satisfactory arrangement – it never is – but it was the best that could be done under the circumstances. On the resumption of play, the Australians, led by Ian Chappell, took to the field with the new, revised total that they had to defend very much at the forefront of their minds. They were surprised, then nonplussed, then dumbfounded by the way the West Indians seemed to be dawdling their way towards a target that was rapidly disappearing over the hill. The Australian consternation immediately turned to outrage when they were told that the match could still run its full, allotted course, even with the break for rain, before the witching hour of 10.15pm. The Aussies had been duped, they felt, by the umpires who had not kept them abreast of what was going on.

Who won? 'The West Indies of course. They had been told of the decision but we had not.' *Why had there been a change in the playing regulations?* 'Kerry, who had been watching, thought that it was such a good game that it ought to go the full distance. He'd told the umpires and the West Indians but not us.' *What was your reaction after the game?* Greg gave a thin smile. 'We were not happy.'

Packer was like this. He was prepared to listen to the informed advice of experts and ex-players but it was his show and everybody knew that. 'He loved being around the players,' said Greg, 'and I think he appreciated being treated no differently from anybody else when he came into the dressing room. He was the boss, of course, but we didn't bow and scrape before him. I guess that fawning attitude happened to him a lot and he was pleased when we weren't sycophantic.' *Did he dare show his face after you were shafted in that match?* Greg laughed. Thereby hung a tale. 'He came in and said bad luck, boys. My brother turned on him and gave him a piece of his mind.' I winced. Along with countless others, I had been on the receiving end of Ian Chappell's tongue out there in the middle and it is not a comfortable experience. 'He told Kerry that there was no bad luck involved. It was all down to the incompetence of the management. Except that he put it rather more forcefully than that.' I could imagine. 'What's your problem, son, Kerry wanted to know. It's not my problem, replied my brother, it's yours and your bad organisation. I was looking at Kerry at the time. His lips moved but nothing came out. I don't think he'd ever been spoken to like that.'

What happened? Were there any repercussions? 'Kerry quit the room. To be fair, he knew there were problems and it concerned him as much as anybody. A few personnel changes were swiftly made and things soon started to improve.' When I recounted this story to Barry, he was highly amused. 'Chappelli could be like that, straight from the hip. Bit like me, really!' I always liked that nickname for Ian Chappell – Chappelli, rather as if he was the Godfather of Australian cricket.

Packer's problems were compounded by the fact that the series between Australia and India had been a nailbiter, which the Aussies had won 3-2. That winter (the Australian winter, that is), Australia undertook a tour of the Caribbean. The Australians naturally did not pick any of the Packer rebels. The West Indian board, which was firmly of the opinion that the dispute between WSC and the ACB was purely an internal affair, gave in to popular pressure and picked their Packer players. The result was fairly predictable. West Indies won the first two Tests comfortably. But then old quarrels and long-standing disputes between the home players and their board resurfaced and political infighting ensued. The West Indian Packer players were sacked and a completely new team picked for the remainder of the series, which provided a closer, if inferior, contest. All the West Indian players signed by Packer had now burnt their boats. They were the money-spinners for his project and present circumstances meant that they were behind him lock, stock and barrels of cash. Even the most purblind of cricket traditionalists must by now have grasped the fact that WSC was going nowhere. And the united front put up by the ACB was beginning to fracture.

The cracks ruptured into wholesale breaches with news of an agreement between Packer and the cricket authorities in Brisbane, Adelaide and Sydney for WSC to use their grounds. The jewel in the crown was Sydney, with its newly installed floodlighting for day/night matches. Packer, with his keen business acumen, had quickly worked out that his one-day matches, particularly the ones under lights, had proved to be more popular than the traditional five-day Supertests. And, with characteristic opportunism and ruthlessness, he accordingly shifted the emphasis of his assault to give greater prominence to the single innings game. It was clearly what the paying public wanted.

What was your opinion of day/night games, Barry? 'Panic!' *I beg your pardon?* That was the first time I have ever, ever, heard Barry admit to anything less than total self-confidence on the cricket field. Of course, he then qualified his assertion. 'Not exactly panic. But I was worried that things were becoming a bit blurred.' He was referring to his deteriorating eyesight, not his post-match carousing. 'Facing 90mph-plus bowling when you're having trouble with your eyes is no joke. And under lights it's worse. Some of the lighting was frankly inadequate. The guy next door in his garden was getting as much light as we were!' The standard of floodlighting quickly improved but Barry still found it difficult. 'That's why I wore a helmet without a grille. I couldn't stand having anything in front of my face.' Batting necessarily became harder. 'The fours became twos, the twos became singles and the blocks became wickets,' he announced, more cheerfully than he must have felt at the time.

And, as ever with Barry, his comments have to be put into context. It is true that he did not set the world alight in the one-dayers, or should I say the day-nighters. But there, neither did any other of the main batters. Viv Richards, the Chappell brothers, Clive Lloyd, Gordon Greenidge and Zaheer Abbas similarly struggled. As I said earlier, this was the Age of the Fast Bowler and in the 50-over format, having only to bowl ten overs, there was little chance of them getting tired. Furthermore, Barry was an opening batsman. 'That meant, as often as not, I would have to go out to bat during the period of dusk, when it's neither light nor dark.' Never having played under lights, I shall have to take his word for it but it makes sense.

What was your daily schedule like? 'Hectic.' *Any days off? Down time?* He admitted that the grind was not nearly so wearing as county cricket but Packer demanded his pound of flesh. 'There were coaching clinics we had to do. I had his son in the nets and that was no easy task, I can tell you.' He remembered with amusement another youngster under his tutelage. 'He kept on slogging the ball out of the net. I told him if he did it again, that would be the end of his batting session. Of course, the next ball sailed out of the net. I hauled him out and he was furious.' That young boy was Steve Waugh and he and Barry still laugh about it whenever their paths cross. 'There were the second teams as well,' Barry pointed out. 'They were known as the Cavaliers and they went up country, playing and coaching and generally waving the flag.' Taking his matches to the further-flung outposts of the game was another indication that Packer was intent on winning – was winning – the PR war.

Where were you based at this time? 'In hotels.' *No, where were you living?* He grinned. 'Dunno. Haven't a clue. Honestly, Murt, it was all a bit of a blur. I think I was based in Perth but I was actually living out of a suitcase. We went round and round in strings and roundabouts.' I had never heard of that expression but it sums up well enough the sprint from dressing room to coach to airport to plane to coach to hotel that had become the norm. The life of a cricketer has many blessings but in the end all get fed up with the travelling and the anonymity of hotel rooms. *Tell me about the routine of a day/night game.* 'The rhythm of the day is different. You don't finish until 10.30pm and then you've got to wind down. At best, you wouldn't be in bed before midnight.' And remember, Barry was no night owl. 'So you'd get up at 9.30am instead of 8am.' I did not admit to him that those hours did not seem to be all that different to the ones I was used to keeping at Hampshire. But there, Kerry Packer was not my boss.

So to the second season. When Packer announced to the world that the devil would take the hindmost, he never considered for one moment that it would be him. 'He was a shrewd operator,' said Barry. 'Tough, ruthless and he knew exactly what he wanted and how to get it. But he was no mindless bully, as his detractors tried to make out. He was canny enough to take on board what his advisors were telling him. And those advisors were current and former players.' That was the difference between WSC and the current establishment boards. 'The three captains – Greig, Lloyd and Ian Chappell, well, four, if you include his brother Greg – had his ear and for the first time the players had a hand in the organisation of the game they played,' Barry continued. 'There was now proper liaison between management and players.'

I note that Mike Denness was your team manager. What was his role exactly? 'He didn't have much to do with coaching or anything.' *I would imagine not. These were all players better than he ever was.* 'Yah, but he was a former England captain and any advice he passed on would have been respectfully listened to. But that wasn't really his role. He was more concerned with the administration of the matches, that all went well, that everything was operating as it should.' *How did you get on with him?* 'He was an absolute gentleman, well respected, well liked.'

First and foremost, Packer and his advisors speedily appreciated that the West Indians were worthy of having a team of their own, making the Supertests a triangular tournament. They were that good and that popular. Secondly, more exposure was given to one-day games. And crucially, the attraction of cricket under lights became unstoppable. It is now widely accepted that the tipping point in the war between WSC and the ACB came on the evening of 28 November 1978. A crowd of over 40,000 flocked to the Sydney Cricket Ground to watch Australia play West Indies under lights. The Sydney night sky was lit up with the million wattage of Packer's broad smile. Greg Chappell remembers standing with Packer on the top balcony of the pavilion watching the lines of people snaking around the ground, queueing at the turnstiles. Rod Marsh was alongside. 'We're back!' he announced with a grin. Packer nodded. He knew he had won. Cricket would never be the same again.

It helped that the official Australian team were currently enduring a torrid time against England (they lost the series 5-1), a humiliation that had a lone trumpeter sounding The Last Post on a sparsely populated Sydney Hill as England won the final match inside four days. With astounding fickleness, the Australian media and public, who had previously been firmly on the side of the ACB, now loudly demanded the reinstatement of the WSC players into the Australian side. Cricket fans were beginning to vote with their feet. The Packer brand with the world's most charismatic cricketers locked in combat, and all the excitement and vibrancy of day/night matches, white balls, coloured clothing, music and of course excellent television coverage, was of increasing appeal to cricket supporters of all ages – and sexes. Cleverly, Packer had targeted women and children in his marketing campaign. Greg Chappell put it rather well. 'There was a phrase going round at the time that the Australian Board were "pale, male and stale."

The promotion of David Hookes as the poster boy of the series was a masterstroke of marketing. The ACB had never advertised cricket for the whole family. The contrast between the exciting WSC and a turgid Test series was stark. Graham Yallop's boys were being pummelled by the Poms, for God's sake, under the captaincy of the pantomime villain, the Ayatollah himself, otherwise known as Mike Brearley, and that was hard to stomach. Looking back, the fight between Packer and the ACB appears to have been a huge mismatch, though it seemed to be anything but that at the time.

Tell me about the coloured uniforms, Barry. I believe that it did not meet with wholehearted approval. He laughed. 'It was the 1970s, don't forget, not an era noted for its fashion sense. All the shirts were tight fitting, with huge collars and the trousers were flared. We played in light blue. That was all right. The Aussies were in canary yellow, a bit bright but just about okay. But whoever put the West Indies in bright pink should have got his marching orders. Let's just say that the colour suggested they were batting for the other side, if you get my meaning. And those guys weren't terribly impressed.' Obviously not. In the second season, the shocking pink had been toned down. A little. For not much about WSC was ever toned down.

Despite the intoxication and the hoopla of the one-day game now so fervently espoused by Packer and so enthusiastically supported by the public, it was still the longer format of the game that most of the top players preferred to judge themselves against. I do believe this still holds true today, despite the fame and fortune that are to be gained playing in the IPL and its corollaries around the world. Barry is no exception. That is why he rates his innings in the final of the Supertests in the 1978/79 season as among his very best. In the preliminary rounds of the triangular tournament, the World XI beat Australia and then the West Indies by an innings and 44 runs, a performance that served to underline the strength of their bowling attack. What captain wouldn't want to have at his disposal the bowlers of the calibre of Imran, le Roux, Rice, Procter and Underwood? The final, against Australia, was played at Sydney – not at a converted football stadium or show ground but at the fabled SCG – in early February 1979.

It was a low-scoring game played on a wicket that was not altogether straightforward and as is often the case in matches of low scores and fine margins, it turned out to be a tense and gripping encounter, about as far away from a 'circus' that the establishment wished to portray as it could possibly be. Australia were bowled out for 172, with le Roux taking 5-57 and Procter 3-37. The World XI fared no better, being dismissed for 168. At one stage, it looked highly likely that Barry would top-score with 28 but an improbable last-wicket stand of 64 between numbers ten and 11, le Roux and Underwood, robbed him of that dubious distinction. Dennis Lillee was their chief tormentor, taking 5-51. In their second innings, Australia only managed 212, succumbing to the irresistible forces of le Roux, 4-44, and Imran, 3-60. The target for victory and the $100,000 prize was 224, the highest of the four innings. 'I just knew it depended on me,' said Barry. 'It was a tricky pitch, the Aussies scented blood and the pressure was enormous. It was no blitzkrieg, I can tell you.' He made an undefeated 101 to usher his team home by five wickets.

How did it compare with the double hundred you scored at Perth the previous year?
'In that innings, I smashed it. To be fair, it was a good, fast wicket and I could go
for my shots. But this was completely different. Not pretty but bloody hard work.
If I got out, the Aussies would win. If I stayed in, we would win. It was as simple as
that.' Simple, no doubt, but not simply done. It would be a searching test of skill
and temperament, the sort of challenge that Barry relished. In an analysis of all his
big innings, there has been this unspoken understanding between us that we take
into consideration many factors at play at the time other than the number of runs
he had posted on the board, the LOD effect I like to call it, the Level Of Difficulty.
The LOD was off the scale that day in Sydney.

*I guess it was a bit like your innings of 37 not out against Northamptonshire
at Southampton in 1973 that more or less secured us the County Championship?*
Enthusiastically, he took up the comparison and ran with it. 'Yes, in many ways it
was. On both occasions, the result of the match more or less rested on my shoulders.
I just couldn't afford to get out. So I had to play within my limits and just concentrate
on correct shot selection.' There is an important point there. Very often, in similar
situations, when a batsman just cannot afford to get out, he eschews all risk and
becomes virtually strokeless and the scoreboard grinds to a halt. Barry never allowed
the bowlers to assume total dominance like this. It went against the grain. Attack was
still his instinct but it was aggression tempered by common sense. In other words, he
had to be patient and wait for the right ball to hit. And in this mood, with this level
of motivation and concentration, there was no one better. That is why the innings
gave him so much pleasure and satisfaction. He had proved to the world, to his World
team, that he was fit to walk with the gods. That magical series against the Australians
nine years ago was no fluke, no passing affair, no shooting star. He really was as good
as everybody had been saying. And as good as he himself secretly believed.

I asked Derek Underwood about this innings of Barry's. Of all the wonderful
knocks he had witnessed from the great man – most from 22 yards away – this he rated
to be up there with the very best. 'I think he was the most...*balanced* batsman I've ever
seen,' said Underwood. 'He seemed to sway either forward or back, depending on
length. He was so poised at the crease and had such natural timing. He didn't crunch
the ball off the bat; it just flowed. In WSC, he stood out, even in that illustrious
company. That innings was simply magnificent. Only Barry could have played it.'

*I see from the scorecard, Barry, that you had a crucial partnership with your old pal, Mike
Procter.* 'Not quite up there with the carefree days of that match for Gloucestershire
against the South Africans back when we were both kids,' he chuckled. When Procter
came in, the World XI were reeling at 84/4, with Lillee and Gilmour in full cry.
Together, the boyhood friends stemmed the tide and when Procter was out with the
score at 175, they were nearly home and dry. Barry saw to it that they really were.
In many ways, it was a poignant moment for both of them. By now, they would
have been considered the elder statesmen of that South African side that had such
a glittering future ahead of them in 1970. Circumstances had denied them that
fulfilment. WSC had afforded them a late, last opportunity to show the world what
might have been. But both were past their prime and had needed to drop the bucket
deep into the well to perform at this level.

As Barry admitted, he was having trouble with his eyes and was not the same
batsman that he was earlier in his career. Procter had simply worn himself out. He
had been tearing in off that long run of his for nigh on ten years now, without a
break. If county cricket had taken a toll on Barry's mental state, it had taken an equal
toll on Procter's body. 'He was knackered,' said Barry, simply. I imagine he had both

senses of the word in mind in describing his friend. 'It was a tribute to his tremendous fitness that he could bowl at all by this stage. He was no longer the out and out fast bowler of his younger days but he still swung the ball at a useful pace. But what a competitor! And don't forget his batting.' Heaven forfend. But some do. It is worth refreshing our memories that he scored 48 first-class hundreds in his career. Barry scored 80 – though we all know he should have scored more. 'WSC was a godsend to Prockie too,' was Barry's generous conclusion.

The conclusion to this extraordinary chapter in cricket's history was not long in coming. That spring, Kerry Packer was to take his travelling circus off to the West Indies – I feel I can safely call it a circus now, on account of its peripatetic identity more than any connotations of the big top and performing animals – where it was, unsurprisingly, a great financial and popular success. The South Africans, equally unsurprisingly, were unwelcome in the Caribbean. The world, so to speak, was left at home. Nevertheless, it was becoming increasingly evident that the war between Packer and the ACB was entering its final phase – total capitulation was not far away. During March, one month after Barry scored his hundred at Sydney, both sides came together for a series of meetings at which a truce was called.

It appeared that the words of John Woodcock, one of the few English journalists to have put his head above the parapet to have a look at what was actually going on, were at last to be heeded, 'They can bargain from a position of strength; they can cut down the bloodshed; they can cleanse the air. For the good of cricket, something must be tried in the near future. It may mean a lot of dismounting from high horses.'

It is difficult to see from today's perspective where and when Kerry Packer dismounted from his. He was granted complete broadcasting rights for his Channel 9 and, what's more, a ten-year agreement to promote and market the game. Truce? I suppose you could call it a truce in the sense that hostilities had ceased. But nobody was in any doubt who was the winner. As Barry had presupposed, once the media mogul had got what he wanted, he immediately called off his tanks and they turned round and headed back to base. But my goodness, how they had churned up the lawn in the meantime.

Before we cast a glance back to the wider ramifications of WSC on the governance and the playing of the game, let us consider Barry's contribution to the adventure, rather than its contribution to him. The World XI had played in six Supertests, won five and lost one. The Australians had played 15 and the West Indians 11. The imbalance was just the nature of the tournament; that the World XI had played significantly fewer matches was no fault of theirs. We can presume that their record would have been proportionately successful had they played more. Barry had played in five Supertests, had eight innings, and scored 554 runs at an average of 79.14. And he was past his prime (so he says)! Furthermore, WSC was tougher than any other cricket played in the world (for this we have the corroboration of many who participated). It makes you wonder what his Test record might have been, in a different, parallel universe. To put it into context, the batting averages for WSC read like this:

Barry Richards – 79.14
Viv Richards – 55.69
Greg Chappell – 56.60
David Hookes – 38.45
Clive Lloyd – 37.94
Gordon Greenidge – 35.90
Ian Chappell – 35.72.
Quod erat demonstrandum.

QED? Well, perhaps not quite. Although the Packer Revolution is remembered clearly, and probably in a more positive light as the years pass, what happened on the field of play is largely forgotten. In a recent edition of *The Cricketer* in England, a list was compiled of all the seminal moments through the whole sweep of the game's history, including overarm bowling, W.G. Grace and professionalism, the inaugural Test match, Bodyline and Bradman, the end of the amateur, the D'Oliveira Affair, advent of one-day cricket, World Cup, Decision Review System, Indian Premier League and many more. At the top of the pile, universally acknowledged to be the single most important event in the game's evolution, was WSC and the way it changed cricket, radically and forever. Yet try and find stories, reports, newsreel, photos, narratives, even books, and the cupboard, if not bare, is poorly stocked. Even these statistics that I have quoted required hunting down. Nowhere in the official records of international cricket will you find any mention of WSC.

It is a crying shame, bordering on a scandal, that none of the deeds performed by the world's best players, in competition with each other, is even considered to be first-class! It is as if the records, if not the consequences, of WSC have been airbrushed out of existence, rather like a party functionary who has fallen out of favour with a despot and suddenly disappears from the official photo. It is perhaps reminiscent of the insensitive and misguided decision by the game's authorities to rescind Test match status for the Rest of the World matches in England in 1970. Barry agrees, but has one caveat. 'WSC was much, much harder. Those matches for the Rest of the World were hastily organised and always had a feeling of ad-hoc encounters. Don't get me wrong. Great players were in opposition and personal pride, if nothing else, was at stake. But WSC was seriously competitive. Ask anyone – Viv, Gordy, Greg Chappell. They all say the same. It was brutal combat out there. Packer would not have it any other way.'

In what ways had the game been changed by this momentous coup by Kerry Packer? Barry is in no doubt that it was for the better. Above all, it came about because of the players' desire to improve their lot, something that he had been striving for through most of his career. Only in England had the concept of professionalism obtained but, as Barry continually complained, the pay was poor and the patricians were firmly in control. Tony Greig could see this as plainly as anyone, though he got little thanks for it at the time. In all other countries, amateurism – or various shades of it – prevailed and the top players were becoming mightily disenchanted. The less gifted players, the journeymen of the first-class game, simply couldn't afford to play for love and left the game early. Packer did not instigate the rebellion. The preconditions were already in place. 'Ripeness is all' as Hamlet most famously observed. You could say that the tree was groaning with over-ripe fruit. The point is, when Packer came along and gave the tree a jolly good shaking, once the fruit lay burst and useless upon the ground was there a new and plenteous crop blossoming?

At first, not much seemed to have changed. Test cricket resumed, and the 'rebels' and the rest often uneasily sharing a dressing room, none more so than the Australians. Unrest persisted for several years, fatally undermining the captaincy of Kim Hughes, who was suspiciously regarded as an establishment figure. But soon, the repercussions of the Packer schism began to be felt. One-day internationals proliferated, more and more grounds installed floodlighting, pitch technology advanced, helmets and protective equipment improved, coloured clothing, white balls, pink stumps, musical jingles, side stalls, intrusive PA, cheerleading, it all soon became commonplace. Test cricket survived but its continued health remains a concern, with dwindling support (outside England) and truncated tours. But undoubtedly, the biggest transformation has been in the marketing and the selling of the game, with considerable knock-on effects to the remuneration of players. As I pointed out earlier, in 1977, Tony Greig was paid £210 to play in the Centenary Test. Within a year or so, the fee per Test had gone up to £1,000. Nowadays, the figure is £12,000. County salaries, incidentally, have increased exponentially. 'Too late for us, eh Murt?' observed Barry wryly.

All this bounty did come too late for our hero. Greg Chappell, Dennis Lillee, Rodney Marsh, Imran Khan, Clive Lloyd, Viv Richards, Gordon Greenidge, Andy Roberts, Michael Holding *et al* had Test careers to return to, with all the attendant endorsements, advertising, sponsorship deals and image rights on offer. They would become rich – their heirs to international stardom even richer – to a degree unimaginable a decade earlier. But Barry's race was run. The challenge and the deep personal satisfaction of having played, and succeeded, in WSC had been financially fruitful for him but he had not made a fortune. Nor would he have the opportunity of doing so, unlike his contemporaries. He was not alone in missing out, of course. There were other South Africans in the same boat. But somehow it seemed to hit him harder. 'Look,' said Garth le Roux, 'I was just happy to play. But with Barry, it was different. I didn't miss Test cricket because I had never played it. Barry had, and that made all the difference.' Quite possibly what made a difference too was that le Roux had a career outside the game.

Of the other South Africans, Clive Rice still had a successful future ahead of him for Transvaal, Nottinghamshire and late on – 'better late than never', said Barry – playing for South Africa on their return to the international fold in 1991. Mike Procter could be said to share Barry's disappointments and poor timing, being an exact contemporary, but I sense that Procter, from all that I have heard of him, never having met him, except unsociably from 22 yards away, is cut from different cloth to his old team-mate. *How do you think Prockie felt about his lost Test career?* 'Hmm... difficult to judge. Sure he felt he'd missed out, like we all did. But he threw himself into his career for Rhodesia and Gloucestershire. We all had different ways of coping with the disappointment.'

Barry then embarked on a passionate critique of his friend's place in the pantheon of great all-rounders. 'People talk of the 1980s as the era of the four incomparable all-rounders: Botham, Imran, Hadlee and Kapil Dev. Prockie was their equal, without a shadow of a doubt. Probably better. With a helmet, because he was a little dubious at times against the short ball, he would have been a great batsman alone. I often felt that because he had knackered himself bowling off that long run, his energy for batting was naturally lessened. And he batted lower down for us – I mean the South African Test side – because we had such a strong batting line-up. He could easily have batted at number four. Wonderful fielder too. And he could bowl spin. People say that Jacques Kallis was the complete package as an all-rounder. Prockie was as good. Probably better.'

In conclusion, the Packer Revolution was important not so much for what it achieved but what it made possible. For the first time, players had an expectation of what they were worth and the insatiable marketing of the game has fuelled, and financed, those expectations. A very good living can now be made from playing; for the top players, the rewards are princely. Few begrudge this. Rare is it that I come upon a former cricketer who resents his modern-day successor his wealth. With nostalgia, and a certain naivety, it has to be said, the stock response is that he played for the love of the game and wouldn't have had it any other way. Barry is more cynical, or realistic anyway. He still remembers having to find his own digs in Southampton when he arrived as Hampshire's first overseas player and asking for a car to get around. Nowadays, the England players are each given a Jaguar. 'And they've all got agents,' Barry remarked. 'Can you imagine Desmond Eagar having to deal with agents?' No, that was a scenario difficult for both of us to envisage. However, for all that, Barry is pleased that his awareness of the role and the value of a professional cricketer has been vindicated, albeit a little late for him. Is it too much to credit him with vision and foresight when others had their heads firmly in the sand? His friends and cohorts believe incontrovertibly that he does deserve this accolade – 'trailblazer' was the word I heard most frequently used to describe him. 'I know I was right,' he says, 'even if I didn't always go about it in the right way. It was a policy – to make the game, the players and the administrators more professional – I tried to continue in my later coaching career.'

So much for the politics and the reverberations of WSC. Though all very interesting and contentious, I was curious to discover Barry's opinion of those whom he played with and against. As a batsman, he was forever watching and assessing his opponents, searching for weaknesses and opportunities to exploit. In the slips, he was quicker than most to surmise what was going on in a batsman's mind at any given moment. As a coach, he was adept at spotting little flaws in technique and good at exploring the mental side of his charges' performances. And as a television pundit, he was excellent at reading the game and interpreting the action clearly and concisely for the viewers. So, like an excited schoolboy, I started to quiz him about the superheroes of WSC.

Having permitted me this slice of self-indulgence, I shall grant myself another. I wanted to start with Imran Khan, someone who has intrigued me ever since we faced each other as schoolboys when I was on a cricket tour of Pakistan. I doubted that he could possibly have remembered me, given my undistinguished contributions to that match, but he did, several years later, when our paths crossed on the county circuit, and a most friendly and companionable fellow he had turned out to be. By then of course, his career was burgeoning, a process accelerated by his association with WSC. 'Suddenly, he got fast,' remarked Barry. Assuming that he was referring to Imran's bowling, not his speed off the blocks in charming seemingly the entire female population of any country he visited, I quizzed him further.

When he came down from Oxford and started playing for Worcester, he was rated as a batsman who could bowl a bit of medium pace. Yet when Packer signed him on, he had transformed himself into one of the quickest bowler around. How? Barry wasn't sure either but had a very firm idea what made Imran such a fearful proposition with a ball in his hand. 'Reverse swing. Sarfraz Nawaz had first developed it in the Pakistan side and he had passed on the technique to Imran, who in turn coached Wasim and Waqar in its mysteries. Basically, it's managing to get late in-swing with the ball when it's lost its shine. At his pace, it's useful.' Useful! Useful enough to take 362 Test wickets, to say nothing of his 3,807 runs, which place him firmly in the elite category of the great all-rounders. Then Barry started to chuckle. 'I remember a cocktail party we had to go to for Channel 9 where there were quite a few nice chicks. Garth le Roux, Imran and I got chatting to them and…' It probably were best I leave the story there but any social event that included those two, claimed Barry, was 'a lot of fun.' And then he added something quite poignant and illuminating. 'Later on, Imran got very involved in that project to build a cancer hospital in memory of his mother. It was a sort of calling for him. It must be nice to have a calling.' The last words were uttered with something like wistfulness in his voice.

What about the other Pakistanis? 'Javed was still young and finding his feet, not yet the dominant personality that he later became in that Pakistani team. *Zaheer?* 'Zaheer had been brought up on Pakistani wickets and had cut his teeth as a county pro for Gloucestershire, who played the majority of their home games at Bristol. Those pitches were generally slow and low and of course the Australian wickets were fast and bouncy so he found it difficult to cope at times.' Given that, Zaheer coped well enough on different pitches to join a select few who have scored 100 hundreds in their career. Majid Khan, however, has always held a high position in Barry's regard. In many ways, this should come as no surprise. Majid was Barry's type of batsman. If not exactly embracing style over substance, he batted with sublime elegance and artistry, albeit with occasional irritating bouts of carelessness and lack of concentration. At first, he batted down the order but soon moved up to open the innings. He played the quicks with ease and a fluency that belied a watertight technique as well as a deep well of courage in those pre-helmet days.

He remains one of only four batsmen (oh dear, it was so nearly five, wasn't it?) to have scored a century before lunch in a Test match, the others being Trumper, Macartney and Bradman. Crowds flocked to watch him take guard. Sometimes, he looked bored, as if his mind was elsewhere. He caught flies at slip and he bowled occasional off spin. He scored 73 first-class hundreds but should have scored more. Remind you of anyone? 'He had such soft, beautiful hands,' Barry remarked admiringly. 'He was one of the best bad wicket players I've ever seen,' said Barry, 'and there were a few around before the days of covered pitches.'

In any discussion that Barry and I have had about his West Indian contemporaries, he has always trodden warily, as well he might, given the political eggshells under his feet. Cricketers are cricketers, he has always maintained, whatever their colour, and it is no fault of his that misbegotten and misguided racial policies of his government (for whom he did not vote) put up this glass barrier between them. 'West Indians are not Africans,' he said, 'not our countrymen. Whatever the quarrel, the problem, the wrong that has been done to them in our name, it has nothing to do with the inhabitants of the Caribbean.' Strictly speaking, he is right of course, but as he well knows, the subject of apartheid is much more complex than that. And annoyingly for him, it just won't seem to go away. It distresses him that he should be judged simply because he is South African and *per se,* he must therefore be seen as perpetually at crossed swords with the West Indians. It was bad enough having to take on their heavy artillery with just a bat in his hand without everybody believing that they were at war in the bar after stumps or at a cocktail party as well. In point of fact, he got on well with the great majority of the West Indians in WSC and they got on with him. The respect, if nothing else, was mutual. 'Gordon, Fruity and I were team-mates at Hampshire, for heaven's sake,' he said warmly.

But what about Viv? Here he drew breath, knowing as well as I did that Viv Richards was nothing if not sensitive about race. At times, it seemed that the raging intensity of his hostility towards racial inequality fuelled the destructiveness of his batting. When he came out to bat, with that slow, languid swagger, his jaw working overtime on a hapless piece of chewing gum, you sensed that he was going into battle not only for his country but for the nobility and self-respect of the black man everywhere. He was going to bend the knee to no one. And he didn't.

Barry understood all this and perforce admired him for it. 'Viv was more political than me. He was vehemently anti-South Africa. He had his principles and I had no problems with that. But we were always respectful of each other as individuals. We weren't bosom buddies because we came from two different planets but that was all right. There was never the slightest hint of animosity between us.' *What about him as a player?* 'He was, what, 27, 28 at the time, right at his peak. He was the standout batter, without doubt. I reckon it was just about the best he ever played.' That comment put me in mind of that exceptional hour of Test match cricket when Barry and Graeme Pollock elevated the art of batting to a totally different plane against the Australians in 1970. Pollock felt that he had to raise his game because the young Richards was about to steal his thunder. Here, nine years later, the younger man was not only stealing Barry's thunder but also his name. So he did something about it. He had to.

With others of the West Indian side, Barry had no such wariness in his social relations. 'I often shared a room with Joel Garner. Great guy. Desmond Haynes too, a really nice fellow. Michael Holding I still see from time to time on media duties and we always stop and have a friendly chat. And of course Garry. In my opinion, he is one of the true gentlemen of the game.' *But Garry Sobers wasn't playing in WSC. He'd been long retired by then.* 'I know. But he would still have scored a few runs even if he hadn't picked up a bat for six years, eh? He just loved cricketers. Maybe it was because I had played with him for the Rest of the World in those games in England and news got around that perhaps I wasn't the devil incarnate after all. But my point is that these guys became good friends. Hartley Alleyne and Collis King too. It's perfectly possible for a West Indian and a South African to be pals. Why not?' Why not indeed?

Needless to say, there was no equivocation in Barry's friendship with the Australians. Or was there? 'Traditionally, Australians and South Africans are meant to hate each other,' he revealed, which was news to me. 'Maybe it has something to do with the intense sporting rivalry between the two, both competing for colonial top dog.' Certainly, the competition between them on the field of play was as fierce as it gets. 'They were always tough opponents,' he continued, 'and they had a formidable team. But genuine dislike between us? Certainly not for me.' Perhaps it was the fact that he had played in the Sheffield Shield, taking them on in their own backyard, so to speak, that had built up respect and friendship. 'The Chappells, Lillee, Marsh – they're all great guys and it is always a pleasure to see them again at functions and reunions.' The amount of time that Greg spared me in the writing of this book, always willing to share memories and anecdotes of their times together, is testament to the regard in which Barry is held Down Under – and those are Greg's words, not mine.

We haven't mentioned Kepler Wessels, who made his name as much as anybody in WSC. Another one of the 'cleansed' South Africans? 'Kepler was Australian.' Aha – yes, of course he was. An odd sleight of hand by the game's politicians. A prolific schoolboy batsman, he made his first-class debut for Orange Free State at 16 and by the age of 18, he had already scored a double hundred in a trial for Sussex. I remember it clearly. A significant portion of his runs came off my bowling. *I'm intrigued, Barry. How did Kepler end up playing for Australia?* Barry laughed and seemed surprised that I did not know the full details of the story. 'It was when I got that 200 in Perth. After the game, John Cornell, one of Kerry's henchmen, came up to tell me that the boss wanted to see me. When I entered the room, Greigy and Ian Chappell were present. The pleasantries were swiftly dispensed with and then Kerry told me I was now going to play for Australia!'

What! I know the Australian team had struggled a bit against the might of the Rest of the World and you had just put their finest bowlers to the sword but you can't just chop and change sides as if you're picking teams in the school playground. 'That's what I thought. When he asked my opinion, I told him I thought it was a terrible idea. It wasn't in the spirit of the whole thing.' To their credit, both Chappell and Greig voiced their opposition to the plan. 'Greigy was shouting, "No no no – he's one of us!"' *I'm sure he did. He wouldn't have wanted to lose his opening batsman.* But Packer's mind was made up and it was not for changing. Barry continued, amused at his memory of the scene. 'Ian Chappell was furious. "But he's not one of us, a true Australian!" Packer just shrugged. "He soon will be. Get him a passport!" he said to one of his assistants. And to me he promised an interest free loan over ten years of $30,000. We shook hands on it.'

For once, Packer changed his mind. Wiser counsel somehow prevailed. Barry wearing the Baggy Green would not have sat comfortably in my eyes any more than had he taken to wearing the green of Worcestershire. 'But he paid up, you know,' Barry was at pains to point out, 'Kerry, once he had shaken hands, always honoured his deals.' *And you carried on playing for the Rest of the World?* He nodded. *And how did Wessels end up playing for Australia?* 'It was Greigy who recommended him. Obviously, as they were both at Sussex, he knew of the lad's potential and he got Kerry to sign him up. He told Kerry that as Kepler was largely unknown, it would create far less fuss in getting him the correct visa and papers than if we had the full story with my face plastered across the front pages of the papers.'

And what a good acquisition Kepler turned out to be. 'Yah, he was the star of the second year.' Following WSC, Wessels played 24 Tests in the Baggy Green before retiring, citing general disillusionment with the Australian Cricket Board. Having re-settled in his homeland, he found himself captaining the new South Africa after their re-emergence on to the world's sporting stage in 1991. He truly was one of cricket's itinerants, more so than Barry. A list of all the teams he represented would take up a whole page. *What was your opinion of him, Barry?* 'Annoying! Bit like Graeme Smith.' Lest anyone should regard this as a little unkind, let me reassure you that he was referring to his batting style, not his personality. 'He had an ugly method of scoring runs but it was very effective.' However, Barry did have reservations about Wessels's opportunism, something that he has been accused of himself, but he begs to differ. 'I never considered playing for another country. It was either South Africa or no one for me.'

Barry is a bit ambivalent about the English players involved in WSC, their contributions on and off the field, for one or two good reasons. 'I reckoned they felt a bit uncomfortable,' Barry suggested. 'Maybe the razzle dazzle was alien to their more conventional, conservative culture. They never really embraced it all in the same way that the laid-back West Indians did.' Furthermore, the English didn't feature much because few were enlisted. Those who were could be said, with some justification, to be in the twilight of their careers and probably believed that they had nothing to lose by turning their backs on the TCCB. Tony Greig (who wasn't English anyway) had played all his Test cricket with Alan Knott, knew him well and trusted him. Through Knott, Kent colleagues Bob Woolmer and Derek Underwood were approached and accepted. John Snow and Dennis Amiss also signed but the rest of the England Test team, including obvious targets such as Bob Willis, Ian Botham, David Gower, Geoff Boycott and Derek Randall resisted the siren cries of Packer's cash. I wondered why. Who better to ask than Derek Underwood?

'It was Greigy who got in touch,' answered Underwood. 'It was a terribly difficult decision, I can assure you. But for once in my life, I had been guaranteed three years' security, instead of shorter contracts with Kent, and of course with England, you never knew from one Test to the next whether you would be selected. If I signed, I knew where I stood and what cricket I would be playing for the next three winters and that counted for a lot.' *Why did you think the younger ones didn't sign then?* 'I think the TCCB were quicker off the mark than other boards to react to the situation. We were getting paid something like £200 per Test. In short order, it had shot up to £1,000. So immediately there was more security for them.' *Did you ever regret signing for WSC?* 'Never! It was good for cricket. And I loved it. It was such an exciting time. We really felt we were part of something new, something radical, a historic time in the game's evolution. And another thing…Barry and Viv were on my side for once, which meant I didn't have to bowl to them!'

Of the English contingent of WSC, only Knott and Underwood featured in the Supertests; the others were relegated to the Cavaliers touring up-country. Barry of course knew both very well from their many years on the county circuit. Alan Knott was supreme as a wicketkeeper in just about everybody's opinion and Barry sought not to demur. 'Knotty was top-notch, no doubt about it. I can't remember him ever dropping a catch.' As a batsman, his powers were in decline, but that hardly mattered, given the depth of talent in the World team. For Underwood, Barry had nothing but the highest praise. 'Yes, he was unplayable on those cabbage patches they played on in Kent. But he could also bowl overseas, which very few of his type manage to do. So he could fulfil both roles, attacking when conditions suited and holding when they didn't.'

Holding! I know he had a long run for a spin bowler but another Michael Holding? 'A holding pattern, I mean. He could tie up one end while the fast bowlers rested. The thing about Deadly,' Barry continued, 'is that he never seemed to bowl a bad ball.' I can vouch for that. On one occasion, I was floundering while facing him, convinced I would never score a run. 'Don't worry, mate,' said Alan Knott genially to me from behind the stumps. 'He's made better batsmen than you look stupid.' Derek claims not to remember the occasion. And that is perfectly feasible, considering how many batsmen in his career he has similarly bamboozled. *How do you feel you coped in WSC?* 'Oh, I didn't have much to do,' he laughed modestly. 'Not with that battery of West Indian fast bowlers in the side. All I had to do was wheel away for a few overs while they had a rest. And when we were playing *against* the West Indies, we had Garth le Roux, Imran Khan and Mike Procter to spearhead our attack. I just provided a bit of variety here and there.'

Underwood is being self-deprecating here. A look at the Supertests' bowling statistics reveal that in five matches, he took 16 wickets at an average of 27.56, not quite in the Deadly class of some of his performances on those wet Kent pitches but on the hard, fast tracks of Australia, very creditable nonetheless. Out of those seven bowlers above him in the averages, all were speed merchants. This was, after all, the Age of the Fast Men.

All good things come to an end eventually. I quizzed Barry about when he became aware that things were being wound up. 'We all knew that the situation was unsustainable and that some sort of agreement would be hammered out. I mean you couldn't have two versions of the game existing side by side. And that's exactly what happened. We were called in and told that our contracts were to be paid out. Packer had got what he wanted and the adventure had come to an end.' Barry is ever the realist and a shrewd analyst of the course of events. It would be a huge mistake ever to underestimate him. That rarely happened on the cricket field but some, even today, fail to understand the sharpness of his mind, mistaking a certain inapproachability for lack of intelligence. All the same, he got the better of Packer, did he not? 'No, I would hardly say I got the better of Kerry,' Barry demurred.

But you secured an extension to your contract? He agreed that yes, he had broached the subject of renegotiating his contract before WSC was wound up and that yes, he had got them to increase his pay for the third year. 'But the deal was not done with Kerry. I negotiated with one of his executives, Andrew Caro. To my surprise, it was agreed. When Kerry found out about it, he was not best pleased.' *Did he pay up?* 'As

I have said before, he *always* honoured his deals. That is not to say that he wouldn't try to negotiate over the terms.' *Did he on this occasion?* 'He said I could either have an agreed sum of money up front or he would pay me the full amount of the contract over ten years. I calculated it was better to take the money on offer immediately and that's what I did.'

I wondered, now the party was over, whether Barry had any feelings of anti-climax. He admitted to some – he was sad that the high profile of the matches had come to an end – but his overwhelming emotion was one of relief. Not that it had finished but that he had been granted two years of international competition at a time when he had long since given up hope and that he had proved his worth. He knew that he was past his best but he had still managed to hold his head up and perform at the highest level. 'I survived on experience,' he said, 'maybe without the panache and domination of old but at least I had lived up to my reputation.' He reckons that the opportunity had come just in the nick of time.

Two years further down the line and he firmly believes he would not have survived. He cites the example of Eddie Barlow for whom WSC had come too late. 'It was such a shame,' said Barlow's former Springbok colleague. 'He was clearly past it. For him, it had come two years too late. He didn't really feature at all. I knew what a fantastic competitor he had been, what a wonderful all-rounder and a tremendously positive influence in the dressing room.' Barry does have a sensitive side and his commiseration for former team-mates and opponents – those whom he respects, mind you – who have suffered misfortune or who have fallen on hard times is genuine and worthy of admiration. 'When you're playing, it's dog eat dog. But when you've finished, rivalries, enmities even, should be put aside. I'm learning that as I get older.'

All things considered, did you enjoy the whole experience? 'Well, it wasn't quite like the carefree joy of that series against Australia back in 1970. But I was much younger then and the whole of my future, I thought, stretched out in front of me. As it happened, it was not to be and WSC offered me the chance for one last shot at glory. But I have to say that it happened at a very exciting and interesting time in the game. You couldn't help but get bound up in the exhilaration of the enterprise.' This is a view shared by his friend and ally, Greg Chappell. 'Times were changing in the 1970s,' he reflected, 'and sport is a mirror of society. The Vietnam protests were going on at the time. Authority was being challenged. There was a lot of change going on and we felt very much in the vanguard of this upheaval. It was a historic moment and we were well aware of our part in it.' Derek Underwood agrees, 'There was a bit of animosity and ill-feeling about it all when we returned to England but personally, I never had a moment's regret at signing up. I loved it, so exciting. And, as things turned out, it was good for the game. People are beginning to appreciate that now.'

How about Barry's assessment of the Packer Revolution and its repercussions on the game? 'I honestly believe that the modern-day players have little understanding or appreciation of the pivotal role that World Series Cricket played in the development of the game. It was the turning point in professional cricket. I'm not saying that it wouldn't have happened anyway over the course of time but the thing was that it *did* happen, all at once, at that place and at that time. And Packer was one of the few men who could possibly have pulled it off.' Barry gets cross when he remembers the bad press that Packer received, especially in England, where the establishment regarded him as an ogre, much like the Big Bad Wolf in *Grimm's Fairy Tales* and countless frightful prophecies from mothers to their children down the ages. Even when reassured that Kerry Packer's reputation in this country has undergone something of a revisionist makeover, he said, 'England is a very conservative country. Look, they still persist in picking blockers to open the batting!' Ouch! Oh, for an English Barry Richards. And both of us agreed that *surely* an England team would be more feared with Kevin Pietersen in the batting line-up, whatever his unorthodox texting habits.

Together, we reflected on the paltry recognition that WSC is accorded in the historical records of the game, almost as if a nasty smell still lingers over the actions of the 'pirates'. Francis Drake was a privateer, a pirate in all but name, but he is credited with defeating the Spanish Armada and saving England from invasion. Tales abound of his derring-do but of the Packer warriors, no such folklore has been spawned, no legendary tales woven over pints of beer with misty eyes and reverential voices. The Supertests have been relegated to a footnote in the history of the game – a significant footnote, it has to be said – but it is not part of the main narrative. As evidence of this, Barry points an accusing finger at the administrators, past and current, who see fit to consign the records and statistics of WSC to the backwaters of statistical data. 'We're not even given first-class status,' he snaps angrily, 'and that's absolute… absolute *nonsense!*' I'm sure you have got to know Barry well enough by now to doubt the authenticity of that last idiom. You would be right, of course; the word he used was much more colourful. But no less truthful for that.

10

Those Two Imposters – Triumph and Disaster 1984–2015

*'Of all the things that have happened in my professional
life, apart from playing, that is, my work for Queensland
gave me the greatest pleasure.'*

**Barry Richards on his time as boss of
Queensland Cricket Association**

*'You just don't get over something like that. The nightmares have
diminished but I still have sleepless nights.'*

Barry Richards on the suicide of his son

IT was a warm, soft evening in late summer such as you only find in England. The shadows from the imposing, red brick, Victorian pavilion were lengthening across the wide expanse of the Oval outfield. Despite its more egalitarian roots than those of its fashionable sister ground north of the river, the Oval has just as much historical significance as Lord's. The first ever Test match in England against Australia was played here in 1880. And less obviously, it was the venue for the first international football match, England versus Scotland, in 1870.

Traditionally, the final Test of the series is played at the Oval. Many famous players down the years have taken their last bow at this ground. It is a fitting place and a fitting time, at the end of the English summer; dusk approaches and the lights in the pavilion glow more brightly. Somehow, one senses that it is time to go. The Oval crowd, ever knowledgeable, appreciate this and the farewells, loudly bestowed, are fair and invariably generous. The most notable of course was that accorded to Donald Bradman in 1948. He was applauded all the way to the wicket, where the England team gave him three cheers. Two balls later, he was on his way back, having been bowled by Hollies for a duck. After a shocked silence for a few seconds, Bradman's reception on his walk back was just as vociferous and moving. And he was the enemy.

South Africa had just bowled out England for a meagre score, no mean feat on a quick and essentially true surface. There had been an irritating last-wicket stand of 46, which had set the teeth of the South African captain on edge. Mentally, he had been preparing himself to go out to face the England opening attack in what was going to be a crucial session, one that if they survived intact, would hand the initiative to the visitors. But they had been held up and their captain, more in annoyance than anything else, had given his bowlers a piece of his mind. Evidently, it had worked because England's number 11 had holed out where before he had been more circumspect. Ten minutes – in point of fact, a minute or two fewer given the many steps from dressing room to pitch side – is never long enough for an opening batsman to gather his thoughts as he hastily straps on pads and fumbles for bat, gloves, helmet. Before he knows it, he is trotting down those steps and stepping out on to the outfield, affecting a calmness he does not feel.

'Come on,' said Barry Richards to his opening partner, Jimmy Cook, who seemed to be dawdling behind him. Barry was keen to get out there and commence battle. He stepped on to the grass, looked up to the sky, squinting in an effort to find the sun and adjust his eyes from the gloom of the pavilion. At first he did not see the England team, lined up in a guard of honour, applauding him to the crease. And when he did see them, he was momentarily nonplussed. And then the significance of what was happening struck home at the same time that he became aware that the whole ground was on its feet, acclaiming every step of his towards the wicket.

He puffed out his cheeks and muttered a curse. This was something that he most certainly wasn't expecting. And to tell the truth, it was something that was not terribly welcome. He had a job to do and he did not like being distracted. But even he, hard-nosed as he was about his chosen profession, felt the emotion percolating through his veins. He blinked furiously. 'Thanks, guys,' he said, to no one in particular.

At last, he reached the crease and was joined by Cook, who had known what was afoot and had deliberately hung back. Barry looked around the packed Oval stands. It had been a generous send-off and he knew it. At once, unbidden, a thought came into his mind. 'Jeez, I hope I don't mess this up and get out for nought, like Bradman did. Had he scored just four, his Test average would have been 100. A duck won't seriously affect my Test average of 60 odd but hell, I've got to get runs here.'

'Hey, Richo! Bet you can't see the ball for tears in your eyes, eh?'

It was Ian Botham calling at him from slip. Barry turned to his genial tormentor and gave him back a cheerful volley of insults. Now the sentimental gestures had been dispensed with, the England players made it plain, by word and body language, Barry's wicket was the one they wanted. 'And they're damn well not going to get it,' he said to himself as he faced up to his first ball. It was – thank you, God – a leg-side half-volley, which he leant into and the ball streaked away across the Oval turf. Four. He was on his way.

Of course, it never happened. But it should have. Putting politics aside for one moment – and how often have we been able to do that in this tale? – few of Barry's contemporaries would have begrudged him a half-decent Test career. Incidentally, it would be interesting to consider how the great South African side of 1970 of Richards, Irvine, Peter and Graeme Pollock, Procter, Barlow, Lance and Lindsay would have coped with the onslaught of Lillee and Thomson of Australia and the four-pronged pace attack of any combination of Roberts, Holding, Daniel, Garner, Croft, Bishop and Clarke of West Indies. And how would this mythical 1984 South African team of Richards, Pollock, Cook, Kirsten, Procter, McEwan, Rice, le Roux, van der Bijl, Hobson and, who knows, one or two black or mixed-race players as well, have performed on the world stage? We shall never know. Such fairy tale contests will have to remain residents of our imagination, just as much as this farewell of Barry's to Test cricket at the Oval.

In point of fact, it was at the Kingsmead Ground in Durban that Barry made his farewell appearance as a first-class cricketer. If not at the Oval in a Test match, then on his home turf was as apt as anywhere. The occasion was the final match of the 1982/83 Currie Cup season against Transvaal. It wasn't a bad game, judging by the scorecard, though Barry has little recollection of the details. In their second innings, Transvaal had declared, setting the hosts 328 to win. That Natal so nearly pulled it off – they lost by 39 runs – was to a great extent thanks to an innings of 82 from Richards, not on this occasion leading the charge from the front but manoeuvring and supervising the middle order from his position of number six. At the top of the order was Robin Smith, just setting out on his journey to prominence, which would take him to England and a hugely successful Test career for his adopted country. He was able to qualify to play for England because his parents were English born, even though he was not.

Barry, of course, had enjoyed no such parental luck. And he has always maintained that he would not have turned his back on his native country, even if he had been afforded the opportunity. And by now, it was much too late anyway. When South Africa were finally restored to the international fold in 1991, Barry was 46. I know Jack Hobbs was still playing Test cricket at that age but that was in another era. Barry had shot his bolt when he was in his mid-30s and he knew his quiver was now empty.

As he wearily removed his cricket gear and no doubt made sure that a warm bath was ready for him to soak his aching limbs, what were his thoughts? 'I thought I scored a hundred in my last innings,' he announced to my surprise. 'I remember it, against Northern Transvaal. Simon Hughes was playing.' A hasty check of the records confirmed that his memory had been faulty; the 82 he scored against Transvaal was indeed his final first-class innings. Of the match and the innings, Barry has no recollection but he does remember how he felt as he packed his coffin for the last time. 'It was time,' he said. 'It had been brewing for a year or two. I didn't really want to practise anymore. I didn't look forward to the games. I didn't want to turn up, get changed, go out there and perform. I had ceased to enjoy it. It's difficult to explain but most players know it when the time comes. The same has just happened to Jacques Kallis. Perhaps he could have gone on a bit longer but he just couldn't summon up the will anymore. Same with me.'

Retirement in any man's life is a strange moment of mixed, conflicting emotions. Some regret the final reckoning, others have been awaiting it impatiently for years but no one can be entirely immune from a degree of soul-searching. 'Have I had, all things considered, a successful career? Has it been worthwhile? Have I enjoyed it? Should I have done something else? And what now? With a bit of good fortune, reasonable health and a following wind, I should squeeze out another 20–30 years before the Grim Reaper comes calling. How shall I fill my time?' For professional sportsmen, needless to say, the crack of doom comes much earlier and the days of restlessness and discontent can stretch into a worrying emptiness. It is a sobering thought that retirement for them is probably going to last a great deal longer than the span of their playing career. The incidence of depression and suicide among ex-cricketers is disturbingly high. It is not like that for everyone; plenty of ex-players find fulfilling occupations. But I know a surprising number who have never really adjusted to a world beyond the dressing room.

As if reading my thoughts, Barry brought up the sad case of Graeme Pollock, who has featured large in these pages. At the age of 19, he scored his maiden Test hundred at Sydney, an innings which had the world's press in raptures. 'Next time you decide to play like that,' commented Don Bradman, 'send me a telegram.' Speaking of Bradman, do I need to remind you that Pollock's Test average of 60.97 lies second only to the great man? Yet life has not been kind to him subsequently.

Various business and financial ventures did not work out. Added to which, he is battling cancer and Parkinson's Disease and has recently suffered a minor stroke. The legend that strode confidently on to the outfield at Newlands in Cape Town in 1999 to receive his award as the South African Cricketer of the 20th Century now has a job to pay his medical bills as his health fails him. 'It's so sad,' said Barry. 'He was once a god. Now he is largely ignored. We've all tried to help financially over the years but you would have thought that Cricket South Africa could have found some sort of ambassadorial role for him.' As Barry will later point out, the current regime that runs cricket in his country largely ignores the Springboks from the apartheid era. If Barry feels sorry for himself, and he has admitted to some bitterness on occasions, he feels desperately sympathetic for his old compatriot. Pollock never left his homeland to fight under a foreign flag, nor indeed ever plied his trade overseas.

So retirement was never going to be a seamless transition for Barry, no matter how disenchanted he had become with playing to empty Albert Halls. It never is. When you put away your bat for good, it feels like an extension of your arm has been removed. Some ex-pros drop down a level, and then another, and then another, and convince themselves they are content with that. They say that they have always loved the game and they still enjoy playing it, though they know in their heart of hearts that their powers are steadily diminishing. Others are too proud to allow this to happen and tell themselves that enough is enough. Ian Botham famously retired on impulse mid-season, never to play again. A friend of mine, no mean player, burnt his cricket gear after his final match. And I shall never forget a former colleague of mine, John Rice at Hampshire, who came off the field after having been dismissed in his last innings, to sit down by the gate to the pavilion at Dean Park in Bournemouth, unstrap his pads, remove his gloves and shove them all, together with his bat, into the nearby rubbish bin, with the words, 'Well, that's my lot then.' And it was.

It was Barry's great fortune that an opportunity in cricket administration at once became available, for the alternatives were thin on the ground. Cricket had been his life and to be truthful, he knew of little else. Natal offered him the job of director of cricket in the province and he jumped at the chance. 'It was a new lease of life really,' he said. 'It was the first appointment of its kind. It encompassed everything, the playing side, coaching, administration, marketing, development.' *I guess your experience with Packer weighed heavily in your favour?* 'Certainly I knew now how cricket could be run and what needed to be done.' He worked for Natal for six years and is proud of the changes he instituted and the progress that he oversaw in his time at the helm. Pride of place goes to the new bank of nets that he had installed at Kingsmead. 'Previously, there was only one net on the ground, can you believe? And that faced the sun!' New stands were erected and sponsorship deals secured, which generated income, putting the old place in far better shape when he left than when he was playing. He refuses to take all the credit but he does believe that his influence was key to setting up planning strategies and supervising their implementation. 'I'd been at the cutting edge of the new philosophy and that's what I wanted to do – to manage the change in Natal from the amateur to the professional era.' He enjoyed that responsibility and felt that he had stumbled upon a line of work, a profession, which suited him down to the ground.

Geoff Boycott always said that, once he had played himself in on a pitch that held no terrors and had got on top of the bowling, he would 'book in for bed and breakfast'. Barry was never one to book in for bed and breakfast. He preferred five-star hotels to B&Bs. In the same way, he would rather play a scintillating innings of 70 or 80 than grind out a featureless hundred – unless the situation demanded it. The same impatience can sometimes be observed in his personality. Perhaps impatience is not quite the right word, but there is a restlessness in his soul that does not permit him to put down roots easily. Certainly not permanently. 'I'm a travelling man,' he said simply. By now, he felt that he had achieved all that he could at Natal and had begun to get itchy feet.

'A guy called Murray Sargent, an ex-player for South Australia, got in touch. I knew him well – he was a selector for the state team. Together with another guy, Ian McLachlan, they offered me the job of coach.' *What, just like that?* 'Well, they knew me from my year playing for South Australia. Ian was chairman of the South Australian Cricket Association.' McLachlan was a former first-class cricketer himself. He had represented Cambridge University and had played for South Australia for a number of years. He was a very successful businessman with a string of awards to his name and later became a Member of Parliament, rising to ministerial rank, for Defence. *Not a man you say no to?* 'Certainly not. In any case, I fancied a change of scenery.'

Hang on a moment, Barry. Were you not married by now? Indeed he was. That happy occurrence had taken place in 1981, to Anne, an Australian. The two boys, Mark, the elder, and Steve were born in quick succession, in 1982 and 84. *How did they feel about being uprooted?* 'No, fine. We were happy in Adelaide. It was a good time for us.' He became almost nostalgic. 'We lived in a lovely place on Opie Avenue, not far from the ground. Mark went to St Peter's College, one of the top schools in the country. Steve was too young to go to school. We had a lot of friends there and enjoyed a busy social life.' I got the impression, over months of conversations with Barry, that Adelaide has always held a special place in his heart, in the way that, say, Southampton never did. Of course it was the locale of his most famous and productive season during his *annus mirabilis* in 1970-71 when he scored that acclaimed 356 at Perth.

But I think his stay in Adelaide meant more to him than sheer weight of runs. Here he got to know Greg Chappell, who has had such an instrumental role in his life and with whom he has maintained a steadfast friendship. There were other good friends too who were, and remain, loyal and well disposed. It was also the dominion of Sir Donald Bradman, who had been such a fervent admirer of the young Barry's enormous talent. 'It's not a big place, Adelaide,' Barry told me, seemingly inconsequentially, 'I was known in cricketing circles as "Number Two".' *Eh? Why?* 'Well, you can guess who was number one, can't you?' *Oh, I see. Still, it's no indignity to be No 2 to the great Sir Don, is it?* Barry laughed. He is never one for false modesty. He is quite clear of his place in the pantheon. And it is not up there alongside The Don.

There is another contributory factor to his fond memories of Adelaide. 'In every Shield and Test match, they invite all the ex-players back and make a fuss of them.' I agreed that this was a splendid initiative, one now replicated in all the counties in England, as far as I am aware, and one whose beneficence I certainly avail myself of at Hampshire. 'But I'm seldom invited back to Kingsmead, you know,' he added. My jaw hit the ground. *You mean that Barry Richards, one of the most famous and most loyal sons of Natal cricket, is not made welcome at his home ground?* He nodded sadly. 'Politics again, Murt, politics.' The significance of what he had just said, and the petty meanness of it all, took a while to subside, all the while as he was calling to mind the list of slights to which he had been exposed.

How would you describe yourself as a coach? He gave this some considerable thought, all the while rubbing the side of his nose. *Not one of the old school, I guess – you know, get your foot to the ball, young man, and show us the maker's name!* His look said it all. 'I suppose you could call me more of a <u>facilitator</u> than anything else.' He was attempting to make it *easier*, less difficult, as he assisted in their progress. What he wasn't doing – it is not in his nature – was barking out stock phrases from a dusty coaching manual. Nor was he sitting on a stool beside the nets (as I saw recently at a practice session for the England team) tapping away on his computer while one of his players, alongside and unnoticed, carried on playing and missing. 'I often think you can over-complicate coaching with all this technology,' Barry claimed. 'Of course there is a place for instant feedback on a computer. Who wouldn't benefit from actually seeing on the screen what you're doing wrong?' I agree with that. No matter how many times you are told that your head is falling away to the off side as you play your shot, it is not until you have actually *seen* yourself do it that the realisation truly dawns. On the other hand, we both agreed that the modern player can look a bit too grooved. Too much time with the bowling machine, I suggest. As for personal stereos and earphones: 'They're all plugged in and don't seem to speak to each other,' Barry despaired.

Not that he was a reactionary old diehard. Far from it. He has always been receptive to new ideas, different methods, flexible reasoning, thinking outside the box. 'I tried to be innovative,' he said, 'to mix up the routine. I liked to design individually tailored sessions, which the guys seemed to appreciate.' As an example of what he meant, he talked about Andrew Hilditch, a fine batsman, who had a distinguished career in Sheffield Shield cricket and played in 18 Tests for his country. Latterly, he has been a selector for the Australian team. 'Andrew was a compulsive hooker,' Barry said, 'so I took him into the squash court and threw specially weighted tennis balls at him, to sharpen up his reactions and refine his technique.'

Did you have a good side there? 'Plenty of fine players but they had been under-achieving. Hookes, Hilditch, Wayne Phillips, Tim May, Peter Sleep, the young Darren Lehmann – we had the nucleus of a good side there. Plenty of batting but a bit thin on the bowling. We relied a lot on Tim May.' And he used the off-spinner as an illustration of his principle, as he calls it, of 'one size does not fit all'. 'Look, May had a dodgy knee. He didn't want to do all the training that the other guys had to. If anybody moaned, I'd say, "What would you rather, knacker his knee so he can't bowl or let him off training and he takes five wickets?" That soon shut 'em up.' *So what did he do? Sit in the dressing room and have a fag while all the others flogged themselves running round the ground?* 'Times had moved on from those Hampshire days, Murt. He practised carefully and alone and that was fine by me. And the others accepted it once the situation had been explained to them.'

Your captain was David Hookes. Controversy seemed to stalk his life, including the circumstances surrounding his death. How did you get on with him? 'He was a charismatic figure. Kerry Packer soon latched on to this and promoted him as the poster boy of WSC. As a captain I rated him. He was aggressive in his tactics, his first instinct was to attack and seek the win, not sit back and react to events. He was my kind of guy and I got on with him. Mind you, he didn't hold back verbally. He gave me as much stick as anybody else. He used to say, "When's the real Barry Richards going to turn up and coach us?" I didn't mind. It was all good banter.'

He never really did himself justice, did he? 'Probably not at the highest level. But he scored more runs in the Sheffield Shield than anybody else – ever! So I would hardly say he underperformed.' Nonetheless, Hookes's record in Test cricket is indifferent, given his enormous talent; in 20-odd Tests, his average hovered around the 35 mark. Not exactly a failure but not exactly living up to the glittering future that was predicted for him after he had announced himself so spectacularly on the international stage by hitting Tony Greig for five consecutive fours in the Centenary Test. He reminds me of two other unfulfilled talents, Graeme Hick and

Mark Ramprakash, who both failed to reproduce their prolific county form in Test matches. 'But Hookesey's contributions to the team, both as a run scorer and as a captain, were invaluable,' Barry insisted. *Was the feeling mutual?* 'How do you mean?' *How did he get on with you?* 'Fine. He respected me, I think.' That is often the way, I sense, with difficult, opinionated, even arrogant, young men; they do respect and listen to, if not their elders, then their betters. I once asked Barry how he got on with a controversial fellow countryman of his, Kevin Pietersen, and he said that Pietersen had never been anything but courteous and respectful towards him. I should jolly well hope so.

That year, you were in with a good shout of carrying off the Sheffield Shield but fell at the final fence. What happened? 'Moody.' *But you're often moody, Barry.* 'Tom Moody! He scored a hundred in both innings. I'll never forget it.' The rules of the competition stated that first and second in the table at the end of the season should play each other in a winner-takes-all confrontation, with the team who had finished on top having home advantage. *Hmm – so they can prepare a favourable wicket?* 'Exactly. It was against Western Australia in Perth and the pitch was so good we could still be playing on it. And, as I said, we had a bit of a weak attack.' The scorecard says it all. Western Australia scored 539 and South Australia 494. The match had stalemate plastered all over it. In their second innings WA had time to score a further 289 for the loss of only two wickets (and yes, indeed, Tom Moody was a centurion in both innings) before stumps were drawn and the game put out of its misery.

For all the heavy scoring in that dispiriting play-off final, one name caught my eye, even though he had only made a modest 17 runs: D.S. Lehmann. 'Yes,' confirmed Barry. 'He was only a youngster, 18 or 19, but his talent was there for all to see.' During a visit to Cape Town in March 2014 to catch up with Barry and to put some of the flesh on the bones of this book, I was invited to attend a charity golf day featuring many of the visiting Australian cricket team, who were about to take on South Africa at Newlands. The name of the charity and Barry's involvement in it shall become clear later on in this chapter but suffice it to say that the regard in which Barry is held by Lehmann, the current Australian coach, and the rest of the Australian team, spoke for itself in the willing turnout on the eve of an important Test match. In the clubhouse, I seized the opportunity to buttonhole Lehmann to explain the reason for my presence there and to ask whether he might be willing to offer an opinion of Barry as a coach at a very formative stage of a young batsman's career. I don't know why I was surprised at his reaction. I should not have been. He had already made a sizeable impression on a recent Ashes series, both for his restorative powers on a demoralised Australian team and for the charm and dignity that he brought to the role. In short, he could not have been more friendly and obliging. He promised to give me as much time as I wanted. 'Anything for the Master,' he grinned. And he was as good as his word.

'Barry was the first full-time coach we had had at South Australia,' he said, 'and he had a huge influence on me as a young player.' I asked him about David Hookes, commiserating with him over his untimely death and the contentious circumstances surrounding that ill-fated brawl outside a nightclub. 'Barry got through to Hookesey,' he went on. 'That was why he was a special coach. He allowed you to expand and flourish. In fact, he encouraged it. He had been a great player himself and he could spot little things that were wrong in your technique that you weren't even aware of.' *What were you like as a member of that dressing room? Shy and retiring?* He gave a huge belly laugh. 'I was a brash and cocky young kid. Bit like Barry was, I guess. He related to me and I respected him.' Lehmann then recounted a story that had a familiar narrative to it. 'I thought I was a pretty good squash player. So I challenged him to a game.' I started to chuckle. I could guess what was coming next. 'He wiped the floor with me: 9-0, 9-0, 9-0. He just stood there on the "T" and made me run and run and run. Afterwards, I threw up in the car park.' I explained that I had had a similar experience with Barry on a squash court but that I had stopped running just in time to spare my digestive system after the walloping. Strangely enough, I too thought that I could play a bit. 'That was his approach.'

What – to make you sick? 'To push you to your limits. To demand your very best. He hated slackers.' *Would you say that you have modelled your coaching style on him?* 'No, not exactly. You take the best bits from everyone who's influenced you, don't you, and model them around your own personality and way of thinking.' His admiration and affection for Barry were transparent and I sensed it had more to do with just cricket. 'Aw look, his son died early. My mum died early. My great mate Hookesey died early. These blows put everything into perspective. So we had an instinctive understanding between us about what's important in life.' Indeed. As it unfolds, we shall see that this chapter is all about that essential verity. *Thank you for your help, Darren.* 'No worries, mate. You do these things for your mates, don't you?'

Fair stood the wind for future success and family contentment. South Australia and Barry seemed a perfect fit, the team was on the cusp of great things and Anne and the children were happy and settled. What could go wrong? What could disturb the professional and personal idyll? Anything and everything is the plain and simple answer. An opportunity suddenly presents itself. You are not seeking change but change comes knocking. Do you stick or twist? Robert Frost puts the quandary that Barry faced much better than me in his poem *The Road Not Taken*:

> **Two roads diverged in a yellow wood**
> **And I sorry I could not travel both**
> **I took the one less travelled by**
> **And that has made all the difference.**

Why on earth did Barry choose the road less travelled? Or, more to the point, why did he choose at this time to take the road less travelled? He had barely started on a job to which he was well suited and which he was enjoying. *Why did you leave South Australia after only one year? Things were going so well.* 'An opportunity arose that was too good to turn down,' he replied simply. In any career, promotion can arise at an untimely moment. When he explained the circumstances surrounding a fateful phonecall, from his good friend, Greg Chappell, the horns of the dilemma did look uncomfortably sharp. The proposition that Greg was laying before Barry was the post of chief executive of the Queensland Cricket Association. The job description took in responsibility for the running of cricket throughout the state, at all levels, not just looking after the First XI. 'It involved setting out a long-term strategy for Queensland cricket, from the grass roots up, not just organising the nets for the lads,' he said.

Greg told me that it was his idea that they approach Barry; he had to convince a few sceptical people because Barry wasn't an obvious choice, not having had experience in the administration of a large organisation. 'But Barry had always been a deep thinker about the game and had always expressed sound opinions on how it should be run so I was sure he was our man,' said Greg, adding for good measure, 'And I was right. We had seven or eight good years with Barry at the helm.'

There was also the carrot of a hefty hike in salary. 'Eighty thousand dollars instead of $40,000,' he answered immediately, as he always did, to my query about salary. *Well, yes, I can understand your decision. Did South Australia try to keep you?* 'Yah, they upped their offer but that wasn't really the point. It was a much bigger job. Look, there are only six CEOs in Australia and most of them had been in their post for 20 years so an opportunity like that only came up once in a blue moon.' The train was about to leave the station, with or without him, so swiftly he hopped on board. And that made all the difference.

He may have hopped on swiftly but it was not without a wistful look back. Adelaide has always held an affectionate corner of his heart. For a start, it is one of the most attractive grounds – or ovals, as they are known in that part of the world – in a beautiful city. He made good friends there and played cricket with the gods at that stage of his career. He had enjoyed his time coaching South Australia and still remembers with a smile giving the young Darren Lehmann his debut for his beloved state.

'Every time I return there,' he said, 'it feels like a homecoming. My times there gave me so much. Perhaps it was the making of me as a cricketer and a person.' Barry is not given to sentimentality and it was a surprise to hear him speaking like this so we can safely assume that his fond memories are genuinely felt. 'Whenever I'm invited back, you know at Test matches and players' reunions, the welcome is always warm. It's a wonderful place and a piece of it is always with me.' *Blimey, Barry, you'll soon be telling me you miss the United Services ground in Portsmouth*. The gist of his response was that probably he would not.

Not unnaturally, his hasty exit left a sour taste in the mouths of his employers and, more upsettingly, the South Australian team. 'Hookes took it badly,' Barry admitted, 'and didn't want me anywhere near the team before I went. And I can understand that. I felt very guilty and I knew it looked as if I'd abandoned them.' But the chance was heaven sent and unlikely to arise again. He had to take it. Ambition goes hand in hand with ruthlessness. I know of no successful man, or woman, in whatever profession or career, who has not stepped on a few toes on the way up the ladder. Barry was not insensitive to how it appeared but the challenge had presented itself and he could no more turn his back on a challenge than park legally. Come on, be honest now. Do you know of any South African who obeys parking regulations?

The scale of the task that awaited him in Brisbane at first took his breath away. Queensland had never won the Sheffield Shield. The competition had been in existence since 1892 and the Sunshine State joined in 1926/27. Since that time, the 'banana benders', as Queenslanders were unkindly called, had been waiting, and waiting and were still waiting when Barry arrived. 'That was all they talked about,' Barry said. 'All they even thought about. When are we going to win the Sheffield Shield?' It had become the Holy Grail and as the prophet brought in from overseas, Barry was expected to lead them to it. But Barry didn't see it quite like that. He believed that the state cricket association ought to concentrate on other priorities, putting in place a plan, a strategy, from the grass roots up, to improve standards at all levels, at the pinnacle of which should be players good enough to represent Australia. From the application of such good practice and custom, success for the state team would automatically flow. 'Stuff all that, mate,' was the message Barry sensed he was getting. 'The Shield is what we want you to deliver.' That he did, while at the same time putting in place his radical blueprint, afforded him as much pleasure and satisfaction as anything he ever did in cricket, save with a bat in his hand. But it took time. And a lot of hard work. 'Not just by me,' he stressed, 'but by my team, all of us.'

On the top of a pile of priorities toppling over in his in-tray was the need to slim down the bureaucracy. The bugbear of any amateur organisation is the proliferation of committees, all manned by enthusiastic and dedicated volunteers no doubt but often lacking in dynamism and expertise. 'Jeez, it was like turkeys voting for Christmas,' exclaimed an exasperated Barry. 'It took us three years to reduce the board from 22 members to ten.' Club cricket was revamped to encourage younger players from outlying districts. He put in place good coaches and managers of the junior sides and kept in close touch with schools cricket. It is a vast state of 500 million acres, most of the interior scrubland and uninhabited, and Barry, even if he was used to long distances, found the huge logistical task of coordinating cricket in such a large area testing. At least the climate was familiar, sub-tropical and similar to Durban. One happy consequence of the warm winters was that training in preparation for the season was never a problem and Barry set great store on the fitness of his players.

What contact, now you were an administrator rather than a coach, did you have with the players? I had a vision of Barry slogging up and down the sand dunes of the Gold Coast together with fit young men half his age but he immediately discounted that unlikely scenario. 'The state players, you mean? They were not my direct responsibility – that was the coach's – although obviously I took a great deal of interest in them, watched them in the nets and during matches. But my role encompassed all players in the state, schools, junior teams, university teams, clubs, representative 11s, so individual contact was less. I wore a suit not a tracksuit.' Now that I would have loved to have seen.

Who was your coach? A pause, while the nose was stroked. 'Jeff Thomson.' *Ye-es? Go on.* 'Look, Thommo is a great bloke, a really, really lovely guy. But his style was a little...well, shall we say outmoded. He was an "up and at 'em" sort of coach, good on motivation but less interested in the detail of technique. We needed an overhaul of how we did things.' He left it there, hanging in the air, but I pressed him. 'The way his departure was messed up caused me grief and I was very sorry about it.' The need for a change had been well signposted. Applications for the job were invited for the end of Barry's first season and there was no reason for Thomson not to make his pitch together with all the other candidates. 'But John Buchanan gave a very good presentation,' said Barry. 'He was the standout applicant and we on the board offered the job to him immediately.'

However, the interviews and discussions had over-run and it was now late, past ten in the evening. Barry fully understood that his duty was to contact Thomson with the bad news. He did not want his old friend to find out from any other source. 'But it was late, man,' said Barry, 'too late to phone, so I got in touch the first thing next morning. Unfortunately, the press had got wind of the decision and got in first.' Apparently, the journalist concerned had had no such scruples about ringing Thomson up late at night and spilling the beans. *How did he take it?* 'Badly. And I felt bad about it too.'

The choice of John Buchanan as coach was an interesting one. Buchanan had played a few first-class games for Queensland in the late 1970s and then concentrated on the coaching side of the game, cutting his teeth in England, taking charge of Oldham CC in the Central Lancashire League and Cambridgeshire in the Minor Counties. As such, he was a relative unknown when the board took a punt on him, having been impressed by his earnestness, his grasp of detail and his zeal for the use of the new technologies now becoming available. He was a controversial choice, owing to a perceived lack of experience playing at the highest level, a disparagement that dogged him in his later time in charge of the national team. 'The only coach you need,' Shane Warne once famously quipped, 'is the one that takes you to the ground.' Ian Chappell was equally dismissive of Buchanan, saying that anybody could have coached that successful Australian team of Warne, McGrath, Ponting Hayden, Healy *et al*.

Barry begs to disagree. 'He wasn't everybody's cup of tea. Andrew Symonds and he didn't always see eye to eye.' That would not be altogether surprising. Symonds, for all his talent, has always been a free spirit, not one to bend easily to rules and restrictions. 'But others thought the world of him,' Barry continued. 'Matthew Hayden was hugely influenced by Buchanan early on in his career. He probably made Hayden the player he became. He was revolutionary in the way he used computer analysis. He was full of new ideas and initiatives and the guys, mostly, responded positively to him. But like all coaches or managers of teams, he only had a certain shelf life. You can't keep on re-inventing the wheel.'

There then ensued one of Barry's riveting monologues, the like of which he was so strangely unwilling to air during his playing days. Out loud, he wondered at the value of a coach to a cricket team. Lest he be accused of clambering aboard Shane Warne's despised bus he immediately spelled out his reasoning and it all had to do with his firmly held belief of horses for courses. There are some players, and as we have mentioned Shane Warne, let us use him as a prime example, who work it all out for themselves and do not greatly appreciate what they see as inexpert meddling. Some need an arm round the shoulder and a boost to their confidence. Others appreciate the technical input and are always looking for advice and guidance on how to eradicate faults in their play. A coach tries to be all things to all men but in the end he has to trust his judgement and get everyone to buy into his philosophy. Barry himself, from personal experience, knew what a difficult, sometimes impossible, job it was. 'Why don't we go down the golf route?' was his surprising suggestion. 'Everyone has his own individual coach.' *But you couldn't possibly have that in a team context, surely? There wouldn't be enough space for them all in the dressing room.* 'Not full time. They could work with each player as and when. And then, every so often, they could all get together under the main man and discuss ideas and progress.' As ever with Barry, he had provided food for thought.

Notwithstanding his critics, would you say that John Buchanan was a success at Queensland? 'Undoubtedly. We won the Sheffield Shield. Twice. We paraded it around Brisbane in the midst of such scenes of celebration you would not believe.' *Similar to the joyous outpouring of euphoria around the streets of Southampton when we won the County Championship in 1973?* It hardly needed his snort of derision but he gave it anyway. 'A guy called Andrew Blucher, our marketing guru, sold me the idea of rebranding the team the Queensland Bulls and we went ahead with it. We were the very first anywhere in the world to do that. Now all teams have a tag name.' *Not Hampshire, I'm relieved to say.* 'I think you'll find they have.'

A quick check on Google proved him right. Previously known as the Hawks, they latterly changed to the Royals. Why, you may ask. Nothing to do with the Royal Family but everything to do with money. It was a marketing initiative to join forces with the Rajasthan Royals of the IPL. 'Look, we had to make money, to pay the bills,' Barry insisted. 'Queensland was the poor relation of state cricket and we needed to increase revenue to afford the improvements to the infrastructure and the operation.' Fair enough. Cricket needs continually to look to its governance and move with the times. Packer taught us all a sharp lesson there. *Incidentally, why Bulls?* 'The bull is the symbol of the country areas of the state.' That seems a sound enough reason. I can find no such justification for the moniker Royals. As far as I know, Her Majesty owns no castle in Hampshire.

First and foremost, the Gabba, Queensland's home ground, needed a facelift. The first Test match at the ground was played in 1931 and it has been a regular fixture in the international calendar ever since. That was the trouble, according to Barry, it had a history but very little else. The stands were dilapidated, the facilities basic, the administrative offices poky and a dog track ran round the perimeter of the playing area. 'And we didn't even own it,' exclaimed Barry. 'We had to negotiate a rent with the state government.' On the premise that, as he was starting from scratch, he could not really fail, Barry set about injecting some life into the sleeping giant. The dog track was dug up. Thanks to excellent work from a first-rate groundsman Kevin Mitchell, the playing surfaces were improved and now his son, also named Kevin, carries on the good work. 'We bought a brothel next door,' Barry announced to my surprise and amusement.

Were the good ladies taken on the payroll and employed as part of the lads' warming-down routines? He laughed. The joke had obviously been cracked many times. 'Woolloongabba, where the ground is situated, is not a very salubrious area. So we bought the premises at a cheap price and converted them into offices. Then we were able to employ more people to put in place our reforms.' They needed another oval, so they acquired a rugby league club that had gone out of business in nearby Albion and constructed two new ovals, one named after Allan Border and the other after Ray Lindwall, two legendary servants of Queensland cricket. 'It's now the National Academy for Australian cricket,' Barry said proudly, 'The facilities are *fantastic.*'

For good measure and increased revenue, the Gabba is the home of the Brisbane Lions, an Aussie Rules football team. For those of us who live in England, the dual use of cricket grounds, whether for football or rugby in the winter, always sends a shudder of dread down the spine. English grass does not recover from such a pounding and as an outfielder myself, I used to hate fielding on a bobbly, rutted outfield scarred by heavy studs. But in hotter countries, it doesn't seem to matter so much. The warm and humid conditions aid growth and regeneration.

All this transformation occurred, or at the very least, was initiated, on Barry's watch. However, he is adamant that it could not have been done without the unswerving support of some very good people. 'Don't think I did it all on my own. I did not. Nobody could. I was lucky enough to have a formidable team with me, on and off the field.' He pays particular tribute to three of his fellow members of the board, Alan Pettigrew, Cam Battersby and Damian Mullins. 'They were great allies. Sadly, all are now dead so they were not able to see the long-term fruits of their labour. And that is a great shame.' In point of fact, Barry had huge respect for all members of the board and the unstinting support they gave him. In any successful organisation, the CEO must feel that those who appointed him and are charged with monitoring his progress are standing foursquare behind him, through thick and thin. Nothing of much value can be achieved if they cut and run at the first hint of trouble. Barry appreciated this and was generous enough to state it publicly.

How would you rate the influence of Allan Border on the team? 'Massive! I can't overstate the impact that guy had.' Border had retired from international cricket the previous season and was therefore able to devote all his time and energy to the cause of Queensland cricket and the pursuit of that elusive goal. On the day that the Sheffield Shield was at last placed in his hands, Border was four months shy of his 40th birthday. *There you are, Barry. If he could do it, so could you. An expensive pair of prescription glasses and you would have been as good as new, hitting it over the top, just like the old days.* 'I've told you – my tracksuit had been binned forever. But it was a great moment for AB. Everybody was delighted for him. Nobody deserved it more.' For his own part, Border was lavish in his praise for what he regarded, first and foremost, as a team effort. As Barry had done, he made reference to the team off the field as well. 'We had a tremendous bunch of players,' Border commented afterwards, 'and really good management.'

It might have been hard for those who knew him as a brash, young newcomer to English cricket in 1968 to envisage Barry as an exceptional manager. But he clearly was. It must have taken considerable vision, conviction, optimism, grasp of detail and political shrewdness to make a success of the job. 'But I'm not a politician,' scoffed Barry. 'Look at how many people I've upset over the years.' Maybe so. But who said that a successful politician spared people's feelings? A successful politician gets thing done, by whatever means necessary. He works out which levers to pull and which buttons to press. So I would disagree with my friend here. He clearly has a shrewd business brain. I remember Barry used to get really animated when he got on to the subject of financial matters when he was a player. I don't mean that he was continually grumbling about the size of his pay packet but that he was keen to discuss the details of commercial deals, sponsorship contracts, financial models, contract negotiations, merchandising opportunities and the like. He had a head for figures and would sometimes groan at the amateurish way that a supposed professional organisation, such as a county club, would fail to maximise its potential. He would leave me floundering in his wake as he attempted to explain the logic of his opinion. And then, as I was pondering this, out of the blue, I received an e-mail from a friend of Barry's in Australia.

Dennis Yagmich (of Croatian descent, I was interested to discover) played a little for Western Australia but not in the same year as Barry was playing Shield cricket. As it happened, during the Packer years, Barry played in a match for the World XI against the WSC Cavaliers. Dennis was playing for the Cavaliers. As Barry strode to the wicket, he passed Dennis and greeted him thus, 'Yag, how ya doin'? You're a long way from Midland.' Yagmich was dumbstruck. He'd never met Barry. Putting two and two together, he remembered that Barry had been living in Perth and had played for the Midland-Guildford club, Yagmich's home team, though he had moved away before Barry had arrived. 'Obviously the Midland boys had told him a few stories about me,' Yagmich ruefully deduced. The two got chatting after the game and a firm friendship was born. After WSC was wound up, Barry returned to Perth and reignited his association with the Midland club. He needed somewhere to live. Where else but to board but with Dennis Yagmich? It was an obvious, yet fateful, fit.

Yagmich's further discourse on Barry's business acumen I print in full. It is worth noting that Yagmich himself is a successful accountant and sits on the Western Australian Board of Commerce, so his opinions bear scrutiny, 'Away from cricket, we would often talk of stocks and shares and property investments in which Barry had a keen interest. Barry showed a flair for business. I often think where he would have ended up had he pursued a full-time career in business. He has a very visionary outlook on things and would have been a good entrepreneur. His astuteness in business and cricket matters led to a succession of senior and prestigious appointments in the administration of the game. The 1987 stock market crash was a good example of when he could see an impending problem on the horizon and he managed to save himself from disaster by selling out prior to the crash.'

So, not only could Barry sense when a short ball was coming, he could also predict the market! Barry laughed when he heard this description of him as a guru of the stock market. 'Not all of my investments were successful,' he said. 'I remember once going on holiday and failing to keep my eye on the price of gold while I was on the beach.' But he did admit to having a bad feeling about the stock market in 1987. 'I just got a sense that things were overheating so I did sell – just in time. I've always worked on the premise that when everyone is selling, that is the time to buy. And when everyone is buying, that is when you sell.' *A nonconformist to the last, eh?* 'Yah, but I made a few errors too. You need careful attention to detail if you play the stock market. And I've not always done that.' Someone who has done more than most to keep Barry on the straight and narrow, or more aptly, as we are discussing the stock market, on an upward curve, is a good friend and confidant, Rob Zadow, his financial advisor. 'These days the business of stocks and shares is much more complex,' Barry informed me. It was my impression that it has always been complex, to me, at any rate.

Such was the wide scope of Barry's remit at Queensland that we have barely touched upon performances on the field. *I assume by now that you were not playing serious cricket anymore? I know you had retired from first-class cricket but were you attached to a club and expected to turn out on Saturdays?* His eyes widened. As if he could ever think of such a thing! He admitted to donning his whites for the odd charity bash or exhibition match but only for 'fun'. His competitive juices he saved for the golf course. Having said that, a distant memory stirred and he smiled. 'It was in a testimonial match for Allan Border. I was batting with Hansie Cronje, both of us wearing helmets of course, and the commentator remarked that it was difficult to distinguish between the current Test player and the long retired Test player. I was pretty pleased about that, I can tell you.'

Although Barry kept himself at arm's length from the state side, leaving the day-to-day responsibility to the coach, he knew he would, in the end, stand or fall by the results in the Sheffield Shield, no matter what good work he was doing behind the scenes. 'We had a good side and had been runners-up a few times before we actually nailed it.' With players of the calibre of Hayden, Love, Law, Border, Bichel and Rackemann, surely it would only be a matter of time. The day of days came at the conclusion of the 1994/95 season. The final was played at the Gabba; home advantage, so no complaints of a dead pitch and a certain draw. Queensland, in keeping with Barry's philosophy, wanted to win the match, and win it well. Victory by an innings and 101 runs would seem to have fitted the bill all right. The supreme irony of it all was that their opponents were South Australia. I know elephants are supposed to have long memories but cricketers do too.

'I don't think they were best pleased,' remarked Barry, with the merest hint of a grin. It was Allan Border's farewell to first-class cricket and success at last was as emotional for him as it was gratifying for Barry. Border was no longer Queensland's captain – Stuart Law had taken over the reins – but he, as much as any player, had steered the state through years of disappointment and near misses to ultimate success. It ended Australia's most famous losing streak and 'the monkey was off our backs at last' as Barry said.

Joy was unconfined. The team celebrated long and hard. The whole state was ecstatic. The Shield went on tour of all the districts and outlying towns. Wherever it was paraded, the crowds were plentiful and noisily appreciative. At last they had shrugged off their tag as perennial losers and the local press went into overdrive. 'It's the equivalent to man landing on the moon,' shrieked one. 'It's the day all those jokes about Queensland stopped,' trumpeted another. And even the academics from the University of Queensland threw off their customary scholarly circumspection.

A Dr Jopling was quoted, 'This Shield success has dramatically changed Queensland in the same way that World Expo in 1988 transformed Brisbane from a backwater into a vibrant city.'

How did you feel, Barry? You must have been over the…, sorry, most gratified. 'I think what gave me the greatest pleasure was that we had put the cricket team firmly on the map. Because of our success, we felt emboldened to seek more state funding from the ACB, which meant that at last we could compete on the same footing.' He was right. Their success was repeated two years later, against Western Australia at Perth. *No Tom Moody to scupper your chances this time?* 'He played – yes. And he got a hundred – a big one. But it wasn't enough, heroic though it was, to deny us for a second time.' Queensland won by 160 runs. Thereafter, they became serial winners, carrying off the Shield more times than any other state up to the present time.

'You know,' said Barry, in serious and reflective mode, 'of all the things that have happened in my professional life, apart from playing that is, my work for Queensland gave me the most pleasure. Batting? Well, that was instinctive, it came naturally. But this took hard work, all that planning and supervision and effort and keeping the faith. And it all paid off.'

As he had made mention of his professional satisfaction with his job, I thought it was high time that I asked him how family life was progressing in Brisbane. It had been something that I had been avoiding, for reasons that shall soon become apparent. *Was everybody happy in Brisbane*, I asked as nonchalantly as I could muster. Barry, by contrast, prefers to meet things head on. That's why he liked to open the batting. It is easier to set the tone, the agenda, from the front. And it was no different now. 'I was happy. We had lots of good friends. Greg Chappell had moved away by this time but there were others we got on with well, particularly Max Walters and Andrew Slack, the former Wallabies captain and his wife, Caroline. Andrew became a great mate. He's one of my most loyal friends. I respect him enormously. We played a lot of golf and had some serious chats as well as a few good laughs. So, yes, it seemed to me the Richards had a flourishing social life. I was away a lot but that was the nature of the job. Besides, as a cricketer, I had always been away a lot.'

What did Anne do? 'You know she was a serious squash player?' No, this was something I had been unaware of. 'She was ranked…number five, I think, in South Africa at one stage. And then, back in Australia, she was the national and world over-50 champion.' I whistled, and then a cheeky thought took hold. *Could she beat you?* I was desperate to find someone who did. He laughed, not wholly convincingly. 'She certainly could once I'd reached 45 or so. The old muscles started to seize up at that stage.'

We pressed on. Mark, Barry's eldest son, was a big chap. I've seen photos of him. He looks bright-eyed, confident, strong. Barry then relaxed, if that is the right word, into telling me about his son and what sort of boy he was. 'He had such quick hands. He was a natural. Being a big lad, 6ft 2in, he wasn't so quick on his feet but he had excellent hand-eye coordination. If he had worked hard at it, he could have been a reasonable first-class player. He was a good-looking lad and very intelligent. It must be difficult for any lad who's the son of a famous father, especially if he's trying to follow in his footsteps. Everybody sees him in terms of his father rather than an individual in his own right. Unfair and unhelpful comparisons are always being made.' *What about Steve?* Barry laughed. 'He asked me whether it was okay to retire from the game early – when he was 12!' *No benefit then?* 'He was a wicketkeeper. It's too damned hot, standing out there for hours on end, he told me. So he spent more of his time playing rugby, Aussie Rules and swimming. He's a very good swimmer.'

After some thought, he gave this assessment, 'Yes, Mark and Steve were two quite different personalities.'

When the Richards family came to Brisbane, Barry sought the advice of his friend, Greg Chappell, as to which cricket club it would be best to enrol Mark at. He was nine at the time and Greg's son, Jonathan, was of a similar age. It seemed sensible and convenient to both families that the boys should play for the same club. Both were later playing in one of the junior sides when Mark was unfortunately run out. 'He was a talented player,' said Greg, 'so the run-out was doubly unfortunate, for the side and for him personally.'

Apparently, Mark took it badly. At any age, a run out is senseless and frustrating. When you are nine, it is the end of the world. Mark was inconsolable and wanted to go home, there and then. Both fathers were at work so it was left to Anne to lay down the law to tell her son that under no circumstances could he go home before the end of the match; he would be abandoning his team-mates and besides, it would be the height of bad manners. So he took himself off to sit under a tree, sulking, still with his pads on. When the time came for a drinks break, Mark ran on to the field and kicked the perpetrator, his team-mate who had run him out, in the shins. 'Fortunately, the boy had his pads on so the damage was minimal,' Greg said, the laughter in his voice scarcely concealed.

Barry took up the story. 'Anne was mortified. I came back from work and went to sit, still in my suit, with the rest of his team while Anne took him home. Apparently, in the car on the way home, Mark announced that he was retiring! When I saw him, I sat him down and told him he had to do three things. First, apologise to the coach. Mark said yes. Second, apologise to his mum. Mark agreed. And third, apologise to the boy concerned. Hmm…Mark admitted he wasn't at all sure he could do that! Anyway, his retirement lasted two weeks. When he went back, all had been forgotten and forgiven. Richo – where've you been, was all they wanted to know.' Barry was laughing at the memory. As was I. So sad that the anecdote, the sort of one that goes down in family folklore, to be repeated *ad nauseam* at Christmas dinners and the like, will always evoke only confused and poignant emotions.

The other story was furnished by Rev. Mike Vockins, former secretary at Worcestershire CCC, rural dean of Ledbury in the diocese of Hereford and an OBE for his services to cricket. One of his many roles was to manage an England Under-19 team on a tour of Australia 'sometime in the early 1990s', he hazarded a guess, slightly rueful at the failure of his memory. 'We had been practising at the Gabba,' he does remember clearly, 'and Barry, as CEO of Queensland was there and was making us all very welcome. Anyway, on our way back to the pavilion at the end of our practice session, we noticed that a guard of honour had been lined up for us, a posse of eight- or nine-year-olds, all in their baggy caps, applauding us as we made our way up the steps. Then a piping voice was heard from one lad in the line, "Come on, you guys, let's give these Pommies some shit!" We were later told it was Mark, Barry's son. Of course Barry was mortified but we didn't mind at all. We found it quite funny.' Mike and I agreed that we could imagine the young Barry passing a cheeky comment like that.

Barry quit Queensland with nothing but happy cricket memories to accompany him. *Why did you leave? All was going so well.* 'As I've said before, I believe that CEOs stay put for far too long. Twenty years some of them had been in the job. That's too long. You stagnate and become comfortable. I thought I had given all that I could. We'd raised the profile of the state. We were now the best team in the land. And the base of the pyramid was broader and stronger and the infrastructure had been improved out of sight.' Chappell agreed. 'They had been successful years. Barry had done a fantastic job, as I knew he would.' Barry had no regrets accepting the position and he had no regrets at the timing of his departure. 'I reckon there's a nine- or ten-year lifespan in that job,' he asserted. 'Three years to learn it, three years to save for it and three years to implement it. I could have stayed but I knew I'd had enough.'

Why move to Perth? 'That was Anne's home. Her dad was ill and she wanted to go back there. I was happy to go. I knew the place and it seemed a good place to live. As it turned out...' His voice tailed off. What was to come was going to be very difficult for him. *Did you have a job to go to?* He shook his head. 'Chris Smith, a former Hampshire player, as you remember, was about to quit as CEO of Western Australia cricket and I thought I was in with a chance of getting the job. But no.' *Any idea why not?* He shook his head again. 'Instead they appointed a complete unknown. And he failed,' he added, with a knowing look.

The tragedy that befell Barry and his family in Perth was a lightning strike of deadly consequences, a catastrophe that shook them all to the very core of their being. As usual, Shakespeare puts it better than most, 'As flies to wanton boys are we to the gods. They kill us for their sport.'

In May 2009, after a long battle with depression, Mark took his own life.

I remember the dreadful news filtering through to us at a players' reunion at Hampshire and the overwhelming reaction was of course one of shock. Few details were available at the time but there was no need for the ghastly fact to be embellished in any way. For any parent, a child predeceasing you is a terrible burden to bear. For a child of your flesh and blood to take his own life is unendurable. People were shaking their heads, almost as if they were incapable of taking it in. Peter Sainsbury voiced simply what everyone was thinking, 'God knows what that poor family must be going through right now.' I guess that was a sentiment shared by many throughout the cricketing world.

The details of Mark's death do not concern us here. The shock, the grief and the guilt of those left behind would have been unbearable. Together, Barry and I were quietly sipping our beers under the shade of the oak trees in a Cape Town hotel. Tentatively, I broached the subject. After some careful discussion, we decided it were best to draw a veil over his family's suffering. The whole thing was understandably still too raw in the memory and that was clearly the right thing to do. But one thing bothered me. Why did he so manifestly and so fiercely blame himself for Mark's death? The look of pain on his face told its own story. He was lost in hopeless and bitter self-recrimination. It was very sad to see. 'All I know,' he added at last, 'was that no one, *no one*, could have done more to save that boy than Anne.'

In Perth, once the job of CEO at Western Australia had not materialised, Barry was left at a loose end. And then Greg Chappell rang – again! *Talk about 'phone a friend' on* Who Wants To Be A Millionaire. *He must have shares in Telecom Australia.* 'Yes, he's been a good friend and has always looked out for me.' *What plan did he have for you on this occasion?* 'He suggested commentating on TV. At the time, television companies were proliferating all over the place and, as Packer had shown, the cheapest way to fill airtime is live sport. And of course, cricket takes place over a long period of time. There weren't that many experienced broadcasters around... well, experienced in the actual game. They were looking for ex-players to act as expert commentators. Greg got me a few gigs and it sort of went from there.' Barry did not work exclusively for one company. He was freelance and took the assignments as, when and where they arose. 'Have bat will travel' had now become 'Have mike will travel'. *A lot of time away from home?* Mournfully, he nodded. 'I wish…I wish…Ach, there are so many things in my life I wished I had done differently.'

At times like this, when personal tragedy has struck, people often immerse themselves in raising money for the appropriate charity. Have you done the same? By way of an answer, Barry told me about Steve's bike rides, back in Perth, that he had organised with his best friend, James Larkan, in Mark's memory. 'I came along to the first one,' Barry said, 'and I could see straight away that the financial challenges of such a venture were enormous. So I broached the idea of a charity golf day, to help fund the project.' And this is a task that Barry has embraced with enthusiasm and diligence. I saw the fruits of his labour for myself when Barry invited me to watch some golf when we met up in Cape Town. *But I don't play.* 'You can watch, though.' *Who's playing?* 'A few of my cricketing friends. Oh, and the whole of the Aussie cricket team.' Now he had me interested. The Australian team were in town for the finale of the riveting 2014 series against South Africa.

Why are they willing to play just before some of the most important Test matches of the year? 'Because Boof promised they would.' Boof, I knew, was the nickname for the Australian coach, Darren Lehmann, the same Darren Lehmann to whom Barry had given his debut for South Australia all those years ago. 'It's for Mark,' continued Barry. 'The proceeds of the day go to Steve's charity.' I needed no further prompting. *Give me the directions.*

A golf day in South Africa for a charity in faraway Western Australia, no matter how noble the cause, would have been a non-starter without a more relevant hook on which to hang the promotion. Accordingly, Barry approached Jacques Kallis, recently retired from cricket, and suggested that they share the proceeds of a potentially lucrative day of golf in Cape Town between Kallis's academy for young, disadvantaged cricketers and Steve's bike rides in aid of youngsters who suffer from mental illness. Enthusiastically, both Barry and Kallis embraced the idea.

Thus I found myself, a trifle nervously, inching my way up the imposing driveway of the Steenberg Golf Club. A lot of golf courses are picturesque, that I have to allow, even though I am no player myself – strangely for a cricketer – but this one, hidden in Constantia Valley, with a stunning backdrop of the Constantiaberg mountains, is jaw-droppingly beautiful. I didn't watch much of the golf. I contented myself with an ice-cold beer, admiring the scenery and buttonholing various friends and former team-mates of Barry's for the purposes of research for this book. Notable among my scalps were Pat Trimborn, Robin Jackman and, yes, the aforementioned Darren Lehmann, who did indeed turn up, his team dutifully in tow. Barry gave a pleasing and articulate little speech, as you would expect of an accomplished broadcaster, outlining the charitable purposes of the day and encouraging everybody to give generously.

The raffle and auction of prizes began. Sometimes they can be a little tedious, especially when the drawing of the winning tickets starts. This one was no different. As stubs were flourished, colours identified, numbers announced, I noticed the attention of several people around me beginning to wander. One by one, they picked up one of the pamphlets that had been generously distributed around the clubhouse and started to read. More and more followed suit until it seemed most of the room were more engrossed in the subject matter of the pamphlet than in the identity of the prize winners. Reading glasses were fumbled for, necks were craned, bottoms shuffled for greater comfort, heads were turned towards more favourable light, eyes were narrowed, brows furrowed. Intrigued, I picked up one myself and started to read. I print it here in full, in the hope that you will understand why a club full of golfers was – for a while – transported to somewhere quite different:

A Touch of Luck

'Howzat!' shouted the red-capped Aquinas players in unison. I knew instinctively as I heard the appeal that the umpire was going to give Andy, our opening batsman, out. He did. With head down, Andy headed back to the pavilion. As I stood and strapped on my gloves, I muttered to myself, 'Right, this is your only chance to show Dad that you can bat.' I had worked hard on my game and this was the first season Dad had been away and hadn't seen me play. I wanted to show him I had it and prove something to myself as well.

As I walked towards the white line, Dad said in his typical South African way, 'Good luck, boy,' and I knew what I wanted to do. I walked out to the far end of the green strip, took guard and looked at the bowler. He ran in fast and sent down the first ball, just short of a good length. I went back and played what I thought was a reasonable shot…but the ball hit the edge of my bat and went straight to second slip. My heart sank. It was a sharp chance but heading for his open hands and he was going to catch it. He didn't. He dropped it. The bowler kept on coming towards me and uttered a few choice words into my face but I just looked him in the eye as Dad had always taught me to do. He stared for a few seconds but had to turn back to his mark. The next ball was a fiery bouncer, which I ducked under. I had survived the first over.

'That was lucky,' said Sam. 'Yeah, I reckon,' I replied. 'Righto, work hard and look for the singles.' That over went quickly, with Sam smashing a cover drive straight to the fielder and then turning one behind square leg for two.

'Keep concentrating, Richo,' said Sam encouragingly as I walked back to face PSA's finest. The first ball of the over was a half-volley, which I managed to squirt behind point for two. Relief. I was off the mark. I wasn't going to get a duck in front of Dad. The next three balls were wide and I left them, the fifth was a bouncer, which I top-edged over the wicketkeeper for four. Not too good but I'll take them any way they come, I thought. The last ball was an attempted yorker that ended up as a full toss. This I hit well through the covers for four.

There were more words between overs but Sam and I ignored them. Sam glanced the first ball down to fine leg for a single. This was it. The bowler I was about to face had got me out the last two times we had played Aquinas and the slip fielders were not afraid to let me know it.

As the lanky Aquinas bowler came charging in, I thought about my father and suddenly making lots of runs didn't seem to matter anymore. At that moment, I knew that no matter how many runs I scored, Dad wouldn't mind, he would still be proud of me. The pressure I had put upon myself fell away. The ball flew towards me and I timed a fine shot for four, one of the best shots I was to play in my innings. After that ball, everything seemed to flow.

On reaching 50, I raised my bat to my team and to my father. He was sitting alone, as he usually did when he watched me. He was clapping and I could tell he was the proudest man there.

I cruised to 70 and then started to not quite middle the ball. I managed to make 20 shaky runs to reach 90. I really had to grind those runs out. Sam was batting soundly and we had a solid partnership going.

I was on 91 when the captain decided to bring on the leg-spinner. The first ball was a half-volley, which I hit through the covers for two, taking me to 93. The next ball he dropped short and I managed a four. I was on 97 and a century was there for me. The leg-spinner started his run-up and bowled another short ball. I couldn't believe my luck, this was my hundred. I stepped back and tried to smash it through the leg side. I tried to hit it too hard. I mistimed it. It went in the air and the fielder at midwicket took an easy catch. I was out. I couldn't believe it. I looked at the fielder in disbelief and he just told me exactly where to go.

As I started to trudge back to the dressing room, I remembered to raise my bat, one of the first things my father told me to do. I looked for Dad. He was over on the bank where he had been since I went out to bat. He had a proud smile on his face. Making a century didn't seem such a big deal anymore. I knew he was proud of me but I was proud to be my father's son.

Mark Richards (Year Ten)

That is a beautiful story, Barry. Did it actually happen like that? 'It was a piece of creative writing that he did at school. He was very artistic like that. I think it was a sort of imagined scene that he would have *liked* to have happened.' But no less poignant for that, I judged.

It was with considerable satisfaction that Barry was able to support Steve and hand over a cheque for $10,000 to Youth Focus in the wake of this emotional golf day, the charity supported by Steve and his bike rides. *Tell me about Youth Focus.* 'It's a wonderful organisation in Perth that helps young people with mental illness. That is why I was able to persuade so many of the Australian guys to come along to the golf day, because it is based in Western Australia. Where it all happened.' He lapsed into silence. I found a lovely photo of Barry handing over the cheque to the CEO of Youth Focus, Jenny Allen. They are both smiling. Sometimes good comes out of tragedy. *How is it now, Barry? How are you coping?* It was a difficult question to ask and obviously a difficult one to answer. 'The years go by. You try to rebuild your life. But you just don't ever get over something like that. The nightmares have diminished but I still have sleepless nights. The guilt, remorse, the self-recrimination will never leave me, I guess.'

Another way to cope with personal tragedy is to bury oneself in work. Barry's services as a pundit on television had been in great demand. I wondered why they had not been in such demand recently. My mouth framed his answer practically at the same time he uttered it. 'Politics!' But then he paused and added this as amplification. 'Perhaps it would not be entirely correct to put it all down to politics. Other factors came into play as well. After a while, you become old hat. The producers want someone younger, more recently retired, an ex-player who knows the guys that are still playing and who can relate better to the younger audience.' In that respect, the changing of the guard is a notion as old as the hills.

Yes, but is there no place in broadcasting for the voice of experience and wisdom? 'Possibly. But you have to fit the mould that has been shaped for you. Or else become a parody of yourself, which isn't true broadcasting. That's more like showbiz. Not a lot of scope for original thought and proper debate there.' He also pointed out that the heyday of commercial television, with its proliferation of channels, was unsustainable in the long run; companies merged and the biggest ones took larger and larger slices of the cake. Thus the cadre of expert pundits started to shrink. *But I repeat, why were you not kept on as one of the favoured few? After all, you had your advocates.* He sighed. 'I dunno, Murt. Perhaps I didn't toe the line sufficiently.' And this is what he means by politics, petty internal politics as well as national ones. *I often wonder whether there's much difference.* 'That would be for you to say, Murt. I could not possibly comment.'

That Barry did have his champions is not in dispute. Robin Jackman shared a microphone with him on many an occasion. 'Barry was one of those colleagues that I always looked forward to my half-an-hour with. He was a brilliant analyst and read the game so well. He never wasted words or could ever be accused of waffling – he was succinct, to the point and spot-on.' *Is that how you would describe your style, Barry?* 'I didn't have any formal training,' he replied. 'It was very much a case of learning on the job. But I soon learnt that there was little point in telling the viewers what had just happened. That they could see for themselves. You had to tell them *why* it had happened.' He admits that he wasn't very good to start with but that gradually he became more comfortable, able to relax and give of his best. *Any major cock-ups?* He started to laugh. 'Ask Greg Chappell.'

So I did. Greg confessed it was not Barry's *faux pas* at all but his. Apparently, in a reference to the sluggishness of the pitch, Greg remarked, 'Well, you have to bang it in to get it up.' You always know when commentators have unwittingly said something *risqué*. You can hear stifled laughter, fits of coughing, snorts of hysteria in the background, followed by an embarrassed silence then a swift moving on. 'The guys at the back were hysterical,' recalled Barry of Chappell's clanger. 'I was crying with laughter and it was a couple of minutes before anyone was able to speak…and we made sure we changed the subject.'

One of the skills of broadcasting that I am ever in awe of is the ability of the presenters to keep talking – sensibly – when a cacophony of voices is assailing them through their earpieces. 'Very difficult to concentrate,' agreed Barry, 'but you somehow learn to cope and block out what's going on backstage.' Rather like batting, I suppose. One got the impression that when Boycott, for example, was at the crease, a bomb could go off in the pavilion and he would not notice.

Another problem that Barry encountered was the pronunciation of the Bangladeshi names. He would write them out phonetically on a crib sheet. He also did not take to presenting or interviewing, preferring to remain in the background as an analyst rather than take centre stage. 'Imagine trying to interview someone who can't speak a word of English. No, far too difficult. I left that to others.' He says that he was no great improviser, able to speak off the cuff and fill in time during breaks in play. 'I needed to be prepared. I wanted to feel confident of what I was going to say.' Mind you, he was not alone in that. He remembers once firing a question at Richie Benaud, the doyen of commentators. Benaud did not reply. Either then or later. He simply carried on as if he had not heard. Never ask Richie a question, he was told, unless you have warned him first.

I believe Barry was, if not quite in a class of his own as an expert critic, then certainly in that exalted bracket of those who talk sense rather than poppycock on the box. His comments were measured, informed, intelligible and fluent. He abjured the commonplace, the inane and the laddish, all of which seem to afflict many of our current pundits. But don't listen to me; hearken to Mark Nicholas, who should know what he is talking about. 'Barry is knowledgeable, articulate and forensically analytical. He can see clearly what's going on and can sense how a batsman or a bowler is feeling at any given moment.' In this, Nicholas compared Barry to Geoffrey Boycott, who is not everybody's cup of tea with his forthright Yorkshire accent and opinion but who knows his onions all right. *How about that, Barry? You and Boycs mentioned in the same breath.* A little laugh indicated that he had appreciated the incongruousness of the comparison.

So what went wrong? How did he become so unpopular, at least on the airwaves of his home country? Opinions are mixed. Even Barry seemed bemused by the ostracism, though he is prepared to hazard a guess. 'I told it as it is,' he said, 'and maybe that was what got me into trouble.' *Do you mean to say that your comments were deemed to be politically incorrect in this post-apartheid age?* 'It got to the stage that if you criticised anybody, you ran the risk of it being taken the wrong way.' He cites as an example his observation on the technique of Hashim Amla, which he believed did not go down well with his bosses. 'Earlier on in his career, Hashim had this habit of twirling his bat. I made the point that to succeed in Test cricket, he will have to tighten up his technique. To his credit, that is exactly what he has done. The twirl has disappeared and look at him now! But my remark was perceived to be disparaging of his Asian background, which is absolute nonsense.' It didn't help, Barry added, that he said this during the Kingsmead Test, and Durban has a large Asian community.

Another controversial episode took place in England, at Headingley in the fourth Test between England and South Africa in 2003. For the first time in their history, South Africa took the field with two black players spearheading the new-ball attack, Makhaya Ntini and Monde Zondecki. 'I was commentating with Mark Nicholas at the time,' remembered Barry, 'and he asked me whether I was pleased to see how well integration was working in South Africa, seeing as two black guys were opening the bowling. Of course I was pleased but I said that the fact that we happened to have a black pair of opening bowlers was not evidence that the system was working at all. It wasn't. What the country needed was not some sort of tokenism but a fully integrated policy of identifying talent, pooling resources efficiently and putting the financial backing, which is considerable, into these academies, nurseries, elite schools – call them what you will – rather than just pouring money indiscriminately into the grass roots of the game and hoping that Test players will grow. Well, you can imagine that my comments went down like a lead balloon with the powers-that-be.'

His was a considered point of view, one that he adheres to strongly even today, but it did not sit easily with the political ethos of Cricket South Africa, the governing body of the game. 'I was sacked by text,' Barry said grimly, 'even though I apologised if I had inadvertently offended anyone. After five years' employment! I don't think Supersport initially had a problem with my comments. But Cricket South Africa certainly did. Well, I guess political pressure was applied and I got the boot.' Since then, he has tried to build bridges. 'But they're not interested. They probably feel I've passed my sell-by date. It's all a bit sad really.'

The lack of black cricketers who make it through to the Test team remains a besetting problem in South Africa. 'Zondeki – where did he go?' was Barry's cry. 'Another one was a guy called Ngam. He was quick, man! I saw him bowl against New Zealand and he had genuine pace. But he was another one who seemed to disappear without trace.' Barry pondered the reason. He speculated that it might have been because they – and one or two others – were not willing, or not able, to assume the mantle of pioneers of fully integrated cricket in the way that Ntini has, joyfully embracing the fame and the spotlight. Correct or not in his assumptions, Barry is convinced that the money being flung at the troublesome question is misdirected. And for his views, he is excommunicated. A man with a world of experience deserves at the very least to be heard.

And here seeps a running sore, one that does not just upset Barry but many others who have the game of cricket in South Africa close to their hearts. For many it is a sad fact that the numbers that the current South African Test players wear on their shirts date from 1991, when the country was welcomed back into the international fold after full integration. Thus, number one is Kepler Wessels, the captain of the team that played in the first Test since reintegration, against the West Indies. In point of fact, he is the 246th player to have represented South Africa (as well as being number 317 for the Baggy Green of Australia, forget not). 'And number two? Do you know who that is?' cried Barry, with understandable exasperation. Indeed, I did not. 'Mark Rushmere!' *Well, I never. So you, Procter, Pollock, Barlow, Bland, to say nothing of the likes of Dudley Nourse, Athol Rowan, Hugh Tayfield, Jackie McGlew, John Waite, Roy McLean, Neil Adcock and Trevor Goddard – none of you played for South Africa?* 'It seems not. We've been airbrushed from history.'

While the new South Africa is a functioning democracy, a beacon of hope for the rest of that continent, by not honouring the contributions of its white cricketers, albeit from a less enlightened age, Cricket South Africa is doing itself, and its country, a huge disservice. After all, what was the Truth and Reconciliation Commission set up to do but to confront and to come to terms with the past? As Desmond Tutu said, 'You cannot forgive what you do not know.' To excise from history those 245 cricketers is not confronting its past; it is pretending that it did not exist. Thus that famous series in 1970 against the Australians never took place. The memorable stand between Richards and Pollock at Kingsmead was but a figment of the imagination. *Wisden* tells me otherwise. But Cricket South Africa is trying to convince me that these great players, and their predecessors, did not play Test matches for their country. Indubitably, this is 'doublespeak'.

Barry does not want to kick at the hornets' nest, not wishing to whip up a turbulence of recrimination and thereby stand accused of bearing grudges. He just shrugs his shoulder at the slight. Just one of many, it seems to imply. But his friends and former colleagues, those whom I have interviewed during my research for this book, have privately encouraged me to speak out on behalf of The Forgotten. Far be it for me to act as an apologist for what went before, in the dark days of apartheid, but that was then. This is now. And it seems to me that the shabby manner in which these past players have been treated is unworthy of any self-respecting board of control. I am not alone in my dismay, far from it. Others, closer placed and better informed, have taken up the cudgels. I recently unearthed an article by R.W. Johnson, the South Africa correspondent for *The Sunday Times*, which appeared in *The Standpoint Magazine* a couple of years ago. In it, he berates the controllers upstairs in the offices of Cricket South Africa for its vindictive treatment of their country's former players.

He attempts to compare the legendary 1970 Springbok team with the current side, always an interesting exercise but one that is inevitably subjective. But in one regard, the difference is starkly illuminated. The current crop are lionised, respected and hugely rewarded. The 1970 veterans – amateurs all, let us remember – are shunned, excluded, frozen out. Some of them have fallen on hard times and were it not for the efforts of friends and well-wishers, they may just as easily have fallen into destitution and penury. And Cricket South Africa does not even lift a finger to help.

The irony of it is that many cricketers of that generation did their best, in a climate of fear and repression, to make their feelings known about the inequity of segregated sport, encouraging the government at every opportunity to soften their stance. The famous walk-off in 1971, by Barry and Mike Procter and the rest of the team, was cited by Johnson as evidence of the liberal leanings of those players, something the rugby players could never be accused of, he observed tartly. And for this, the Pollocks *et al* are cold-shouldered by the present administration. Johnson calls this a 'scurvy treatment of old heroes' and goes on to list a shocking catalogue of indignities and kicks in the teeth.

Roy McLean, South African batsman of the 1950s, enjoyed being invited back for Test matches but when he requested a ticket for his wife because, as an old man, he needed looking after, his request was refused and he was told that people like him were 'beyond the pale'. Lee Irvine confirmed that his privileges such as free seats at Test matches had been withdrawn. Jimmy Cook and Kevin McKenzie offered to help with coaching but were just told, 'It's our time now.' Irvine's offer too was spurned. 'We don't need you,' he was informed. And there wasn't a man jack in that 1970 side, asserts Johnson, who voted for the government and apartheid. 'When it was recently proposed that a stand at Newlands cricket ground in Cape Town be named after Basil D'Oliveira, this was vetoed on the grounds that D'Oliveira had refused to follow the ANC party line.' All the honours boards in all the Test match venues have been removed, as well as all the old photos of past players. 'This was more than many could bear. When Graeme Pollock remonstrated about the hurt done to many who had simply been sportsmen doing their best for their country, in front of many members, he was dismissed with the words, "You guys had your day. Now it's ours."' The hot indignation of the article exudes from every paragraph.

Politics, as Barry says. Except that it is politics from one side being replaced by politics from the other. And Barry and his colleagues are forever caught in the middle. I asked him whether any of this rang true. He smiled wearily and produced one or two stories of his own. The reference to the mooted D'Oliveira Stand jogged his memory. 'Bryan Waddell, the New Zealand commentator, was on air at one of the South Africa Tests. "What's all this with naming stands over here after maps? You know, North, East, South, West? Or pointless notions like the Friendship Stand or the Centurion Stand? Why can't you guys name stands after heroes like Graeme Pollock and Barry Richards? Like we do back home. And everywhere else in the world." Well, the silence at the back was deafening. Everybody was curled up with embarrassment. He'd said the unsayable, you see.'

Barry was pleased to hear that, at last, the authorities at St George's Park in Port Elizabeth have relented and named one of the stands after their most famous old boy, Graeme Pollock. But for the Barry Richards Stand at Kingsmead in Durban, the world still waits. And it is likely to be a long wait. How do we know? Because, in a modest attempt, the proposition was scuppered before it even got off the ground. The Kingsmead Mynahs Club, whose history we know, wanted to honour their patron by naming a room – just a room, mind you, not a stadium, or even a stand – in the ground at Kingsmead the Barry Richards Room, with a brass plate with his name on the door. He was invited to lunch during a Test match, for its official opening. But the ground authorities got wind of the plan and all hell broke loose. The club was informed that under no circumstances could that action be countenanced. Under the threat of having their certification removed, the Mynahs had no option but to shelve the project.

When he was playing in Australia, Barry was presented with a signed, mounted and framed photograph of Sir Don Bradman. It was a memento that Barry cherished – and he doesn't usually get misty-eyed about trophies, medals and trinkets – but this one was special. After careful consideration, he felt that it would be appropriate to ask for it to be put on display in the pavilion at Kingsmead, the home of Natal, *his* home, which he had served loyally for 30-odd years. Later, he discovered it, up-ended, in a puddle of water, rotting behind a fridge in the kitchens of the pavilion. He rescued it, restored it and now it is displayed proudly at his old primary school, Clifton, in the Barry Richards Pavilion. 'At least something's named after me,' he added ruefully.

I think this slight by Natal upset Barry more than he was prepared to let on. 'Do you know,' he announced sadly, 'I've had more recognition from Hampshire than I have ever had from Natal? I'm rarely asked back. My early offers to help, my wish to advise, all my experience and knowledge, were consistently ignored.' At Hampshire, he was asked to become president, which he did, from 2007–2008, but at Natal, he is a non-person. 'No, no!' he disagreed, 'Not a non-person. Just an ex-player who is not…not…' He left it unfinished but uncherished would have been my term.

A prophet is not without honour save in his own country, says the Bible, and Barry at least had the compensation of being honoured in another country, namely England ('I've never been so cold in my life as over there'), more specifically, London ('Livelier than Southampton, hey?'), precisely, Lord's ('Must be great to bat there in front of more than one old man and his dog.'). He was invited to join the MCC World Cricket Committee by its chairman, none other than Tony Lewis.

There is a happy symmetry here. Tony Lewis was the despairing MCC captain of a ragged and perspiring bowling attack that was assaulted by Barry in one of his most spectacular innings at Lord's on that bitterly cold day in April 1974. Lewis's account of this innings forms the opening lines of the preface to this book. The purpose of the committee was to act as a sort of independent think tank, pondering the big issues of the game throughout the world and making recommendations for its improvement. It was specifically non-political and had no authority, other than having the moral weight of MCC behind it, the guardian not only of the laws of cricket but its conscience too.

Who else was on it? 'Geoff Boycott, Martin Crowe, Mike Brearley, Steve Waugh, Majid Khan, Anil Kumble, plus others. And the woman in the photo, who you didn't recognise, by the way, is Charlotte Edwards.' *So it is. Very natty white strides you're wearing, sitting there in the front row, if I may say so, Barry.* 'Thank you, Murt. You know me, always cutting a dash on the sartorial front.' I forbore from reminding him of the flared flannels he used to wear. Instead I quizzed him about the purposes of the committee and its workings. It meets twice a year, once at Lord's and the other time in any one of the cricket-playing countries. Its remit is broad and unspecified, basically anything to do with the game and its welfare. It can only advise and has no executive powers but it is hoped that the reputation and status of its constituent members will make people sit up and take notice.

And did they? I mean, was it an effective mouthpiece? Did it have any effect? Barry was dubious that the committee made a huge difference worldwide, not one that was immediately obvious, at any rate. 'I felt it was too big, too many voices, a bit unwieldy in its structure. Some made enormous contributions; others less so.' The trouble was that the governing body, the ICC, the power brokers who do have authority and clout, saw it as a rival and tried to sideline it. 'Which was a pity,' said Barry, 'for we were in no way trying to compete or to take over. We saw ourselves solely as an advisory body.' In order to effect more of a working relationship with the ICC, David Richardson, the CEO of the ICC, was co-opted on to the MCC committee and things immediately improved, Barry thought.

I asked him about the sort of subjects that came up for discussion. 'Anything and everything. The future of Test cricket to the IPL.' He went on to list a number of burning issues: match fixing, anti-corruption measures, Pakistan's refusal to take the field at the Oval in 2006, four-day/night Test matches, high visibility pink balls, Decision Review System, T20 and the Olympics, expansion of the women's game. *And you don't think your views – not yours personally, but those of the committee – were listened to?* 'No, I didn't say that. I meant that the effects were not always immediately obvious. But there's no doubt in my mind that the influence of the committee's recommendations slowly seeped in, behind the scenes rather than on the front page, if you see what I mean.' *Did you enjoy being involved?* 'I loved every minute of the seven years I did it.' It was therapeutic being closely involved in the game once more. He was fascinated by the contrasting perspectives offered by people from different countries and cultures. And it gave him a platform to air his views and to bounce his ideas off people whose judgement he respected.

For Barry is a deep thinker about the game, possessing an analytical mind that is not always immediately apparent to the casual observer or the passing acquaintance. Those of us who played with him, at Hampshire, and no doubt team-mates elsewhere, shamefully, and to our detriment, did not pick his brains enough when we could. Those who have heard him commentating on the television and radio will know that he is thoughtful and incisive and comes over as knowledgeable and articulate. But there remains a perception that because he was a genius with the bat in his hand he really wasn't aware of how and why he played as he did – a talent that was born out of pure instinct. That is a misconception.

Mark Nicholas believes that Barry is one of four of the foremost thinkers about the game alive. *Who are the others?* 'Ted Dexter, Shane Warne and Martin Crowe,' he answered without a moment's hesitation. 'All of them, in their different ways, have this ability to think outside the box, to question and to look ahead. Barry, in particular, is knowledgeable, lucid and forensically analytical. He's of course perfectly capable of seeing and commenting on what is going on, what is happening at any given stage in a match, like all reputable pundits. But he can also think laterally and put ideas in your head that you've never thought about before. I think he's a brilliant communicator.'

Many were the times during our lengthy conversations when Barry would ask whether I was still with him. I certainly was. My silence had only betokened an unwillingness to interrupt, to cut short the stream of consciousness as he cogitated about this or expounded on that. 'What's the point of leg byes?' on one occasion he suddenly flung at me. 'I mean why should it count as a run? The ball has beaten the bat. It hasn't hit the stumps, which would have been out. It hasn't missed everything and gone through to the keeper – a moral victory for the bowler but a dot ball. But if it hits the leg and dribbles away on the on side and the batsmen take a single, it's a run to the batting side. Why? Why should a good ball that has beaten the bat be punished by the award of a run to the other side? Now tell me, where's the logic in that?' I opened my mouth but nothing came out. I could think of no sensible answer.

'And another thing,' he said, warming to his task, 'What's happened to swing?' *Well, after its heyday in the 1930s, its popularity declined in the war years because many of the musicians were on active service.* He ignored me and carried on. 'The art of swing bowling seems to be withering on the vine. What's happened? There was a time when swing bowlers were in evidence all over the place. All right, Jimmy Anderson can swing it round corners when the conditions are right but where are the rest of them?' He thought that the increase in the one-day game might have had something to do with it. 'Pitches are flatter. You can't have a side being bowled out for 80. That's pretty well the end of the game before it's started. And the bigger bats mean that players look to hit it out of the ground more. So the bowlers have to bowl a yard shorter as a result and they get used to bowling that length. And you can't swing it if you don't pitch it up.'

He also pointed the finger at the machine manufacturing of the balls. 'They used to be hand-stitched and even a craftsman does not stitch any two balls exactly the same. There is always going to be a fraction of difference in the seam if the ball is made by hand.' On this occasion, I found my voice, if only to agree with him. Lots of variables come into play to make a ball swing: position of the wrist at the moment of delivery, angle of the seam, good polish on one side and roughness of the other, atmospheric conditions, wind direction, pace of the ball, different make of the ball, proximity to the sea (honestly) – the variables are endless. I remember one occasion at Dean Park in Bournemouth on a hot, sunny day in conditions not generally regarded as being conducive to swing bowling, when the ball, in the middle of the afternoon, suddenly started to swing all over the place. Nobody could control it. Bowlers, batsmen, fielders, umpires were at a loss to explain the phenomenon. In discussion at the bar after play, we came to the only logical explanation – it was just a rogue ball. But Barry was right in his calling into question the dearth of swing bowlers. It is an art but one that is in decline. And that is a pity. If its demise is the consequence of machine-made balls then that is another nail in the coffin of individuality and variety in the game. And Barry hates conformity, uniformity, sameness.

The theme of variety exercises him a lot. Remember that he always regarded himself as an entertainer rather than a gatherer of runs. He was sometimes accused of getting out because he became bored. That was quite possibly true. If the game had become predictable, meaningless, all spice and competition squeezed out of the tussle between bat and ball, then he probably would throw his wicket away. He couldn't see the point. Massaging his average had no interest for him. That is why he believes that the balance between batting and bowling is crucial for the game's vitality and subsistence. All right, on occasions the balance is weighted on one side or the other but that is the nature of a game that relies so heavily on the weather. Sometimes batting can be a nightmare if the pitch is awkward but sometimes, if the wicket is a belter, batting can be a delight. Swings and roundabouts.

But if the perennial struggle between bat and ball is consciously tampered with and altered artificially, the game becomes all too predictable. Boring, in other words. 'The proliferation of limited overs cricket has shifted the equilibrium,' Barry maintains. 'Everything is now in favour of the batsman. Covered wickets, slower wickets, helmets, bigger bats, shorter boundaries. Also, people are getting bigger, physically stronger, able to hit it further. People want to see sixes now. They're no longer interested in wickets falling or even a batsman struggling to survive against a hostile spell of bowling.' He's right of course. Some of the most riveting passages of play have been when, ostensibly, nothing much is happening. But the mental tussle between a bowler with his tail up and a batsman having to dig deep into his reserves of skill, technique and courage, just to survive, can be more engrossing than someone slogging the ball out of the ground.

Do you fear for the future of Test cricket? 'Yes I do. Look, most players still regard Test cricket as the ultimate examination of how good they are. But the IPL has had so much publicity, with all its razzamatazz and high value placed on entertainment. The experience of the occasion is all that counts, not the result. Whoever wins doesn't really matter and rarely stays in the memory. All people want to see is that white ball soaring up into the air, lit up by floodlights, to land in row Z of the stands. It's a batter's game. All the bowlers do is rock up to the wicket to get smashed out of the ground. Where's the real drama in that? It's no more than a game of rounders. Perhaps that is what the present generation demands, instant gratification,' he broods. That is not to say that he believes there is no place in the schedule for 20-over cricket. But he is firmly of the opinion that it necessarily lacks the intensity, the emotion, of Test matches, of playing for your country. He believes that cricket has missed a trick by not agitating for T20 to become an Olympic sport. 'They should have gone for franchises, rather than countries,' he asserts. 'Towns versus towns. Think what a marketing dream it would be to have Sydney v New York or Cape Town v Los Angeles or London v Miami. Even if it meant importing the star players to get it off the ground. They say they want to spread the bible, take the game to new outposts.

That would have been the way to crack the US market. But the genie's out of the bottle now by making T20 internationals.'

Another of his gripes is that the administrators are killing the goose that lays the golden egg. In his assertion that too much cricket is being played between too many teams, he is at least being consistent. He was voicing his concerns back in the early 1970s. For a start, he accuses, as he has always done, county cricket. Eighteen fully professional counties is simply too many. And the glut has spread to other countries. 'There are just too many teams. So what used to be first-class – *properly* first-class – is now no more than club level. So goodish players do well and then, when they make the step up to Test cricket, they're way out of their league. Many of them are no more than first-class cricketers in drag with a fancy name.' This made me laugh. The image of county cricketers in drag was more than my equanimity could bear.

But yet again, I found myself in broad agreement. I am frequently asked how county cricket today compares with the game as played by my contemporaries (you will note that I did not say as played by me). The answer is that it cannot possibly compare. Back then, all the great players played county cricket. Every team (save Yorkshire) had two, sometimes three, overseas stars, not unknown Kolpak mercenaries or Second XI internationals that nowadays masquerade as overseas signings. Furthermore, all the England players, when not on Test duty, were playing. 'It was the same in the old Currie Cup and Sheffield Shield,' Barry asserts. 'All the top players played. They don't anymore. Central contracts, in many ways a good thing, have put paid to that. So it cannot be of such a high standard as before. Can it?' Barry's scorn at the level of competition is not reserved exclusively for the first-class game. He points another accusatory finger at the calibre of some of the Test matches today, the erosion of the gold standard, you might say. He believes that a two-tier structure would be more realistic. Clearly, Zimbabwe and Bangladesh do not deserve full Test match status but two divisions, with promotion and relegation, might encourage the junior members of the club, such as Ireland and Afghanistan, to shoot for the stars. 'But don't call that second division Test matches!' he stated vehemently.

It would not be an exaggeration to say that, by now, I was reeling from the intensity of his forensic dissection of the modern game and my wrist was aching with scribbling down notes as he spoke. I was beginning to understand what Mark Nicholas meant when he said that Barry was up there among the best of cricket theorists and philosophers. As he had the wind in his sails, I challenged him about the vexed question of quota systems in the selection of South African teams. He was unequivocal in his opposition to any manipulation of the racial make-up of any side. 'My view is, and always has been, that selection should be done solely on merit. Race should have nothing to do with it. Is he good enough? That ought to be the sole criterion.' The trouble is that in the bad old days of apartheid, race *did* have something to do with it. And whether a quota system is a form of reproach for racial discrimination in the past or a healthy shove in the right direction for previously disadvantaged players, it does have its supporters in the political hierarchy of Cricket South Africa. But Barry believes they are barking up the wrong tree.

It is an uncomfortable fact that fewer than expected young black players are making the grade. You have to examine the reasons for this, he asserts, with a keen eye and calm judgement, putting aside political prejudices. The explanation leads on directly from what he was saying about the dilution of standards in the domestic game. As a result, a young player with promise is lauded to the heavens as the next superstar, with very little authoritative evidence to support the claim. Admittedly, a young Barry Richards only comes along once in a blue moon but look at the number of runs he scored in a very competitive Currie Cup before he was picked for his country. You could hardly say that his elevation was based on a hunch and a promise. Yet the latent talent in South Africa is there, surely, lurking somewhere in the *bundu*. Why is it not being unearthed and cultivated?

Barry's conviction is the one that got him into trouble with Cricket South Africa in the first place, that the finance being expended in this mission is being unwisely spent. 'It's no use chucking huge amounts of money at the townships like Soweto or Langa in the belief that you're watering the grass roots of the game. The thing to do is to identify talent early on for specialised coaching in the proper environment. Cricket is a complex and difficult game and it needs time and manpower to be taught properly. At the moment, the only places where it's being effectively developed are in the private schools.' *Er, South Africa is not the only country where that seems to be happening, Barry.* 'Well, whatever, wherever…Call these centres of excellence what you will, academies, schools, coaching hubs, foundations, but target your resources more sensibly. And if the guys can't afford the fees, let the government provide scholarships. There's enough money sloshing around.'

And then he used a vibrant metaphor that I could not possibly have bettered. 'It's hopeless lighting a lot of fires all over the place. You need to pile up your wood in fewer places to fuel a much bigger bonfire.' I suppose you could say that his proposal is elitism in all but name but what is Test cricket but the best players in the world in competition with each other? I know this point of view does not sit easily with the more egalitarian, socialist, populist policies of government, particularly in South Africa, hence the unpopularity of Barry's views but he remains convinced that cricket cannot be delivered in bite-sized chunks to everybody on an equal basis. 'Talent needs nurturing,' he says, 'and this demands commitment, money and time.' That is his message.

Politics as a motif has threaded its way through this book. Can I ask you about your own politics? To rummage around in a person's political persuasions is always a risky business, no more so, perhaps, than in South Africa, a country bedevilled by its controversial history. Barry stroked his nose nervously. I have encountered such edginess before with denizens of his homeland whenever the subject has cropped up. In the past, it would be an understandable unease, talking openly in a divided nation whose state authority was enforced by violence and repression. Latterly, even in a true democracy, the fear is of offending the sensibilities of those who were formerly downtrodden and are now in power. After some thought, Barry clearly opted for plain speaking. 'Why change the habit of a lifetime?' he smiled and commenced to voice his concerns for the future. 'The present lot have had the reins of government now for 20 years. That is surely time enough to have got a grip of things. Are we in a better position than we were before? Yes, of course, in some important respects, we are. But wherever I look I see mismanagement, inefficiency, even corruption. Everyone who fought the good fight gets the jobs, irrespective of merit.'

He cited a surprising example – textbooks in schools. 'From central government to local education departments to printers to deliveries – all the way down the chain, people take their rake off. So those at the bottom get **** all. Either there are not enough textbooks to go round or, surprise, surprise, they never arrive.' I don't know why I should have been taken aback that he used schooling as an illustration. He has spent most of his adult life since he stopped playing educating the young how to do things the correct way. 'Education is at the heart and soul of any civilised country and to deny your people that is to renege on your responsibility as an elected government.' Phew! Far from the usual smart alec comment that I might have made here, in view of his self-confessed lack of diligence as a student himself, I found myself nodding in vigorous agreement. It wasn't the first time that he had vehemently espoused the crucial role of education in society.

Would you say that most of your friends are in broad agreement with you over your less than sanguine hopes for the future? 'I don't know about that,' he laughed. 'All I know is that Ingrid has barred me from discussing it at home. Let's just say that we agree to disagree!' Ah yes, Ingrid, his partner. I was curious how they met and he was happy to fill me in. Following the break-up of the family and the inevitable distressing fall-out, both personal and domestic, he lived for a while in Perth with a fellow South African, Grant Dakin, who was similarly down in the dumps with personal misfortune.

Dakin? That's a familiar name in South African cricket. No relation to Geoff Dakin, by any chance? Geoff Dakin was a big cheese in the Eastern Province Cricket Association when I was playing over there. 'Grant is Geoff's son. Well, we were being miserable together so he said to me we might as well be miserable together on the golf course. Let's get out of here and go back home. The change of scenery will do us good. And you know, he was right.' Barry did not move lock, stock and barrel straightaway back to South Africa; it happened in stages over several months. While playing golf, he met Ingrid, a golfer herself, and they stayed in touch. In point of fact, she had been for 18 years the CEO of one of the country's premier courses, Fancourt Golf Resort, in George in the Western Cape, with all three of its courses named in the top 20 in South Africa. 'You don't get to run a place like Fancourt for 18 years,' Barry told me, with some pride, 'without being a very competent administrator. She now runs her own consulting and events business. She took over and completely turned around the fortunes of another big golfing complex around here, the Pezula Golf Club.'

He is in no doubt that their relationship rescued him from profound melancholy, perhaps even worse. 'When I met her, I was in a deep, dark place. Who knows what would have happened otherwise. Perhaps I could have sunk so low that the same fate as my son awaited me. Is that exaggerating how bad I felt? I dunno. It was about a year after Mark died and I was as low as I believe it was possible to be. Ingrid was my saviour.' She helped him to clear his head, to accept what had happened and to move on with his life. They now live on an island by the lovely seaside town of Knysna on the Garden Route in the Western Cape. 'With golf courses all around.' *Of course, Barry, of course. How many?* 'About ten!'

In order to make his point, he picked up his computer, on which we were communicating by Skype, and pointed it at the blue skies and sea. I know Knysna because I have been there and I agree that it is God's Own Country, which was just as well, because what Barry was showing me was a blank screen. *Er, turn on the camera, old son.* 'Eh, what's that? Oh, right…now how do I do that?' Thereafter, his virtual tour of the delightful Knysna Heads turned into something of a farce. Eventually, I got a glimpse of sky. At least I think it was sky; it was unbroken blue but it just as well could have been a snapshot of their curtains. Content with that, he sat down again and the screen resumed its usual picture of the wall above his head. Not for the first time, I reflected that my friend's expertise with the computer did not match his with the bat.

'I've always punched above my weight, you know.' *What! Don't tell me, it was Cassius Clay who spotted something of the fighter in you all those years back when you bumped into him in Earls Court?* 'With the women, I mean.' I chuckled. *Come off it, Barry, we were informing you of that fact throughout your Hampshire career!* 'No, seriously, I've been very lucky with the ones I've had proper relationships with. I'm not sure why.' If he wanted to be serious for a moment, let me too. It should not be forgotten that Barry turned heads in his time, a glamorous figure, not conventionally handsome but a striking presence, with his shock of blond hair and his trim, six-foot physique, glowing with health and vitality. His South African-ness added a degree of fascination, allure and dare I say it, a hint of danger. Added to which, Barry was only the best batsman in the world, with God-given gifts, an artist of unparalleled poise and elegance, who could reduce the fastest bowlers to raging impotence. The guy possessed charisma all right. Eyes would swivel when he walked into a room. The men admired him for his deeds on the cricket pitch, the women for his appealing mixture of shyness and self-confidence. And he kept everyone guessing; none of us could predict what he was going to do next. An intriguing man, then and now, an impression that has not altered by the writing of this book.

How do you fill your days? 'We play golf, go for bike rides, have coffee in the café and read the papers. We live on an island and there are lots of lovely walks in the nearby forests. It's very quiet here. I'm at that stage in my life where I can do what I want.' *Any commentating or media work?* 'Bits and pieces here and there, when anything crops up. Which isn't very often these days.' As it happened, an old friend from the Australian Broadcasting Corporation, Jim Maxwell, contacted him to do some stints on the radio for the South Africa versus Australia Tests very soon after we had this conversation. 'But the regular gigs have dried up,' he assured me. 'But, hey, I've had my time. I've now reached the biblical span of three score years and ten, so I can't complain.' *You often got bored and got out for 70, Barry. I don't want you playing any loose shots at this stage of your innings.* 'Don't worry, buddie. Ingrid keeps an eagle eye on me. I'm lucky I met her. And I've got three lovely daughters.' *Daughters? I thought you only had two boys, Mark and Steve.* 'Ingrid's daughters, I mean. And two grandchildren.' What a lovely slip of the tongue, to omit the 'step' in stepdaughters. Was this truly Barry Richards who was speaking? I had rarely heard him so at ease with himself.

Taking advantage of his tranquil mood, I asked the question that went to the heart of it all really. *Are you happy, Barry?* A frown creased his forehead, not of annoyance but of concentration and reflection. 'I shall never get over what happened to Mark. I don't think anyone could get over that. That tragedy remains with you for the rest of your life. So, no, I can't say that I am happy. That is a state of mind beyond me now. But I am content…yes, I think I can say that I feel contented.' *People say that you're still bitter.* 'What about?' *Oh, you know, having your Test career snuffed out at birth. And not being properly appreciated in your own country.* He gave that some thought too. 'No. Bitter is the wrong word. Disappointed, sad, upset at times, but not bitter. Life's too short for that. In any case, Mark's death put all that into perspective. Mark is my bitterness, not cricket.'

At that very moment, my attention was diverted by some grainy, black and white footage of a cricket match appearing on the large television screen above the bar of the café where we were seated, supping our beer. Actually, the pictures were brown more than black and white and bizarrely, as I looked more closely, the subject matter was the fabled 1970 series against Australia. Specifically, Graeme Pollock was being featured; there was that familiar crunching drive off the back foot past extra cover. I drew Barry's attention to the coverage. Briefly, he glanced at the screen. *Cricketing Legends* was the caption. A flicker of interest in the eyes as the camera zoomed in on GP and then the light went out and he turned away. It was as if all exasperation, all anger, all bitterness had been extinguished. Even curiosity. That was another age, another world, another century even. Life had taken its toll.

I felt sad. Not so much that cricket, once his very lifeblood, had ceased to course so fiercely through his veins but that nobody in that room had noticed. Not even casually looked up at the screen. A legend of that series had been saluted, albeit briefly, in that clip and here he was, unheralded, in their midst. The hum of conversation continued uninterrupted. Barry shrugged and gave a thin smile. It was as if he had heard the whispered words of the slave in his ear as he drove his chariot through the triumphal arch of Rome after his greatest feat as a general on the battlefield: *Memento Mori* – Remember thou art but a mortal man. Except that Barry never had his triumph.

APPENDIX

BARRY RICHARDS CAREER AVERAGES
Compiled by Bob Murrell (Official Hampshire CCC Statistician)

BA Richards – first-class

	Mat	Inns	NO	Runs	HS	Ave	100	50	Ct	Balls	Mdns	Runs	Wkts	Ave	5W	Best
South Africa – Tests	4	7	0	508	140	72.57	2	2	3	72	3	26	1	26.00	-	1-12
South Africa – other	6	10	1	252	66	28.00	-	2	4	-	-	-	0	-	-	-
Rest of the World	6	10	1	338	81	37.50	-	2	4	36	1	39	0	-	-	-
Hampshire	204	342	33	15607	240	50.50	38	91	264	3708	194	1675	46	36.41	1	7-63
Natal	91	160	20	8321	219	59.43	27	41	72	1830	65	890	24	37.08	-	4-50
South Australia	10	16	2	1538	356	109.85	6	3	10	300	5	145	5	29.00	-	3-29
DH Robins' XI	2	4	0	235	102	58.75	2	-	2	30	0	29	0	-	-	-
Gloucestershire	1	1	0	59	59	59.00	-	1	-	-	-	-	-	-	-	-
International Wanderers	1	2	0	178	110	89.00	1	1	1	-	-	-	-	-	-	-
Invitation Section A XI	1	1	0	100	100	100.00	1	-	-	-	-	-	-	-	-	-
SA Board President's XI	1	2	0	86	58	43.00	-	1	-	18	1	19	1	19.00	-	1-19
South African Colts XI	1	2	0	76	63	38.00	-	-	-	24	1	11	0	-	-	-
South African Games XI	1	2	0	35	25	17.50	-	-	1	18	2	3	0	-	-	-
South African XI	2	4	1	272	107	90.66	1	2	2	6	0	2	0	-	-	-
South of South Africa	1	1	0	0	0	0.00	-	-	1	-	-	-	-	-	-	-
Transvaal XI	1	2	0	207	140	103.50	1	1	-	-	-	-	-	-	-	-
South African Invitation XI	6	10	0	546	180	54.60	1	4	3	84	2	47	0	-	-	-
Overall averages	339	576	58	28358	356	54.74	80	152	367	6126	274	2886	77	37.48	1	7-63

BA Richards – Limited Overs

	Mat	Inns	NO	Runs	HS	Ave	100	50	Ct	Balls	Mdns	Runs	Wkts	Ave	5W	Best	Econ
South Africa	10	10	0	399	102	39.90	1	3	4	6	0	10	0	-	-	-	10.00
Hampshire	186	183	15	6708	155*	39.92	13	37	82	215	4	139	6	23.16	-	2-8	3.87
Natal	26	25	2	1020	152	44.34	2	6	16	3	0	5	0	-	-	-	10.00
South Australia	2	2	0	89	89	44.50	-	1	1	16	0	15	1	15.00	-	1-15	5.62
C Wesley's XI	3	3	0	64	27	21.33	-	-	2	30	1	16	0	-	-	-	3.20
SA Board President's XI	1	1	0	63	63	63.00	-	1	1	-	-	-	-	-	-	-	-
South African Invitation XI	4	4	0	130	67	32.50	-	2	1	-	-	-	-	-	-	-	-
South African XI	1	1	0	33	33	33.00	-	-	-	-	-	-	-	-	-	-	-
Overall List A averages	233	229	17	8506	155*	40.12	16	50	106	270	5	185	7	26.42	-	2-8	4.11

BA Richards – World Series of Cricket

	Mat	Inns	NO	Runs	HS	Ave	100	50	Ct	Balls	Mdns	Runs	Wkts	Ave	5W	Best
5 day Supertests	3	5	0	338	207	77.60	1	2	1	-	-	-	-	-	-	-
4 day matches	3	5	0	60	37	12.00	-	-	-	-	-	-	-	-	-	-
3 day limited overs*	2	4	0	221	93	55.30	-	3	2	-	-	-	-	-	-	-
2 day 1 innings matches+	6	6	0	307	87	51.17	-	3	4	-	-	-	-	-	-	-
2 day match†	1	1	0	40	40	40.00	-	-	-	-	-	-	-	-	-	-
Limited overs matches	34	34	0	835	92	24.56	-	6	12	-	-	-	-	-	-	-

* In these matches each first innings was limited to 40 overs, each second innings to 75 overs.

+ These matches were 75 eight-ball overs in 1977-78 and 100 six-ball overs in 1978-79

† Two day match with no overs limitation

Data from CricketArchive 3 December 2014

Highest Test match averages

Player	Seasons		Mat	Inns	NO	Runs	HS	Ave	100	50
DG Bradman	1928	1948	52	80	10	6996	334	99.94	29	13
BA Richards	1969/70		4	7	0	508	140	72.57	2	2
CS Dempster	1929/30	1932/33	10	15	4	723	136	65.72	2	5
BH Valentine	1933/34	1938/39	7	9	2	454	136	64.85	2	1
*Mominul Haque	2013	2014	12	23	4	1198	181	63.05	4	7
SG Barnes	1938	1948	13	19	2	1072	234	63.05	3	5
AJL Hill	1895	1896	3	4	0	251	124	62.75	1	1
Taslim Arif	1979/80	1980/81	6	10	2	501	210*	62.62	1	2

RG Pollock	1963	1969/70	23	41	4	2256	274	60.97	7	11
GA Headley	1930	1954	22	40	4	2190	270*	60.83	10	5
H Sutcliffe	1924	1935	54	84	9	4555	194	60.73	16	23
E Paynter	1931	1939	20	31	5	1540	243	59.23	4	7
*KC Sangakkara	2000	2014	128	221	17	11988	319	58.76	37	51
KF Barrington	1955	1968	82	131	15	6806	256	58.67	20	35
ED Weekes	1948	1958	48	81	5	4455	207	58.61	15	19
WR Hammond	1927	1947	85	140	16	7249	336*	58.48	22	24
GS Sobers	1954	1974	93	160	21	8032	365*	57.78	26	30
JB Hobbs	1908	1930	61	102	7	5410	211	56.94	15	28
CL Walcott	1948	1960	44	74	7	3798	220	56.68	15	14
L Hutton	1937	1955	79	138	15	6971	364	56.67	19	33
JH Kallis	1995	2013	166	280	40	13289	224	55.37	45	58
GE Tyldesley	1921	1929	14	20	2	990	122	55.00	3	6
CA Davis	1968	1973	15	29	5	1301	183	54.20	4	4
VG Kambli	1993	1995	17	21	1	1084	227	54.20	4	3
GS Chappell	1970	1984	87	151	19	7110	247*	53.86	54	31
AD Nourse	1935	1951	34	62	7	2960	231	53.81	9	14
SR Tendulkar	1989	2013	200	329	33	15921	248*	53.78	51	68
*Younis Khan	2000	2014	96	172	16	8327	313	53.37	28	29
*S Chanderpaul	1994	2014	158	269	49	11684	203*	53.10	30	65
BC Lara	1990	2006	131	232	6	11953	400*	52.88	34	48

This table includes all players who have a batting average of over 60 and have at least 4 completed innings plus those with averages down to 53 who have played at least 20 innings. Data taken from ESPNCricinfo.com 3rd December 2014.

Players marked with an * are still playing Test cricket.